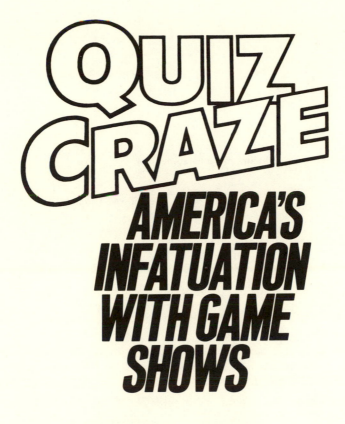

QUIZ CRAZE

AMERICA'S INFATUATION WITH GAME SHOWS

THOMAS A. DeLONG

New York
Westport, Connecticut
London

Library of Congress Cataloging-in-Publication Data

DeLong, Thomas A.
    Quiz craze : America's infatuation with game shows / Thomas A.
DeLong.
        p.   cm.
    Includes bibliographical references and index.
    ISBN 0-275-94042-X (alk. paper)
    1. Quiz shows—United States.   I. Title.
PN1992.8.Q5D44   1991
791.45'3—dc20   91-10573

British Library Cataloguing in Publication Data is available

Library of Congress Catalog Card Number: 91-10573
ISBN: 0-275-94042-X

First published in 1991

Praeger Publishers, One Madison Avenue, New York, NY 10010
An imprint of Greenwood Publishing Group, Inc.

Printed in the United States of America

The paper used in this book complies with the
Permanent Paper Standard issued by the National
Information Standards Organization (Z39.48-1984).

10 9 8 7 6 5 4 3 2 1

Every reasonable effort has been made to trace the owners of copyright materials in this
book, but in some instances this has proven impossible. The author and publisher will
be glad to receive information leading to more complete acknowledgments in
subsequent printings of the book and in the meantime extend their apologies for any
omissions.

For
Sarah
and
Elizabeth,
viewers and players

Contents

Photographs appear on pages 79–88 and 187–197.

Preface

For well over half of the twentieth century, the quiz show has thrived, testing contestants, offering prizes, hawking goods and entertaining listeners. America's fixation on television and radio games and their quizmasters and prizes remains as strong as it did in the days of *Pot o' Gold, Stop the Music!* and *The $64,000 Question.* Contests measuring mental prowess and physical proficiency continue to draw and energize vast audiences as well as to attract eager players. Be it a trivia question or hidden-word puzzle, the challenge with its inexorable suspense and excitement has captured the eyes and ears of millions who every day tune in on the dozen or so games broadcast throughout the country. Even the discovery in the late 1950s that a number of big-money, prime time quizzes had been rigged failed to alienate audiences from viewing habits or the television screen. Quiz shows soon regrouped into new formats and time slots. By the mid-1960s game shows were again growing and prospering as daytime fare alongside the equally proliferating soap opera.

Whether an airing of *Password, Tic Tac Dough* or *Card Sharks*, a TV game above all must entertain and enlighten while providing an opportunity to play along with, or against, on-screen contestants. A successful game series generates a variety of emotions—tension, joy, disappointment, anger, pride. The strength of such responses often determines the durability of a program, be it the knowledge-probing *Quiz Kids* or the value-guessing *Price Is Right.* Fortunes have been made, careers built, merchandise promoted, even lives changed, by broadcast games and contests. Moreover, no other type of program on the air has attracted and embraced such a diversity of professional talent, ranging from comedians and bandleaders to newscasters and academicians.

Never has there been a bigger crowd-pleasing spectator sport in any American arena—a field where the voice of the people can be heard and common people have a chance to "come on down" and play.

I am very grateful for the recollections, insights and anecdotes of many who brought this genre to listeners and viewers. Producers, directors, gamemakers, writers, M.C.s, panelists, announcers, musicians, engineers, advertisers and publicists have contributed to this narrative on a segment of programming only now being seriously documented and analyzed. They include Mel Allen, Morey Amsterdam, Kay Armen, Harry Babbitt, Bob Barker, Vanessa Brown, Ward Byron, Frankie Carle, Peter Cranford, Bill Cullen, Dresser Dahlstead, Clark Dennis, Douglas Edwards, Win Elliot, Dan Enright, Clifton Fadiman, George Fenneman, Emerson Foote, Walter Framer, Anne Golenpaul, Mark Goodson, Lester Gottlieb, John Green, John Guedel, Harold Hackett, Merrill Heatter, Horace Heidt, Ed Herlihy, Bob Howard, Dennis James, Bob Jensen, Gary Johnson, Dick Joy, Joseph Kahn, Joseph N. Kane, Sammy Kaye, Tom Kennedy, Mort R. Lewis, Art Linkletter, Ted Malone, Wink Martindale, Randy Merriman, Vicki Mills, George Murphy, Jan Murray, Ken Murray, Jack Narz, Robert Noah, Walter O'Keefe, Johnny Olson, Richard Osk, Ralph Paul, Jim Perry, Sarah Purcell, Don Reid, Rosa Rio, Kenneth Roberts, Harry Salter, Dan Seymour, Bob Shannon, Bernie Smith, Derek Smith, Jay Stewart, Mike Stokey, Ralph Story, Bobby (McGuire) Van Deventer, Peter Van Steeden, Frank Wayne, Dwight Weist, Burt Wheeler, Ireene Wicker, Gene Wood and Chuck Woolery.

Former contestants (and family members) offered reminiscences: Nancy Ahillen (*Wheel of Fortune*), Margaret Allen (*Name That Tune*), Paul and Sally Bennett (*The Big Payoff, To Tell the Truth*), Grace Bulkley (*Winner Take All, What's in a Word*), Lewis Fox (*Split Second, Password Plus*), Senator John Glenn (*Name That Tune*), Karl-Erik Gude (*Do You Trust Your Wife?*), Paul Kane (*The $64,000 Question*), Edward Letteron (*To Tell the Truth*), Janne Loh (*Camouflage*), Thom McKee (*Tic Tac Dough*), Shirley Morabito (*What's My Line?*), Stephen O'Hanlon (*The $64,000 Question, The $64,000 Challenge*), Martha Parker (*Wheel of Fortune*), Jon G. Smith (*The $100,000 Big Surprise*), James B. Taylor, III (*Double or Nothing*), Winona Thiel (Colgate-Palmolive '49er Gold Rush contest) and Dr. Jack Weiss (*Break the Bank*).

Noteworthy organizations in the broadcast field provided important research materials: The Museum of Television and Radio, New York; Pacific Pioneer Broadcasters, Los Angeles; Radio Advertising Bureau, New York; Broadcast Pioneers Library, Washington, D.C., and especially its director, Catharine Heinz; UCLA Film & Television Archive, Los Angeles; and the Society to Preserve & Encourage Radio Drama Variety & Comedy (SPERDVAC). I am grateful to Friends of Old-Time

Radio and founder Jay Hickerson for the opportunity to organize and moderate a panel on quiz programs at its 1987 convention.

Diverse and farflung libraries furnished resources and documents: New York Public Library, including the Billy Rose Theatre Collection at Lincoln Center; Los Angeles Public Library; Fairfield University Library, Fairfield, Connecticut; Columbia University Oral History Research Office; The Pequot Library, Southport, Connecticut; Knox County Public Library System, Knoxville, Tennessee; Ross Library, Lock Haven, Pennsylvania; Fairfield (Conn.) Public Library; Truth or Consequences (N. Mex.) Public Library; University of Wyoming Division of Rare Books and Special Collections; Georgetown University Law School; Otis Library, Norwich, Connecticut; Fort Worth Public Library; National Association of Broadcasters Library, Washington, D.C.; and Paley Library, Temple University, and its Urban Archives Center acting head, George Brightbill.

The exceptional cooperation and resources of the *Los Angeles Times, St. Louis Post-Dispatch* and *Miami Herald* brought to the text a more sweeping overview of game popularity and audience response. I am also beholden to the *Chapel Hill* (N.C.) *Newspaper;* Conde Nast Publications, Inc.; Hubbard Broadcasting Company; Lewis-Howe Company; NBC Program Information; King World Productions; Station KMBZ, Kansas City and Cheryl Jackman of its programming/promotion staff; and *US* Magazine and editor Lynn Dorsey.

Scores of individuals have helped with information and suggestions. In particular, I wish to thank Harry Ackerman, Phil Cohan, Howard W. Hays, Jeanne Brown, Martin Halperin, Liz Martin, Gene M. Gressley, Thomas A. Greenfield, Thurlow O. Cannon, Miles Kreuger, Rich Conaty, and Bill Johnson, son of *Vox Pop's* Parks Johnson, and Richard Lawrence, son of quizmaster-announcer Mort Lawrence.

I am indebted to Judge Joseph Stone and Timothy Yohn for their studied comments on the section covering the quiz-scandal investigations.

Exposure to the contemporary world of TV games—along with interviews and program data—was provided by Mark Goodson Productions, Reg Grundy Productions, John Guedel Productions, Barry-Enright Productions, Merv Griffin Enterprises, Ralph Edwards Productions, Martindale Enterprises and Bob Stewart Productions. I am grateful to these organizations and the assistance of their associates.

I especially have valued the interest and enthusiasm of Chris Lembesis for this subject. Greenwood Publishing Group's Marilyn Brownstein, Judith Lipner, Andrew Schub and Mary De Vries provided immeasurable guidance and direction. Finally, but assuredly firstline, has been the ongoing encouragement, time and energy given to this work by my wife, Katharine R. C. DeLong.

›1‹

Quiz Roots

Quiz, a succinct, sonorous, one-syllable word, begins and ends with two of the least-used letters of the alphabet. These consonants, *q* and *z*, give a unique ring to a word that arouses various and often contrasting emotions: fear, anticipation, distaste, pride, envy. Actually, it is a word with an uncertain origin. Where it came from, nobody really knows. One colorful, although undocumented, story of Gaelic origin persists.

In the late eighteenth century James Daly, the manager of a theater in Dublin, after imbibing a quantity of Irish whiskey, made a rash wager. He bet that he could introduce a word into the language overnight. Moreover, he wagered that this would be a word absolutely without meaning. There were takers for his bet, so Daly had to make good his boast. He hired scores of the city's street urchins and sent them out into the night with instructions to chalk a single word on every wall in Dublin. The word was *quiz*.[1]

As a result of Daly's scheme, *quiz* was on the lips of all Dublin within days.[2] Interestingly, the word sprung from theatrical turf some 150 years before *quiz* became associated with "show" and mass entertainment.

But initially, the word became synonymous with "practical joke." Daly had played a prank on the people of Dublin. Later, *quiz* came to mean making fun of a person by verbal bantering. By the twentieth century, *quiz* took on a new shade of meaning. To quiz meant to question a person in order to learn the extent of his or her knowledge. Academia picked up this connotation. As a result several generations of students have encountered the quiz as an accepted part of the process of becoming educated.

Also, with the growth of urban newspapers early in the twentieth century, many publishers adopted the quiz, or question-and-answer feature, to provoke reader interest and boost circulation. Quizzes on news and current events appeared regularly. As photojournalism evolved, quizzes built around pictures were introduced. More and more daily papers and periodicals soon added word, picture and news puzzles. A number of publications ran reader contests in connection with a quiz, spotlighting prizewinners to gain greater circulation and, in turn, more revenue.

The most popular and enduring quiz in print remains the crossword puzzle. A word game devised by Arthur Wynne, an editor of the Sunday section of the *New York World*, it was introduced in the paper's Christmas supplement in 1913. Wynne's quiz used a diamond-shaped diagram of squares. Both his clues and answers were simple. The little geometric game fascinated enough readers to warrant a second puzzle the following week.[3]

Originally called "word cross," it was renamed through a typographical switch of the two words. In 1914 Wynne challenged his readers to construct their own crossword puzzles and send them to the paper. He soon had more contributions than he could possibly use.[4]

Crossword puzzles flourished and, in the 1920s, became a national craze. Once a newspaper or magazine added these word teasers, few were able to drop them. The puzzles became as much a fixture as the daily weather map, and doing the crossword puzzle became a daily habit.

In 1924 the first crossword puzzle book appeared. Published by the newly established firm of Simon & Schuster, as its very first book, the publication sold a staggering 350,000 copies that year. Every morning for weeks, mailbags of orders actually blocked the door to Simon & Schuster's small office. A volume of crossword puzzles became a perennial addition to the firm's list of new books. Some 135, edited chiefly by pioneer puzzle maker Margaret Farrar, have made this series the longest-running, uninterrupted collection in American publishing history.[5]

Aside from the printed puzzle, Americans in the early 1900s amused themselves with age-old parlor games. Young and old often joined together to play impromptu pastimes such as ghost, hangman, 20 questions, charades, categories, anagrams and tic-tac-toe.[6] Theatrical performers in vaudeville and burlesque also adapted a number of these games into a routine or specialty number. The seeds of future radio and television game and audience-participation shows were being nourished in the home and on stage long before Dr. I.Q. quizzed a lady in a balcony.

Spelling bees, too, were as American as the little red schoolhouse. Generations of youngsters competed in classroom spelling contests, and every graduating class honored its prize speller. In the 1920s a National

Spelling Bee brought together in Washington, D.C., scores of students between age 10 and 15 to participate in an annual competition, sponsored since 1941 by Scripps-Howard Newspapers. Radio would take notice of the popularity of these spelling contests and introduce its own "bees."

Crossword puzzles, photo quizzes, spelling bees and parlor games satisfied a competitive urge. Not a great deal of thought was given to prizes. On the other hand, card games, such as poker and black jack, had long attracted money seekers and gamblers.[7] Their eye was on a "jackpot." Among avid poker players, and later bingo devotees, this jackpot referred to cumulative stakes or a pot of money.

With the development of mass, instantaneous communications and the appearance of broadcast quizzes, *jackpot* took on a broader meaning. It signified a coveted big prize or prizes, often a lot of "jack" or "dough." Radio and television would also transform parlor games and quizzes into carefully produced and timed "programs." The broadcast media formalized contests and games of knowledge, skill and derring-do, greatly expanding the number and scope of participants and listeners and viewers.

A journalist of the early 1940s once described radio quiz contests as a new and easy road to riches, in contrast to the old Horatio Alger formula of hard work. The major effort, this newspaperman observed, was a willingness to devote nights listening to the radio and anticipating a telephone call from a quiz show master of ceremonies. Such calls, indeed, might bring a windfall to a lucky and knowledgeable listener.[8] But long before America's telephone began to ring, radio first had to grow from a makeshift novelty into a workable vehicle of communications, an accepted form of entertainment and a widespread means of advertising.

› 2 ‹

Different Wavelengths

In the beginning there was the word—lots of words and chatter, babble, small talk, even hot air. Like its older sibling, the telephone, radio carried spoken messages and conversation. A "wireless" apparatus that evolved from Marconi's Morse code signals first beamed across the Atlantic in 1901, radio gradually developed into a device able to transmit the human voice on wavelengths. Its early practitioners were wireless operators aboard ships or ashore, eagerly communicating among one another. Experimental breakthroughs by inventors Ernst Alexanderson, Reginald Fessenden and Lee de Forest advanced the value of radio as a remarkably different method of transmitting words and sounds.[1]

In 1910 the first broadcast test outside a ship's radio room or an experimental station picked up the singing of Enrico Caruso from the stage of the Metropolitan Opera House. Lee de Forest piped it to a nearby laboratory and from there put this "remote" on the air. Only a handful of the two dozen or so receivers in the New York area picked up the faint sounds of the great tenor and his coartists.[2] Aside from the technical shortcomings broadcasting as entertainment was still unexplored and hardly dreamed of. Nevertheless, the wireless telephone—as radio was then called—grew into a fascinating and time-pleasing hobby among amateur operators or "hams" setting up transmitters and receiving sets in their homes.

Radio broadcasting remained erratic. At one minute signals would be clear; the next, they would fade into silence or turn into static. In 1914 a patent was issued that would help correct this deficiency and start to take radio out of the earphone and crystal set stage. This invention, the superheterodyne of Edwin Armstrong, made true broadcasting possible.[3] In the wake of this advance, amateur stations sprung up on college campuses and in equipment-testing laboratories. But when the United States entered World War I in 1917, the government outlawed all ham operators and stations. Two years later, it allowed them to return. Among the first transmitters to reappear in the postwar period was a home-based experimental station of a Westinghouse Company engineer.

Dr. Frank Conrad, Westinghouse's chief assistant engineer and a radio buff, set about improving the sending of radio signals. He gathered together a group of hams in the Pittsburgh area to listen and report on his nightly experimental broadcasts. Conrad sent out test signals in both Morse code and his own voice. His listeners urged him to broadcast more sounds, not dots and dashes. He talked at length, reading weather, crop and local news reports. Often his voice grew hoarse, and to relieve the strain he played records on a phonograph placed near his transmitter.[4]

Conrad's small audience welcomed the mixture of talk and music, and so the first disc jockey was born. He settled down to spinning records two nights a week. A Pittsburgh music store soon supplied new records in exchange for an on-the-air announcement of the shop's location and a description of merchandise. Thus Conrad unknowingly delivered the first radio commercial.

A month or so later, a department store ran a newspaper ad offering radio equipment capable of picking up Conrad's broadcasts. Westinghouse, manufacturers of radio electrical equipment, was so pleased with the outcome it appropriated money for a 100-watt station. As KDKA, it quickly became the earliest and biggest name in radio in the early 1920s. The Pittsburgh transmitter compiled an impressive list of radio "firsts," including broadcasts of the first religious service, sports event, bedtime story, farm program, outdoor concert and marriage ceremony.[5]

As scores of stations popped up throughout the country, more and more Americans discovered radio and brought it into their homes. The newly formed Radio Corporation of America, makers of radio sets and supplies, also encouraged interest in this area by backing the publication of a new consumer magazine called *Wireless Age*. This monthly specialized in articles on how to build a radio, constantly stressing the joys of owning a receiver. Those lucky enough to have a radio, the magazine emphasized, would attract lots of friends who would gather next to the receiver, press a headphone to their ear and wait to pick up broadcasts such as a health talk by a representative of the Association for the Prevention and Relief of Heart Disease, vocal selections by a conservatory student, a report on weather and climate conditions by an amateur meteorologist, a piano solo by a part-time musician, a lecture on getting women to vote by the League of Women Voters, dinner music from a salon orchestra in a downtown hotel, a talk on the value of effective speech over the telephone by a staff announcer, a discussion of growing flowers by a garden magazine editor, a violin interlude by the station manager's nephew and a review of baseball by a local sports reporter.

Talk programs—often overly wordy—filled much of the daily log. Both recognized experts and self-appointed authorities spoke. Assigned station personnel with little or no knowledge of a subject frequently extemporized at a microphone. Listeners accepted advice and commentary from both professional and amateur alike. Few questioned its content.

More and more stations came on the air with the backing of equipment manufacturers, department stores, schools and newspapers, all of which generally thought of their transmitter as a promotional tool or public service endeavor. As money to operate stations began to go out, however, it occurred to most station owners that some revenue had better come in.

In the summer of 1922, the first program with a commercial sponsor went over the air. New York station WEAF, owned and managed by the American Telephone & Telegraph Company, offered time to a real estate firm eager to tell would-be home buyers of a great opportunity. The Queensboro Corporation bought time for a series of ten-minute broadcasts at the rate of $35 each. The programs consisted of one long commercial on the benefits of owning a home in Jackson Heights, a short commute from Manhattan.[6]

Other outfits took notice as the Queensboro realtor talks boosted property sales. Companies hesitantly began selling their wares to an unseen yet apparently responsive audience. Newspapers and magazines especially discovered the promotional value of going on the air. In doing so, to their later chagrin and dismay, they strengthened a future competitor in the communications field.

Time, a weekly newsmagazine started in 1923 by two young Yale graduates, Henry Luce and Briton Hadden, used a current-events quiz over radio to build readership. *Time* circulation manager Roy Larsen wangled free time on the New York-area station WJZ. The magazine called its quiz *The Pop Question Game.* Hadden would read a question and Larsen would strike a musical chime. As the last note faded, the listener was expected to have provided an answer before Hadden read the correct one. The quiz ran as a regular feature for nearly three years, until late 1926. A variant of the quiz was staged by *Time*'s promotion-minded founders at Chamber of Commerce luncheon meetings throughout the country. These "skull tests" of questions and answers led to reader questionnaires to ferret out marketing information and later to *Time*'s popular current-affairs test used extensively in schools.[7]

WJZ listeners with a musical bent tuned in *The Brunswick Hour Mu-*

sical Memory Contest, sponsored by Brunswick Records. Offering a grand prize of $5,000 every month to a listener who identified both music and performers, and then wrote an essay on a particular musician or singer, the quiz aired musical questions based upon its catalog of available discs waxed by John Charles Thomas, Mario Chamlee, Elizabeth Lennox, Frank Munn and other artists. This short-lived promotional vehicle produced at least one big winner—a young salesman who had absorbed a wealth of musical knowledge from ushering at symphony concerts.[8]

WJZ's close competitor, WEAF, already had added a question and answer feature to its pioneering daily news program called *The Radio Digest*. On the West Coast a station had introduced a program based on the highly popular question-and-answer books *Do You Know* and *Ask Me Another*. Station KMTR in Hollywood took advantage of this quiz-book craze by urging people to organize "quiz parties" around their radio and entertain each other by calling out answers before the announcer did. But the idea did not catch on.

By the late 1920s coast-to-coast broadcasting was a reality. Two major networks, the National Broadcasting Company and the Columbia Broadcasting System, tied together strings of far-flung stations, making possible instantaneous national hookups. Big advertisers and their agencies now flocked to network flagship microphones in New York, Chicago and Los Angeles. The greatest stars of the stage, movies and concert hall followed. Fees from radio broadcasting alone meant a weekly income of $1,000 or more for headliners such as Rudy Vallee, Paul Whiteman and B. A. Rolfe.

The day of the run-of-the-mill amateur—even the budding semi-professional—on big-time radio was clearly over. Advertisers and listeners alike expected polished, established performers on well-scripted and produced presentations. The proverbial man-off-the-street stayed on the curb.

Weekly network shows for the 1929–30 season emphasized top-flight music and comedy. *The Majestic Theatre Hour* starred the Two Black Crows. General Electric sponsored a symphony led by Walter Damrosch. *The Blackstone Program* headlined Broadway's Frank Crumit and Julia Sanderson. The pioneering Roxy and His Gang maintained its well-earned popularity. *The Cuckoo Hour* bowed with the witty Ray Knight. The Cities Service orchestra spotlighted Jessica Dragonette.[9]

In the midst of a wealth of programs, the stock market crashed and rocked the country. Billions of dollars of paper profits evaporated. Virtually every industry suffered from shock waves—except radio. The ensuing economic slump actually favored broadcasting. A growing army of Americans were losing jobs and savings. Forced to stay at home, they turned to a radio set to provide daily entertainment and a measure of relief from the problems and woes of the Depression. Comedians found a favored spot on the dial. Eddie Cantor, Amos 'n' Andy, Fred Allen, Jack Benny, Burns and Allen and Jack Pearl brought smiles and laughs, a welcome tonic to tough times. Frequent musical interludes, too, relieved burdensome worries. Kate Smith, Morton Downey, Bing Crosby, the Mills Brothers, the Boswell Sisters, Arthur Tracy, Russ Columbo and Lanny Ross sang their way into millions of homes. Big band remotes, sports events, soap operas, minstrel shows, news and commentary, and homemaker talks rounded out daily schedules.[10]

The lingering Depression gradually affected new types of presentations. Dramatic and often escapist fare took hold. *The First Nighter, Eno Crime Club, Roses and Drums* and *The Shadow* appeared and grew in popularity. To compete with the increasing variety of programs, free at the turn of a dial, movie theaters reacted by featuring contests, bingo games and bank nights. Prizes ranged from household goods and groceries to gift certificates and tickets to upcoming double features. This extra fillip kept audiences in the moviegoing habit. At the same time, newspapers ran special giveaway contests to keep their readership.

While motion pictures and publications struggled to maintain a hold on the public, radio truly entered a golden epoch. The average American made listening to this ethereal medium a favorite pastime. Much of the country sought to be a party to actual broadcasts from the country's major radio centers. What to do with the multitudes of radio fans wanting to observe an actual program had perplexed broadcasters almost from the start of network radio. Two factions fought over the question of whether to allow spectators in a studio. Many producers and performers believed that an audience distracted an artist and not infrequently spoiled work before a microphone. Gum chewing, whispers, wiggles, sneezes, coughs—all seemed to disturb, even mar, a performance. Engineers, too, regularly vetoed the idea of an audience. Noise from a large group, they explained, interfered with the quality of transmission.[11]

On the other hand, radio VIPs and headliners wanted to build a big following for programs and sponsors. Studio audiences, to them, seemed an important part of a show. The networks decided to open their doors a crack or two. For its most popular shows, NBC compromised. In its large studio on the roof of the New Amsterdam Theatre on New York's 42nd Street, the network installed a heavy four-ton glass curtain between the performers and the audience. Few singers or musicians expressed objections to this blanketing device, which smothered applause. But radio comedians had other thoughts. Eddie Cantor and Ed Wynn, two of the biggest names on Broadway, broadcast several times behind NBC's glass wall. After every funny line or joke, they naturally paused for a laugh—that special stimulant and signal of success. Not hearing a reaction threw their timing off and rattled their composure. Like all true comedians, they thrived on an audience's response. It inspired a better performance. The Cantors and Wynns made it clear: they wanted no part of broadcasting if a barrier separated them from an audience.[12] Faced by their imminent departure, NBC removed the cumbersome glass curtain, giving comedians as well as all performers a truly "live" audience.

By 1933 applause and laughter were the order of the day. "Silence Please" signs were removed. Now there was no urgency to choke a cough, stifle a laugh or restrain a clap. The extraneous sounds humanized radio.

At the same time that the pros and cons of studio audiences were being weighed, broadcasters began to grow curious over how many people were actually tuned in to a particular show. Advertisers were spending large sums on programs, and they, too, were curious to know more about their listeners.

Stations, large and small, wanted evidence that they had an audience. The general manager of 1,000-watt KMBC in Kansas City, Arthur B. Church, typified station executives, as he wondered if any significant number was listening. One day he discussed this concern with his friend Frank Russell, a local candy maker.[13] Russell suggested that a box of chocolates be offered to those early morning listeners who wrote a note to the station requesting this gift of sweets. Russell would provide the candy at no cost. Church agreed to the idea. The day after KMBC's staff announcers told listeners about the offer a sack of mail arrived at its studio on the top floor of the Aladdin Hotel. Soon hundreds of letters from Kansas City listeners as well as from residents of surrounding counties piled up. Within days, several thousand requests poured in.

Arthur Church, overjoyed with the deluge, studied the various addresses to prepare a geographical breakdown of his morning listeners. Frank Russell faced the mountain of mail with trepidation. If he filled all two thousand requests, it would put him out of business. He and Church devised a way to honor their pledge. Each listener would receive a box of candy—containing one large chocolate.

"No one complained," recalled the candy maker's son Alden Russell many years later. "They really didn't expect anything to begin with."[14]

A year or so later, young Alden, who was now broadcasting at KMBC under the name Ted Malone, devised the first of numerous schemes of his own to determine listenership. To launch a breakfast food called "Dwarfies," the cereal maker agreed not to sell the product in Kansas City until Malone went on the air to introduce the new cereal. To test audience reaction and promote the brand, Malone explained that the first 20 listeners to bring in the names of local grocers carrying the cereal would receive $5. Of course, no local stores had stocked "Dwarfies" before the announcement. But following Malone's broadcast, they rushed to fill their shelves. It seems hundreds of listeners had made a beeline to grocery stores asking for the new cereal. When the "Dwarfies" salesman paid a call, Kansas City merchants placed large orders, demanding immediate delivery to please eager customers.

Ted Malone, who became best known for his poetry reading on *Between the Bookends* over the networks, came up with some solid demographics. Apparently, listeners felt an important part of KMBC programs and activities.

Network shows, especially daytime serials and soap operas, also approximated the size and enthusiasm of an audience by special offers and giveaways. In 1934 Ireene Wicker, on her daily NBC storytime for children *"The Singing Lady,"* told youngsters to write in for a songbook. Her sponsor, The Kellogg Co., was amazed at the response. When requests totaled more than 14,000 in less than a week, Kellogg quickly hired dozens of women to handle the mail.[15]

In the early 1930s, few broadcasters gave any thought to using such listener response, enthusiasm and loyalty directly before a microphone. As CBS and NBC vied for stations for their chains, competition grew more intense, particularly in the evening prime-time hours. Station managers and network executives feverishly sought new ideas, material and formats. Curiously, the question-and-answer program never came under much serious discussion. The broadcast industry generally had associated quiz and game shows with lotteries and eyed them as not in the public interest. It pointed to the radio lotteries that had briefly surfaced on scores of local stations in 1930 and 1931. These contests—generally viewed as against the provisions of the Federal Radio Act of 1927—risked the renewal of a station's license from the Federal Communications Commission.[16] Broadcasters now avoided promotional sweepstakes, as well as all types of games.

Meanwhile, hoards of fans surrounded radio studios. Tens of thousands sought tickets to shows every week in New York alone. NBC and CBS recognized the publicity value and goodwill stemming from a theater full of exuberant spectators. NBC's parent company, RCA, already had assigned a dozen floors to radio broadcasting in its new skyscraper at New York's Rockefeller Center. Known as Radio City, it contained 35 studios—many with large seating areas. CBS acquired a handful of studio theaters in mid-Manhattan. By 1937 practically all network programs except newscasts and serials aired before audiences. Access to broadcasts also encouraged countless would-be performers to "break into" radio.

Notwithstanding, the major stations shied away from inexperienced and untrained talent. The very concept of coast-to-coast programming embraced top-drawer performers and established stars. Nevertheless, closed doors did not discourage singers, comedians, sportscasters, actors and announcers. When auditions were announced, they came by again and again. Reputedly, one capable Chicago soprano even endured 49 auditions in three years without arousing network interest.[17]

Untried and untested talent generally had greater opportunities to gain a "voicehold" at local and regional transmitters where the pay, however, was small or nonexistent.

Struggling to compete with star-filled, prime-time network shows, WHN turned to the clusters of would-be performers beating a path to its studios in midtown Manhattan. Owned by Loew's Theatres and located atop their headquarters on Broadway, the 1,000-watt independent station attracted little attention. In 1934 Major Edward Bowes, manager of the chain's Capitol Theatre, was given the responsibility of boosting WHN's low ratings. Bowes knew radio. Since 1925 he had broadcast a moderately successful Sunday morning variety show called *The Capitol Family Hour* over WEAF. The talent at his microphone was often amateurish—but on Sunday mornings no one really cared.

For WHN Bowes also devised an evening program to showcase strictly amateur acts. He called it *The WHN Amateur Hour*—the word *original* was later added when dozens of stations copied the idea. Long a staple in vaudeville, the amateur night competition quickly caught on among New York listeners and had the entire Northeast dialing the station.[18] Within a year, Major Bowes sold the show and himself to NBC and sponsor Chase & Sanborn Coffee.

Until Bowes, the very thought of amateurs on any network had been heresy. But so completely alien to the air, the show fascinated listeners. *The Original Amateur Hour* turned the spotlight on new and generally unpolished acts and gave them coast-to-coast exposure. It also started a trend toward participation by listeners, who could actually cast a vote by telephone, telegram or letter for their favorite amateur. The telephone especially would play an increasingly vital role in game and giveaway programs emerging in the wake of Bowes' phenomenon.

Voted the most popular show of 1935, *The Original Amateur Hour* broadcast from NBC's biggest studio theater where 1,200 occupied seats guaranteed thunderous applause and cheers as Major Bowes introduced the dozen or more acts. He routinely asked every neophyte why he or she wanted to go into show business. The major's repartee helped "humanize" the proceedings, which attracted countless struggling and hard-pressed prey of Depression times.

On a broadcast in November 1938, Major Bowes introduced a young dancer and asked how he became interested in dancing. "My parents sent me to dancing school," the chap replied. "When I first saw the girl students in shorts, I ran away."

"But," twitted Bowes, "you came back for more!"[19]

For another show, a teenage contestant had hitchhiked from Philadelphia to audition for the major. "It was Mom who told me to take a shot at it, even if I had to crawl here. Pop says the radio is nothing but a kid's gewgaw. He wants me to be a chemist or scientist of some sort. But I bet he won't stay sore if I came back with a singing contract in my pocket and my name in front of the theatres."[20]

Some critics claimed that Major Bowes shrewdly exploited the unimportant talents and naive ambitions of the great unwashed. Nevertheless, win or lose—or immediately strike out at the sound of the major's brass gong—they were grateful for a chance to be heard by millions of fellow Americans. *The Original Amateur Hour* brought a solid measure of democracy to the entertainment field when the American way was being sorely challenged and threatened.

The enormous popularity of Bowes' show and the many other amateur programs that followed gave rise to an offshoot: the community sing. People were invited into a studio or theatre and instructed to sing-along with well-known show-business personalities who directed this "working" audience. Everyone enjoyed the novelty of "being on the air."

In 1936 Milton Berle emceed the *Gillette Community Sing* with the venerable radio team of Billy Jones and Ernie Hare, "The Happiness Boys." Evangelistic song leader Homer Rodeheaver and announcer Tiny Ruffner cohosted the *Palmolive Community Sing*. Unschooled, off-the-street voices dominated these weekly proceedings, but producers often scattered professional singers throughout the audience to encourage spontaneous and full participation and to offset the tinhorns. The pros picked up an easy $15 a broadcast. The latest radio vogue, singalongs never lacked audiences to lift their voices in new and old songs.

Radio again took another look at how such staunch and energetic fans might be used at a microphone. Once more, it turned for ideas not to the denizens of network radio centers but to the pilots of modest-sized regional transmitters.

›3‹

Vox Populi

In Houston, Parks Johnson and Jerry Belcher, with the help of a radio engineer, strung a microphone line from an upper story window of KTRH to the sidewalk in front of the busy Rice Hotel. The two broadcasters hoped to attract enough passersby to chat on the air for ten minutes. As soon as people noticed the mike, held by 41-year-old Johnson, they stopped to watch and listen. He and Belcher randomly stopped several pedestrians, and before these Houstonites fully realized what was going on, they were on radio.[1]

The show's mastermind, Parks Johnson, a local one-man advertising agency and son of a Georgia circuit-riding preacher, developed the sidewalk "remote" with the help of Belcher, a former newspaperman and farm journal reporter. It was during the time of the hotly debated 1932 presidential contest between newcomer Franklin D. Roosevelt and President Hoover. They had tossed around the idea of on-the-street interviews on the election, with a quiz segment or two.

The broadcast from downtown Houston blossomed into a daily half-hour, and both serious and humorous queries came into the popular sidewalk discourses:

- Is fear or desire the stronger?
- How many feathers are there on the average hen?
- What is the difference between lingering and loitering?
- How wide is a half-dollar?

From close contact with people on the street, Belcher and Johnson soon had a mental portfolio of various types regularly encountered, along with an ability to recognize them at a glance and separate the bashful boy from the smart aleck, the worldly-wise from the kindly soul. Without realizing it, the two Texans were pioneering a new departure for radio. Out of those curbside question bees developed to a large extent the quiz program and the audience-participation show.

To reflect the "voice of the people" theme, they named the show *Vox Pop*, dropping an earlier tag, *Sidewalk Interviews*. In July 1935 the advertising agency J. Walter Thompson and a sponsor, Fleischmann's Yeast, brought the series from Houston to the NBC network in New York as a summer replacement for comedian Joe Penner. The first Manhattan pick-up originated from Columbus Circle, a haven of long-winded soap-box orators in the 1930s. Luckily, the sight of a microphone generated enough "mike fright" apparently to nip in the bud any overbearing pavement philosophers in the crowd.[2]

Variety called the program "a distinctly new and probably refreshing type of program to the majority of dialers."[3] This trade review, however, voiced a suspicion that the program was overstaged and not spontaneous. In a sense, his observation reflected favorably on Johnson and Belcher who were already masters at ad-libbing and handling the unpredictability of a makeshift gathering.

Vox Pop rewarded individuals interviewed. At first, a dollar bill went into their pocket. But Parks' wife, Louise Johnson, had a better idea. She would buy gifts for participants. Louise joined the *Vox Pop* staff, purchasing dozens of unusual items, ranging from puppies and silverware to lawnmowers and rugs. Her weekly budget eventually grew to $1,000 or more and was spent locally for each show when it traveled around the country in the 1940s. Sponsors' products were duly distributed too. The recipient of a package of Kentucky Club Tobacco once remarked, "I'm a Mormon missionary and I don't smoke—but I'll take it anyway. I hear this kind of tobacco is very good for sick cattle."[4]

At the close of *Vox Pop*'s first season on NBC, Wallace Butterworth, a radio singer turned announcer, replaced Jerry Belcher who had developed a serious drinking problem. Belcher periodically came to the program tipsy and even missed broadcasts. Butterworth and Parks Johnson made even a stronger team, alternately conducting interviews and lining up participants. By 1938 the program had become less impromptu and more preplanned. Guests were scouted and screened in advance, and the cohosts learned about their background and experiences before each broadcast. Yet the program retained much of the naturalness and levity of the old catch-as-catch-can days. *Vox Pop* often lined up a broad spectrum of people on a single show. A typical tantalizing array of the late 1930s included hopeful Irish sweepstakes winners, the sister of a missing Loyalist Spain volunteer, a New York mother on strike against having babies and a man who served on a jury with eleven women.[5]

The series prospered and grew in stature. Johnson decided it had to reach out to the people and travel to points of interest and present more authentic stories by those actually living that experience. "The average man is just as interesting as any celebrity," he'd often say.[6]

On January 25, 1940, he broadcast his first "road" show—an interview with a "typical American co-ed" on the campus of Rutgers University. Billed as "The Show That Travels America," it soon attended a lawn party of Rhode Island Governor William H. Vanderbilt in Newport, visited the New York World's Fair Aquacade, stopped by the Democratic Convention in Philadelphia, explored the U.S. Naval Academy in Annapolis and participated in a rodeo in Deadwood, South Dakota. The show frequently covered the premieres of motion pictures based on America's early history and heroes. For these events *Vox Pop* journeyed far and wide—to Charlottesville (for "Virginia"), Cincinnati ("Mark of Zorro"), Tucson ("Arizona"), New Orleans ("Birth of the Blues") and South Bend ("Knute Rockne").

West Coast announcer Dick Joy recalls the world premiere of "Santa Fe Trail" on December 12, 1940, and the special train that carried the cast and producers of the Warner Bros. film from Barstow, California, along the famed pioneer route to Santa Fe:

> Harry Spears, CBS chief engineer, and I drove from Los Angeles to Barstow for the broadcast, getting in shortly before airtime. Harry was dismayed to find he had to lay power cables across several tracks to reach the parked train. My biggest problem came when I couldn't hear Johnson or Butterworth over the hubbub in the club car. They had to wave at me to come to the observation platform to deliver commercials. I totally missed one because of the crush of stars and publicity people, most of whom were enjoying a very long "happy hour." Errol Flynn created the principal obstruction.[7]

By 1948, when it left the air, *Vox Pop* had broadcast in every state except North Dakota, Nevada and Utah and had traveled to Canada, Mexico, Cuba, Puerto Rico, France and England. While covering plenty of ground and meeting many famous notables, it remained, in the words of Parks Johnson, "a down-to-earth, honest and reliable program."

The notion of an inquiring reporter on a sidewalk spread to other stations not long after *Vox Pop* burst upon the network lines. By 1937 more than 50 cities had at least one man-on-the-street broadcast. WJBK Detroit originated *What's Your Opinion?* giving street interviewees an opportunity to speak up, along with rewarding listeners a dollar for submitting questions used. Jerry Belcher took his verbal byplay from *Vox Pop* to WGY in Schenectady, New York. Fitch Hair Tonic sponsored his new series *Interesting Neighbors*. In Cincinnati, *Man in Your Neighborhood*—Red Barber—visited homes, carrying a hand mike attached to a mobile unit parked on the street. In signing off, Barber named the neighborhood he would visit the following day and advised listeners to "look for the big white WSAL mobile truck."[8]

In downtown Charlotte, North Carolina, Leo Kirby nabbed passersby and propounded questions, puzzles and riddles. The midday WBT feature depended on the quick response and wit of those interviewees buttonholed. New York's WMCA took a different tack. On *Gangplank*, it "spot-interviewed" well-known individuals—authors, actors, diplomats, society figures—as they departed or arrived by ship or airplane. Ingenious WMCA recorded the interviews on discs and rebroadcast them at open time slots later in the day.[9]

A man-in-the-street show in Kansas City encountered a difficult, almost morbid, situation one December morning in 1936. An unsigned note, in a woman's handwriting and received by WHB, threatened suicide. The message urged the program to air a pro and con discussion of her intended suicidal action. Believing the note to be authentic, the station pulled out all the stops on the street to persuade her to reconsider. Had the suicide given her name and address with her note, a reporter wisecracked, she would have won a pair of silk stockings and a chance on a diamond ring.[10]

Early in his very successful broadcast career, producer Walt Framer conducted a sidewalk audience participation program in Pittsburgh called *Have You Got It?* The show aired in front of the sponsor's jewelry shop and was based on the premise that a person would swap something of little or no value for a chance of getting a couple of silver dollars or theater tickets. Framer did the show with a young announcer named Bill Cullen.

"It was his first radio job," says Framer, who later produced such leading network quizzes as *Strike It Rich* and *The Big Payoff*. "A theatre owner had called me to give a big build-up to this kid whose father ran a local Ford agency. I was program director at a small independent station, so I agreed to see him."[11]

Bill Cullen, Jr., appeared at Framer's office boasting, "I'm the best sports announcer in the world."

"Where have you been doing your announcing?" Framer asked.

"Nowhere, but I'm still the best. Try me."[12]

Walt Framer did. He hired the brash youngster at $18 a week. Bill Cullen, however, broadcast few, if any, sports events but came into his own as a dependable and versatile staff announcer. When Framer left for New York in the early 1940s, Cullen followed.

Other broadcaster interviews occasionally came up with a new twist. They forsook the curbside and remained in a studio with a telephone next to the mike. Irv Abeloff at WRVA in Richmond, Virginia, sold the city gas works on the idea of sponsoring two or three calls to local users of gas heating. During a ten-minute show, Abeloff asked opinions on current interest topics. The station, however, faced a major hurdle on airing the interviews. Telephone company regulations prohibited the broadcast of an actual "live" telephone conversation. WRVA got around the ban by recording the conversation and airing it an hour or so later.[13]

A similar program in Dayton worried the Ohio Bell Telephone Company over possible litigation if a hot-tempered subscriber or one of an uncertain sense of comedy exploded or said something off-color while being interviewed. Station WHIO also met this obstacle by recording calls for later broadcast.[14]

The great fear of producers and station managers had been largely overcome at regional transmitters, but a degree of apprehension remained among their network counterparts over "live" interviews. An embarrassing word or a suggestive remark loomed as a possibility, and the thought sent shivers up and down the backs of radio executives. Engineers were instructed to cut off a program if a smutty remark reached the microphone. Even cinema siren Mae West's suggestive drawl while performing a brilliantly humorous—and fully scripted—takeoff on the story of Adam and Eve on the Edgar Bergen-Charles McCarthy show so outraged listeners that she was excluded from radio for a dozen years.

In practice, broadcasters rarely had to pull the switch. During the first three years of *Vox Pop*, for example, only one man ever used the word *damn*, and then he didn't realize he'd said it. "They were always so busy trying to answer our questions," Jerry Belcher said, that "they hadn't time to think up anything smart or smutty."[15]

People off the street, it seems, were on their best behavior, and this, now more than ever, encouraged producers to seek new formats to bring them to a microphone.

An age-old parlor and school game became one of the new entries in audience participation activities. The spelling bee appeared on coast-to-coast radio in late 1936. Dr. Harry Hagen brought the idea to CBS. A physician who first went on radio to give health talks and present exercise programs, Hagen found a Sunday afternoon time slot to conduct a word bee among children. The format caught on with listeners of all ages. Within six weeks other stations featured spelling bees. NBC rushed to the air with a competition hosted by Paul Wing, a staff director and author of children's books. Elsewhere, WBBM Chicago invited groups of well-known wrestlers, artists, jockeys, actors and baseball players to participate as teams. This approach apparently pulled in listeners who delighted in a chance to hear a celebrity made to look a bit dumb. At WAPI in Birmingham, Alabama, a college professor refereed teams from schools, community organizations and newspapers on *Spell-a-Bee*.

Chase & Sanborn Coffee sponsored a one-hour contest at WMCA in New York. Dr. Harry Aiken played the pedagogue, herding together more than 50 contestants from metropolitan schools vying for a grand prize of $25. In nearby Bridgeport, Connecticut, George A. Patridge and WICC's Joe Lopez conducted a Monday evening contest from a hotel ballroom.

After a season as quizmaster, NBC's Paul Wing formed some opinions on spelling. "Good spellers are born, not made. The person who spells words at random, that is, without grouping them in syllables, is much more apt to make mistakes. A good speller is picture-minded. He visualizes the word before him as if it were spelled out on an imaginary blackboard."[16]

People came from near and far to match their spelling skills. Others with unusual stories, backgrounds or talents found a new network variation of the audience-participation format. Phillips Lord, with programs such as *Gangbusters* and *Seth Parker* to his credit, came up with an interview show inspired in part by variety-show host Rudy Vallee's frequent weekly feature of bringing an unknown but interesting person to his microphone. CBS liked the concept and agreed to hire newscaster Gabriel Heatter to handle the job on a scripted program called *We, the People*. Most guests were lined up weeks in advance to ascertain an interesting cast of characters. On one particular broadcast, they included a lady with a southern drawl who spoke on adoption of unwanted babies, a champion liar, a legally authorized yodeler, a housewife who didn't think her clownlike husband was funny and a veteran rider of the Pony Express days.[17]

We, the People stagehands at the Columbia Radio Playhouse called it the craziest show on the air mainly because they had to build so many special pieces of equipment to accommodate guests. The crew made a huge chair for Robert Wadlow, an eight-foot, nine-inch tall man from Alton, Illinois, and on other occasions constructed a cage for a gorilla and a complicated wire and glass enclosure for a colony of bees.[18]

The whole idea of the show—to present a cross-section of American life—allowed nearly anybody with an interesting story. Each week, a research staff read hundreds of letters by people who thought their lives were unusual. This staff also searched newspapers and magazines for likely prospects and sent about 50 suggested names to the producers every day or so. Out of them, seven or eight were selected for a single show.

The producer assigned members of his staff to meet out-of-town guests when they arrived two days before the broadcast. Taking care of these people was not always an easy task. One particular guest could not be left alone because she had a knack for getting lost in hotel lobbies and on city streets. Another fellow got grumpier and grumpier as broadcast time approached. Nobody could figure out his problem, until a staff member discovered that he wasn't satisfied with his meals. He was taken to a steak house and fed a dinner that would have nourished six truck drivers. After that he was happy.[19]

Writers for *We, the People* prepared rough scripts for each guest. Coaching and rehearsal sessions preceded every show. If necessary, sections of each script were revised to fit individual personalities; then more rehearsals followed. Adding to the demanding agenda was a rebroadcast to the West Coast three hours after the initial airing at 9 P.M. in New York. On several occasions a guest appeared on the first broadcast but failed to show up at midnight for the second. Frantic manhunts ensued. If unsuccessful, someone had to be hastily summoned to read the script in place of the missing guest. Once a taxi driver failed to arrive for the rebroadcast; it was assumed that he picked up a fare and got caught in traffic. Director Joe Hill ordered an assistant to rush out into Times Square and grab the first cabbie he could find.[20]

"As a fully scripted show, it undoubtedly lost some spontaneity," admits 1940s program host Dwight Weist. "From time to time, a guest could not read, and thus had to be carefully coached in order to get in the key facts and the tag line. In my time with the show, it always included a celebrity or star, usually in the next-to-last segment."[21]

Generally, when a star finished his work at the mike, he or she rushed out of the playhouse to avoid the usual crush of fans and autograph seekers. "Most took off without a 'thank you,'" Weist says. "The only celebrity who ever expressed any appreciation while I was M.C. was prize fighter Joe Louis."[22]

Weist also recalls a near-explosive incident at a rehearsal with seasoned performer Milton Berle a year or so before his great television success.

"Why are we reading this script?" Berle asked the production staff.

"For timing," replied a young assistant, holding a stopwatch. "It's necessary for a radio show."

"Just tell me how many minutes I have for my bit," said Berle. "I'll watch the studio clock and get on and off on time. I just can't deliver the jokes without allowing time for laughs."

The guileless timekeeper looked up from his watch to ask, "Well, Mr. Berle, how do you know there's going to be any laughs?"[23]

Vox Pop and *We, the People* provided recognition and inspiration to many, but countless Americans were equally intrigued with the thought of winning a prize, especially cash. Few outright question-and-answer shows had as yet bowed on radio. But by the latter half of the 1930s, in spite of possible FCC opposition, the radio dial could not resist a basic formula that attracted the public: the chance to win a prize. Cash awards enabled the Depression-laden to buy a much-needed pair of shoes, treat their family to dinner or pay a landlord back rent. Five or ten dollars made a big difference when most weekly paychecks averaged $30.

The first genuine money quiz arrived in the form of *Professor Quiz*. Conceived by the promotion manager of WJSV (later WTOP) in Washington, D.C., the quiz combined inquiring interviewer and spelling-bee techniques. Emceed by an ex-vaudeville monologist, Jim McWilliams, and sponsored by G. Washington Coffee, it brought contestants before a microphone and plied them with questions such as "Are black and white colors?" and "What officials in France correspond with members of the U.S. Congress?"[24] The game attracted a sizeable studio audience. Listeners, too, had an opportunity to receive cash for questions submitted and used. Studio contestants who answered the highest number of questions won ten silver dollars. To increase listenership, the sponsor added a half-dozen or so other CBS outlets and then moved the show to a nationwide hookup.

On March 1937 *Professor Quiz* came to CBS in New York, bringing a WJSV announcer named Arthur Godfrey to deliver commercials (and often heckle contestants). "His you-all Dixie accent is quite novel," noted *Variety*.[25] The professor's very first quiz question read: "What is the difference between a lama with one 'l' and a llama with two 'ls'?" The contestant failed to come up with the answer: A lama is a Buddhist priest or monk in Tibet and Mongolia; a llama is a South American animal related to the camel.

The success of *Professor Quiz* made broadcasters and sponsors realize they had an answer to the continual challenge of developing new audience-building shows.

In fact, *Professor Quiz* had been so popular in Washington, D.C., that CBS sought to collect a royalty when the program sponsor told the network that it "probably would be moving to NBC."[26] Because the show had originated on a Columbia station, CBS claimed ownership of both the idea and the title. During the confab, McWilliams became ill and apparently was dropped. However, he soon reappeared on NBC with *Uncle Jim's Question Bee*. A new Professor Quiz, Craig Earl, replaced him, although his identity remained concealed for several seasons.

The quintessential question-and-answer man, Earl had played vaudeville as a magician. With his neatly trimmed moustache, wire-frame glasses and bright bowties, the genial trouper easily assumed the role of a professor. He brought a measure of jollity and drollery. Earl's wife assisted, acting as scorekeeper for the fast-paced game. CBS soon assigned its versatile staff announcer Bob Trout to help the duo. Trout had spent several years in Washington where he covered President Franklin D. Roosevelt's first inauguration and introduced FDR's famous informal radio talks to the nation as "fireside chats." He transferred to Columbia's key station in New York in 1935 and quickly established a reputation as a highly capable newscaster and specialist in man-in-the-street interviews.

Professor Quiz and his associates selected five members from the studio audience to answer a half-dozen questions on all sorts of subjects. Generally in the form of riddles and trick puns, they were quite easy. The best score won $25, the second $15. To supply 40 silver dollars each week, director Lee Little tracked them down in dozens of New York banks. He finally arranged for a single banker to provide the silver. When the quiz went on tour, as it frequently did, Lee carried around a bagful of silver so as not to be caught short in a town where these increasingly scarce coins were unavailable. During his first four years on the air, *Professor Quiz* gave away a total of 65,000 coins to both contestants and listeners who supplied questions.[27] In a short time, quiz prizes had leaped from a dollar to much bigger rewards—and the public loved the idea of real money floating around.

Professor Quiz piqued the interest of audiences from the very first broadcast. The question-and-answer motif caught fire immediately. Within two years, there were more than two hundred variations—a bumper crop ranging from a multitude of unimpressive, quickly passing gambols to a roster of spirited, long-lasting brain-twisters.

›4‹

Quiz Craze

"I have a lady in the balcony, Doctor."

This catchphrase became the most repeated line emanating from any pre-TV quiz, perhaps from all of radio in the early 1940s. First spoken by an announcer with a portable microphone in a Chicago theater, these words identified the question-and-answer format of NBC's *Dr. I.Q.*, "The Mental Banker." Introduced in April 1939 as the genial master of wit and information, *Dr. I.Q.* broadcast from a crowded motion picture theater. Four or five assistants roamed the house with hand-held mikes as members of the audience eagerly volunteered to answer short, snappy questions.

A correct answer could win as much as 23 silver dollars. Even wrong replies garnered a box of Milky Way candy bars and two tickets to a show at a local movie theater. Listeners at home could participate by sending in tongue twisters, true or false statements, or biographical clues identifying famous people—special features that paid them up to $50. For the theater audience, a "mastermind" award of $100 awaited those correctly completing 12 difficult questions on cards distributed at the box office before the broadcast.

Like *Vox Pop*, *Dr. I.Q.* originated in Texas. Lee Segall of Houston developed the idea and packaged it for a sponsor as a burlesque-type act on several regional stations.[1] The tremendous success of *Professor Quiz* had already created an interest in similar shows, and *Dr. I.Q.* soon landed on a national hookup with Lew Valentine of San Antonio as the doctor. This good-looking, 26-year-old M.C. with experience as an announcer, singer and dramatic actor, as well as station production manager, had no trouble jumping into the role as major domo of a fast-moving quiz in a large auditorium.

Audiences both at broadcasts and at home relished this latest contest. Too popular merely to remain limited to a single theater in one city, *Dr. I.Q.* spent many months on the road. Large crowds of would-be contestants frequently necessitated extra performances apart from the weekly broadcast. In Louisville, Kentucky, an overflow audience in the lobby of Loew's State Theatre was given a chance to play. One woman in that mob won 50 silver dollars—a big windfall in those preinflation times. Her joyful cry turned to a sigh of relief. Totally broke, she said the money would enable her to return to her family in Atlanta.[2]

Dr. I.Q.'s assistants had an extra chore in Louisville. A new Kentucky law required winners to fill out a card in order for the state to record the 15 percent tax due on such prizes.[3] The show's roving broadcasters were also complaining that the $50 or more in silver required reinforced pockets on their tuxedo jackets. Moreover, the heavy coins, they added, made them look droop-shouldered.[4]

An ill-tempered crowd once greeted "The Mental Banker" in Portland, Maine, at a benefit performance. Most of the 2,500 ticket buyers were led to believe that show would be an actual broadcast, namely, that they would have a reasonably fair chance of being quizzed over the air. When it became apparent that only a tiny handful would play and no one would be heard outside the theater, a sea of disgruntled, moody faces glared at the doctor. Having paid 75 cents—double the price of a local movie ticket—the audience griped over the longshot odds of winning some silver, even a candy bar, let alone being short-changed out of an actual network broadcast.[5]

The incident made *Dr. I.Q.*'s producers and other radio executives wonder: Do nonwinners ever go away happy? Does the mere fact that a show is being broadcast keep an audience satisfied? What does an advertiser gain by associating his product with odds that are painfully long, however much the presence of them may be concealed by quiz-show trimmings?

As more and more quiz programs landed on the airwaves and provided greater opportunities for would-be contestants, answers to these questions soon became less pressing.

The fact that game and audience-participation shows cost significantly less than most prime-time presentations contributed to the surge. "Sustainers" and nonsponsored trial balloons could go into production on a modest budget of $300 or $400. Not infrequently, a show went on the air for the sole purpose of establishing a prior claim ahead of somebody else, who might have a similar format in the pipeline.[6]

General Foods, for one, faced anxious moments over a contract that its agency, Young & Rubicam, had prepared for the MCA-packaged *What Would You Have Done?*[7] Upon learning that others claimed ownership to this audience-participation game, General Foods even insisted on a bond indemnifying it from any lawsuits arising on the question of piracy.

A basic yes-and-no game entitled *True or False* encountered no threats of thievery or plagiarism. Harry Hagen, after a year of spelling bees, inaugurated this generic-type contest over the recently established Mutual Broadcasting System and staged the team-organized contest in different cities. Players on two six-man teams were often recruited from employees of local telephone exchanges, officers of chambers of commerce and editorial staffs of newspapers. Although Hagen's questions were presented simply as statements, they increased in difficulty. Every player, win or lose, received $5; the best guesser, $25. Those on the losing team each picked up a True or False I.Q. board game, a program giveaway that set a merchandising precedent for future quizzes.[8]

Another prime-time entry, *Ask-It-Basket*, had M.C. Jim McWilliams backed up by an expert who answered questions that contestants missed. Sponsored by Colgate Dental Cream on CBS, it featured a round of questions on a specific subject; listeners were invited to send in their own puzzlers on a particular topic.

The 1938–39 season also witnessed the arrival of *Guess Where*, a geography quiz conducted by Budd Hulick of the Colonel Stoopnagel and Budd comic duo. Shirley Booth and Charles Cantor were cast as Mr. and Mrs. Stowaway in skits that contained clues to the city or country where they were. Booth combined this radio job with a leading Broadway role in Katharine Hepburn's play "The Philadelphia Story," necessitating a ten-minute dash from the microphone for an 8:40 P.M. curtain. Sponsor Philip Morris cigarettes took an unusual step to accommodate *Guess Where* fans. They were allowed to observe Friday afternoon rehearsals.[9]

Bob Hawk's *Quixie Doodle*, built around trick questions, pitted a team of question makers against a team of respondents. When the sponsor decided to inject humor into the Mutual program, Colonel Stoopnagel (Frederick Chase Taylor) replaced Hawk, interpolating questions with gag material. The appeal of the show, noted *Variety*, was limited because of the many competing—and better—quizzes, but, it surmised, "touring the broadcast to different originating points on its 10-station net may hype considerable interest."[10]

New, but far less compelling, formats vied for an audience. *Answer Auction*, *Whodunit?*, *Fun in Print* and *Youth vs. Age* appeared and sunk in a season or less. Other entries merely surfaced as summer replacements for Jack Benny or Fred Allen and then faded at the first frost.

Independent stations lost little time jumping on the gamewagon. A regional contest sometimes revealed more originality and spontaneity than many network presentations. *Treasure Hunt* at KSD, St. Louis, began with a 15-minute segment at 6:30 P.M. when announcer Frank Eschen

rattled off the treasures that contestants needed to win. On one particular show, the 75 or so players had to find a baseball bat, bean bag,
tea kettle, 12-inch board with 25 carpet tacks and necklace made of 20
different buttons; find the numer of Caseys listed in the local telephone
book; determine the number of black squares on a checkerboard and
the number of trees surrounding a nearby plaza; then write a 25-word
paragraph on the merits of the sponsor's Cremo Cigars and finally,
return wearing the largest possible artificial flower.[11]

Each week more than 500 spectators crowded the radio studio to
await the contestants' reappearance and awarding of prizes. A forerun-
ner of *Truth or Consequences*, the attention-getting *Treasure Hunt* offered
fun for players and observers on Saturday nights.

By 1940 sponsors faced a flood of mail from listeners sending in quiz
questions, requesting tickets, and commenting, pro or con, on the latest broadcast. A veritable "matterhorn," the weekly mountain of letters
approached, and sometimes exceeded, 10,000 pieces for big network
quizzes. Overwhelmed by the volume, some producers opened only
the first 500 letters and tossed aside the rest.[12] Handling tons of listener
correspondence became a major, and generally tedious, part of the price
of success.

A program that virtually depended on listener letters—in fact, they
were the very premise of the show—was *The Answer Man*. Started in
1937 by Albert Mitchell, a former musician, conductor, composer and
master of ceremonies in vaudeville, and by Bruce Chapman, a radio
producer, it first aired as a weekly unsponsored feature at WICC in
Bridgeport, Connecticut. Mitchell as "Answer Man" asked listeners to
send in any factual questions that they wished to have answered over
the air. Connecticut audiences took him up on this challenge, creating
a hit in less than a month. Mutual and its New York station WOR
wasted no time in bringing Mitchell to a bigger forum. Network sponsor Provident Loan Society made possible a large staff of researchers
who came up with answers to what would number in the 1940s a quarter
of a million questions each year.[13]

This "braintrust" of about 20 people found answers to approximately
65 percent of all questions. But for the remainder, it turned to a long
list of reliable authorities—experts such as Dr. William Bridge of The
New York Zoological Society (who once determined that the average
parasol ant walks 720 feet per hour) and Dr. William H. Crew, physi-
cist at New York University (who confirmed that a barrel of beer would
float in seawater). In turn, well-known figures in many fields turned
to *The Answer Man* when they were puzzled over a factual question.
Novelist Kenneth Roberts, author of *Northwest Passage*, regularly cor-
responded, and one time asked to know who made George Washington's false teeth (the answer: dentist John Greenwood).[14]

During a daily 15-minute broadcast, some 40 questions of general interest were broadcast; questions not aired, nevertheless, were answered by mail. Mitchell, however, refused to respond to queries by telephone, and legal and medical questions were unacceptable. Only once, apparently, was Al Mitchell ever stumped. A Boston listener asked: "Did Paul Revere's friend wave his lantern up and down or sideways to signal the arrival of British Troops?" As a reminder of his fallibility, he had the question written on parchment and framed.

During its 13-year run, *The Answer Man* stood as an unusual educational and trivia feature as well as an argument settler—even a voice of prime authority. Such stature brought an occasional brickbat. "I wish you would fall off a cliff," a Nyack, New York, breadwinner wrote. "My wife and kids used to take my word for things, but no more. No, they write you instead. You're a homewrecker!"[15]

Al Mitchell's creation encouraged producers of other so-called intellectual quizzes and led to a very popular panel show that meshed entertainment and information in a skillful blend. This unlikely hit stemmed from the imagination and determination of one individual, a dabbler in radio and a self-proclaimed "idea man."

Born in New York at the turn of the century, Dan Golenpaul attended Columbia University and then managed local political campaigns and speakers' forums. A fascination with early radio led to an involvement with public service programs on several independent stations, including WBAT and WHN. His *Magazine of the Air* was an innovative if short-lived feature with advertisers paying for segments on current events, literature, sports, theater and music.[16] With the encouragement of New York University and The New School for Social Research, he produced and aired programs on education and government.

Carrying around a pocketful of ideas from station to station, Golenpaul finally sold one called *Raising Your Parents* to NBC as a ten-minute sustainer on Saturday mornings. Milton Cross presided over a panel of youngsters suggesting solutions to problems sent in by other children. A child psychologist provided professional commentary at the conclusion of each discussion. With *Raising Your Parents*, Golenpaul almost struck paydirt.

"When NBC hired Toscanini at $40,000 a year, beginning in 1937," Golenpaul always insisted, "many sustaining shows were dropped as a cost-cutting measure. So the Maestro put me out of work. But not *Professor Quiz* who was big at that time. I used to get annoyed when he made such a great fuss over the fact that a contestant didn't know an answer. A bit sadistic, I thought."[17]

Golenpaul wondered why people exposed themselves to such situations. "I wish I had these quizmasters and so-called experts in front of me," he thought. "I'd like to ask them some questions. They're probably not much brighter than the average listener." [18]

The idea of turning the tables and putting the bigshots in a hot seat intrigued Golenpaul. He outlined a format whereby the average person—the underdog—could stump the pros. At the same time, he wanted the experts to be interesting, funny and spontaneous. For listener identification, he recognized the importance of lining up the same group of experts week after week. NBC took a dim view of a stodgy group of esoteric windbags. Too highbrow, the network pointed out. Nevertheless, it told Golenpaul to go ahead within a budget of $400 a week. He already had its name, *Information Please*, but now he faced the problem of how to find personable and erudite panelists. Would such individuals be willing to go before millions of Americans and take on a question that clearly might reveal outright ignorance in their particular specialty or sphere of knowledge?

For help, Golenpaul turned to the book editor at *The New Yorker*. Clifton Fadiman had had some radio experience. He briefly had reviewed books over the air. Although the feature didn't catch fire, Golenpaul liked his flair and wit, especially in debates with other literary critics. He visualized "Kip" Fadiman as a quizmaster presiding over a handful of congenial authorities and masterminds.

"It was a crazy idea and I told him so," Fadiman claimed some 50 years later. [19] "No one but Dan had much faith in the program. A shoestring project, it seemed to have no chance of finding an audience or picking up a sponsor. By necessity, the first panelists were journalists, high school teachers and other educated unknowns. Only Franklin Pierce Adams—the great F.P.A. of 'The Conning Tower' column in the New York *Post* and a member of the famous Round Table at the Algonquin Hotel—measured up. Exceedingly witty and highly urbane, Adams excelled from the very beginning and was invited back."*

Fadiman—introduced as the "Toscanini of Quiz" on the premiere, May 17, 1938—presided over an exhilarating half-hour. "A pip novelty," said critic Robert Landry. [20] Yet there were a number of "bugs" to work out. Golenpaul had solicited on-the-air questions from the studio audience. To pull it off, he corralled everyone he knew to come and act as "ringers" by asking questions he had prepared in advance. He soon switched to listener-submitted questions to exercise more control and continuity. At the same time, Golenpaul found the makings of a permanent panel.

Along with Adams, he chose John Kieran, a sportswriter for the *New York Times*, and Oscar Levant, a concert pianist and musicologist.

---

*Adams flopped as a quizmaster when he hosted a spelling bee and word-usage contest called *The Word Game* for CBS.

The fourth chair was reserved for a different well-known guest each week.

Putting such people on the spot paid off. "It's the same element that makes for success of the amateur hour, but in this case the 'amateurs' are 'experts' and the gong that signifies error is the cash register," wrote Orrin Dunlap of the *New York Times*.[21] "Furthermore, the quiz is educational as well as entertaining. . . . This is no 'background' or 'atmosphere' program; to enjoy it the listener must give undivided attention. He cannot be reading, playing bridge or visiting with friends. This quiz is a concentration program; it exercises the mind."

Listeners had an opportunity to hear what the experts knew, what simple questions they missed and what complex ones they answered correctly. The expert became a mirror for the listener, who at the end of the program was pleased if he found himself with a higher score than those of the panelists. Listeners rallied to the crowing rooster and the words of announcer Milton Cross, "Wake up, America! It's time to stump the experts!"[22]

Clifton Fadiman remained the fulcrum, bringing to his weekly assignment a measure of liveliness, informality and drollness. His friendly approach made it seem as if the program were being played by family and friends in a living room.

"The program developed a cult," Fadiman says. "It received good reviews and press coverage, in part because F.P.A. and Kieran were journalists and knew so many newspaper people. Certainly we were all radio neophytes. But it clicked, and off we went. By the fall of 1938, we were sponsored by Canada Dry Ginger Ale, and moved into the money and the top ten."[23]

Questions submitted by listeners were selected by Golenpaul, his wife, Anne, and their editorial advisers. They paid $5 for every question used. For every one the panel failed to answer, they sent $10 and a multivolume set of the *Encyclopaedia Britannica*.

"The panel had a wealth of information," Fadiman points out. "But the show was no mere recitation of facts and knowledge. How they answered a question was really more important than a correct answer. My job was to get the best out of the quartet and generate an interplay of spirited and unrehearsed commentary."

John Kieran, in addition to a vast knowledge of sports, had an impressive grasp of the natural sciences and Shakespeare. Cheerful and mild-mannered, he was an omnivorous reader with a depth of knowledge of many subjects and was the hardest panelist of all to beat. One of seven children of James Kieran, a school principal who later became a professor and then president of Hunter College, he grew up in a home where good books were a way of life. At the age of 46, Kieran began leading the double life of sports columnist and panelist for a suddenly very popular program.

In Oscar Levant, *Information Please,* in the words of Kieran, "found a positive genius for making off-hand cutting remarks that could not have been sharper if he had honed them a week in his mind."[24] Many thought him strange, eccentric and a bit crazy, but never boring. As the youngest and most uninhibited member of the group, he was constantly referred to as "l'enfant terrible."

Once, when questioned to name the author of an autobiography that began, "I was born an ugly duckling," Levant unhesitantly replied "Eleanor Roosevelt." Democrats all over the country quickly called to protest. The opening line came not from Mrs. FDR's writings but from the life story penned by veteran actress Marie Dressler.[25]

Levant was thought by many to be the nearest to a real genius on the panel. Born in Pittsburgh, he was a musician from his early childhood and had studied in Europe with composer Arnold Schoenberg. He didn't have much formal education after that. Oscar's keyboard talent took him to Hollywood where he worked in early sound pictures. A close friend of George Gershwin, he became identified with the composer and his works, frequently performing "Rhapsody in Blue." Born with a prodigious memory, he picked up a lot of information and facts just from talking with the celebrities that frequented his life, and many appeared as guests on *Information Please.*

Famous authors, actors, scientists, professors, playwrights, congressmen and musicians eagerly joined the panel because the show was both literate and fun—not to mention a prestigious, albeit low-key, showcase for their latest book, composition, film, play or legislation. "Giving a right answer was the least important contribution by any guest or regular on the panel," John Kieran wrote in his book of recollections *Not Under Oath.* "It was generally more fun when the answer was wrong, especially if the culprit tried to wriggle out of it. An uproarious error or a brilliant bit of irrelevance was rated far above any dull delivery of truth."[26]

Everyone seemed willing to get into the spirit of the proceedings, although most were invariably nervous at first. Many stumbled over easy questions. Economist Stuart Chase didn't know that "multiple shops" was British for "chain stores." Dramatist George F. Kaufman was asked to name the only distinctive thing about his play "Deep Tangled Wildwood." While he pondered, Kip Fadiman twitted him with the sad truth: "George, it flopped." Author John Gunther once identified Reza Pahlavi as the ruler of Persia. "Are you Shah?" grinned Fadiman. "Sultanly," quipped Gunther.[27] A serious Gracie Allen revealed a surprisingly broad grasp of politics, aviation, literature, music and even pediatrics.

Few politicians or government officials passed up an invitation to appear. Governors Harold Stassen and Wilbur Cross and Senators Henry Cabot Lodge and James Fulbright joined the panel. When the United

Nations began meeting in New York, Lester B. Pearson, Ralph Bunche and Sir Gladwyn Jebb appeared. U.S. presidential hopeful Wendell Wilkie became a leading Republican contender in 1940 after his visit.

"But politicians in general," Fadiman points out, "had the dullest minds. Along with bankers, they usually fell flat at our microphone. Perhaps they were too used to appealing for votes and avoiding anything too controversial."[28]

In November 1939 Roosevelt's Postmaster General James A. Farley came on. His lack of knowledge of the Federal Postal Service became apparent by the end of the show, but he did impress some listeners by identifying Dr. Crawford Long as the inventor of anesthesia.[29]

One of the most engaging and flamboyant politicians, New York Mayor Fiorello LaGuardia, also muffed several questions on his city. On another broadcast he had better luck. He submitted a question and won $10 by stumping guest Maury Maverick, mayor of San Francisco.[30]

Musicians often came aboard too. Artur Rubenstein answered questions on music as well as European royalty, an area of special interest to this world-renowned concert pianist. For a musical question, NBC staff musician Joe Kahn, who regularly provided *Information Please* clues on his keyboard, played a few bars of a piece.[31] Fadiman first asked Rubenstein if he liked Kahn's brief rendition.

"No!" exclaimed the great virtuoso.

The studio audience laughed. So did Kahn. Then he quickly realized he had been insulted in front of millions of listeners. Rubenstein realized his blunder and attempted to withdraw his curt observation of a fellow artist and member of the prestigious NBC Symphony.

"I thought you asked me whether John Kieran could play that piece."

A rather lame coverup, thought Kahn.[32]

That week Golenpaul's office was swamped with letters and postcards in Joe Kahn's defense. "We didn't realize that the program had that loyal an audience," Kahn says in recalling the incident. "I certainly was not in competition with Rubenstein; I idolized him."[33]

The most uproarious evening unfolded when Harpo Marx occupied the visitor's chair. He stayed in character, never uttering a word. The mute Marx Brother answered questions by sounding his old auto horn, then whistling bits of familiar songs.

Before long, a small coterie of bright, articulate and witty regulars stood on call to fill in, especially when Levant's concerts took him away from New York. They included Deems Taylor, John Erskine, Russel Crouse, Grantland Rice, James Mitchener, Louis Bromfield, Christopher Morley, Lillian Gish, Cornelia Otis Skinner and Fred Allen.

The first sponsor of *Information Please*, Canada Dry, basked in the high ratings and widespread press coverage. The show boosted sales of their ginger ale by 20 percent during 1939, and the company considered the $10,000 in weekly production costs money well spent. Promotional spinoffs and premiums created a bustling sideline for Dan Golenpaul and his wife, Anne. They offered Information Please games, and with John Kieran, prepared an annual *Information Please Almanac and Year Book*. Pathé and other filmmakers produced a total of 50 Information Please shorts for theater release.

The country's newspaper editors voted the program the best radio quiz of 1939 and the fourth best show in all of radio, surpassed only by Jack Benny, Bergen & McCarthy, and Bing Crosby. Kip Fadiman found himself among the poll's "New Stars," receiving more votes than Bob Hope, Kay Kyser and H. V. Kaltenborn and only a few less than Orson Welles. In 1940 the *Saturday Review of Literature* gave *Information Please* its award for distinguished service to literature.[34] On many campuses, undergraduates voted the show their favorite program, as did numerous alumni.

Overseas, a British version called *Any Questions?* came into play over the BBC in the early 1940s (and rebroadcast as *Brains Trust* in New York by WNEW). *Any Questions?* gathered a blue-ribbon panel of professors, scientists, military leaders and statesmen who, after facing questions, gave a long-winded discussion of the subject matter. Popular in England, it failed to win Manhattan listeners who anticipated a more stimulating contest among Anglo brains.[35] A similar presentation, *Transatlantic Quiz*, with competing panels on each side of the Atlantic, aired simultaneously over NBC and BBC.[36]

Information Please sponsors and networks changed throughout the 1940s. Golenpaul contributed to periodic moves by upping the price for the services of his panel and staff and by inviting guests unpopular in radio's executive suites. FDR New Dealers, such as Harold Ickes and Ellis Arnall, often brought anguished outcries. In 1940 Lucky Strike, the leading brand of American Tobacco, picked up the sponsorship, integrating its strident, hard-hitting commercials into the proceedings. Cigar-smoking Golenpaul took an immediate dislike to his new backers and refused to shift loyalty to the company now paying his bills. "Every brand of cigarette is as bad as every other brand," he often repeated.[37]

A special promotional slogan, "Lucky Strike Has Gone to War"—referring to a wartime switch from the traditional green and red pack to a colorless wrapper—constantly annoyed Golenpaul. He wanted the oft-repeated line off his show, claiming it "loused up" the dignity of the presentation. The tobaccomen refused, so Golenpaul sued them. The controversy made the front pages and actually generated much favorable publicity for the program. American Tobacco insisted it had bought the air time and could say what it pleased about its product. Both parties eventually settled the confab out of court.[38] But Lucky Strike did not renew its contract. Actually, few sponsors pleased Golenpaul.

In the late 1940s he battled Parker Pens and CBS when they injected product plugs into actual panel questions. In 1947 *Information Please* switched to Mutual, which resulted in multiple sponsorship. Its trouble-prone creator expressed his dislike of this co-op arrangement and slapped a half-million-dollar suit against the network. It sounded the death knell for the now-fading series. Revived briefly as a local WOR sustainer and telecast as a CBS summer replacement for Fred Waring, it failed to captivate audiences in the early 1950s.

"We had ten good years with a significant impact and influence," Fadiman emphasizes. "The program gave the American public new role models beyond those in sports, politics and films. Suddenly, intelligent men and women were looked up to and emulated. And most came across as 'regular guys.' We'd get fan letters saying, 'Our son, or daughter, could not live without listening to you every Tuesday night.' Maybe we demonstrated that education is worthwhile and can be fun."[39]

Beyond *Information Please*, Clifton Fadiman added to his popularity. He hosted an early television series *This Is Show Business*, a season of *Quiz Kids*, and a radio feature called *Conversation*. But *Information Please* remains the program for which he is remembered. He is often asked if it would prove successful today.

"Conversation was in a general state of decline even before 1938," he believes. "*Information Please* actually helped to revive it." Television definitely stifled intelligent conversation, Fadiman believes. "In an age of TV talk shows, why converse when you can get other people to do it for you. Moreover, there's an absence of a solid, broad-based frame of reference for literature, history, political science and geography. Even the wit and humor of *Information Please* might confuse them," he adds. "It's impossible for an audience to respect the mind of a F.P.A. and, at the same time, admire the lack of a mind of a John Belushi."[40]

"*Information Please*," he concludes, "came across as a family show, attracting listeners of all ages, levels of education and degrees of knowledge. It wouldn't have much appeal today."[41]

Clifton Fadiman might have noted that even in 1940 the program was looked upon by some as an aberration—an oasis among banal gag and empty-talk quiz shows. While thousands were sending in questions to stump the experts and win $10 and an encyclopedia, millions were vicariously participating in a mental crap game or merely sitting between a radio and a telephone waiting to win ten times that amount.

›5‹

"Hold It, Horace!"

A troubled housewife glanced at the stack of bills on her kitchen table. Among them was a notice of long-overdue telephone charges. It was the one bill she desperately wanted to pay. The telephone company now asked for immediate payment; if the account was not paid in full, the telephone would be disconnected.

The wife called the local telephone office and pleaded to be allowed to keep the telephone for just one more week—at least until the following Wednesday morning. The telephone representative reluctantly agreed.

A few days later, on a Tuesday evening, the wife and her husband sat listening to their radio. They enjoyed the popular musical selections, but it was a spinning wheel at the broadcast studio that held them spellbound. They visualized this wheel coming to rest at a number that would correspond to their telephone listing in the local directory.

"Somewhere in this broad land a phone is going to ring," the radio announcer reminded them.

The large wheel spun for the third and final time to pick the actual telephone listing on the particular page number selected by the second spin and from the city or area directory chosen by the first spin. Seconds after the selection wheel stopped at a number, the couple heard their name spoken by the announcer. They shouted with joy. Soon the telephone rang. This was the moment they had hoped and dreamed of for months. The call would pay off their debts and help them get back on their feet.[1]

"This is the *Pot o' Gold*," the caller proclaimed. "And you have just won $1,000 in cash!"

The bills were paid, and the telephone stayed in that household. The couple typified most Americans in the late 1930s. They clung to their telephones. Along with the radio, the telephone was a device to help endure the rough days and maybe even lead to a windfall. Once broadcasters realized that the telephone could be used to bring hundreds of thousands, even millions, of new listeners to their radio receivers, Bell's invention would never be very far from the microphone on a quiz or giveaway show.

By 1939 there were more than 20 million telephone subscribers in the United States. Fewer and fewer households lacked a telephone. Through the AT&T system, an operator could easily connect a caller with virtually any place in the country within a minute or less. Radio's *Pot o' Gold* was among the first to tap the tremendous audience-building potential at the end of a telephone receiver. This innovative breakthrough delighted stations, sponsors, producers, performers and listeners. At the same time, the *Pot o' Gold* and similar radio giveaways caused government investigations, individual lawsuits, theater-owner threats and audience complaints. From the day an ingenious fellow by the name of Robert Brilmayer walked into the office of The Music Corporation of American (MCA) and presented his idea of a radio giveaway, the airwaves would never be the same again.

MCA's Harold Hackett had been assigned the supervision of radio programs for big band clients. Every bandleader sought a commercial show. It was Hackett's job to devise an attention-getting format to spotlight the maestro and his musicians. To Hackett, a visit by Robert Brilmayer seemed just another attempt by a guy off the street to show the professionals how clever he was. Hackett greeted the young man and asked what he could do for the big bands.

"There are millions of telephones in homes throughout the country," Brilmayer said. "Why not select one or two phone listings every week on a musical show. Call the party and have the bandleader give away $1,000 for just answering the phone."[2]

Hackett thanked him for the suggestion but expressed doubts over whether MCA would be interested. Nevertheless, the concept of a giant giveaway among U.S. telephone subscribers intrigued Hackett. With MCA's okay, he decided to buy the suggestion, agreeing to pay Brilmayer several hundred dollars a week if the idea went on the air.[3]

Hackett looked over the roster of bands under MCA management; they included Benny Goodman, Guy Lombardo, Sammy Kaye, Tommy Dorsey and Eddy Duchin. Horace Heidt had been a client for several years with better-than-average success. He had been in the band business for more than 15 years.

Heidt, while a student of the University of California in the early 1920s, started a four-piece band for engagements in nearby Oakland. He played there in clubs and theaters for most of the decade. In 1930 he traveled to New York with a 12-man outfit for for an eagerly sought engagement with comedian Ken Murray at the Palace Theatre. The orchestra was a hit, staying 16 weeks. From there, it went to Monte Carlo. A year later, the group came back to New York where, this time, they totally flopped. Heidt's band soon broke up. He returned to California where he conducted a pit band in San Francisco. Heidt then organized a youthful aggregation, sparkling with talented performers and adept showmanship. It led to theater, hotel and radio work and frequent record dates, including the waxing of his theme "I'll Love You in My Dreams" and his 1938 hit "Ti-Pi-Tin."

His troupe—at first called the Brigadiers and then the Musical Knights—was a diversified, familylike outfit, full of individual talent, including at one time or another, singer Larry Cotton, pianist-composer Frankie Carle, trumpeter Bobby Hackett, baritone Gordon MacRae, vocal quartet The King Sisters, guitarist Alvino Rey, whistler Fred Lowery, singer-mimic Art Carney and canine mascot Lobo.[4] They contributed to the solid, old-time showmanship that characterized the Heidt stage band. But his weekly radio broadcasts had generally failed to catch on big with coast-to-coast audiences. Harold Hackett approached the bandleader, who was eager to vie over the air with the Dorseys, Benny Goodman, Fred Waring and other reigning organizations of the late 1930s.

Heidt reminded MCA that he had initiated one of the earliest audience-participation shows on radio. It happened at the Drake Hotel in Chicago in 1932. During a broadcast remote from the hotel, a microphone fell off the bandstand onto the dance floor. To cover the embarassing moment, Heidt jumped down off the bandstand, picked up the mike, and started to converse with several couples as to what kind of a time they were having, where they lived and what song they would like to hear played. An accident, it started a whole new feature for Heidt and his nightly broadcasts. Heidt called it "Answers By the Dancers." Listeners liked hearing the ad-lib comments of the people dancing to Heidt's music. Dancers soon crowded the Drake ballroom and competed for Horace's attention at the microphone.[5]

A year or two later, the engaging, friendly maestro expanded on the feature, which was now widely imitated on other programs. Heidt decided to interview only people who were celebrating their anniversaries or people about to be married. Games were played for prizes, and the one who failed to answer the questions correctly was make to "walk the plank"—a strictly audio gimmick that tested the versatility of the radio sound-effects technician. This anniversary night program led to "The Treasure Chest," whereby winning contestants reached into a drum to select valuable gifts, such as theater tickets and luggage. Heidt relished the spontaneous repartee and enthusiastic response of the people who came to his microphone.[6] Yet by 1938 he wanted a new and dramatically different feature to capture a bigger audience.

At the same time, a small and relatively inconspicuous manufacturer of drugs in St. Louis sought new ways to stimulate sales for its products. The Lewis-Howe Company had been founded by a doctor and a pharmacist at the turn of the century to produce a vegetable laxative called Nature's Remedy. A new product was added in the mid-1930s as the result of President James Howe's wife. The couple had traveled to Europe and on the return voyage, Mrs. Howe had become ill with stomach cramps. When Mr. Howe reached home, he went to his basement workshop and mixed a compound for his wife to try. The mixture gave relief to her indigestion. Howe decided to manufacture commercially the compound, which chiefly contained calcium carbonate. Formulated into an antacid tablet, Howe called his new product Tums, which, he pointed out, sounded as if it were a solution for a sour tummy.[7] The candylike concoction joined Nature's Remedy on drugstore shelves.

The laxative would soon be overshadowed by Tums. Nature's Remedy, because of broadcasting bans against laxatives, could not be advertised over network radio.[8] Tums, on the other hand, could be plugged on the air as much as Life Savers (which they resembled in package and in price). In 1938 Lewis-Howe spent more than $400,000 for radio time for Tums. The following year, the company sought a new coast-to-coast hookup to stimulate sales in drug and cigar stores. With a half-dozen years of attention-getting audience interviews and quiz segments to his credit, Horace Heidt offered an opportunity for Lewis-Howe to make Tums a bigger name. The company could not have anticipated the instant acclaim as well as the chronic headaches from the *Pot o' Gold*. On some days the firm surely wished it had concocted a head remedy, not a stomach soother.

Lewis-Howe proceeded cautiously once Heidt and producer Ed Byron had been signed for the new 1939 radio series. The company eased him and his aggregation into the program by sponsoring his "Answers by the Dancers" during the slack summer listening period. At the same time, the Tums makers started a program called *Quicksilver*, broadcast over 29 NBC outlets from Chicago. The series was broadcast from the Chicago & Northwestern Railway station where travelers, commuters and trainmen were briefly interviewed and asked a riddle.[9] If the contestant answered correctly, the M.C. gave five silver dollars plus a roll of Tums. Listeners were requested to send in original riddles on the chance they would be used, thus earning the listener $20 and a package of Tums.

In the fall, the major emphasis would be placed not on *Quicksilver* but on Horace Heidt and the new NBC series tagged *Pot o' Gold*. A mammoth game, based not upon quizzes or riddles or stunts, it focused on a giant multinumber wheel of fortune.

Heidt's orchestra furnished music between and during turns of the giant wheel. Announcer Ben Grauer and vocalist Larry Cotton spun the selector three times during each broadcast. The first spin "picked" a volume from the vast collection of telephone books. Another spin picked a page of the book. The last spin picked a line on the page, giving a telephone number. Then the call was placed.[10]

"The *Pot o' Gold* show was the first radio program to extend prizes beyond a studio audience to listeners across the country," remarked Horace Heidt 45 years after the inauguration of this big radio giveaway.[11]

> When the trade first heard of the idea of utilizing the telephone to hand out money, some people speculated that the show might never air because of the networks' policies outlawing contests based on chance. But NBC pointed out that it was no contest, merely a windfall if a home telephone happened to ring. You didn't even have to be listening to the show to win. However, there were repercussions and objections from areas we never dreamed of. The immediate response, of course, pleased us all. I had guaranteed Mr. Howe that the show would get Tums from the back shelf of drug stores to front counter beside the cash register. Within a month or so, most outlets had placed Tums on the counter in full view of every customer. The plant in St. Louis expanded almost overnight, turning out tens of millions of Tums tablets a week.[12]

With very few exceptions, the lucky winners called by the *Pot o' Gold* needed the $1,000 prize and were overjoyed to get it. Mrs. Ben Kluding of Norwalk, Ohio, and the mother of eight children, ages 11 to 26, spent it on groceries and clothes. Her husband had become disabled and had not worked in four years.[13] For some, the money provided cash for an unplanned vacation, as it did for an exterminator in Jacksonville, Florida. He mapped out a trip to New York.

Heidt remembered one call in particular to a far-from-needy couple in Beverly Hills. When the call was answered, he asked for the man of the house.

"Yes, this is his residence," a woman replied.

"You have just won the Pot o' Gold! This is Horace Heidt calling from New York. You have just won $1,000. What does your husband do?"

"He works out in the garden."

"Oh, he's a gardener."

"No," the wife abruptly answered. "He's not a gardener. He's out in his garden watering plants."[14]

The Beverly Hills woman had never heard of the *Pot o' Gold* and the $1,000 was only seed money to the affluent couple. Heidt ended the telephone call fast.[15] In this case, the thrill and excitement of winning just didn't materialize.

On another occasion, a husband refused to answer the *Pot o' Gold* call. His wife was away, and, it was later discovered, he was spending that evening entertaining a girlfriend. He passed up the $1,000 fearing the notoriety might expose his philandering.[16]

The majority of Americans stayed next to their radios every Tuesday night between 8:30 and 9:00 P.M. eastern standard time—and kept a clear path to their telephone. Calls dropped noticeably during the half-hour. Theater owners complained of a dip in attendance. Dozens piped the show into the lobby and delayed the start of movie presentations. Other managers offered $1,000 to any patron called while in their theater.[17] A delighted Bob Hope, who followed *Pot o' Gold* on Tuesdays over NBC, called Heidt to exclaim that his comedy-show rating had gone up eight points after a month or so in the wake of the phenomenal giveaway.[18]

Heidt's ratings soared too. Only the *Fitch Bandwagon* surpassed Heidt among musical variety shows. His popularity rose so quickly that the network seemed a bit unprepared for the widespread attention. NBC and Lewis-Howe, still uncertain whether the proceedings were not a lottery, actually considered ways to bring down the ratings so that the Federal Communications Commission would not become alarmed and perhaps take the *Pot* off the air.[19] Meanwhile, a flurry of similar programs sprung up at large and small stations throughout the United States. Reports came to the trade of variations of the Tums idea, twists on bingo and a general outbreak of merchandizing enthusiasm for cash come-ons.

At WOAI in San Antonio, *Popsicle Pete's Money Box* dialed local numbers and asked if there was a child between 5 and 17 years of age at home. If so, he or she received a check for $2.50 and a merchandise prize.[20] Kay's jewelry store in Providence, Rhode Island, used radio and telephones to distribute five dollar bills to numbers called on its program *Buy on Credit*. Oddities multiplied. In Bridgeport, Connecticut, according to *Variety*, "the punchboard gentry" were making book on the state the Tums winner would be in.[21]

Complaints by would-be winners and disgruntled theater owners and various antilottery segments kept the *Pot o' Gold* and similar giveaways boiling. Even after six months on the air, Heidt wondered if the ax would suddenly fall through governmental intervention.[22] In the spring of 1940, the Justice Department finally informed the Federal Commu-

nications Commission (FCC) that punitive action need not be instituted.[23] The program's technique did not include "consideration," an
element in a game of chance and, in this situation, meaning active participation by a contestant. Some experts, however, felt that the listener
actually answering the telephone could be construed as consideration.[24] The question of what did or did not constitute consideration
would be raised and debated beyond the halycon days of radio and
well into the formative years of television.

Peeved almost-winners had raised Wednesday morning havoc and
created unpleasant headlines almost from the first Tums telephone call.
J. A. Planting of Anaheim, California, was dining at home with his
family when the *Pot o' Gold* rang from Philadelphia.[25] He ran to his hall
telephone. He heard a long-distance operator say that there was so
much music, noise and confusion on the caller's end that "they" could
not hear Mr. Planting and that "it would be taken care of tomorrow."
The local operator repeated the words of the Philadelphia operator. By
now Planting realized that Horace Heidt was calling. He stood to lose
a grand by someone's mistake or bad hearing. He asked the Anaheim
operator to connect him with the exchange manager, but he wasn't in.
He asked her to please make a record of the call.

In the meantime, announcer Ben Grauer had shouted, "Hold it, Horace . . . stop the music! I think we have a winner."

After a pause, Grauer reluctantly stated that the Plantings did not
answer, that they evidently were not home. Western Union, he noted,
would be delivering a consolation prize—a money order for $100.
However, it was no consolation to Planting.

Almost immediately, his telephone rang with callers, ribbing him about
not staying home and answering his telephone. Everywhere he went
for weeks, someone would yell, "Hey, Planting, why didn't you answer your phone?" It wasn't so funny to Planting. He complained to
Tums, NBC and the telephone company. Their reply—he never answered the telephone—only angered him more. The press took up his
cry and told his story throughout the country. But he failed to prevail
against the giveaway masters. The $100 money order was his only re-
ward.[26]

Several thousand miles to the east, on an earlier broadcast, Mrs.
L. G. Gantz of Marietta, Ohio, met a similar fate. Her dog whined at the
kitchen door soon after Heidt came over the radio. She had the mis-
fortune of stepping out with the pet when both Heidt and nature called.[27]

On the evening of January 9, 1940, the *Pot o' Gold*, broadcasting from
Hollywood, proceeded in its usual style with the spinning of the selector. The consecutive spins of the wheel resulted in the selection of the
name of Cornelius C. Dumont and the number 4-6097 in Albany, New
York.[28] Mr. Dumont was at home smoking his pipe and apparently

waiting for just such a call. The long-distance operator rang the number. No one answered.

A perplexed Cornelius Dumont had heard his name over the air, but the number, he quickly realized was his old listing, given up when he moved to a new address in Albany seven months earlier. About a month before Heidt's call, a new telephone directory had been issued for Albany in which Dumont's new address and number were listed. His old number had been assigned to someone else. Who was entitled to the $1,000 windfall or the $100 consolation prize?

Dumont immediately complained to NBC, which pointed out that the program only selected telephone numbers, not the name. Moreover, all calls were placed station to station. In the event the telephone was not answered, the consolation money was sent to the name opposite that number in the telephone book used. This almost-winner, however, refused this explanation of being the man who wasn't there. He obtained a writ of attachment under which a levy was served by the local sheriff's office on an account owed to the Lewis-Howe Company by a local dealer. Since the Tums firm was a Missouri corporation, it was necessary to find some property in New York as a prerequisite to serving a summons. Dumont charged the defendant with carelessness and negligence in failing to ascertain his correct telephone number in the then-current directory. He demanded payment of the $1,000.[29]

The Tums makers refused to pay off. They also reminded Dumont that, inasmuch as the jackpot was an outright gift, neither he nor others had any cause for complaint.

For nearly a year he sought $1,000 or nothing. Not long after the *Pot* began its second year on the air, his lawyers advised him to drop his suit and accept the $100 consolation prize. Cornelius Dumont conceded defeat in the much-publicized controversy. Two months later, on December 10, 1940, the "little man who wasn't there" died of pneumonia . . . and perhaps frustration.[30]

The brouhaha stirred up similar complaints when telephone calls placed by the *Pot* were misrouted or disconnected. Listeners not owning telephones out of preference or economics also felt cheated. Tums acknowledged the millions of listeners without listings and contemplated a plan for including them in the periphery of perspective winners. The sponsor found a solution to bring in more of the American public. Horace Heidt carried his giant wheel into theaters throughout the country and, as part of an on-stage movie-house presentation, spun the selector for strictly local audiences. Heidt and his troupe toured the United States, preceded in city after city by an advance staff of a dozen or so promoters who alerted managers of drugstores of the upcoming arrival of the giveaway. A solid distribution system for Tums was built up; at the same time more people in an area were offered an opportunity to participate at much more favorable odds.

NBC and Lewis-Howe also made efforts to ease their giveaway off the full network. When stations in Baltimore, Kansas City and Detroit canceled the show because, in their words, "it was not in the public interest," the network and the sponsor were not alarmed or dismayed.[31] They now placed more emphasis on regional radio versions, particularly for New York listeners.

With some 10 million people in the metropolitan New York area alone, Tums spun off a duplicate *Pot o' Gold*, originating at WMCA and broadcast over two other independent stations, WNEW and WHN.[32] Tommy Tucker and his orchestra and announcer Rush Hughes presented the regional version, which scaled down the giveaway to $500 per program.

Although the U.S. Department of Justice had announced that it would not institute "prosecutive action" against the *Pot*, program supervisor Harold Hackett still worried about a possible antilottery ban by the Roosevelt administration. One day he picked up a newspaper and read a story announcing that President Roosevelt's son James had become a movie producer. Hackett was struck with an idea. He approached young Roosevelt and asked, "How would you like the hottest property in America for one of your first pictures? However, there's a slight problem because the Justice Department is looking us over."[33]

The possible crackdown by Washington was no hindrance to James Roosevelt. He bought the screen rights to *Pot o' Gold*, signed James Stewart and Paulette Goddard for the leads, hired five screenwriters (including originator Robert Brilmayer) and added Heidt and his Musical Knights.

Heidt played himself, staying pretty much in the background of the story. "Pot o' Gold," released in April 1941, proved to be a muddled musical melange with a banal plot. "As for Horace Heidt," observed critic Howard Barnes of the New York *Herald-Tribune*, "he may be a good band leader, but he doesn't know any more about screen acting than James Roosevelt does about screen producing."[34]

For Horace and his aggregation, it was the first and only exposure to moviemaking. The film, however, did not hamper its future prospects for television.

Meanwhile, the fiscal aftereffects for the *Pot* continued well into the 1940s. A winner in 1941 named Pauline Washburn was still arguing with the federal government five years later over whether she had to pay taxes on her $1,000. The IRS wanted $180 of her prize. She claimed the windfall was a gift and thus tax free.[35] Such disputes the revenue service usually won.

Harold Hackett discovered the hottest radio property of 1939–40, and he later developed other question-and-answer formats, *If It's the Last Thing I Do* and *What Would You Have Done?* But his great success with the *Pot o' Gold* did not carry over to them. "They were corny," he admitted. "The 'dogs' of all radio quizzes."[36]

›6‹

Wunderkinder

"I went through a period of several years after leaving radio when I suppose I was experiencing a classic let-down, like a lot of child actors who have achieved too much, too soon," revealed Harve Bennett Fischman, an ex-Quiz Kid, in an interview at the age of 49.[1] A successful middle-aged television producer, he remembered a time when his appearances on the *Quiz Kids* troubled him greatly. Concerns over the expectations heaped upon him, Fischman explained, were the reason he flitted from profession to profession, before eventually settling into TV production (and creating the concept of a miniseries with *Rich Man, Poor Man*). "I was a has-been at 15. It took me 20 years to figure where the attention and adulation had put me."[2]

The use of bright and gifted youngsters on radio met with less resistance, say, than the airing of grown-up amateurs and people off the street. Tots and preadolescents at a microphone stood on a different level. They were handled more as a commodity—a stock in trade that, for the most part, was readily interchangeable. Moreover, their time in the spotlight was comparatively short, ending in the teen years, and their exposure generally fell into nonprime-time periods of the broadcast spectrum. All in all, in contrast to their widely cheered and highly paid counterparts in films and on the stage, radio-based youngsters gleaned modest acclaim and rewards.

Before radio discovered the appeal of youngsters as quiz contestants, panelists and all-round wunderkinder, they often surfaced as entertainers on amateur hours and kid shows. *The Children's Hour*, sponsored Sunday mornings by Horn & Hardart restaurants on stations both in New York and Philadelphia, and *Coast-to-Coast on a Bus*, also a Sunday morning excursion, allowed budding singers, dancers, musicians, comics and actors to display their wares. *Let's Pretend*, a Saturday storytelling session over CBS, featured many young thespians, including 12-year-old Roddy McDowell and nine-year-old Billy Halop. Daily programs such as *The Singing Lady* occasionally brought small-fry members of Ireene Wicker's audience to the microphone as participants in her beguiling tales and true adventure stories.

In 1939, station WXYZ in Detroit, home base of *The Lone Ranger* and *The Green Hornet*, brought together some 40 juveniles for its *Radio Schoolhouse*. Musical numbers and dramatic skits occupied the large cast. As adult quiz shows grew in popularity, host Dick Osgood, as "The Professor" outfitted in academic gown and mortar board, injected a segment wherein he fired questions at members of the school-age audience. A few small city transmitters, too, like WHEC in Rochester, New York, with *Children's Recess*, had already launched local quizzes for youngsters.

In Chicago, a publicity man for Kay Kyser's band, the Stevens Hotel and the Aragon and Trianon Ballrooms took notice of such programs, as well as NBC's *Information Please*. Louis Cowan, a radio buff since the 1920s when he first operated a crystal set, wanted to create something new and special for the air. With a large inheritance from an uncle, he had already produced three unsuccessful quiz shows, *Who Said It? Play Broadcast* and *Musico*, before age 30.[3]

"It seemed to me that if one had any kind of creative talent at all, it might be possible to create something for radio that might become a property," he remarked many years later.[4] The idea of a version of *Information Please* using kids fascinated Cowan. Nobody ever pays any attention to bright youngsters, he thought. He set about developing what comedian Fred Allen would soon call "*Information Please* in short pants."[5]

With Chicago journalist Pence James, Cowan searched area schools to round up an interesting mix of winsome and intelligent children. They settled on four: 13 year old Van Dyke Tiers, a spelling and geography whiz; 7 year old Gerald Darrow, a bird expert; 14 year old Cynthia Cline, flutist-composer-poetress; and 13 year old Joan Bishop, an occasional piano soloist with the Chicago Symphony Orchestra. Cowan made a demo disc of the youngsters in an actual question-and-answer session to play for ad agencies. He made little progress until Miles Laboratories, maker of Alka Seltzer and One-a-Day vitamins, expressed interest. They were looking for a summer replacement for pianist Alec Templeton and his Friday night series over the NBC Blue Network.

Miles signed Cowan for ten weeks at $1,000 a show. To come up with a title for his program, he brainstormed guests during a·family get-together. Cowan's wife and her sister ran the gamut of names, beginning with "Our Children" and "Examination Time" and then considering "School Kids Questionnaire" and "The Kids Knew." Inspired by the current film success, "The Wizard of Oz," they toyed with "q" and "k" sounds: "Quizard of Oz," "Quizard of Kids," and finally "Quiz Kids."[6]

"That's it!" Cowan shouted across the dinner table. As the *Quiz Kids*, his brainchild bowed in June 1940; it quickly attracted national attention and soon coined a new phrase. (He also discovered a local program, *Kiddy Quiz*, in Minneapolis, but secured from its creator an okay to use his similar-sounding tag.[7])

Audiences took immediate delight in the panel of alert, unhesitating and exceedingly bright students. More than 15,000 letters arrived the first four weeks, supposedly a record for a new show. Many contained a question to ask the Quiz Kids with the hope that its sender might receive a Zenith radio if it was used on the air. The summer fill-in easily made the transition to a year-round feature on Sunday afternoons.

Early critics suggested a panel less inclined toward sheer brilliance and a bit more normal. Skeptics voiced doubts whether the show was truly spontaneous and on the level. To assure listeners, Cowan invited a professor of psychology at the University of Chicago to talk to the youngsters before the program and make on-the-air comments at the close. The weakest part of the program during the first month or two seemed to be the jittery M.C., whom *Variety* described as "definitely poor" and "incapable of exploiting his opportunities."[8]

Joe Kelly had been an odd choice for quizmaster. Louis Cowan auditioned a range of talents, from college professors and lecturers to newscasters and authors. They all apparently flunked Cowan's test, as did Chicago announcers Harlow Wilcox and Durward Kirby.

Cowan's choice of Kelly surely flaunted the image of an erudite Clifton Fadiman type. For one thing, Kelly had not gotten beyond the third grade in school and often had difficulty in reading the questions.* He frequently brought up insignificant points and overlooked the important ones. Yet his cheerful disposition, easy manner and reassuring tact compensated for these shortcomings and carried him through the early weeks of the program and on to an association of 13 seasons. In 1947 he even survived the unpleasant notoriety surrounding the shooting of two prowlers discovered in the kitchen of his Chicago apartment. Kelly grabbed and fired his .38 caliber revolver, killing one and wounding the other.[9]

Born in 1901 in Crawfordsville, Indiana, Kelly left school at age eight when his father, a brewery truck driver, died. Young Joe had an ap-

---

*Kelly once misread a question from a printed card: "What is the difference between a simile and a metaphor." Kelly thought "a simile" was a typographical error and changed it to "assimilate."

pealing voice; to support his mother, he joined a traveling stock company and then a minstrel show. He learned practical arithmetic by paying his own hotel bills, acquired an ability to express himself by writing letters home to his mother, and with the aid of a ten-cent-store dictionary read stories of Horatio Alger. At 12 his boy soprano voice broke, and he left the stage for the humdrum of preadolescence.

Joe worked as an office boy and, in his spare time, learned how to play a piano by ear. Although he couldn't read a note of music, he formed his own band, Kelly's Klowns. At 17 he returned to the footlights with a stock company and, five years later, married the troupe's secretary. Kelly promised his bride that he would quit show business. Settling in Michigan, he sold pianos and phonographs and then managed a men's clothing store. When radio came to the small-sized cities of the Midwest, Kelly teamed up with a partner for a comic singing act called "The Two Lunatics of the Air," broadcasting from Battle Creek. They received $12 a week for six 30-minute shows, plus all the milk they could drink from the sponsoring dairy company. Four years later Kelly left the act to join the announcers' staff of Chicago's WLS. There he became "Jolly Joe" on a morning kid show. In the early 1930s Kelly was chosen as M.C. for the Blue Network's Saturday night hoedown, *The National Barn Dance*.[10]

Still there were times during that first summer with the Quiz Kids when Kelly devoutly wished he had not wandered out of the *Barn*. On one broadcast he got caught in a cross fire between two youngsters, Van Dyke Tiers and Gerald Darrow. The question was: "Define a dodo, a dido and a dado." Darrow confidently answered the first part, "A dodo is a prehistoric bird," and added, "I think he had a harsh call."[11]

"Not exactly," injected Tiers. "The dodo is extinct but not prehistoric."

"That isn't what it says in my encyclopedia," countered Darrow, looking to Kelly for support.

"Well," Kelly drawled, hunting frantically through his cards and notes, "I guess there isn't much difference, eh?"

But Tiers was not to be put off. "Mr. Kelly, I would like to submit to you that all prehistoric animals are extinct, but all extinct animals are not necessarily prehistoric."[12]

There was another incident in an early broadcast that Joe Kelly would not easily forget. It was the day when he unknowingly reshuffled the sequence of his question cards and was unable to complete a question on dogs and their masters.

After the program, Kelly believed he would be tossed out as M.C. But Cowan and the sponsor disregarded all negative reaction, declaring that Kelly was at least himself with the kids.[13] But to avoid a similar mishap a research staff was ordered to come up with all possible answers to future questions. Kelly, in turn, would study and review this material the day before each broadcast. As a precaution against further loss of face on the air, Kelly bought an unabridged dictionary to keep at his side. Apparently, it helped; he had little or no trouble in getting future questions and answers down pat. Kelly really admitted that he learned plenty from the kids every show—and what an unusually gifted and outspoken contingent they were!

Some 600 kids competed on the program during its run on radio and television. But only about two dozen became "regulars" and nationally known. At least 50 applications for would-be Quiz Kids came in the mail each week, usually recommended by proud teachers or doting parents. Contestants were drawn chiefly from the sons and daughters of farmers, businessmen, teachers, ministers and writers living in and around Chicago. Every potential player took a written examination and was interviewed by Cowan and executive producer John Lewellen, a former Time-Life employee. A display of prodigious memory weighed heavily in the selection process, but some evidence of imagination, reasoning and musical ability counted too.

In her 1947 book on the Kids, program assistant and researcher Eliza Hickok described the ideal Quiz Kid as a normal, healthy youngster in the right grade at school, who regarded the broadcast as a happy extracurricular activity on Sunday afternoons.[14] But was a genius-level I.Q. normal?

The proud mother of seven-year-old Ruth Duskin, for example, wrote the producers of her daughter's accomplishments in reading and writing and her "genius rating" by the Chicago Board of Education. Duskin's letter sparked an interest in her offspring; a questionnaire came in the mail, along with the request for a 250-word essay by Ruth on "Why I Should be a Quiz Kid." The real test was participation in a simulated broadcast. "Brain power and book learning did not assure acceptance," Ruth later wrote in a book of recollections called *What Ever Happened to the Quiz Kids.* "Poise, originality, humor, modesty and mike sense were more important than profundity. It helped to be young and/or small—the ability to wow the audience bore an inverse relation to size and depth of voice. . . . Showmanship was critical. . . . Showoffs and smart-alecks were crossed off at once."[15]

But it apparently helped to have an I.Q. near or equal to little Ruth's 200. When she joined the quintet of young achievers in November 1941, this daughter of a high school chemistry teacher was the first little girl on the program. (The scarcity of strong female contenders was a continual headache for Cowan.) Skeptical listeners insisted she was a midget posing as a youngster. On her initial appearance Ruth answered enough questions to place her among the top three contestants and thus, according to the program's rules, was invited to return the following week.

She became the top female panelist by the time she turned 16 and "retired" in 1950. By then she had accumulated a drawer full of $100 U.S. Savings Bonds, one for each of the 157 shows in which she participated.

A number of program "regulars" tallied similarly long runs, becoming small-fry celebrities and model-child wonders. Joel Kupperman, a math whiz, lasted ten years. Lonny Lunde, a musical prodigy, appeared 235 times over seven years. Naomi Cooks, a literature specialist, chalked up some 120 sessions in the years 1946 to 1953. Harvey Dytch, an animal expert, bridged the gap from radio to TV, rarely missing a weekly show. Other well-known participants were the future film and television actress Vanessa Brown, Nobel Prize winner in medicine James Watson, engineer Claude Brenner, diplomat Richard Williams and theologian Jack Lucal.

"We Quiz Kids, as a group," observed Ruth Duskin, who in her "retirement" became a schoolteacher, wife and mother, "have neither fulfilled the highest hopes nor realized the worst fears laid upon us three or four decades ago."[16]

The Kids, after all, were entertainers, while bringing untold bits of information to a "gee whiz" audience. Youngsters tuned in were alternately inspired or repelled.

Chicago radio personality Chuck Schaden recalls the effect of Ruth and the *Quiz Kids* in his home. "Naturally, my folks always enjoyed the broadcasts. They would make sure we tuned in every week and would always comment on how smart those youngsters were and how proud their parents must be. And then they would give me 'that' look. A look that said, 'So how come *you're* not a Quiz Kid?' "[17]

But secretly, Schaden admired Joel and Ruth and Pat and Lonny. "They may not have been my intellectual equal, but they did represent the Kids of America and if grownups were surprised that any kids could know so much and be so smart, well score one for our side."[18]

Illinois Governor Adlai Stevenson, a special guest in early 1952, expressed the thought of many fans when he remarked that the proceedings encouraged children to be keen and clearheaded. He spoke for adults too: "It even makes me want to be as wise and intelligent as the Quiz Kids."[19]

Throughout the 1940s, these radio wunderkinder contributed to a sizable cottage industry of program spinoffs. The Kids seemed to pop up everywhere. They made movie shorts and record albums, were turned into cutout and follow-the-dot book characters, appeared in a special *Quiz Kids Magazine,* inspired toys and games and sweatshirts and badges. Quiz Kid dictionaries, anthologies and syndicated columns touted their young talents. The famous and celebrated vied to meet them on stage and off, and headliners such as Bob Hope, Fred

Allen, Ralph Edwards, Eddie Cantor and Bing Crosby sought guest appearances as quizmaster.

One of the funniest Jack Benny radio shows of the 1940s was patterned as a contest between the Kids and Benny's cohorts, Mary Livingstone, Phil Harris, Dennis Day and Don Wilson. The youngsters answered genuinely tough questions, while grownups as the Jello Kids floundered on the most palpable kind of setups—all obviously rehearsed but hilariously funny.[20]

Soon after school bells rang for the start of the very first fall semester of the *Quiz Kids*, carbon copies appeared at a number of regional stations. Teams of youngsters from nearby cities and towns within driving distance of WGY Schenectady, New York, competed in *The Little Red School House*. A panel of moppets billed as *Kid Wizards* fielded questions from a child psychologist at WHN New York. *Recess Time* over WSCH Portland, Maine, combined quiz segments with songs, claiming it had started its format nearly two years before Cowan's.[21]

The most successful kiddie panel show, apart from the *Quiz Kids*, came to Mutual in the mid-1940s. Jack Barry gathered a group of five articulate and attractive preteenagers and let them voice their opinions on the problems of their peers. Barry hosted his *Juvenile Jury* and, along with cocreator and producer Dan Enright, selected the questions from the thousands regularly sent in by children, parents and teachers. The responses of the *Jury* were spontaneous and original and often humorous. Like Cowan's Kids, Barry's troupe gained a solid following among audiences of all ages.

In 1946 Cowan inaugurated a special annual feature to honor the teaching profession. He asked every schoolchild in the country to nominate "the teacher who has helped me the most."[22] A fourth-grade teacher in Jackson, Mississippi, Aline Neal, won first Teacher prize. Chosen from 33,000 nominations by a committee of educators, the 49-year-old Neal was brought to Chicago where Joe Kelly presented an award of $2,500 for advanced study at any university of her choice. In 1950 a teacher of blind students in Youngstown, Ohio, Pauline Powers, was selected. The nationwide contest, according to Cowan, gave scholarships to worthy elementary and high school instructors while focusing on the issue of low salaries among all teachers.

Not surprisingly, a higher percentage of ex-Quiz Kids pursued teaching careers than any other profession. (Law was a close second.[23]) Outfitted in academic gown and mortarboard week after week, many moved on at age 16 to a lifetime amid academic ivy. Yet for Joel Kupperman, a professor of philosophy at the University of Connecticut in the 1980s, memories of his time fielding questions from "Professor" Joe Kelly seem painful. In an interview in 1982 he said that the program "may have done some good for the idea that education is a good thing, but being a bright child among your peers was not the very best way to grow up in America."[24]

For original Quiz Kid Gerald Darrow, a celebrity at 7 and the subject of a *Life* cover story at 9, coping as an adult proved a bitter experience. Once the center of attention and almost singlehandedly responsible for the show's initial overwhelming success, Darrow spent his postcollege years as a classical music disc jockey. But at 36, his broadcast career ended. Estranged from his family, he drifted from one menial job to another, living in cheap rooming houses. "I can't forgive those who exploited me. . . . I wish it had never happened," he wrote in 1976. Three years later, ill, alcoholic, and on welfare, Darrow died alone in a Chicago hospital.[25]

Gerald Darrow's teammates survived, and the majority had few regrets over their exposure as a whiz kid. Most sought recognition for real accomplishments as adults, rather than living off past acclaim for a good memory and a quick comeback. But virtually all could never escape the indelible stamp: Quiz Kid.

›7‹

"Aren't We Devils?"

The lure of a chance to be center stage and in the spotlight and to win a prize spilled over from the comparatively straightforward question-and-answer show into the out-and-out physically focused contest. People seemed willing to subject themselves to demanding and demeaning pranks beyond a basic quiz session. Audience participation in this area grew so attractive and appealing, both on the part of program developers as well as would-be contestants, that it soon became apparent that visual stunts and derring-do had a place in a sound-only medium. The impetus toward off-beat challenges, outright dares and frenzied hijinks gained momentum in the early 1940s.

The chief promulgators and mainstays of such madcap antics gained their start in radio as studio announcers and on-the-street interviewers. They readily honed their innate skills and instincts for handling people into broadcast features that brought a new dimension to network radio and were later carried over into television.

One evening in late 1939 Ralph Edwards taxied home from the New York studios where he spent hours as as announcer on a flock of daytime shows, including *Life Can Be Beautiful, The Gospel Singer, Against the Storm* and *The Children's Hour*. Twenty-six year old Edwards had landed a full-time announcer's job with CBS the year before, after working at regional stations in California. He was well paid for the 40 or more shows a week and claimed that he announced more commercial programs than any other person in America. But the work was fairly repetitive and anonymous. A successful program innovator, on the other hand, could pretty much call the shots and focus on one or two major undertakings.

Information Please and *Professor Quiz* were the radio sensations of that season. Radio people were continually fretting over coming up with new program ideas for important sponsors. Anyone with a really fresh idea—a family-type show—could gain a hearing with the executives. Edwards kept dreaming about a new quiz or contest or game to break into the ranks of creator-producer.[1]

As he came through the front door that evening, threw his hat on the foyer table, and started down the hall to say hello to his wife, Barbara, and her parents, who had come to town for a visit, it hit him.

"Heavy, Heavy Hangs Over Thy Head!"

He went through the usual motions of acknowledging the presence of the others in the living room. But for nearly an hour he didn't hear much of anything that anybody said. Later he went to the telephone and called the radio director at the Compton ad agency.

Edwards outlined an old childhood game that he had played as a ten-year-old farm boy in Colorado. A popular parlor game called Forfeits, it brought together a group of boys and girls who each handed over a personal object. The youngster, whose turn it was to play, was seated in a chair behind which the leader stood with one of the articles collected held over the subject's head and singsonged "Heavy, heavy hangs over thy head. Is it fine or super fine. Tell the truth or pay the consequences." If they thought it was a boy's article, the person would say "fine." If the person said "fine" and it turned out to be a girl's handkerchief or similar item, the player would have to take the consequence. Usually, in those days it was running around the farmhouse twice, or sitting on the girl's lap or doing some other little stunt of that nature.

The Compton agency liked the idea and asked for an audition. Edwards and his wife quickly went to work to dream up consequences and then tried them out on family and friends.

A few weeks later Ralph made arrangements to keep the audience from the Sunday morning *Children's Hour* in place for an extra 45 minutes to provide contestants for an audition run-through. He also called upon fellow announcer Andre Baruch and his wife, Bea Wain, to participate as celebrity contestants.

"The audience was willing, but this was new stuff," Edwards later recalled. "Nobody had played this old game in public before."[2]

The first contestant, a smiling round man, missed his question. Ralph explained his consequence. He would pretend to be a radio announcer, but because his partner, who had all the sound effects, was stuck in an elevator, he had to make all the sounds vocally himself. "Do you understand the consequence?" Ralph asked. The contestant's only response was an almost inaudible "haw." Edwards plunged on desperately, reading now from the script.

"It is a windy day in New York." Edwards paused for a wind effect, which was not forthcoming. "You hop into your car." Silence. "You are in the car, roaring down Broadway." Silence. "You put on your brakes, and toot your horn. TOOT YOUR HORN!"

At that moment Ralph wheeled around in back of the fellow and jabbed him hard with a pencil where it would do the most good. Out came a loud: "Yipe!" It was ear-splitting, and the audience roared.[3]

The ad agency heard the record the next day and hurried it off to a sponsor. Proctor and Gamble liked the results. Four weeks later, on Saturday night, March 23, 1940, the show went on CBS for Ivory Soap with Edwards and staff announcer Mel Allen.* The initial silly but entertaining session had participants who fizzled on questions put to talking and spelling words through the impediment of an all-day sucker, imitating a one-man band with dishpans and coffeepots and conducting off-the-cuff interviews with strangers. The rewards were modest—$5 for those who went through with the consequences and $15 for a participant who answered the question. There was also a grand prize of $20 for the stunt that got the most applause. Listeners were offered $5 for each question used and $10 for a consequence.

"Edwards," noted *Variety*, "proves a fit choice for the assignment. He's fleet of tongue, a suave party man and adept at keeping things moving snappily."[4] The studio audience enjoyed itself immensely, and so did the home-based listeners. The laughs, screams, groans and cheers of the studio observers registered well with those at home and added greatly to the interest in the house-party proceedings and boosted its popularity beyond all expectations. It was quickly discovered that contestants would deliberately fail to answer a question in order to pay the consequences.

"Aren't we devils?" exclaimed Edwards at the start of each consequence.[5] Some of the humorous and crazy stunts that brought the program to peak insanity included a woman who had to portray the role of Juliet in the "Romeo and Juliet" balcony scene, interspersing her lines with commercial plugs for her father's fur shop. A burly Brooklyn construction foreman was told to imitate a baby crying for his bottle. A man who admitted he could play the piano well was made to perform upside down. A bachelor was required to put a diaper on a young pig as a first lesson in baby care. A golfer was told to drive golf balls across the country. A fellow was asked to get in a bed with a seal at a downtown thoroughfare. A contestant was promised $1,000 if he fell asleep during the program.

The elaborate preparations frequently involved live animals, segments piped in from street corners and railroad terminals, ongoing progress report "remotes" from contestants, surprise celebrity gags and, with it all, large expenditures of money and effort.

*Allen's sister Esther left their home in Alabama to help the show contrive "consequences." She came up with one that ultimately led to Edwards' *This Is Your Life*.

Why do people clamor to appear and submit voluntarily to getting dunked in a tank of water and similar indignities, asked some critics? The search for an answer seemed likely to "make sociologists and psychologists shudder," wrote one newspaperman.[6] "As I see it," observed Ralph Edwards, they do it "because it is a challenge to their courage; because it affords them an opportunity to express themselves in a grand manner; and because it is a lot of fun. What's so deplorable about that? These people aren't psychopathic—they're just everyday lawyers, preachers, salesmen, housewives, cab drivers—out for a little fun, and perhaps a cash prize."[7]

Perhaps Edwards *himself* was one explanation. "In five minutes he seems to lead his audience into a world where the demented situations," wrote *Life*, "are not only lots of fun but also the essence of normality."[8]

Edwards, who in the 1930s had hitchhiked to the East in search of a radio job, had lived out of a Manhattan church and had eaten meals in Bowery handouts, analyzed the program's tremendous appeal and the public's feeling for it. "By an overwhelming majority," he said, "the listeners agreed on two things: the program was a welcome relief from the unhappy news of world affairs; and it was accenting the importance of the long-neglected front parlor, making it once more the friendly room, wherein family ties are formed."[9]

The weekly antics of *Truth or Consequences* often made newspaper headlines. On one particular broadcast from New York, a contestant was told that money was waiting for him at the corner of Prospect and Walnut in Holyoke, Massachusetts, where it had been buried earlier by a member of the program's staff. This anxious player boarded a train immediately for that city. But Edwards had not reckoned with the local citizenry. It had its ears glued to the program that night. A handful of people with shovels—and a few clad only in pajamas—rushed to the designated street corner and started to dig. One enterprising listener even brought a bulldozer! One of the first on the scene—a carpenter's helper—dug into the soil and found the buried cash, a bag of one thousand silver dollars. The show's contestant never had a chance.[10]

During the war years Edwards helped promote official messages and campaigns formulated in Washington. A Staten Island housewife was chosen from the audience as a contestant one Saturday because she was the mother of the youngest serviceman in uniform. She failed to give the right answer to her question, "How many kings of England possessed the name Henry?" Her consequence was quite unusual. Edwards ordered her to do something about getting scarce pennies back in circulation. He suggested that the radio audience send her copper pennies to buy a war bond for her 17-year-old son in the Marines.

The results alarmed even the irrepressible "man who dishes out pleasant punishment." Within two or three days, nearly 20,000 letters arrived at her home. For a week the mail poured in. The beleaguered mother called Edwards for help, and he gathered a dozen or more men and women to open envelopes and count pennies. There were more than 300,000 one-cent coins, and some of the 130,000 letters contained quarters, half-dollars and dollar bills. Gifts of neckties, handkerchiefs and other apparel were in the mail too.[11]

The young Marine appeared with Edwards the following Saturday night to accept the coins and gifts. For every fifth penny of the $3,000 or more he received in one week, the GI said that he would spend it to buy sports equipment for Camp Lejeune. Director of the U.S. Mint Nellie Taylor Ross wrote that the outpouring of pennies was very gratifying to the government because it promoted the effort to keep these coins in circulation. "Every penny hoarded," she pointed out, "means that another must be made from scarce metals urgently needed for the war."[12]

By jarring so many pennies out of piggie banks and people's pockets, *Truth or Consequences* aided the war effort through bringing a lot of copper out of hiding places and encouraged the purchase of bonds, along with boosting the well-being of a serviceman and his military unit. "Without question," concluded reporter John K. Hutchens, "the show won more publicity than any other radio performance since Orson Welles's celebrated—and considerably less happy—'War of the Worlds,' back in 1938. Few of his colleagues in radio, so far as is known, have begrudged Mr. Edwards the gratification and rewards of his triumph."[13]

The triumphs of *Truth or Consequences* sparked the development of a parallel format by a very energetic and likable radioman. This program, similar to Edwards' in its approach to people and human nature, proved that there was room on the dial for more than one zany audience-participation show in prime time.

People Are Funny had a much slower vegetation period than Edwards' parlor game. It grew from several regional studio features on the West Coast. One of them was a San Francisco program called *Who's Dancing Tonight?* with a youthful and loquacious personality called Arthur Linkletter. A variation of the ad-lib third-degree interrogation of dancing couples, it was already being done by Horace Heidt in New York hotel ballrooms and elsewhere. Linkletter's refreshing charm attracted local listeners. He rarely stumbled nor was he at a loss for words or wisecracks, and he readily put those quizzed at ease.[14]

Film and radio scriptwriter John Guedel happened to switch on Linkletter on his car radio while riding to work. He liked the friendly voice and made a mental note that he wanted to meet the fellow behind the voice. Two years later, in 1941, they met through a mutual friend.

Guedel had left college when his well-to-do family was wiped out in the Depression. He turned to writing and through a chance meeting got a job on "Our Gang" comedies at the Hal Roach Studio. The lot closed periodically whenever Roach took a holiday, and with it, John lost his job a half-dozen times. Finally, he turned to radio through an ad agency, where he penned nothing but jokes. Then the enterprising Guedel got an opportunity at more serious material and wrote half-hour dramas for Forest Lawn Memorial Park.

The idea of an audience stunt show came to him while doing research on President James Garfield in the public library. He accidentally pulled out an old book called *Games*. This gave him the idea for a switch on straight quiz shows. They weren't new ideas, just twists on old ones, he later explained.[15]

Guedel developed a stunt show called *Pull Over, Neighbor*. An early gag was simple, but it presaged big things to come with *People Are Funny*. A contestant sang "Smiles" and at the end of each line, John shoved an ice cube in the man's mouth. It brought down the house, as much as a pie thrown in the face convulsed a vaudeville crowd.

Meanwhile, Linkletter was compiling countless hours of extemporaneous talk over the air. He entered radio while a scholarship student and English major at San Diego State College and remained at a microphone instead of taking a teaching position. Radio paid $5 more a month, and that simply changed the direction of his career. In the mid-1930s he worked as radio director at the Texas Centennial Exposition in Dallas and for the San Francisco World's Fair. In 1939 he became a freelance announcer and M.C. and soon chalked up more than 15 shows a week.

"I never considered it work," Linkletter later recalled. "There wasn't any stress involved. It was all ad lib. Besides, it paid amazingly well for something I would have done for practically nothing."[16]

His interview and news features included *Are You a Genius? What's Doing, Ladies?* and *What Do You Think?* One of his San Francisco shows was announced by a young Mark Goodson.

Linkletter recalls one particular incident that happened while interviewing a recently engaged couple at the St. Francis Hotel. He suggested that they come back in a week and have the marriage ceremony right in the lobby.

"You can consummate your wedding vows right here in the main lobby," he announced.

With that remark, Art built up a tremendous audience for the event. "Everyone wanted to hear them consummate their marriage vows," he recollected of this early faux pas. "I thought it meant to plight one's troth!"[17]

A full schedule of creating, producing and hosting programs was a made-to-order experience for the network show to come with John Guedel in 1942. A show focused on human nature, *People Are Funny* evolved from Guedel's and Linkletter's then-current regional programs and was built around four stunts. "Human nature, that's the whole key," realized Guedel.[18]

The program bowed over NBC for Wings Cigarettes in a Friday night slot. From *Pull Over, Neighbor*, Guedel brought in M.C. Art Baker and, from San Francisco, his new friend Art Linkletter. The two Arts co-hosted the first six shows. But Guedel realized they were not a good match. NBC opted for the better-known Baker; Guedel preferred Linkletter who ad-libbed skillfully and actually tried out many of the stunts himself. So for 18 months Baker emceed the increasingly popular show.

"But we had to write out everything for Art Baker," Guedel says. "He was a script person."[19]

In October 1943 Guedel fired Baker, so abruptly in fact that Baker sued, charging that Guedel had broken his five-year contract and brought back Linkletter at a lower salary. "But it all came to naught, and suddenly *People Are Funny* was Linkletter's show," writes radio historian John Dunning. "Linkletter became so well established as the genial *People Are Funny* host that even its longtime listeners eventually forgot that the show had once been handled by someone else."[20]

The Guedel-Linkletter partnership was an exceptional match from the start. The gags developed by this duo—along with much help from Guedel's father who in the wake of losing his shirt in the Crash discovered a new career—lived up to the program's title. During each preshow warm-up the studio audience picked the broadcast contestants from those given trial runs.

"The audience acted as a jury," Linkletter recalled in 1987. "We eliminated the smart alecks and stiffs, and got the best people. Today, contestants are auditioned, tested, coached, even threatened, well in advance. The interview was the most important element for us; today, in TV, it is the device, the jackpot, and the competitive angle."[21]

The program also went through a preview two days before the Friday broadcast to determine how the stunts really worked. In addition to the advance preview and the full-scale warm-up, *People* did a repeat broadcast for the West Coast several hours after the initial airing for Eastern listeners. The same stunts were used but different contestants were chosen. "The second airing was not as important," explains Linkletter. "The big audiences and agencies were in the East. The second show often had a whole different flavor; some of the cast and staff killed time between the two broadcasts at the bar at the nearby Brown Derby, and a few never even remembered doing the repeat."[22]

On those early shows people were moved at a fast clip, according to Linkletter, "as you would move horses along a chute." The proceedings evolved from crude, simple "pie in the face" gags to more complicated and original stunts from playing word-association games to stealing a house, from cutting off a gentleman's necktie to registering a seal as a "girlfriend" at a posh hotel. "Often the very description of the stunt and its outcome was better than seeing it," Linkletter points out. "It was an incredible 'theatre of the mind' for those individuals listening at home."[23]

The production teams of *People* and *Consequences* chartered courses remarkably parallel. Whereas Guedel eliminated any pretense of quizzing participants, Edwards maintained a brief question-and-answer segment for each contestant. Both hosts enjoyed high ratings and readily capitalized on many peripheral and spin-off opportunities that beckoned. Both wrote books based on their programs (*The Truth or Consequences Party Book*; *People Are Funny*) inspired film adaptations ("Seven Days' Leave"; "People Are Funny") and initiated charitable fund-raising projects (the "Hush" mystery personality contests; the CARE "new lease on life" giveaway). Of more significance to the evolution and growth of the quiz and game show is the fact that both of these trail-blazing programs became a breeding and testing ground for new formats, ideas, and concepts. No two "people" shows gave rise to more viable offshoots in both radio and television.

In 1948, for example, Edwards injected a "consequence" whereby a contestant was surprised and honored by family and friends. The mini-tribute soon developed into the heartwarming and entertaining weekly program *This Is Your Life* with Edwards as host and producer. He has long pointed out that a handful of shows on radio and television have stemmed from segments that he developed on *Consequences*. When asked why he didn't turn those stunts into game shows of his own, he answers, "I didn't want to dilute the property."[24] He holds no ill will against those who did go and turn basic *Truth or Consequences* stunts into successful programs. His preference has remained for his "people" type of shows, which expanded to *Crosswits, It Could Be You* and *People's Court*. He is extremely proud that the once undistinguished resort town of Hot Springs, New Mexico, changed its name to the more picturesque-sounding Truth or Consequences in 1950 and each spring holds a Fiesta honoring Edwards and the show.

People Are Funny gave rise to the extemporaneous *House Party* with Art Linkletter, wherein Guedel featured contests, musical auditions and question-and-answer sessions. Various and sundry *People* stunts brought forth one of the most successful quiz and comedy shows of all time, *You Bet Your Life* (and its secret word). When television took hold, it looked back to old Linkletter stunts and came up with programs such as *What's My Line? Let's Make a Deal, The Gong Show* and *The Newlywed Game*, all with parentage traced to Guedel-Linkletter.

"We never did an entire show with one single game," explains Guedel, "and we didn't spin off these formats because they were good regular features for us, and I didn't think it was fair to our sponsor. Columnist Harriet Van Horne once came out and proclaimed *People* stole *To Tell The Truth*. She suggested that Goodson-Todman sue me. But it was just the other way around. That show stole from us, and we initiated a suit against Goodson." [25]

The madcap, implausible but generally laugh-provoking consequences and situations on both the Edwards and Linkletter shows seemed natural entries into television. Edwards bowed on the screen in 1950 with an array of stunts he had been saving for TV.

On the premiere, a blindfolded man was persuaded to kiss a cow under the illusion that it was a pretty girl, and the main stunt consisted of dressing a lot of contestants in outlandish clothes and perpetrating them as a serious dance group. Critic John Crosby concluded at the close of the telecast: "I'm afraid I can't agree that 'Truth or Consequences' is a natural for television. The radio version, which is still on the air, was the ultimate in silliness, but at least it was decently veiled. Its television counterpart is a monstrosity of vulgarity." [26]

NBC audio engineer Bob Jensen long remembered the challenge of handling such "live" remotes. He faced complicated feed-ins and switchovers. Concealing microphones and hiding cameras were demanding tasks. Jensen often spent hours in advance of a broadcast installing lines to bring to viewers a street "consequence." One memorable remote involved a cab and its driver and a woman and her pet boa constrictor. She asked the cabbie to take her and the snake to the Los Angeles airport. The surprised and terrified driver finally agreed but only if the passenger held the snake's head out the window. [27]

It soon became more and more difficult to create new and amusing stunts for TV. Man-on-the-street gags and situations had worn thin, and they also had grown more taxing and costly.

Interest by viewers quickly dipped too. Edwards even tried to get attention for the program by promising a young woman $100,000 if she could break out of a hypnotist's trance during the show; she failed to do it. Edwards also found that the preparation of two weekly TV shows proved too exhausting. He opted for the more uplifting (and Emmy-winning) *This Is Your Life*.

Several years later, in 1954, he brought *Consequences* back; this time it was hosted by Jack Bailey, who lasted several seasons. Still another attempt to revive the show took place in the late 1950s. Edwards hired an unknown disc jockey from Missouri named Bob Barker. Dynamic and ingratiating, Barker recognized that the proceedings needed the full, whole-hearted participation of the audience to make it jell. So before every program, the show's staff plunged in to create a madcap atmosphere, just short of Olsen and Johnson's classic Broadway may-hem called "Hellzapoppin'." The Barker-emceed edition prospered as a daily series and then as a syndicated show, until 1974. It soon re-turned as *The New Truth or Consequences* again in the late 1980s with host Larry Anderson, a comic magician who had had a supporting role on the short-lived *Life with Lucy*. The program never really departed from its original premise of Edwards that it should show America hav-ing fun.

People Are Funny waited to watch its rival try television. When it ini-tially stumbled, Guedel decided *House Party* would make a better video series. But in the fall of 1954 he and Linkletter started a seven-year run with *People* on Sunday night. It fared well but not with the reception accorded *House Party*, which Art preferred because it was more open-ended and free-wheeling. "People make themselves funny," he often remarked of that varied human-interest series, which, with 26 years on the air, became one of the longest-running shows in broadcasting.[28] *People*, too, resurfaced years later. In 1984 NBC launched an updated, pretaped version, hosted by black comedian Flip Wilson. The majority of the footage took place outside the studio with something of a "can-did camera" flavor. An amiable half hour, it, nevertheless, paled as a prime-time Saturday entry and soon departed.

Perhaps Ralph Edwards' most memorable and solid legacy from his audience-participation show is the string of sensational coast-to-coast telephone contests. Beginning with the "Mr. Hush"(Jack Dempsey) riddle in January 1946 and including the highly compelling "Walking Man" (Jack Benny) contest, these events electrified the country. Each week a person was called and given a chance to identify the mystery figure and win an enormous jackpot of prizes. Each contest employed the same technique: a mystery voice and a riddle with an increasing jackpot and new clues each week.[29]

Listeners had an opportunity to participate by writing a 25-word sen-tence on why the work of a certain national health organization was so vital. Edwards suggested that each letter writer enclose a donation for the particular cause. The "Mrs. Hush" (Clara Bow) and "Miss Hush" (Martha Graham) contests in 1947 produced some $1.4 million for the March of Dimes. "The Walking Man," "Whispering Woman" (Jeanette MacDonald) and "Mr. Heartbeat" (Edgar Guest) raised more than $2.5 million for the American Heart Association, and the money truly put that organization in business on a national basis.[30]

The identification of the mystery person was front-page news, and winners such as Ruth Subbie of Fort Worth and Florence Hubbard of Chicago became instant celebrities, as well as the owners of autos, mink coats, travel vouchers, airplanes, motorboats, house trailers and jewelry.*

Ralph Edwards proudly points out that his two audience-participation programs of the 1940s and 1950s raised more money for charity than any other ongoing series. A solid $8.3 million contributed in small amounts by his legions of listeners benefited an array of medical and educational causes and institutions.[31]

The potential comic aspects of quiz and game formats were developed further as producers combined the straightforward panel show with gag questions, jokes and punchlines, often submitted by listeners. Panelists were drawn from the ranks of comedy and joined together on a podium of zany and mirthful entertainment. The two leading practitioners of this humor, *Can You Top This?* and *It Pays To Be Ignorant*, came to the air in the early 1940s—and the public eagerly wrote some of the script. These two "clowntable" discussions on humor were preceded by a short-lived takeoff of *Information Please* called *Stop Me If You've Heard This One*.[32] This comedy quiz of 1939–40 had Milton Berle as the Clifton Fadiman of the program and Harry Hershfield and Jay C. Flippen as members of the board of experts, along with a guest gagster each week. Listeners submitted jokes to the panel, and after Berle told the first part of the joke, its members had to come up with the right tag line to win. Outside of the contributed gags, most of the entre-act humor was set and rehearsed rather than spontaneous. Berle's tendency to stress personal insults in his remarks bothered many listeners. This was his first commercial radio series since his association with the *Gillette Community Sing* three years earlier, and his return to the dial coincided with his appearance on Broadway in "See My Lawyer."

Variety concluded after its first broadcast that *Information Please* was getting much humor out of strictly general questions. Therefore, *Stop Me* had the potential of even a higher score with its hokey content once the pacing improved and hyperactive Berle settled down.[33]

On the other hand, *Can You Top This?* was an immediate success. Listeners again provided the jokes. M.C. Peter Donald told them (often in a dialect), with the studio audience's reaction registered on a laugh meter. Whereupon, the three panelists—Harry Hershfield, Senator Ed Ford and Joe Laurie, Jr.—fished into their memory banks to bring up a joke on the same subject that could top the initial gag on the laugh meter. The size of the cash prize was affected by the gagsters' success

---

*A 68-year-old widow earning $30 a week as a sales clerk, Mrs. Hubbard also "received" 40 proposals of marriage by mail. "Postscript," *New York Times*, May 30, 1948, p. II-9.

or nonsuccess. The purpose of the program was simple—to make people laugh—and not to educate them or trick them. "It's an engaging half hour that provided that expensive radio luxury—humor—at minimum cost and production headache," noted critic Robert Landry. "It's all easy-going, angled for giggles and very listenable."[34]

A quiz to end all quiz shows soon followed. Full of frothy gags, farfetched puns, ancient wheezes and inexpert chatter, *It Pays to Be Ignorant* was a broad caricature of those pretentious information-filled programs. It brought together a panel of three low-brow burlesque-bred comics: Harry McNaughton, George Shelton and Lulu McConnell, shepherded by an irascible quizmaster, Tom Howard. This illegitimate quiz originated with Howard's daughter Ruth Howell and her husband, Bob, who was manager of a New Haven station. They mapped out the format of a board of experts "who are dumber than you are and can prove it." A rough script of the proceedings proved saleable. WOR picked it up. Ruth Howard Howell saw no reason why the Howells shouldn't go to New York and write the show. She became one of the few woman gag writers. Before long, her father was helping with the creative chores, each working separately so that they "didn't beat each other's brains out" until the final draft, when they got together to see that the gags didn't overlap.[35]

Howard, as ignoramus-in-chief, would open the tomfoolery by asking, "What animal do you get goat's milk from?" or "Who wrote Mendelssohn's Wedding March?" From this spring board his delightfully cuckoo cohorts plunged into a whirl of jokes and nonsense. A veteran of many years of burlesque, vaudeville and musical comedy, Howard had a theory. "I hit 'em in the eyes with the satire, while I kick 'em in the pants with the gags. I deliberately picked old timers for my experts. I figured their experience in show business would make the program sound ad libbed."[36]

Not being a real quiz show, the program, however, was carefully scripted and rehearsed.[37] Not ad-libbed any more than Jack Benny's was ad-libbed, *It Pays to Be Ignorant* was a well-prepared comedy show, as well as a takeoff of radio's lofty IQ programs that often left listeners with an acute sense of inferiority. "Probably no hokier comedy can be heard on the air," *Variety* stated when the program acquired a sponsor in late 1942. "But it's skillfully done and funny. And, more than incidentally, that libelous commercial copy should be effective advertising."[38]

Usually, there was ample room for injections of humor, both planned and unexpected, within most quiz and game programs. But before 1940 and the likes of Ralph Edwards, John Guedel, Art Linkletter and Ruth and Bob Howell, few broadcasters thought the deliberate marriage of quiz and comedy, contest and nonsense, had much of a chance.

›8‹

Smoke Rings Musical Knowledge

Melody filled the air, night after night, week after week. After sundown, the big bands found the kind of exposure that money couldn't buy. Broadcasting over a network line or a local hookup—usually from ballrooms, nightclubs and college campuses—these musical aggregations nurtured a following and developed a staying power. At the same time, they filled a need of most stations by occupying blocks of unsponsored air time.

A radio line in the swing era of the late 1930s carried bands of every size and style into countless, far-flung homes while providing an extraordinary outlet for a range of new and old pop tunes. Post prime-time "remotes" on a typical late night—say, May 23, 1940, from New York—aired the music of Charlie Barnet, Eddy Duchin, Orrin Tucker, Tommy Dorsey, Bob Chester, Van Alexander, Ted Fiorito, Bob Zurke, Will Osborne, Gray Gordon, Phil Harris and Red Nichols.[1]

Every up and coming band worth its weight in shellac sought that all-important network "wire"—a hookup that spelled more and better paying bookings, a lucrative record-making contract and perhaps a movie deal. Just as significant, a late night pickup from the Aragon Ballroom, Glen Island Casino or Elitch's Gardens could lead to a choice prime-time commercial series.

By 1938 sponsors and ad agencies were lending a closer ear to the output of those mesmerizing fast-tempo swingsters as well as the smooth middle-of-the-road musicmakers. A straightforward program of popular melodies and vocal selections, introduced and closed by a readily identifiable tag song, developed a musically keen following. But many sponsors, especially cigarette makers, sought an even wider audience. Comedy delivered by a Hollywood attraction or Broadway celebrity midway in the musical offerings often upped the ratings. Dramatic skits or playlets, current events summaries or sports news capsules added broader interest too. But when Professor Quiz came to the air, it didn't take a Dr. I.Q. to figure out the tremendous drawing power by combining a quiz card with a musical score.

Musical games among the big band fraternity sprung from informal gatherings of sidemen. Chicago probably contributed more than any locale to what would become structured melody-guessing quiz programs. During the city's World's Fair in 1934, musicians from all over town stopped at the Blackhawk Restaurant on their night off, traditionally Mondays. Many carried their instruments to join the current house band, Kay Kyser, for impromptu sessions.[2]

Kyser, then a comparatively unknown band, broadcast musical guest nights over WGN. Diners picked up the habit of calling out tunes to see if Kyser and his eager-to-please group could play them off the cuff.[3] The hardworking bandleader went along with the spontaneous round of requests, and the contest soon became a regular feature with Kay's band. The game had all the earmarks of a quiz, but no one picked up the idea as a bona-fide program.

A year or two after the World's Fair closed, a young band booker and publicity man for the Music Corporation of America, Lew Wasserman, came by the Blackhawk to see Kyser, a new client. On the way over, he had listened to *Professor Quiz* on his car radio. Upon meeting Kyser, he asked, "Why don't you do a Professor Quiz with music?"[4]

Kyser remembered the enthusiastic response from the earlier "play that tune" challenge. He called the band's local press agent, Lou Cowan.

"What do you think, Lou?"

Cowan thought the idea had the earmarks of an audience-building gimmick—a contest that soon evolved into Kay Kyser's *Kollege of Musical Knowledge*.[5]

For nearly ten years, Kyser had struggled to gain a foothold in the band business. A native of Rocky Mount, North Carolina, he attended the University of North Carolina, where he planned to study law but then switched to liberal arts. He had his first taste of show business as the university's head cheerleader. In his junior year in 1926, he organized a campus band that within a semester had gained a local following. After graduation, the group stayed together to play one-night stands across the country. Chicago became home base in the mid-1930s, and there the band caught on and broke attendance records at the Blackhawk. His informal musical open houses were so successful that at one point Chicago musicians union chief James C. Petrillo issued an edict: no more celebrity nights with musicians performing without pay. If Kyser wished to continue this type of entertainment, the fun and games must be "programmed" and all musicians added to the payroll.[6]

Lou Cowan, however, felt Kyser's own musicians without any outside help could easily handle a musical game. He prepared a script with quiz questions and arranged to air what was first tagged a "Klass and Dance" program over WGN from the Blackhawk. Wearing an academic cap and gown and wielding an instructor's pointer, Kay played the role of the "Old Perfessor" while band members, dressed in collegiate sweaters and beanies, provided musical clues and cheered contestants on. In his down-home Carolina drawl, he greeted "students" with cheery "Even' folks, How y'all? Come on, children. Let's dance."[7]

Audiences took to Kay's easygoing, often kidding, way of handling contestants, practically giving the answers to slow participants. The broadcasts ran four months without a sponsor before MCA's future chairman, Lew Wasserman, sold the program in early 1938 to the American Tobacco Company. The Lucky Strike cigarette maker prepared a short trial run over Mutual. Cowan later revealed that Lucky Strike carried the show with a short-term commitment because a new radio comedian, Bob Hope, had a program shared with singer Frank Parker on NBC that wasn't doing very well, and the network was looking for something else that could replace it in case Hope didn't pan out.[8] (In the fall of 1938, Hope signed a contract with Pepsodent toothpaste for a different format and build-up that paid off in spades.)

Kay's musical classroom angle won over both music fans and quiz buffs. Most questions concerned composers, musicians, song titles and lyrics and were fairly simple, thus appealing to the knowledge of the average listener. Six weeks of high ratings led the tobacco company to switch the program onto the more prestigious NBC chain.

The quiz segment remained at the core of Kyser's show, with a quarter or so of the hour-long broadcast devoted to his sweet-band arrangements and brisk melodies. Kay also originated the stunt of introducing song titles by having them sung off-key by vocalist Harry Babbitt.[9] The aggregation's other prize "pupils" included singers Ginny Simms and Sully Mason and comedian Ish Kabibble.

The popularity of the *Kollege of Musical Knowledge* pushed Kay into the movies, despite his protests that he couldn't look romantic, act romantic, or be anything but himself. He starred in seven films, including "That's Right, You're Wrong" (his frequent quiz catchphrase), "Carolina Blues" (which introduced the tune "There Goes That Song Again") and "You'll Find Out" (with Boris Karloff and Bela Lugosi for scare tactics.) Kyser and his band also enjoyed a number of hit records: the inspirational "Praise The Lord and Pass the Ammunition," the nonsensical "Three Little Fishes" and the romantic "Slow Boat to China."

Featured on numerous songs in the 1940s were two of his discoveries: Mike Douglas, who later became a television talk-show host; and Georgia Carroll, a Powers model, who became Mrs. Kyser in 1944.

Kyser's weekly program picked up as many as 20 million listeners, and in 1940 he grossed the princely sum of more than a million dollars.[10] In Washington, D.C., a handful of U.S. senators and congressmen, including Harry Truman and Sam Rayburn, picked up the show's title and formed a select group called The Bourbon and Branch Water College of Congressional Knowledge.[11] For 13 seasons Americans smiled at Kyser's familiar greeting "Stoo-dents!" They responded to the warmth of his natural pattern, homespun friendliness, and spirited music, comedy and games. After a brief and unsuccessful foray into television, Kyser longed to retire and settle down in North Carolina. At age 45 he played his theme song, "Thinking of You," for the last time.

"He gave it all up to come to Chapel Hill, to raise a family, and get closer to his God," observed newspaper editor-publisher and friend Orville B. Campbell.[12] "The first few years were really tough. He was nervous and couldn't stay still. He had lived such a hectic life that the motor within didn't want to stop running."

He soon found himself in front of an audience again, this time leading them with a Bible rather than a baton. He became a Christian Science practitioner and, in 1974, head of the Film and Broadcast Division of the national church based in Boston. He traveled throughout the country as one of only 35 Christian Science lecturers in the world. During one of these addresses in Milwaukee, he suddenly made a rueful confession.

"I never learned how to read music or even play an instrument, although I made a lot of money leading a band. I can brag about it now, but I was anxious to hide it back then."[13]

Next to his family and church, the greatest thing in his life was the University of North Carolina, where he established scholarships, helped build the medical center and organized the school's public television station.

"I'm a lucky man," Kyser said many times before his death in 1985. "When the time came to bow out of show business, it didn't ruin my life because there was so doggone much work to be done."[14]

Kay Kyser's first sponsor, The American Tobacco Company, did more than any other commercial enterprise to bring dance band music to radio. The Lucky Strike Dance Orchestra, led by B. A. Rolfe, bowed on NBC in 1928, and as tastes in music changed from brassy, almost martial, music to more subdued ballads, the company inaugurated a suspense-building presentation of songs based on weekly popularity surveys. Behind this series called *Your Hit Parade* stood an aggressive sales and marketing dynamo named George Washington Hill.

The son of the president of the American Tobacco Company, Hill had joined the business as a $5-a-week trainee after attending Williams College for two years. Young Hill supervised and devised campaigns for the company's expanding cigarette line of Pall Mall, Sovereign and

Lucky Strike, working on many aspects of the product, from package design to distribution. When Hill succeeded his father as president in the late 1920s, he quickly gained a reputation as a ruthless and eccentric nabob.[15] Hill, who during the depths of the Depression averaged more than $400,000 a year in salary and bonuses, stopped at nothing to get what he wanted. No sales, marketing or promotional detail was overlooked.

For the *Lucky Strike Dance Hour*, he personally evaluated both the melody and tempo of the selections for each broadcast. During rehearsals Hill insisted that NBC personnel dance to the orchestra's music. Secretaries and script girls were obliged to try out the tunes on a make-shift dance floor.

Hill—who later inspired the portrayal of the advertising Holy Terror in Frederick Wakeman's novel of the late 1940s, "The Hucksters"—continually sought new radio formats to maneuver his brands into first place. Big-band popular music attracted the kind of attention he relished as his minions extolled on the virtues of smoking.

In 1937 Hill and his ad agency, Lord and Thomas, picked up an idea that had been tried on the California-based Don Lee Network. The creation grew into the first large-scale musical quiz of radio, and a West Coast radio executive planted the seed.

After ten years with NBC in New York and San Francisco, producer-director Ward Byron had joined MCA and had opened its Beverly Hills office. One of his first assignments was writing and supervising a new feature using MCA clients in Hollywood. Byron and his staff devised a musical game whereby a song title was suggested through the presentation of a skit. With humorously twisted music-clue lines, these playlets provided a challenge to contestants. For example, a two- or three-minute skit about a couple describing the "lovely view" from their home gave clues for a song title, such as Jerome Kern's "Lovely to Look At." Once a contestant came up with an answer, an orchestra played the song.[16]

Ward Byron wrote six or seven playlets for each show. "It was a horrendous job for one person," he recalls.[17] "I had to carry it off virtually singlehandedly. If the program had originated in New York, we would have had a bunch of writers working on it." Byron called the series *Scripteasers* and brought in crooner Buddy Rogers as M.C. "He had a winning personality, but was too wooden and couldn't ab lib well. Then we signed comedian Benny Rubin, but he was just too exuberant and hammy. There was a sense of relief when Hill took a liking to the program and carried it off to New York and the promotional aegis of his tobacco empire."

Fascinated with the idea of suggesting song titles, Hill changed the name of the program to *Melody Puzzles* and took it to WOR. He chose

Richard Himber and his musicians to provide the melodies and Fred Uttal as M.C. The mixture of music and quiz carried an interest-tugging quality and provided Hill with still another platform to plug Lucky Strike.

Melody Puzzles and *The Kollege of Musical Knowledge* gave an impetus to other musical games. A Cleveland-born bandleader had been playing one-nighters since graduation from Ohio State University in 1933. Sammy Kaye, a civil engineering major, became involved in musical activities as an undergraduate and put together a band to play for school dances and proms. His rhythm makers became so popular with the student body that he helped to open the Varsity Inn, a campus nickel-a-dance hangout.[18] With his musical crew intact, Kaye went on to whistle-stop bookings and then to comparatively choice locations where radio stations did remotes.

By late 1936 Sammy Kaye's orchestra had a Mutual wire from Bill Green's Casino in Pittsburgh to WGN in Chicago. The station picked up Kaye as a daily sustainer each afternoon at 3:30. Many listeners compared his styling and tempo to Kay Kyser, then at the Trianon in Chicago. Even Sammy's theme song—"Kaye's Melody"—sounded reminiscent of the Kyser theme, they noted. Kaye, too, had the same trick of singing and reciting the title and the same slightly sentimental handling of the brasses and saxophones.[19] Audiences especially liked Sammy's informal remarks and song introductions. One night, during an engagement at the Cabin Club in Cleveland, an announcer happened to invite his audience to "Swing and Sway with Sammy Kaye," and the tag stuck.

MCA signed the 13-piece band for a big buildup and steered it into Cleveland's Statler Hotel for a period of "seasoning" before opening at the Commodore Hotel in New York. Kaye followed Tommy Dorsey who had played in the hotel's Century Room for a highly successful two-year run.[20]

One night in 1938 not long after we opened at the Commodore, a guy came up to the bandstand to ask if he could lead the boys. He had a very pretty girl on his arm, so I said, "Sure, if you let me dance with your date." I was eager to get to know the gal. But as we danced, she absolutely ignored me and watched her boy friend on the bandstand. Actually, the band played quite well and at tempo. The fellow got a good round of applause. I began to think if someone wants to conduct a band that much, why not make a game out of it. I asked the hotel manager to give me a bottle of champagne as a prize for the best leader of the band from a handful of volunteers. He agreed. The next night, we started our audience-participation novelty, So You Want to Lead a Band.[21]

The highly entertaining gimmick became an instantaneous hit, and MCA made it a feature of Kaye's stage routine and remotes. People from every walk of life vied to lead his musicians. Celebrities, too, stepped up to test their skill. Jackie Gleason, Ethel Merman, Arnold Palmer, Red Skelton, Perry Como and Carol Channing, along with governors, industrialists, even other bandleaders, came by at one time or another. By 1984 more than 200,000 amateur conductors had waved a baton to produce the "Swing and Sway" sound.

"So You Want to Lead a Band" became the high spot of every broadcast and personal appearance. Radio listeners let their imagination take over as they visualized the gyrations of a contestant beating his way through 16 bars of an old standard like "Alexander's Ragtime Band" or "Bill Bailey" or one of Kaye's hits such as "Daddy," "Harbor Lights" or "It Isn't Fair." Although the band took direction from the contestant, the first trumpet and the drummer kept the tune going. But every contestant had to get the first downbeat and cut the band off at the end of the melody; no one could just walk away and expect the music to stop.[22]

Aside from his ingenious audience-participation stunt, Kaye made sure his orchestra stayed on top of the music business. In January 1940 he garnered his first regular commercial program bringing melodically catchy and rhythmically appealing numbers to dialers coast to coast. Some of his band doubled as a glee club, many sang solos and practically all played several instruments. Among the best-known vocalists were Don Cornell, Tony Alamo, Nancy Norman, Billy Williams and Jimmy Brown. In addition to having a weekly commercial series and frequent late-night remotes, the band presented *Sunday Serenade*, a tuneful afternoon interlude punctuated by readings of poetry by Kaye. This led to a best-selling book of poems culled from the series and a Kaye-backed national poetry contest.

Year in, year out, Sammy Kaye always returned to "So You Want to Lead a Band." Sponsors on both radio and television, ranging from Richard Hudnut Cosmetics to Brillo Pads, and including a predominance of cigarettes—Old Gold, Sensation, Kent and Chesterfield—benefited from his podium stunt and his special knack to adapt to changing tastes in listening and dancing. Whether it was a Heart Fund benefit in Miami, a Jets football game celebration in New York, a Composer's Showcase in Cleveland or an Inaugural Ball in Washington, Kaye always accommodated the people out front with his satisfying sounds and famous baton-waving novelty during one of the longest-playing careers in the big band arena.*

---

*Kaye also played in Palm Beach in 1984 for the first fundraising gala of The Big Band Hall of Fame, founded by Composer's Showcase organizer Sally Bennett.

A high-water mark for combining big bands and musical games was reached in the early 1940s (although a second wave would pound the dial at the end of the decade). Nearly every month a new quiz appeared on the bandstands of many of the country's musicmakers. Ben Bernie and "All the Lads" linked up with a contest called *Musical Mock Trial*. The American Tobacco Company bankrolled the idea, which set up six jurors to pass on musical clues, detect the name of the tune and then declare the defendant guilty or not, and why. Maestro Ben Bernie and his music were buried beneath the complexity of this format, causing its writers to switch to write-in plots from listeners with tunes for plaintiff and defendant.[23] A "trial" for everyone—even George W. Hill pleaded guilty to this miscarriage. The bright spots stemmed from the vocal cords of Bernie's new and relatively unknown bandsinger, Dinah Shore. Late in 1940 Bernie returned for Bromo Seltzer for a second go-round—a straightforward question-and-answer quiz built around tunes performed by his musicians and songstress Carol Bruce.

As a 1940 summer replacement, Philip Morris cigarettes concocted a quiz called *Rhymo* for the accomplished maestro of its regular weekly shows, conductor-composer-pianist Johnny Green. He made his first appearance as a master of ceremonies on this pleasant 30 minutes, building on his year as Jack Benny's musical foil on *The Jello Program*. *Rhymo* contestants supplied the last line, or a last few words, for a four-line jingle, using the name of a song that Green's orchestra played for a clue. Green worked diligently to make it a success, even using entirely different rhymes for the West Coast repeat in order that people who heard the first broadcast didn't try to get into the studio audience at the second and know all the right last lines.[24]

A surprise entry spotlighted the danceable music of a well-established group, its vocalists and a rising young M.C. This contest, called *Beat the Band*, was the first that pitted band personnel against listeners who supplied the questions. As an added gimmick, the musicians played against each other, tossing a half-dollar on the head of a bass drum every time a question was fumbled, with the kitty going to the sideman who piled up the largest number of correct answers. To keep the music flowing, a musician was required not only to provide the song title suggested in a question but to play, hum or sing it.

Beat the Band introduced an unusual and engaging radio game as well as a new General Mills breakfast food—Kix, a ready-to-eat, popcorn-flavored corn cereal toasted into round bubbles. Kix faded from most grocery shelves by the mid-1940s, but three featured performers on this Sunday evening presentation made lasting impressions through an initial assist by the show's maestro.

Ted Weems and his brother Art had directed a college band at the University of Pennsylvania some 20 years earlier. After leaving school, they formed their own aggregation and lined up dates in the Midwest. In 1924 the brothers signed a recording contract with Victor and then moved into radio. Deft sidemen, such as Country Washburn on tuba and Andy Secrest on cornet, joined whistler Elmo Tanner and vocalist Parker Gibbs to add a distinctive touch.

In 1936 Ted Weems signed up a little-known singer from Freddy Carlone's band to replace baritone Art Jarrett. An ex-barber from Pennsylvania, the newcomer was Perry Como. Not long after, Ted and Art added an eye-catching ballad singer with the intriguing name of Marvell Maxwell. In a few years she would achieve movie fame as the glamorous Marilyn Maxwell. The choice of young Garry Moore as M.C. launched an exceptional career for this radio jack-of-all-trades from Baltimore. Droll and whimsical, Moore deftly handled questions such as "Suppose a small fur-bearing animal gets so angry he explodes. What song title is suggested?" and the response from violinist Red Ingle: "Pop Goes the Weasel." [25]

Using the talents of Como, Maxwell and Moore, *Beat the Band* moved into the ranks of the top six quiz shows of 1941. But the series was short-lived. World War II carried off several younger musicians, and Weems and the rest of the band opted for service in the Merchant Marines. The program resurfaced with a new tempo when an entertainer whom Walter Winchell wrote "sings like Garbo looks" replaced the original troupe. [26]

Hildegarde proved an able commander of her audience in her first radio series. Assisted by announcer Radcliffe Hall and Bob Grant's band, the Milwaukee-raised song stylist and pianist upgraded the questions, as *Variety* noted "for those of above the I.Q. of a songplugger fresh out of Lindy's." [27] Hildegarde's version of *Beat the Band* soon evolved into a decidedly new format. The loquacious chanteuse and her manager, Anna Sosenko, sold Raleigh Cigarettes on the idea of re-creating the atmosphere of a swank supper club not unlike New York's Persian Room where Hildegarde frequently held court. *The Raleigh Room* proved a good merchandising vehicle. Backed by Harry Sosnick and his music, Hildegarde herself gained more opportunities to sing and to welcome guests such as Leo Durocher, Irving Berlin and Willie Howard. Scripted by Lee Segall and Alan Lerner (before he teamed up with Arthur Loewe), the program registered so well with listeners that the high-rated *Beat the Band* was quickly forgotten. [28]

Musical quizdom welcomed a unique and decidedly highbrow feature during the 1939–40 season. *So You Think You Know Music* began when originator Ted Cott joined New York City municipal station WNYC as announcer, production manager, director, actor, scriptwriter, commentator and assistant to the office boy—all reputedly without salary for some two years. Born in Poughkeepsie, New York, and raised in

Brooklyn, Ted picked up a cursory knowledge of music by working in his father's radio and record shop.

One Saturday afternoon, a last-minute cancellation left Ted to fill two hours of WNYC air time. He grabbed five people from the studio and rapidly jotted down several dozen questions for a music quiz session. The filler went off without a hitch and even raised a flurry of mail. Cott decided that he had the nucleus for a new program and made no bones about borrowing questions from a book called *Answers to Questions* by Frederick J. H. Hoskin.[29] This musical "Information Please" made an impression among New York listeners, and CBS hired Cott to air it as a Sunday sustainer.

So You Think You Know Music focused on classical works and composers with a musicologist (critic Leonard Liebling) as the final arbiter of answers. Contestants usually came from the music section of metropolitan dailies or the staff of music journals. Audience-submitted questions that stumped the pros garnered symphony tickets, opera librettos and records. When Schaefer Beer picked up Cott's show in the fall of 1940, format, prizes and timeslot changed.

At NBC on Tuesday evenings, the program became part of a half-hour musical revue featuring Allen Roth's orchestra and tenor Felix Knight. Competing teams came to the microphone from two groups: professionals, such as composers and performers, and music fans from the studio audience. A frequent contestant in the former ranks was Leonard Bernstein, then a student at The Curtis Institute of Music in Philadelphia. Cott devised what he called "Serutan Concertos" for Bernstein—music segments played backwards. "Bernstein was brilliant at identifying such pieces," said Cott in an interview years later.[30]

At ease with both novice or savant, Cott tried to be neither facetious nor too dignified. His musical attainments were limited to playing chopsticks on the piano. "And the only place I can carry a tune is to oblivion," he joked. "I don't know much about music, but I know what I like."[31]

Cott believed that there was no reason for approaching a symphony concert or an operatic performance on bended knee. "The great composers created music to give pleasure and joy," Cott reminded his audiences.[32] At one point, when the quiz lacked a sponsor and left the air, his diverse fans, ranging from hardware dealers, bankers and salespeople to high school students, clergymen and housewives, wrote CBS and forced it back on the dial. One of the strongest and more amusing pleas came from a girl in Toronto, who wrote: "I have the mumps. I am eight-years-old and I love your program. I hope you will get enough letters so you can be on the air, as I am not taking piano or anything about music, so you see I am learning a lot over the radio, so I hope you will be on the air and so does my mother and friends."[33]

Education by radio in 1940 remained nebulous as it always had. But Ted Cott's musical game generated considerable attention and serious discussion. His technique of combining entertainment and knowledge demonstrated that Americans yearned for some self-improvement, even "capsule culture."[34] "A fact is a fact," *The New Republic* observed, "and we cling to it, whether it be buried in an encyclopedia, enticingly hidden in 'Ask Me Another' books or picked out of the ether by the turning of a knob."[35]

›9‹

Right, with Eversharp

"Take It or Leave It," adman and program packager Milton Biow proudly noted, "was the birthplace of 'The $64 Question,' a phrase that became part of the language—the tough, imponderable question. Everybody used it, including President Roosevelt and Winston Churchill. It even made Bartlett's 'Familiar Quotations.' "[1]

Biow's *Take It or Leave It* grew out of a basic question-and-answer format. By responding correctly to seven questions, the prize money doubled every time, from $1 to $64. Contestants were picked from the studio audience and could stop at any level and carry off their winnings or risk everything on the next question. The audience was always in there pitching. They either cheered the players on with "Take it, take it," or called in unison, "You'll be sorry!" Concluded Biow: "It was a lively show, fun for everyone who had a hand in it and everyone who heard it."[2]

The germ of the idea stemmed from the musings of a clinical psychologist in Atlanta, Georgia. Twenty-nine-year-old Peter Cranford worked as research director for the Georgia Education Association. This assignment included arranging forums and radio programs to promote better education. The philosopher-psychologist William James played a subliminal role in the development of the $64 Question. Cranford subscribed to James' belief that anything was possible with enough thought and effort.[3] So the young educator set a goal: making a million dollars.

"Times were hard in 1939 and I had to make it without any capital," Cranford recalled.[4]

> I picked the entertainment field. I had heard that radio networks and advertisers were looking for ideas, so I went to the library

and read everything I could about programming. I pondered the question: Why do people listen to one show and not another?

I concluded that what an interesting program needed most was audience identification or participation. I studied every game there ever was. The most intriguing centered on a pair of ordinary dice. But how could I put a crap game on radio?[5]

If questions asked by a quizmaster were substituted for rolls of the dice, thought Cranford, an existing new program could be developed. The idea of gambling, of doubling the reward for each successive question, was a natural suspense builder. He peddled the game at Atlanta stations, facing constant resistance to a gambling-type formula. Then he took his craps quiz to New York after hearing that the Milton Biow Company was looking for novel program ideas. The ad agency liked the "double or nothing" concept and sent Cranford a check for $75.

The Georgia educator had no intentions of selling out; he wanted to lease the property on a royalty, or share-the-profits, basis. Biow next agreed to a payment of $25 a week for the first 26 weeks, for a total outlay of $625.

Cranford again objected to the deal. Having just lost his job, he wanted a measure of long-term security. While he and Biow continued their negotiations, Cranford agreed to let the agency bring *Take It or Leave It* to the air. Then, not long after its bow, a station in Washington, D.C., sued Biow, claiming it owned the idea. The adman reluctantly sought Cranford's help in defending the suit. Given a bargaining wedge, the psychologist insisted on his terms. Eventually, he won out. Cranford received $50 for each broadcast and a one-third share in all monies taken in for licensing the program idea elsewhere.[6] This covered the sale of movie and board-game rights, as well as future TV adaptions.

Peter Cranford never quite made his million from the $64 Question. Nevertheless, he collected an estimated $225,000 from the original show and subsidiary sales. From television in the 1950s, he drew a much greater windfall—until the quiz scandals wiped out *The $64,000 Question* and its spinoff, *The $64,000 Challenge*.[7]

From time to time, Cranford attempted to translate other games to radio and television, namely, a version of bank night, but had little or no success. But his professional career flourished. He wrote several well-received books, including *How to Be Your Own Psychologist* and *How to Discipline Children*.[8]

If *Take It or Leave It* provided a firm cushion for its creator, it proved a bonanza for its ad agency and its sponsor. Biow sold the show to Martin L. Strauss, president of Eversharp Pen and Pencil. In 1940 his company was slipping downhill fast. Strauss had about $300,000 to spend for advertising that year. Biow suggested that Eversharp put it all to use in six months.

"Why wait a whole year to lose money," Biow reasoned, "when you can lose it in six months? Then you have six months left to make back your money. I have a hunch *Take It or Leave It* will make it."[9]

Biow placed the show on CBS Sunday nights, directly after Fred Allen at NBC. The program worked like magic. Before the six months had passed, business started to go up and up some more.

Take It or Leave It attracted an army of new Eversharp dealers. In six months they grew from 400 to nearly 5,000, and sales mushroomed from $2 million in 1940 to more than $20 million by 1944.[10] Everything was right—and write—with Eversharp. Biow, too, grew substantially, gaining new accounts, such as Pepsi Cola, Anacin, Ruppert Beer and Lady Esther cosmetics. Throughout the 1940s, it ranked as one of the top ten agencies with billings of some $50 million.

Milton Biow took a proprietary interest in *Take It or Leave It*. He auditioned scores of announcers for the all-important M.C. role, finally deciding on Bob Hawk, who already worked for Biow on a Philip Morris program called *Name Three*. Earlier, Hawk had conducted the unsuccessful *Fun Quiz* and *Foolish Questions*. In the 1930s he had started as an announcer in Chicago radio where he developed a glib, freewheeling approach. He once scooped the broadcast world by interviewing Roosevelt on the day of his nomination in 1932 by meeting his plane at Gary, Indiana, while everyone else had expected a landing in Chicago. He also conducted man-in-the-street interviews and one day blocked traffic in the Chicago Loop when screen siren Jean Harlow stopped at his mike.[11]

Bob Hawk reputedly suggested the idea of placing the choice of categories on a blackboard to avoid repeating them for each new contestant. With Hawk in charge, the show never took itself too seriously. "Hawk is a bit fresh at times," *Variety* noted after the show's first 13 weeks, "but his al fresco manner, albeit a bit unorthodox in comparison to radio's heretofore circumspect manner of treating the customer always 'right,' is a relief. In fact, this may keynote the humanizing factor in 1940 radio."[12]

A year after Hawk brought the show to a spectacularly high Hooper rating, a rift developed between him and Biow. Neither would sign a new two-year contract. The quizmaster (or glibmaster, as Hawk preferred to be called) believed he deserved more money. Biow disagreed. Hawk apparently stalled negotiations long enough to find another quiz called *How'm I Doing?*, sponsored by Camels. Undaunted by the news, Biow brought in an M.C. of star caliber, the well-known Broadway comedian Phil Baker. *Take It or Leave It* continued its upward climb, and Baker became the host most closely identified with the series. ("Of all the emcees—and they later included Garry Moore, Eddie Cantor and Jack Paar," Cranford once said, "Bob Hawk, in my estimation, was the best."[13])

In 1942 Hawk appeared headed for the ratings basement with his new CBS game. It was dropped, so he helped to package another quiz for Camels called *Thanks to the Yanks*. This timely World War II series let contestants choose "three-carton, five-carton or ten-carton" questions. If answered correctly, they could choose servicemen as recipients for the highly rationed cigarettes. The program became *The Bob Hawk Show* at the war's end and ran another eight years for Camels. Winners on each show were designated a "Lemac" to the accompaniment of the audience's singing "You're a Lemac now" ("Lemac" was Camel spelled backward).[14]

Phil Baker emceed *Take It or Leave It* longer than anyone and handled it skillfully, with a great sense of timing. Before joining the show, he had searched around for a new vehicle to resuscitate his flaccid career. The old vaudeville days almost seemed bright by comparison. In its heyday, he had teamed up with an obscure violinist named Ben Bernie and then developed his own act of songs and jokes, underscored by accordion playing. Featured in Ziegfeld and Shubert productions, he went on to star in "Artists and Models" and "Crazy Quilt." With Broadway in the doldrums in 1933, Baker entered radio with a series built around him and a stooge and called it *Bottle and Beetle*. After several years of lackluster ratings against the likes of Jack Benny, Burns and Allen and Fred Allen, he quit the air. But when Biow offered him the quizmaster post in late 1941, he relented, calling the show "an impelling challenge for a comedian."[15] Besides, the pay was good.

Baker made the $64 Question part of the vernacular of everyday conversation. He truly enjoyed seeing a contestant win as much as possible and often helped them with broad hints. There always was the standard Baker bailout question for a dollar: "Who's buried in Grant's tomb?" A facile ad-libber, he had to admit that 75 percent of the show was prepared in advance by gagwriters such as Hal Block. "The remaining 25 percent is off the cuff," he told a reporter, "and that 25 percent sheds heavy pounds."[16]

Congenial Phil Baker termed his six years as M.C. as getting paid for learning. He acquired a liberal arts education by asking some 40 general information questions each Sunday night. "Before I joined the program, if you asked my anything about anything outside of show business," he remarked in 1943, "I would answer you with a brilliant, 'huh?' In the set I traveled, nobody ever gave a straight answer. Either they didn't know, or it was funnier the other way. Don't think for a minute that I know the answers beforehand. I probably wouldn't know more than a very few unless they were neatly typed out and handed to me before each broadcast."[17]

Every once in a while, Baker would try to show a flash of erudition and wind up getting into trouble. For a set of musical questions, Jacques Renard's orchestra played "In the Merry, Merry Month of May." The contestant hemmed and hawed trying to recall the song title. In an effort to be helpful, Baker said, "Don't you know your Gilbert and Sullivan?" CBS switchboard operators went slightly crazy as listeners called in by the thousands to correct him; the tune was *not* written by the duo who created operettas such as "H.M.S. Pinafore" and "The Mikado."

During World War II he asked a serviceman to tell him whether or not Romulus and Remus discovered Rome in fact or in fable. "In fable," the contestant replied. Baker's answer card read "in fact" and he went on to the next contestant. He received letters and calls from hundreds of indignant listeners who had no idea the mistake stemmed from a careless researcher or typist. He brought the GI back the following week and started over with a new set of questions. He won $64, and everybody was happy.

Milton Biow once played a joke on Baker. On the eve of his 44th birthday, August 23, 1942, he filled the studio full of Bakers, 750 of them. Naturally, every contestant was named Baker, and six of the seven players hit the $64 jackpot.[18]

"My only word of caution to Baker and every M.C. was," Biow recalled, " 'Don't tell jokes for jokes sake. Build them only out of the show so the show keeps moving—and moving fast.' "[19]

At the peak of its popularity, Biow featured celebrity guests. Jack Benny, introduced as a violinist from Waukegan, selected the category of musical history. After correctly answering the $1 question, he insisted on stopping and leaving with his winnings. Baker convinced the radio-created parsimonious character to try for $2. Benny did and won. Baker urged him on to $4, then $8 and on to $32. A gag question stumped him at $64—all according to the prepared script. Only Benny could get away with a "rigged" show and make it "pay."[20]

Phil Baker left *Take It or Leave It* in 1947 for guest appearances and work as M.C. of a short-lived giveaway called *Everybody Wins*. He returned to the show in 1951—by then it was renamed *The $64 Question*—replacing Eddie Cantor who had abandoned his variety series. A year later Biow packed up the 1940s' highest-rated audience-participation question-and-answer program. Not long after, Biow disbanded his entire ad agency and retired—but not before selling a half-interest in his popular and lucrative *$64 Question* to those who would soon develop the quiz crap game into a national mania and ultimately a national disgrace.

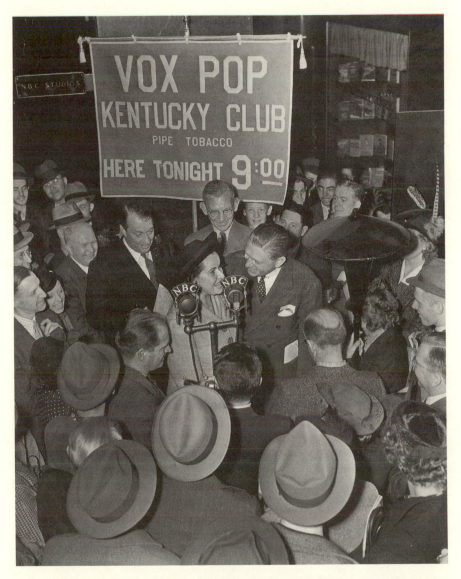

Vox Pop reaches out to people via a remote from the lobby of the RCA Building, New York. Clustered about the microphone for this 1938 broadcast are announcer Graham McNamee, and co-emcees Parks Johnson and Wally Butterworth. (Courtesy Bill Johnson.)

Quizmaster Bob Hawk spells out the category choices for contestants on *Take It or Leave It*, radio fore-runner of *The $64,000 Question*. (Courtesy Temple University Libraries Photojournalism Collection.)

"The Old Perfessor" Kay Kyser introduces his *Kollege of Musical Knowledge* singers Harry Babbitt and Ginny Simms. Lucky Strike and other cigarette brands regularly sponsored musical games in the 1930s and '40s. (Courtesy Harry Babbitt.)

Bandleader Cab Calloway (right, with bassist Milt Hinton and trombonist Tyree Glenn, left) played quizmaster on *Quizzical*, a black "Kollege of Musical Knowledge" of the early 1940s. Calloway was the first black host of a network game show. (Frank Driggs Collection.)

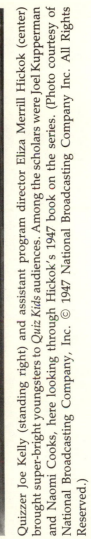

Quizzer Joe Kelly (standing right) and assistant program director Eliza Merrill Hickok (center) brought super-bright youngsters to *Quiz Kids* audiences. Among the scholars were Joel Kupperman and Naomi Cooks, here looking through Hickok's 1947 book on the series. (Photo courtesy of National Broadcasting Company, Inc. © 1947 National Broadcasting Company Inc. All Rights Reserved.)

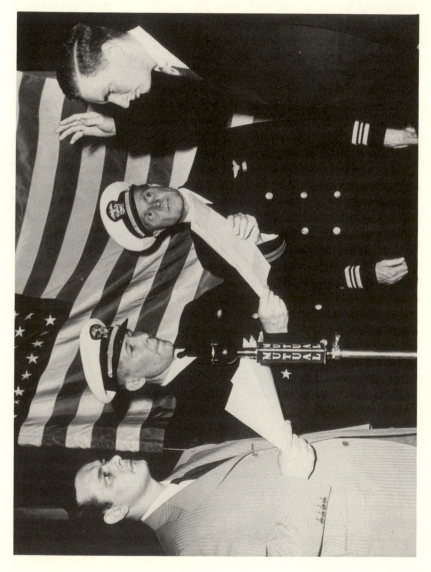

Quiz shows boosted the war effort and morale. In 1942 *Double or Nothing* and host Walter Compton (left) gave airtime for the swearing-in of Naval air recruit James B. Taylor, III (right) by Lt. J. Clement Boyd. Observing the milestone is Lt. Cmdr. James B. Taylor, Jr., a World War I flying ace and test pilot. (Courtesy James B. Taylor, III.)

GIs fill CBS studio for Ken Murray's wartime quiz *Which Is Which?* Film star Olivia de Havilland joins the popular comedian for this Hollywood-based show in 1944. (Courtesy Bette Lou Murray [Mrs. Ken Murray].)

Bud Collyer re-enacts studio audience interview of *Break The Bank* winners Edith and Jack Weiss. Navy physician Weiss carried off a grand prize of $5,220—the biggest cash giveaway in the first 20 years of network radio. (Author's collection.)

ABC's leading game show hosts, Groucho Marx and Art Linkletter, pose for a publicity shot in 1949. (Courtesy John Guedel Productions—Temple University Libraries Photojournalism Collection.)

In the film "The Jackpot" James Stewart guesses a mystery melody, winning a houseful of prizes that, in turn, brings domestic disharmony and havoc. Barbara Hale played his wife in the sobering takeoff on postwar giveaways. (Author's collection.)

› 10 ‹

Service with a Smile

Radio stations, large and small, reinforced America's determination to win a war that had engulfed the world by the end of 1941. So did program content. Quiz programs and audience-participation shows stressed themes of patriotism and sacrifice, while boosting morale and offering a measure of "escapist" cheer. Very early in the war, quizzes, along with whodunits, headed a poll of shows that listeners described as conducive for tuning out the real world. *Dr. I.Q.* and *The Quiz Kids*, *Sherlock Holmes* and *The Thin Man* struck them as ideal fare to block out reality. A trend appeared in the making. The CBS script department was flooded with a rash of chillers and the Blue Network faced a similar pile of mystery plots. The Blue's continuity editor, Dorothy Kemble, also observed a rise in game-show ideas, pointing to two or three quiz suggestions in the mail every day, whereas a year earlier they averaged only two or three a week.[1]

During the ten months preceding the attack on Pearl Harbor, quiz and game shows had already grown to represent approximately 25 percent of the 200 or so sponsored programs on the networks.[2] Only newscasts and news commentary experienced a greater surge, stemming in great measure from the Munich crisis in the fall of 1938 and the German invasion of Poland a year later.

In truth, the war years would see the introduction of only a handful of new quizzes. Audiences seemed satisfied with the wide choice of existing games. These established quizzes provided a pleasant respite from grim world news. But, of course, there was no way the war could really be tuned out. People in uniform popped up everywhere and couldn't be ignored as contestants. Washington soon viewed a quiz forum as a salient factor in meeting wartime goals. It strongly encouraged quiz producers to inject patriotic themes and morale-boosting campaigns into their air time. Picking up the cue, quizzes quickly spot-lighted members of the armed forces, encouraged enlistments, added questions on the course of the war and awarded war stamps and bonds as prizes. Not infrequently, a contestant, celebrity guest, question or stunt would tie into the war effort, occasionally with dramatic results.

Double or Nothing wasted no time to do all it could "for the duration." Originated by Walter Compton in 1940 as a substitute for the weekly "bank night" at a Washington theater, it appealed to a basic gambling instinct. Compton modified the contest for radio by requiring a winning player to talk extemporaneously for one minute on the subject of his question. For each pertinent, informative or amusing fact brought out in this ad-lib monologue, Compton arbitrarily handed over extra dollars.[3] If the contestant correctly answered one final question, his winnings doubled. The format proved an ideal showcase for the swelling number of GI participants.[4] The broadcast of May 3, 1942, for example, left no flag unfurled to uplift the spirits of Americans and aid the conduct of the war.

Aired from Mutual's New York studios, *Double or Nothing* that day saluted the American Legion and its million-plus members—virtually all World War I veterans. A Legion official spoke on home-front measures, explaining that 11,000 Legion posts stood on 24-hour call for civilian defense work. Many veterans had signed up as plane spotters and air-raid wardens. The Legion Auxiliary and its junior members, he continued, were selling war bonds and caring for disabled vets, war widows and orphans.[5]

A team of World War I doughboys played *Double or Nothing* and their winnings went to help servicemen recuperating in a nearby hospital. Another contestant, the Navy Relief poster girl for 1942, won U.S. war stamps. Celebrity guest Woody Herman picked up $35 in stamps and turned it over to the Navy Relief. The show also introduced a special song dedicated to the aviators of the U.S. Navy. Written by singer Frank Forrest, "Silver Wings of the Air" was a buildup to what would follow: "A special and exclusive event," disclosed host Walter Compton.

Lt. J. Clement Boyd, a member of the Naval Aviation Selection Board, came to the microphone to describe the need for 30,000 new pilots by the end of 1942. Young men, age 18 to 26, were sought, if they were U.S. citizens, physically fit and single. For the first time, applicants needed no college education. The Navy Air Corps would now welcome high school graduates.

To dramatize this significant recruitment change, Boyd swore in the first candidate, a 20-year-old flight mechanic at Grumman Aircraft on Long Island. The first noncollegian air cadet, James Blackstone Taylor III, took the oath as millions of *Double or Nothing* fans listened.[6] Witnessing the milestone was Taylor's father, a well-known test pilot and

World War I flying ace—a proud moment for Lt. Cmdr. James B. Taylor, Jr., who had flown and tested nearly 500 planes. Yet it would be one of the very last meetings for the Taylors. Three weeks later, while engaged in a test of a new fighter plane, 44-year-old Taylor crashed into a New Jersey marsh. Dozens of nearby schoolchildren witnessed the fatal accident.*

But at one point just six months earlier, game and audience-participation programs faced the very real threat of going off the air. After the attack by the Japanese on December 7, 1941, broadcasters everywhere were jittery and worried. That very day, the FCC ordered West Coast stations to shut down for brief periods. Would California be the next target of enemy fighter planes, they wondered? Or hit by acts of sabotage?

A week later, stations in Spokane, Washington, got orders from the army to pull their switches. The Northwest military command worried about Japanese aircraft being guided to their targets by radio signals. For several nights, blacked-out Spokane stations picked up their usual network programs but could only air them within the confinements of their studios. So they invited local listeners to come by, pull up a chair near an audio speaker and listen to the usual lineup of network favorites.[7] Few took advantage of the offer.

Ad-lib and informal shows, such as quizzes, disc jockey request shows, forums and interviews, came under close scrutiny—more than any other type of program. The availability of an "open mike" to convey secret, coded messages from a contestant or interviewee to an enemy spy or undercover agent alarmed Washington. The government now had to weigh the possibility of this security-threatening use of the air against maintaining a long-established, censorship-free medium and come up with some answers.

A month later, the Office of Censorship in Washington released its nervously awaited guidelines on radio content.[8] Broadcasters from Vancouver to Key West generally read them with a sigh of relief: quizzes and audience interviews, for the most part, could remain on the air. Nevertheless, the government ruled out certain features and added a few precautions.

All audience-participation quizzes originating as "remotes," either by wire, transcription or short wave, must be dropped. (Military installations and hospitals would remain exceptions.) Any program that permitted public accessibility to an open microphone was described as "dangerous and should be carefully supervised." The greatest danger, the regulations pointed out, "lies in the informal interview conducted

---

*Taylor's son earned navy wings and survived the war to become president of Gates Learjet.

among a small group—10 to 25 people." Any quiz drawing upon such a narrow segment—especially when no arrangement existed for investigating backgrounds of potential participants—ended. This virtually eliminated man-in-the-street interviews.[9]

"In all studio audience-type quiz shows, where the audience from which interviewees are to be selected numbers less than 50 people," the guidelines stated, "program conductors should devise a method whereby no individual seeking participation can be GUARANTEED PARTICIPATION."[10]

This loomed as no handicap to network shows; without exception, they were conducted before audiences of at least 50. A group of ad agencies issued a statement on the selection of contestants. If any modifications were necessary, they would "take them in stride and also adopt all precautions necessary without causing any diminution of entertainment value to the program."[11] At NBC instructions were issued to producers, announcers and M.C.s on audience participation shows to veer away from all subjects that the government regarded as sensitive. NBC added that it had already carried out a degree of self-imposed censorship.

The regulations struck hardest at local stations. Curbside and railroad terminal interviews fell by the wayside. Song requests to disc jockeys by telephone ended. Requests by mail were okay but were tabled for a length of time before reaching the air. Similarly, "lost and found" and community meeting announcements had to be in writing. Foreign-language programs came under tight supervision. Full transcripts, written or recorded, had to be kept; any deviation from a script, it was thought, might be relaying a secret message to the enemy. Some situations even demanded birth certificates from its foreign-language broadcasters.[12]

Studio tours ended at several major stations, including the pioneering KDKA in Pittsburgh. A number of transmitters installed huge spotlights to discourage any attempts of nighttime sabotage. Additional guards appeared everywhere to watch over key equipment and installations. Radio City alone hired 100 or more men to supplement its security force. NBC immediately barred all visitors from the floor housing its master control complex.[13]

In actual practice, studio-based quizzes on the networks survived intact, and many flourished with the influx of contestants in uniform. Military leaders and government authorities not only permitted game shows in the prewar mold but encouraged the appearance of servicemen and defense workers. Washington facilitated the airing of entire shows from naval bases, army camps and air force fields. Policy and logistic hurdles fell as quizzes took to the road.

After December 7, 1941, *Vox Pop*—"The Show That Travels America"—rarely broadcast from a CBS studio. Few U.S military and defense installations now were out of reach or bounds. The first to beam a program from an army training camp, the program gave equal time to the Air Force, Marines, Navy, Coast Guard, Merchant Marines and Seabees and then focused on specialty outfits such as submarine crews, medical corps, ski troops, infantry rangers, nurses, B-24 pilots, chaplains, army engineers, quartermasters and dozens of other service units. Ft. Belvoir, Randolph Field, Great Lakes, Ft. Bliss, Camp Devens, Walter Reed Hospital, Manhattan Beach and Patuxent became familiar places to listeners. Three or four programs originated at Floyd Bennett Naval Air Station; one such remote shared the experiences of a coastal patrol bomber crewman, a marine home from Guadalcanal, the sole survivor from the radio room of a damaged cruiser and a WAVE who conducted courses in antiaircraft fire.[14]

Actually, on July 4, 1940, some 18 months before the country entered the war, Parks Johnson broadcast from the Merchant Marine's *Empire State* moored at New London, Connecticut. This infantry captain from World War I felt the American public should be mobilized for a preparedness crusade and know and understand the activities beginning to gain momentum in camps and armament factories. *Vox Pop* brought thousands of GIs and defense workers to tell their human interest stories to its microphone during the years 1940–45 as it traveled more than 280,000 miles throughout the United States and Canada.[15]

Early in the war, 39 year old Warren Hull, best known as "The Green Hornet" and "The Spider" from movie serials and M.C. of radio's *Show Boat*, replaced Wally Butterworth. The gruelling travel schedule demanded unusual equilibrium and stamina. Butterworth apparently took to steady drinking to ease stress and fatigue but merely jeopardized the quick thinking needed on an ad-lib program, as well as the wartime security consciousness required on all assignments.[16] The producers turned to the personable, Quaker-trained Hull with a sense of relief, knowing his questions would be amusing and searching; his comments, apt and well-timed.

Kay Kyser and his *Kollege of Musical Knowledge* also stood among those to answer the call from military outposts. Kyser's troupe brought jive and laughter to training camps months before the shooting war when morale was low and recognition of these citizen-soldiers perfunctory. On February 26, 1941, Kyser first broadcast from a military base, a pickup from San Diego that ushered in what would ultimately number nearly 500 troop shows and hospital visits by his Kollege.[17]

Next, Kyser heard about the need for a swimming pool at a Navy hospital in Oakland, California. He played a dance, making in four hours more than $26,000, money enough for a pool *and* a recreation hall. That year, he also joined a Broadway-bound delegation of stars to open the Stage Door Canteen and then gave his services to appear in a fund-raising movie of the same title. Not long after, he acted as master of ceremonies of a three-week war-bond sales tour that touched every large U.S. city.

For several years, Kyser sought to take his Kollege overseas. Finally, in 1945, when transportation became available, the Kyser aggregation jumped from one Pacific outpost to another. His greatest thrill came while performing in northern Luzon, just behind the battle lines. There, he got word of the first tentative offer by the Japanese to surrender and broke the happy news to his GI audience. His troupe covered more than 30,000 miles and played more than 70 shows to nearly 1 million men and women in uniform. During this Pacific tour, Kyser decided to wind up his contractual obligations back home and then retire. Hoping for a release from his radio contract, which still had 26 months to run, he, nevertheless, was persuaded by his sponsors to keep the Kollege open for several more seasons. They reminded him that it would be a year or more before most GIs gained discharges and entered civilian life. After a long rest, Kay Kyser and his troupe returned to the air as well as the road. Ex-servicemen never forgot Kay's efforts on their behalf. For the next 40 years, rarely a week passed that he did not receive a letter from a veteran who simply said, "Thanks, perfessor. You helped me through some mighty tough times.[18]

On the home front, the *Quiz Kids* went on the road from time to time to sell war bonds in San Francisco, Pittsburgh, New Orleans, Richmond, Des Moines, Philadelphia, Boston and other large cities. Audiences ultimately bought $120 million in bonds as admission to watch the Kids in action. In many cities, a local youngster chosen by vigorous testing and interviews joined the panel. At New York's Stage Door Canteen, the Quiz Kids and a sultry Tallulah Bankhead as chief quizzer created a riotous question-and-answer session that no GI or home listener would easily forget.

"Hello darlings," she drawled at the outset. "Don't ask me any questions. I'm to do the asking. Now, let's get acquainted."[19]

"How do we do that?" Gerald Darrow asked.

"We talk, darling."

On a fund-raising par with the *Quiz Kids*, the erudite *Information Please* panel raised like amounts for war-bond drives and community charities. On their initial foray, the program journeyed to Boston's Symphony Hall in December 1942 where the sales of seats, priced from $25 to $50,000 each, raised nearly $4 million in one evening.[20] With Treasury Department encouragement, other cities bid for the show. Staged in large auditoriums, the show added a half-hour prebroadcast warmup with local celebrities on the platform, in addition to Messrs. Kieran, Adams, Fadiman, and Levant, who usually interjected a piano piece or two.

On September 27, 1943, more than 3,270 people crowded into the Mosque Theatre in Newark to witness *Information Please* with Arkansas Congressman James W. Fulbright and Vice President Henry A. Wallace. Clifton Fadiman happily announced the purchase, an astounding $277,398,975 in war bonds, chiefly by local business concerns.[21]

In the spring of 1943, *Truth or Consequences* left on a 14-week cross-country tour to boost the current Treasury Bond Drive. Along the way, Ralph Edwards also stopped to entertain at service camps.

"The people outside New York, Hollywood and Chicago want to see what they hear on radio," Edwards explained. "That you can sell bonds at the same time is a happy association of ideas, because they realize they are not actually paying out of pocket money for admission. And the result is thousands of people who bought bonds before they have been given just the little incentive they need to make the purchase. . . . It makes everyone realize it is his war and he is doing his share to finance it."[22]

In Topeka, Kansas, a city of 73,000, more than 9,000 people participated in the bond campaign. They came early in the afternoon, with lunch baskets, and sat on the grass outside the auditorium waiting for the doors to open for the Saturday night broadcast. In Denver, the local committee inadvertently oversold 1,500 tickets. So on Friday night, Edwards added a stage version of *Truth or Consequences* and chalked up an extra $1 million for the U.S. Treasury. The program's tremendous drawing power ultimately contributed more than $180 million to the war effort.[23]

Programs aided the war effort in many ways, blatant and subtle. An offbeat appeal, an oft-repeated tag line, a GI-coveted jackpot prize or a morale-lifting special contest reminded listeners that everyone could, and should, pitch in. When a shortage of paper stopped the manufacture of playing cards, Bob Hawk on *Thanks to the Yanks* asked for spare decks for patients in military hospitals. Tom Breneman on his *Breakfast in Hollywood* requested bath towels for the Hollywood Canteen. Harmonica player Larry Adler, while a *Quiz Kids* guest, pleaded for spare instruments for those GI overseas who could pass many a dreary hour by toying with a song on a mouth organ.

When musician contestants on Hildegarde's *Beat the Band* missed a question, they tossed a pack of Raleigh cigarettes on the head of a bass drum for the boys in uniform to smoke. *Double or Nothing* boosted the role of America's allies by selecting contestants representing an allied nation. British stage star Gertrude Lawrence and Australian opera singer John Brownlee, for example, helped remind listeners of those partners in battle overseas.

Take It or Leave It encouraged servicemen and women to come forward as contestants and as a result even inspired a wartime movie based on the appearance of a fictitious GI. Many questions reflected an increased interest in world geography, battle sites and military leaders. M.C. Phil Baker, a sailor in World War I, was especially kind to fighting men. Once a bewildered gob from Nebraska chose an unusually tough category that offered no chance to pick up pocket money. Baker merely handed the question cards to the sailor and said, "Here, you quiz me." Baker supplied the answers and then handed over the $64 prize money.[24] Baker never failed to sign off every broadcast with the reminder, "Bye, Bye . . . Buy Bonds."

Battle of the Sexes regularly pitted combat veterans against field nurses, airplane spotters against canteen hostesses, pilots against distaff factory workers. "Who is the smarter, the women or the men?" asked M.C. Walter O'Keefe at the beginning of each program. A marine in World War I, O'Keefe once gave special attention to the 167th anniversary of the founding of the corps. Besides quizzing three marines, he sang two choruses of "The Marines Hymn."

Announcer Ben Grauer closed this show by prudently pointing out that "the appearance of Marine Corps personnel does not necessarily involve the endorsement of the sponsor's product [Mollé Brushless Shaving Cream] by the Navy Department."[25]

Blind Date offered servicemen on leave a chance to meet girls for an evening at New York's glamourous Stork Club, courtesy of sponsor Hinds Lotion. Hosted by Arlene Francis, the show selected two personable GIs who verbally competed by "phone" for a date. A partition on stage separated the participants. Only when the girl made her choice of an escort did they meet. The series constantly touched on the admirable service records of these much-decorated GIs.

Another gender contest, *The Better Half*, emerged near the end of the war. A quiz between husbands and wives, it often featured a GI and his spouse and a gag where the loser was forced to pay a penalty. On one show, the losing husband was placed in a box with holes in it. Every time he stuck his neck out, his wife beat him over the ears with a stick. Practical jokes and stunts occupied most of this *Truth or Consequences*-type mayhem. Its obvious visual appeal led "The March of Time" filmmakers to select the program as an example—some said "horrible" example—of contemporary broadcasting.

A series directed at families and friends of GIs, *This Is Fort Dix* reported on the activities of these men in uniform. It didn't matter whether a serviceman had been a mail carrier, shoe clerk or president of the New York Stock Exchange. At the Fort Dix mike, he was just another GI reporting to the folks back home. Only once did a GI interview backfire. An infantry veteran related so stirring a tale of derring-do and bravery that M.C. Tom Slater later spoke to the GI's commanding officer (CO) to suggest a promotion or at least a commendation. The CO looked into the matter. Soon the FBI investigated. Then the Medical

Corps took charge. The medics discovered that the private suffered from certain delusions of grandeur and suggested immediate treatment.

NBC and Clark Candy offered *Service with a Smile*. This short-lived traveling show with Ben Grauer and Garry Moore spotlighted the cerebral skills of a GI along with his talents as a performer. Employees of government agencies in Washington, D.C., gained recognition too. WTOP's *Battle of the Bureaus*, with quizmaster Lee Vickers, lined up two civilian teams for questions on sound identification, word spelling, music and general information. Ted Malone's *Yankee Doodle Quiz* on American history occasionally handed out items in short supply, one time even a live pig.

The war years produced very few dynamic formats; the pre–Pearl Harbor games continued to lead the pack. Nevertheless, broadcasters never stopped introducing a new twist or two.

Former *Vox Pop* cohost Wally Butterworth used a deck of playing cards from which contestants drew questions with the face value keyed to various prizes, such as tickets to "Oklahoma" or dinner at the Waldorf. But *Take a Card*, even with an assist from comedian Lew Lehr and model "Honey" Johnson, collapsed like a house of cards.

Stooperoos, a comedy quiz with Colonel Stoopnagel, didn't fare any better. Perhaps this CBS feature was ahead of its time. Here, two contestants, a man and a woman, were asked how each would react to some bizarre situation. The degree of the participants' success was determined by the screwiness of the answer and the counterqueries put to Stoopnagel Audiences decided the winner.

Perhaps the most acclaimed new game to emerge took on the proportions of a national, albeit brief, epidemic. *Scramby Amby* started on Cincinnati's WLW, then mushroomed onto NBC's Pacific Coast network and soon reached greater heights on the coast-to-coast ABC chain. A radio anagram, conducted by Perry Ward and Larry Keating, it tossed scrambled words at contestants who had three opportunities to win cash. The first clue was a musical selection; the second a daffy rhyme; and the third, a dictionary definition of the scrambled word. Puzzlers came from listeners who submitted them by the thousands each week. This parlor game gave rise to wartime Scramby Amby clubs that gathered in homes on Wednesday nights to vie for group prizes and jackpots. With pencils in hand, word devotees strove to outdo studio contestants and each other.[26] Sponsored by the Manhattan ("Sweetheart") Soap Company, the show actually never achieved a broad-based listenership and was abruptly dropped in early 1945.

One of the few major wartime network quizzes on the West Coast, *Which Is Which?* had the ingredients for a top-rated guessing game. Originating from Hollywood—a wartime mecca for servicemen—this

CBS production drew a standing-room-only audience of GIs. Comedian Ken Murray hosted and was backed by the orchestra of Richard Himber.

By 1944 Murray had enjoyed a long career in vaudeville, on radio and in films. Early in the war, he opened his celebrated "Blackouts" at a theater just off Sunset Boulevard and drew capacity crowds night after night. In the midst of a demanding schedule of producing, directing and starring in this frequently revamped revue, Murray sought a radio series. A year earlier, he had held the reins of a modest-budgeted KNX quiz called *Stop or Go*, a weak imitation of *Take It or Leave It* that comedian Joe E. Brown later took to ABC.

On *Which Is Which* Murray brought a new twist by having GI contestants try to identify well-known radio and film performers and personalities with only their voices as clues. Alfred Hitchcock, Jack Oakie, Basil Rathbone, Olivia de Havilland and Marie Wilson were among those hidden behind a screen as they spoke. A "mistaken identity" feature had GIs guessing if the actual celebrity was talking or merely being impersonated by someone else.[27] Sponsored by Old Gold, the game appealed enormously to the studio audience, but listeners at home lost interest in spite of an array of popular show business "names" that only Hollywood and Vine could turn out.

Upon signing the contract for *Which Is Which?*, Murray said: "If I set a good pace the audience will not be bored. If the audience is not bored, it will have fun and if it has fun, it will tune in again. I want people, as in the case of the 'Blackouts' at the end of a performance, to look at their watches and say 'It can't be that late.' "[28] But Murray's listeners *were* bored, looked at their watches and switched to NBC's *Mr. District Attorney*, a guessing game of another sort. Ken Murray had to wait for television to showcase his special comic-M.C. talents. By 1950 his GI fans were out of uniform, back home, and eager to settle down in front of a video screen—and Murray would be there, and to better advantage.

›11‹

Prized Events

Listeners tuning in special events in the last days of the war could have few doubts that the world was now at their doorstep. In the spring of 1945, the networks picked up a potpourri of many languages by broadcasting the charter meeting on their shores of the United Nations. Representatives of 50 countries gathered in San Francisco as the final drive to crush the Axis powers accelerated. On May 8, 1945, Germany stopped fighting. Three months later, radio beamed to freedom-loving peoples everywhere the message that Japan had surrendered.

The close of the war by no means ended the visits of performers at the front or what had been battlefields. *Information Please* toured the American Zone of Occupation in Germany with a two-hour show that included a piano segment by Joe Kahn, a vaudeville routine by Reginald Gardiner, songs and recitations by Beatrice Lillie as well as the quiz session. "We didn't take the questions too seriously," John Kieran noted in his autobiography, "and, if we had a choice, we gave the answer on the lighter side."[1]

A half-million GIs heard the program over the Armed Forces Radio Network in August. Those lucky enough to witness an actual recreation of the panel game never forgot it. *Information Please* built strong ties with its homeward-bound audiences, who would soon face a period of worrisome readjustment. Quizzes and audience-participation shows geared up to play a postwar role that had yet to be fully defined or blocked out. A handful of young, energetic game hosts, including Bert Parks and Bud Collyer, and a cluster of seasoned pros, led by Walter O'Keefe, Jack Bailey and Bill Slater, set the pace.

Among the returning GIs was Win Elliot, a former radio announcer and M.C. He had signed up with the Merchant Marines late in the war, after trying to enlist in other branches. But both Army and Navy doctors turned him down because of below-par vision. The future sportscaster and erstwhile game host had had a promising career before going to sea.

Lanky, bespectacled Win Elliot had been near a microphone for nearly a decade. A zoology and chemistry graduate of the University of Michigan, he returned to his home in Boston in 1937 determined to go into radio. He had no broadcasting friends to badger nor any discernible talent as a musician or actor. But he had a solid education, a pleasant voice, good diction, and plenty of ambition and perseverance. Elliot found a spot with a small Boston station where he broadcast a nightly half-hour dissertation on words and their derivations. During three years at WMEX he also wrote, produced, emceed and announced countless shows. "But one day I was fired. I had started to think of myself as basically a comedian, and apparently the station thought otherwise."[2]

Enroute to a potential job in the Midwest, Win stopped off in Washington, D.C., for some sightseeing. On the spur of the moment, he walked into the NBC building, presented a summary of his experience and asked for work. The supervisor indicated that there might be an opening. This encouraged Win. He was ushered into a studio and told to assume he was on the air to cover the upcoming 1941 inaugural of President Roosevelt. Meanwhile, the supervisor secretly piped the audition into the office of general manager Carlton Smith.

Well-versed from countless hours as Boston's *Wordcaster*, Elliot readily ad-libbed a hypothetical ceremony from the steps of the Capitol. After 30 minutes of nonstop commentary, the program chief shouted, "You've got the job!"

Win soon learned the post was probably only temporary. "The regular announcer Charles 'Bud' Barry had taken a three-month leave. As it turned out he never came back, having negotiated a contract with ABC in New York."[3]

Win then received an offer to become assistant news editor at station WFBR in Baltimore. He took it and within six months had his own afternoon variety show. With *Club 1300*, Elliot found a highly creative niche as M.C., producer and writer.

After a successful and widely publicized booking of *Club 1300* at the Baltimore Hippodrome, Win received a call to audition for Ralph Edwards and the producers of *Truth or Consequences*. Win did a complete show in New York before a studio audience to test his mettle as a stuntmaster.

Two days later Edwards called. "As you know, Win, I'm slated to go in the Army soon.* You are the best we've auditioned to replace

---

*Announcer Harry Von Zell filled in for Edwards, who in a matter of weeks received a deferment from his draft board.

me. But I can't give you the show. Nobody outside of Baltimore knows you. But, believe me, I'll do something as soon as I can."[4]

That something was a job at ABC in New York and a chance with a show called *Fish Pond.* An impromptu amateur half-hour, it invited members of the studio audience to sing, tell jokes, read poetry or perform in some way. If a contestant came across well, the precoached audience yelled "Reel him in." If an act failed to gain interest, the *Fish Pond* audience cheered "Throw him back." Cash prizes were determined by a formula tied to the contestant's weight. More pounds meant more bucks.

In its initial tune-in *Variety* noted: "Should prove to be an okay entry in the quiz ranks if the quality of the contestants holds up. . . . Win Elliot does a good job, keeping things moving along at a good pace, but some of the high-powered corn he dispenses could stand distillation."[5]

So in 1946, with some experience in Radio City, war veteran Win did have an edge. Hearing that *County Fair* at CBS was looking to replace Jack Bailey, he auditioned and won the M.C. assignment. Sponsored by Borden, this Saturday stunt show combined zaniness with a degree of grass-roots psychology and public service consciousness. Win contributed many audience-participation ideas to the production staff.

"I had spent many an hour watching vaudeville as a kid. That helped me come up with gags and contests. And a string of science courses in college gave me a keen analytical approach to everything."[6]

On one show, Win wanted to find out if women, in general, fibbed about their weight. On another occasion, he sent a contestant out on the street to sell hot cakes to test the old saying "selling faster than hot cakes."

Ideas for audience involvement stemmed from other assignments. While covering a hockey game in Boston, Win came up with a unique idea for *Country Fair.* A teenage fan stuck his head into the broadcast booth during a break and, in a nasal, clipped jargon, complimented Win on his sports reporting.

"I'm Bernie," the youngster added.

"What are you interested in?" Win asked

"I wanna be an umph."

"You, what?"

"An umph."

"What's an umph?"

"Ya know—'ya out; ya safe.' "

"Oh, an umpire!"

Elliot decided to bring Bernie to *Country Fair* to measure how much a person's speech might be improved through weekly diction lessons. For his first appearance Bernie read a commercial in his own picturesque vernacular. It was recorded for a comparative replay a week later after he had taken his first instruction. Week after week, he came back to help with a commercial. His progress was remarkable, and by the end of six months, a smooth, clear-speaking Bernie delighted Win and his listeners. Not long after he completed his stint on *County Fair*, he dropped the thought of becoming an umpire. Bernie decided on a teaching career and eventually rose to dean of students at a large Eastern university.[7]

In 1947 Elliot also replaced Ken Roberts as host of the fast-moving adult quiz, *Quick as a Flash*, at Mutual. A charade game, it gave prizes to the first person guessing a dramatized subject, such as a current event, famous moment in history or book title. The payoff line from the playlets was usually not too obvious, and a listener on his toes enjoyed a real sense of participation. The closing segment gathered a group of actors from a well-known detective or suspense show to create a whodunit. Leading stock players—Santos Ortega, Jackson Beck, Julie Stevens, Everett Sloane, Mercedes McCambridge, Sam Levene— welcomed this chance to work in takeoffs of nursery rhymes or fairy tales. Who would forget "Little Miss Muffet" done in gangster style!

Elliot gained a deserved reputation as a glib M.C. and proficient jokester. But on one noteworthy broadcast, he faced more roars of laughter than ever before. The giggles started just before the first commercial break. Boy, he thought, I'm a veritable Bob Hope tonight. Then announcer Cy Harrice nearly broke up trying to read copy on Helbros Watches. Stepping to the side, Win wondered what was so damn funny. Was his last joke that great?

Meanwhile, producer Dick Lewis waved Win offstage. There, Lewis pointed down to Win's fly. It was wide open, and his broad pleated trousers accented the unzipped zipper. By then, everyone in the audience knew why Win had been almost pulled backstage. Of course, he had to go back to face them for the second half of the show.

Cheers broke out as he moved toward the mike. Win rose to the occasion. "And now continuing with 'Quick as a Flash' ", he said, "we zip into the next puzzler."[8] It was a day made for television.

Radio in the first half of the 1940s shifted much of its content into a unifying, patriotic timbre. Broadcasting in the second half of the decade, reflecting the country's collective triumph in war, reverted to time-tested appeals to individualized pleasures and pursuits. The countless large and small self-denials by warrior and wife had brought about victory; now it was time to settle down in that proverbial vine-covered cottage—a dwelling furnished with all the appliances and accessories American industry had promised. Would radio help make this dream possible? Might radio games provide some wherewithal to attain such rewards in this bright postwar age?

Eager homemakers now stalked the prize-filled halls of radio as broadcasters moved to give them their due.

Even before V-J Day, the networks began to recognize the importance of greater involvement of the distaff side in audience participation. But before 1945, few national programs had focused on the housewife, and when they did, often she was the object of parody and pratfalls. *Ladies Be Seated* seemed a step in a new direction. Although it grew out of a daily afternoon show called *Ed East and Polly*, which in turn, stemmed from East's comic takeoff with Ralph Dumke of household hints on *Sisters of the Skillet*, ABC's *Ladies Be Seated* with Johnny Olson engaged in fewer silly pranks and stunts in exchange for highly coveted merchandise.[9]

Queen for a Day showered an audience-selected "queen" with household goods and clothes and fulfilled her special wish—but for a price. Contestants often had to bare their souls as they explained their innermost hopes and desires to host Dud Williamson. After the war, the program settled in Hollywood where a new M.C., Jack Bailey, commenced a career built on misery-filled interviews. During 20 years, he crowned nearly 5,000 teary-eyed Queens and gave away some $5 million in intensely desired gifts and "wishes."

Constantly criticized for capitalizing on the maudlin sob stories of prayerful, sometimes desperate, women, *Queen for a Day*, nevertheless, gave their counterparts throughout the country a vicarious thrill and a longed-for hope of such royal recognition.[10]

How did perennial host Jack Bailey view the proceedings? "If you can put it in words," he said on the 15th anniversary of the show in 1960, "it's like giving real, sincere good help without being a Pollyanna. It's not so much the wish as the why of the wish. Many women put on their cards that they'd like an ironer to make their work lighter. Who wouldn't! But the woman who wants an ironer so she can take in ironing to help the family finances, that's a different story."[11]

Program assistant Jeanne Cagney added these words: "It's a heartwarming experience . . . but I often think of the runners-up and hope that maybe it helps them just to come on the show to tell someone about their problem."[12]

Participants in *Bride and Groom*, which bowed at ABC in November 1945, drove off with a truckload of household appliances and furnishings. Newlyweds came to the microphone immediately after a marriage ceremony in a chapel adjacent to the studio and faced host John Nelson and a barrage of questions on their first meeting and courtship. An ordeal for some duos, it paid off handsomely in still-rationed washers and refrigerators.

A variation on the theme of *Bride and Groom* and *Queen for a Day*, *Second Honeymoon* broadcast square in the center of a panoply of desirable merchandise—a large department store. Aired by the independent New Jersey transmitter WAAT, this giveaway originated from sponsor L. Bamberger's Newark emporium. Every show opened with Bert Parks' question, "Who's the pillar of American society?" An audience of homemakers bellowed back, "The Housewife!" [13]

A half-dozen women stood at the microphone each morning to tell a panel of five judges why they'd like a second honeymoon. "I was married during the war and there wasn't any leave time for the first one" was a frequent reason. Prizes—perfume, jewelry, record albums, coffee urns—readily passed into the hands of participants. But the coveted jackpot of a three-day honeymoon plus a new wardrobe reinforced the program's stated aim "to teach husbands how to be romantic again." [14]

Mom was finding a place in the sun at many microphones. John Reed King, an M.C. well liked by homemakers, took his *Missus Goes a-Shopping* into New York supermarkets. With shelves of canned goods within easy reach, it made prize giving that much more efficient and exciting, while promoting a variety of consumer brands. King also hosted another daytime game, *Give and Take*, providing women with another opportunity to bring home the bacon.

Cash prizes from the expanding lineup of giveaways certainly had not lost any favor. *Double or Nothing*, as a Monday-through-Friday series, handed over dollars, along with cartons of the sponsor's Campbell Soup. The program built a loyal audience in the years after originator Walter Compton left, and John Reed King and Todd Russell took charge. But the time was ripe to beam *Double or Nothing* more to the ladies.

Veteran entertainer Walter O'Keefe signed a contract to host five afternoon *Double or Nothing* sessions per week. (By 1950 they were expanded to ten programs a week when Campbell Soup decided housewives wanted morning quizzes too.) O'Keefe had been away from a regular series for three years; his last job had been as M.C. of *Battle of the Sexes*. Then he substituted for vacationing Don McNeill on *The Breakfast Club*. Walter was never at a loss for words whether creating show skits at college (Notre Dame), playing a nightclub (Barney Gallant's), writing song lyrics ("Henry's Make a Lady Out of Lizzie"), preparing a syndicated newspaper column (Scripps-Howard) or performing in Broadway revues ("The Third Little Show"). But he claimed he found his natural metier on an ad-lib quiz. He instructed his agent to line up another game, preferably from Hollywood because the climate alleviated his younger son's asthma. Once O'Keefe took over *Double or Nothing*, he had no trouble in building it into a top-ten daytime feature.

It was hard to believe that at one point he had harbored an antipathy of giveaways. In a sense, they had bruised a flourishing radio career. It had taken off when he filled in for Fred Allen on *Town Hall Tonight* for five months when the comic went West to make a film with Jack

Benny. That led to a season on the Packard *Mardi Gras* with tenor Lanny Ross and, in late 1938, to *Tune-Up Time* with conductor Andre Koste-lanetz. A year later, he took over the CBS Lifebuoy Soap program from Al Jolson, revamped it and opened with Mary Martin as costar—in a time slot *directly* opposite NBC's *Pot o' Gold*. The $1,000 giveaway spelled an ignominious defeat for Walter.[15] He spent the war years doing radio guest spots, charity events, and camp and hospital shows along with a season of *Battle of the Sexes*. Increasingly, he turned to drinking to fill time. Years later he explained:

"In the natural kindliness of Irish humor the Celt has a habit of glossing over whatever is unpleasant or obnoxious by draping it in a fancy phrase or facade. For example, the Irish comment on a man who drinks too much is not a harsh one. When they see a tosspot lying in the gutter, filthy, unwashed, unshaven and vulgar, they say, 'He has a very strong weakness.' "[16]

O'Keefe was a man with a very strong weakness and not until the mid-1950s did he overcome his drinking problem. For the next 30 years, until his death in 1983, he devoted much of his time to helping other alcoholics recover. Besides chronic alcoholism, O'Keefe was a survivor of numerous calamities during his 82 years: infantile paralysis, six kidney-stone operations, five heart attacks, two cancer operations, three broken legs, asthma, pneumonia and arthritis. Through it all, he remained active and optimistic and never more so than when handling his daily quiz show.

M.C. O'Keefe was put to it on *Double or Nothing* as few hosts had ever been pressed. A waitress came to the mike to play the money game in October 1948. Walter asked if she had any unusual customers.

"Well, Mr. O'Keefe, yesterday a man asked me a question. He had a sick friend needing advice. This friend can't go out nights, can't eat, can't do nothing. Even had to send his wife away on a vacation. This guy asked 'What do you think we should do with him?' I said, 'I didn't really know.' 'Well,' he replied, 'I think he should get a good-looking girl like you and take her home and just have a big screwing party.' I said: 'What! Why don't you go down to the hardware store and get some . . . a screw . . . and go home.' "[17]

O'Keefe swallowed hard and took a deep breath, and moved into one of the fastest question-and-answer sessions on record. Most of the studio audience seemed to have missed the drift of the waitress's tale. But listeners at home reacted fast, lighting up the NBC switchboard with a myriad of complaints. After a dozen years of audience-participation programs, this was reputedly the first blatantly suggestive episode to hit the airwaves.

A handful of sports and "brain" contests nuzzled the burgeoning sweepstakes during the immediate postwar days—generally without

much success. *Right Down Your Alley* traveled to New York City bowling lanes where contestants were quizzed briefly by Bill Slater and Don
Gardner and then rolled to match a precalculated score. This Sunday
afternoon sports show chalked up many strikes for participants. But
for ABC, it was a spare attraction.

The network tried again, this time with an appeal to bookish listeners on Sunday afternoons. Short story editor Sidney Mason presided over a panel of three authors who were given 30 seconds to for-
mulate a complete original story from suggestions supplied by the
audience. Designed to test the imagination and ingenuity of writers,
Stump the Authors merely caused writer's block.

Once more, ABC scratched out a new game, an attempt to build a
contest around the movies. *Movie Quiz* with Jack Bailey tested contestants' ability to identify stars and scenes from current attractions by
hearing excerpts of the film sound track. But "The End" came quickly
for this quizzer.

WOR, considered one of the most "wordy" stations in the country,
entered the Sunday cultural ghetto with *Take a Word*. This answer-man
type program dispensed thought-provoking research on the origins of
words found in the average person's vocabulary. Why was Cinderella's
slipper described as "glass?" Why is a tuxedo "wolf's clothing?" Listeners seemed not to care and opted for the Sunday papers.

Mutual turned to the legal profession on *Lawyer Q* with the reenact-
ment of an actual criminal case. Practicing lawyers appeared following
the dramatization and offered opposing summations to a jury of 12
members of the studio audience. Each of the jurors then made a decision. If it followed the outcome of the original case, they split a jackpot. The verdict of listeners, however, soon sentenced this game to
unpardonable oblivion.

Nevertheless, a solid mind-stretching game appeared over Mutual's
WOR outlet. An old-fashioned parlor game, *Twenty Questions* would
have seemed an ideal property for early radio. Yet no one stumbled
across the venerable animal, mineral or vegetable quiz until the mid-
1940s. The idea for the program originated with the family of Fred and
Florence Van Deventer of Princeton, New Jersey. The Van Deventers
and their children, Nancy and Bobby, regularly played the game around
the dinner table. One evening, a guest joined them to discuss a game-
show proposal with Fred, a radio newscaster. Fifteen year old Nancy,
always quick to voice her opinions, told the visitor his ideas were stale
and overused.

"If I were planning a quiz program," she pointed out, "I'd try something new like our game Twenty Questions."[18]

Fred and Florence interrupted their daughter before their guest's ego
suffered further deflation. But they realized she had hit on a viable

idea. Fred took it to Mutual where plans for the program started immediately.

Twenty Questions bowed on a Saturday evening with the Van Deventers on the panel. A fifth player, Herb Polesie, was recruited from the ranks of producers (and reputedly because of a voice similar to Oscar Levant's).[19] A kind of reverse quiz, the game allowed the group to ask M.C. Bill Slater up to 20 questions, to which he answered "yes" or "no." From these answers, the panel had to deduce the subject they were seeking. Once the overall category of animal, mineral or vegetable was provided, a mystery voice off-stage let listeners in on the answer at the outset. (Studio audiences were secretly informed of the topic by a placard down-stage.)

Although the Van Deventer family ties were no secret, Mrs. Van Deventer assumed her maiden name of Florence Rinard, and her 13-year-old son took his maternal grandmother's surname to become Bobby McGuire. Bill Slater also brought *his* family into the proceedings. The wife of this West Point-trained officer cum broadcaster prepared all his notes and spent hours researching the subjects each program covered. Slater knew his replies had to be scrupulously accurate. One wrong or even semicorrect reply often threw the panelists completely off the track. Although one of the best ad-libbers on the air, Slater proceeded with caution. When he was asked if the subject—"The Spike on the Devil's Tail"—was human, he answered after a little hesitation . . . "well, not quite human." Any confusion stemming from Slater's replies brought hundreds of letters from annoyed listeners who often accused him of perpetrating an injustice toward the panel.[20]

The hardest items to guess were the "class categories" or subjects that had no personal or functional association. "To get a subject like 'a can opener,' Fred remarked, "is practically impossible. Once we got to the point where we knew we were after some kitchen utensil, we could have named every pot, pan, knife and fork in a typical kitchen. These class categories are haphazard guesses to us, and the audience is always surprised when we miss them because they seem so easy."[21]

Twenty Questions won praise beyond the norm. The American College Association cited its educational value, and the National Parents and Teachers Association rated it "recommended listening." Fred Van Deventer even received an honorary degree from Rider College in New Jersey, and with his augmented income from sponsor Ronson Lighters he acquired a ranch-style house he called "Twintegspel," a Dutch word for "a game of twenty." The popular show inspired several imitators overseas. The BBC introduced a quiz modeled after it, and other versions mushroomed in France and Japan. From a simple pastime for the Van Deventers at meal time, *Twenty Questions* evolved into a family-based commercial venture that lasted a decade.

The only prize money on *Twenty Questions* went to listeners who submitted an apt subject to challenge the panel. These rewards remained miniscule compared to the cash being handed over to contestants on the first of the big postwar quizzes, *Break the Bank*.

The idea of winning $1,000 or more on a single program staggered listeners. But aside from the awe-inspiring sums, this production shaped up into a well-assembled and compact giveaway that stimulated one's mental prowess.[22]

A fairly simple format, it brought in elements of "take it or leave it" and "double or nothing." In a selected category, a contestant could reach the top figure of $1,000 plus whatever amount remained in the pot through default by previous players. Eight questions starting at $5 led up the ladder to the top amount. Aside from the cash and questions, *Break the Bank* discovered a way to build audience suspense from week to week. If a player had not finished the game at sign-off, he had an opportunity to return the following week and complete his round. This quiz took a cue from the daytime soap operas; listeners would have to tune in again to find out if a contestant won or lost.

The creative team for *Bank* stood together as one of the best ever assembled for a radio quiz. Led by producer Ed Wolfe, the program moved into high gear through the efforts of energetic aides such as promoter Walter Framer and director Jack Rubin. The show still remained in an embryonic form when a friend of Wolfe's walked into the producer's office carrying a large phonebook-size folder with the outside lettering "Break the Bank."

"This is a compendium of every quiz game ever done on radio."

Walt Framer turned to Wolfe. "Ed, it's a great title. Why don't you use it?"

Ed Wolfe bought the show name, paying a weekly royalty for the use of those three key words, "Break the Bank."

Walt Framer worked closely with the writer who researched and prepared the questions. Joseph N. Kane, a newpaperman and author of the 757-page reference work *Famous First Facts*, had been selling questions to radio shows for years. At one point, he had had his own show *What's the Fact?*, and another program based on his book on who did what first. Most quizzes pushed a set of encyclopedias and reference tomes in front of a recent college graduate and told this fledgling to dig out 100 or so questions a week.

Kane took a different approach. He may not have turned the preparation of questions and answers into a profession, but at least he honed it into a well-crafted trade. The precise wording of a question had to convey no ambiguities. "A slight vagueness in the phrasing of a question," he reminded his employers, "can generate two or more answers. In writing a question, you must come up with an obvious answer, not an esoteric one." Kane worked one full day to write 30 questions for *Break the Bank*. "I don't think I was well liked because I was in a position of some authority," he observed many years later. "I could kill a question without any explanation."[23]

Although *Bank* did not win any awards from the PTA, it did amuse and enlighten and get talked about. The original Mutual Saturday-night entry brought together Bud Collyer as M.C. (in one of his first important non-Superman radio assignments), John Reed King as quizmaster and Hank Sylvern as organist for musical questions. When Wolfe's budget expanded during the first season, the *Bank* moved to ABC and signed up Bert Parks as quizzer and Peter Van Steeden and his orchestra as musicmakers. Then on August 30, 1946, a man known within his family as "Uncle Information Please"—because of his avid interest in quiz shows—walked off with the biggest jackpot in the first 25 years of radio.

Commander Jack A. Weiss of the U.S. Navy and his bride, Edith, had been given a pair of tickets to the show at New York's Ritz Theatre, a primary location for programs with large audiences. A physician, Jack Weiss was about to be discharged and ready to resume his practice in Chicago. A few minutes after Jack and Edith took their seats, Bud Collyer came down into the audience to choose people as contestants. His preliminary candidates had to stand up and tell Bud and Bert Parks their name and hometown. Several were asked a simple question and, if answered correctly, received a dollar bill.

"We need someone who knows geography," Collyer asked. He looked at Weiss and grinned. "There's a Navy man—he ought to know something about the world and the seven seas."[24]

Commander Weiss chuckled to himself. His years in the service had been spent in the United States, except for a few months on the Caribbean island of Trinidad. But he did know his geography; it had been one of his favorite subjects at school. So Jack Weiss stood up and told them his name and where he was from.

"How long have you been in the Navy?" Collyer asked.

"Four years, three weeks and one day," Weiss replied. The audience liked that answer. Collyer herded Jack and Edith down the aisle to the stage.

Forty years later, Weiss still remembered all eight questions, especially number six, which gave Bert Parks a chance to sing before he asked, "Where is the road to Mandalay?" The Bank-breaking question, "Where is Lake Maracaibo?" and Weiss's answer, "Venezuela," made the Weisses $5,220 richer.[25]

The next day Weiss deposited his jackpot check in a Fifth Avenue bank. The excited teller proudly pointed him out to everyone.

"This is the man who broke the bank for $5,000 on radio last night!"

A punctilious clerk looked over. "May I clarify that," he injected. "Actually it was five thousand, *two hundred and twenty dollars.*"[26]

It seemed as if all America had been listening—and counting—and rubbing their hands.

›12‹

The Whole Sears, Roebuck Catalog

In November 1946 the powerful and much-maligned Office of Price Administration closed shop in Washington, D.C. This federal agency had successfully fought to keep a tight lid on consumer prices during the war and in the period of immediate readjustment as the economy turned its sights from tanks to autos. For the first time since 1941, manufactured goods for civilian consumption moved into the marketplace without restrictions.[1] A pent-up demand and readily available cash overwhelmed the still-limited supply. Prices immediately rose on every imaginable product in an ongoing contest of consumer catch-up.

Manufacturers of household goods, nevertheless, anxiously advertised and promoted their postwar line. The makers of stoves, vacuum cleaners, freezers, phonographs and other appliances rushed to radio to remind Americans that it was business as usual or close to it.

In return for little more than having their products mentioned on the air, manufacturers collectively provided game shows with tons of merchandise every day. Some 40 companies supplied *Queen for a Day* with prizes totaling $250,000 in a single year. For coast-to-coast "plugs" that otherwise would cost as much as $5,000 each in air time in 1947, *Bride and Groom* received Oshkosh luggage, Kelvinator refrigerators, Bulova watches, Kimball pianos, Kaiser-Frazer cars and Bendix washers—with a total price tag of $500,000.[2] Prize coordinators and brokers opened offices in New York and Hollywood to stockpile and funnel such items into the growing whirl of giveaways. A firm called Prizes, Inc., supplied $1 million in prizes for games on some 100 independent stations.[3] Another, V.I.P. Services, Inc., specialized in procuring items in short supply and creating a multigift jackpot called the "Cinderella weekend." For stocking and handling prizes, these agencies receive a set fee from a producer and often an extra no-strings shipment of goods. A number of sponsored five-a-week giveaways paid as much as $1,000 a week to a prize broker, and he, in turn, usually charged a manufacturer from $25 to $200 per plug.[4]

In 1948 the four major networks gave away an estimated $90,000 a week in merchandise spread among 54 programs and totaling by year-end $4.5 million. Mutual led with $1.4 million for 14 shows; CBS was a close second with $1.3 million and 13 programs. In addition, independent stations in total dispensed $20,000 or more in goods each week, and that did not include cash prizes. Network and local giveaways awarded still another $2.3 million in currency that year.[5]

If a deep freezer or lawn mower seemed a bit mundane, other prizes revealed imagination, showmanship and sometimes plain bad taste. Among the more ludicrous were a fully equipped dental chair and a deed of ownership to an Alaskan glacier.

Comedians Abbott and Costello, in addition to having their Wednesday night program, hosted a Saturday morning children's show with a gamut of prizes ranging from a house trailer to a pygmy elephant. The afternoon serial *Jack Armstrong* announced a contest offering 1,000 bicycles to young fans. Paul Whiteman's coast-to-coast afternoon disc jockey session ran a four-week memory lane music game. The 410 prizes, valued at $22,000, included a cabin cruiser, a grand piano and a suite of furniture. Sunday evening's *Hollywood Calling* departed from a conservative stance in prizes to a jackpot of some $30,000, the largest one on NBC.[6] Actor (and future U.S. Senator) George Murphy telephoned listeners to ask questions about the movies and Hollywood stars, some of whom appeared on the show to hype their latest celluloid effort.

"Why I Like . . ." written contests for listeners swept the country. Major radio sponsor Colgate-Palmolive awarded Winona Thiel, a 23-year-old secretary to the mayor of Norwich, Connecticut, a sack of 49,000 one dollar bills for writing a prizewinning Supersuds endorsement "in 25 words or less."[7]

Second Honeymoon left Newark for New York and a big ABC buildup. Bert Parks welcomed the musical accompaniment of organist Rosa Rio as he serenaded his ladies and handed over a larger bounty, including a honeymoon trip now extended to a week from three days. ABC's *Go for the House* looked beyond the nuptials. Prizes consisted of all sorts of household goods, clothing and, in fact, anything that the prize coordinator could get his hands on for John Reed King to dispense. The jackpot trophy was a real bonanza—a completely furnished $7,000 house on a plot of ground. With a million families searching for a dwelling in the suburbs, this offering stood as the answer to many prayers.

The generous distribution of what often was tagged "loot" accelerated, and the titles of two 1948 giveaways summed up radio quizzers' philosophy: *Get Rich Quick* and *Everybody Wins*.

The bank-night orgy reached a postwar peak from the introduction of a telephone call contest giving listeners a chance, albeit slim, to hit pay dirt. So in 1948 when announcer Doug Browning first shouted, "Stay right where you are because here comes *Stop the Music!*" millions of Americans obeyed.

Of the hundreds of network quizzes brought to the air in the 1930s and 1940s this music game endured a longer and more arduous incubation than probably any format. At the close of the war, conductor Harry Salter, with an assist from *Hit Parade* bandleader Mark Warnow, came up with an idea combining elements of that tune-filled Lucky Strike show with the big giveaway appeal of *Pot o' Gold*. Salter, an old hand for podium assignments for *Hobby Lobby* and *Mr. District Attorney*, had followed the rise in popularity for a Hollywood-based offering called *What's the Name of That Song?* This Mutual quiz with Dud Williamson challenged studio audiences to identify songs and then sing their lyrics. Cash prizes of $5 to $50 went to contestants and to those mailing in questions. The combination of music and quiz on this low-budget show struck Salter as having the ingredients for a big-time hit if a telephone broadened the pool of players.[8] The time seemed right for Ma Bell to reenter the game.

During the war the demand for new telephones rose to record highs. But home installations could not be carried out to any extent. In 1942 the War Production Board rationed equipment and allocated telephones to priority situations. At the same time, use of existing telephones—especially for long-distance calls—grew. Subscribers picked up the habit of dialing near and far. In the first postwar year there were 7 billion *more* calls of all kinds than in 1945.[9] It became evident that telephone use would continue to increase, and more and more Americans would be installing equipment. In fact in 1946 more than 4 million new telephones were delivered—at the rate of more than 25 a minute every working day, bringing the total U.S. telephones to more than 25 million.* Nearly all parties who wanted their own line had one by 1948.

Harry Salter devised a system similar to the telephone-directory selection process used on the old *Pot o' Gold*. With the help of producer Mark Goodson, he made a demo record, complete with music, telephone calls and sound effects and asked advertising executives to listen. Practically every agency on Madison Avenue played the disc but showed no interest. Completely discouraged, Salter turned to Louis Cowan, who had put out the word that he was looking high and low for new program ideas, especially to bolster various weaker time frames on all the networks. He spun the oft-played record. After about five

---

*In 1939, the year *Pot o' Gold* burst onto the air, there were 16.5 million Bell telephones in service.

minutes, the Quiz Kid creator reputedly exclaimed, "This is a hit show!" and ran into the offices of his associates to rave about the demo.[10]

Cowan took *Stop the Music!* to Bud Barry, program supervisor at ABC, who had frantically been seeking a vehicle to run against NBC's Fred Allen and Charlie McCarthy on Sundays from 8 to 9 P.M. In contrast to those comedy characters, the Columbia net offered two popular mysteries that hour: *Sam Spade* and *The Man Called X*. ABC had practically resigned from the competition, filling its time with concert selections by major symphony orchestras or groups of staff musicians.

At one point, Barry pursued Rudy Vallee to host a variety show similar to his long-running *Fleischmann Hour* of the 1930s. Negotiations broke down with the entertainer who was now directing his attention to an acting career in films. Suddenly, ABC had virtually nothing but chamber music to fill its Sunday slot, Barry discovered. A quiz show with plenty of music at least could use the large aggregation of house musicians. Barry decided to pick up and expand *Stop the Music!* to a full hour to gain more impact against the other nets. ABC guaranteed Salter a minimum of 13 weeks, with or without a sponsor. At the start of the 1947–48 season, ABC president Robert Kintner could only point to columnist-broadcaster Walter Winchell as the sole ABC Sunday feature of any consequence. Winchell had been complaining about the classical music preceding his 9 P.M. gossip and news.

One night, Winchell, who as a rule spoke of himself in the third person, rushed out of the cubicle where he always prepared his 15-minute show and shouted to everyone in the studio, "Do ya hear that symphony fune-real music? But Winchell gets top ratings just the same!"[11]

Kintner worried over losing his Sunday star attraction but realized that ABC had little existing ammunition against NBC's kings of comedy. He addressed his colleagues with this analogy: "If you have a carnival midway, you don't try to sell the second fattest woman in the world along side the very fattest. You don't get a comedian to compete; you get something totally different." Kintner turned to *Stop the Music!*"[12]

Early in 1948 Mark Goodson revved up the promotional ballyhoo to attract ABC affiliates and sponsors. A sneak preview at station WAGE in Syracuse, New York, gathered a very favorable response from the area's 1,200-family listener panel maintained by agency Batten, Barton, Durstine and Osborn. Meanwhile, Harry Salter lined up 23 staff musicians to form an orchestra and commenced auditions for two lead singers. An unknown singer, Dick Brown, came aboard as male vocalist. The search for a more versatile female counterpart took longer. Salter needed a voice that could handle semiclassical selections as well as the popular field, including blues and swing. Candidates inside ABC and out sang for Salter. Patti Page and Lisa Kirk were only two of the many hopefuls who auditioned. Mighty in vocal stamina and physical stature, Kay Armen wondered why she was one of the few available artists overlooked. For five years she had performed on every type of ABC musical feature, from country and western to opera. Taking matters in her own hands, she set up an audition under the false name "Gwen Hamilton." At Salter's microphone, Kay proved the existence of an unusual singing ability and quick-study skill. Plucky Kay Armen got the job.[13]

Choosing the M.C. remained in the hands of Lou Cowan. Bill Slater moved forward as a strong candidate, until Goodson suggested Bert Parks of ABC's *Break the Bank*. "There was something in his voice we liked," Cowan said. "We thought of him as a version of Li'l Abner because he was young, virile and good-looking. Bert had a warm personality, combined with infinite enthusiasm and solid singing ability."[14]

By 1948 Bert Parks stood shoulder to shoulder with radio's top five or six game-show M.C.s. His unflagging pep kept many broadcasts moving at a swift and upbeat pace. Only 33 years old, Bert had been in radio for more than 15 years, starting as a teenager at a small station in Alabama. At age 18 he filled an opening on the CBS staff in New York where he became one of Columbia's busiest announcers and often seized the opportunity to sing with Benny Goodman and Xavier Cugat while handling their bandstand remotes. After serving as an army captain overseas, Bert returned to New York in 1946, just in time to fall into the frenzy of giveaways. Guest M.C. spots on several quizzes tested his ability, and he soon found a new vocation taking shape.

Stop the Music! premiered on March 21, 1948, before a large theater audience and, in the words of Parks, "starring you—the people of America." In a room backstage ABC telephone operators dialed the first of hundreds of numbers that would be picked at random that year. A listener first had to identify a qualifying tune, winning a washing machine, radio phonograph, silverware or roaster oven. This allowed a chance at the "mystery melody" and a kingsize jackpot. (On the first broadcast, it consisted of a $1,000 U.S. savings bond, a Knabe spinet piano, a Kaiser auto, a diamond ring and a 38-day steamship cruise.)

For the initial program, 6 of the 12 individuals called knew the preliminary song but all missed the jackpot melody. For each incorrect qualifying attempt, a studio contestant, in turn, had a stab at the song title and the prize. But no one in the audience was ever given a crack at the "mystery melody."

"Even for a listener without a telephone listing," *Variety* wrote, "the show seems moderately lively and entertaining. Since the·many numbers are necessarily short and are interrupted by the telephone question gimmick, the show is jumpy and the otherwise good music suffers. . . . The phone call gimmick multiplied the old pot of gold climax 12 times."[15]

As with calls placed by Horace Heidt, telephone hookups lost much of their life because only Bert Parks' side of the conversation could be broadcast.

An unclaimed jackpot grew enormously week after week. It soon sounded like the whole Sears, Roebuck catalog to *New York Times* critic Jack Gould. "Obviously the giveaway trend cannot be stopped now," he feared, "until some master of ceremonies forgets himself and throws in Radio City, too."[16] Lou Cowan contended that people would tune in and be entertained even if they couldn't possibly win. "After a half dozen or so years of rationing and empty shelves, people just hearing the prizes mentioned gained a certain sense of 'Well, it's great to be able to have these things again.' "[17]

For Harry Salter, the program's musical content required the selection and rehearsal of 15 songs a week. Although the preliminary numbers were well-known standards or at least current hits, the "mystery melody" contained all the familiarity of an Eskimo love song. The very first mystery tune, "The Vision of Salome," was an oft-heard number accompanying most belly dancers, but apparently few people knew the exact title. Weeks went by and no contestant could identify it. The show needed a jackpot winner, so Cowan gave the answer to Winchell, who placed it in his widely syndicated column. Listeners now knew in advance the name of the melody. Clues and answers regularly leaked to the press generated jackpot winners about every month.[18]

Salter remembered a particular show when two jackpots were won back to back. It dumbfounded everyone. The name of the ongoing "mystery melody" had appeared in the tabloids for weeks, and a listener tagged it correctly. Later in the show, Salter played the new mystery tune for the first time. A contestant named it right off the bat. Two jackpots carried off on a single show without a chance to leak the latest title to the press![19]

Audience complaints apparently overlooked such leaks and expressed dismay because Armen and Brown never got a chance to do a mumber as it could or should be done and without "la la de duming" the song title. Everytime they got into a song, listeners pointed out, Parks shouted "Stop the Music!"

ABC expected a solid Hooper rating of 4 or 5—double the pallid 2.5 from the earlier symphonic offerings. When the numbers came in, they jumped fivefold from the old basement-level ratings and within eight weeks topped those of NBC. Sponsors who had ignored the program during its first month or so now rushed to buy time; Old Gold cigarettes and Spiedel jewelry led the pack. During the summer of 1948, the demand for studio tickets so overwhelmed ABC that Cowan and Goodson moved the game onto the Capitol Theatre stage on Broadway where every day for several weeks thousands had a chance to play and compete for prizes, including a $5,000 jackpot. Between performances, audiences calmed down from the intoxicating contest by viewing the latest Esther Williams aqua-opus from MGM, "On an Island with You."

For the first time in his long radio career, Fred Allen faced a road-block. At first, he ignored the much-discussed ABC upstart, honestly believing his many fans would remain in Allen's Alley. One of radio's original wits, Allen soon discovered that money could talk louder than humor, especially when the money was in the tens of thousands of dollars.

"Did you folks like the $1,000 bills you found on your seats when you came in?" he sarcastically asked his studio guests before a broad-cast.[20] On his first program for new sponsor Ford, he parried the giveaway threat with comic Henry Morgan, as a burbling Parks, in a spoof called "Cease the Melody" with gag prizes such as 12 miles of railroad track, a saloon and bartender, 20 minutes alone in Fort Knox with a shovel and the gangplank of the *Queen Mary*. Driven down in the ratings from the top 10 to 38th place, he offered a $5,000 insurance payment to anyone who could prove loss of a *Stop the Music* prize be-cause of listening to his show.[21] But fighting giveaways with giveaway offers undermined the aims of protest, and Allen canceled the bond after a few weeks. Bergen and McCarthy had already seen the writing on the studio wall. They left NBC by the close of the 1947–48 season and then waited a year before resuming a new series over at CBS.

Angry and frustrated, Allen aimed his guns at the procedure whereby *Stop the Music!* contestants were actually alerted hours before a broad-cast and told to stand by for an on-the-air call. Consequently, he pointed out, millions of hopeful listeners, sitting by their radio, were wasting their time. They would never be called. Many poor people had tele-phones installed hoping they would be called and find themselves wealthy. "Give-away programs," he concluded, "are the buzzards of radio. As buzzards swoop down on carrion so have give-away shows descended on the carcass of radio. . . . Radio started as a medium of entertainment. The giveaway programs have reduced radio to a shoddy gambling device."[22]

ABC publicly denied that preliminary calls were standard operating procedure. In truth, the producers telephoned contestants on Sunday afternoon to alert them to remain at home and be there to answer their telephone between 8 and 9 P.M.[23] These initial contacts weeded out a lot of time-consuming, unanswered calls, discontinued numbers and out-of-order equipment problems.

In September 1948 a worried, nerve-wracked Allen returned after his usual summer hiatus. He still battled a mania unlike any other on the air. Could he push back a truckload of quiz wares? Allen's Alley and its picturesque cast of characters never regained its pre-March popularity. The following June, his highly original stock company left radio. Allen, bitter and perplexed, predicted that millions of listeners would soon tire of giveaway programs and then radio itself and turn to television. Lou Cowan regretted Fred's departure. "It was always a matter of considerable regret to me that my show led to diminishing the talent of one of the very great individuals broadcasting ever knew."[24]

For nearly two years *Stop the Music!* created more national excitement than any other game or contest in the country. Amid the widespread hysteria, a chorus of critics began to echo the sentiments of Fred Allen. Ben Gross of the New York *Daily News* termed giveaways "a major calamity," lamenting that most operated on the premise that jackpot prizes were more important than talent.[25] His counterpart at the *Times*, Jack Gould, wrote that *Stop the Music!* "has adopted the press agent's oldest stratagem of strewing coins on the street to attract a crowd."[26]

Contestants and would-be players added fuel to the growing fire of controversy. Two men in Boston claimed a prize of $15,000 from *Sing It Again*, Columbia's answer to *Stop the Music!* The dispute started when the telephone rang in the pastry shop of Rocco Rotondi, the party called by the producers. He thought it a gag and handed the receiver to his friend, William de Marco, who identified a "phantom voice" as that of Grover Whalen, New York City's longtime official greeter. Rotondi, thinking that the jackpot was his because he paid the telephone bills, dragged his buddy into court.[27]

On another *Sing It Again* broadcast, as a contestant in Cheyenne stood by her telephone to give the correct answer to a big jackpot question, the line went dead. She threatened to sue the local telephone company and CBS for somehow disconnecting the call and causing her to forfeit $24,000.[28]

The flood of giveaways gave rise to a ruse to defraud housewives. So-called representatives of a radio sponsor knocked on the doors of homemakers to inform them that they would be tapped in six hours by a well-known gift-giving show. All Mrs. Jones had to do was answer the telephone and give her name. But first a special interstate tax on the merchandise had to be collected before its delivery. The housewife usually forked over $10 or $20 for the "tax" for a soon-to-arrive washer or refrigerator. The call never came, nor the goods.

Legitimate winners sometimes found themselves scraping to pay bonafide taxes. Ola Peth of Cleveland discovered that she owed Uncle Sam $6,000, although most of her *Stop the Music!* windfall of $25,000 was in merchandise. To pay the government, she hustled to sell a sewing machine and a slightly used $4,000 wardrobe.

The Brooklyn Public Library soon reminded people that employees at its 35 branches would not supply answers to radio quiz questions. The chief librarian noted that questioners telephoned at the rate of three or four a minute, thus tying up circuits and interfering with the regular work load. Across the river in Manhattan, burglars reportedly broke into the office of game producer Walt Framer, stealing a list of quiz questions and answers.

The giveaway boom turned into a gold rush for the select coterie of glib-tongued M.C.s, a number of whom were pocketing more cash than the president of the United States. John Reed King, Bert Parks, Bud Collyer, Jack Barry, Johnny Olsen and Bill Slater each handled at least three programs a week, banking from $250 to $400 per show. CBS newcomer Bill Cullen had quickly entered the top echelon with three or four programs, including *Catch Me if You Can*, a long-distance telephone quiz.

With more than a dozen years on the game field, Bob Hawk knew which side his bread was buttered on. "A quiz can't be beat," he exclaimed. "It can't be touched, it stands by itself. It's a people's program. That's what a good quiz should be called, 'A Program for the Common People.' "[29]

In the face of negative criticism, quiz producers joined together to stress the positive aspects of giveaways. Audience involvement, they explained, was a widely accepted aspect of radio entertainment. Games appealed to people's sense of sportsmanship. Who could pass up those quiz-time moments of drama and suspense? "People do not tune in to the biggest jackpot," they emphasized, "but to the show which entertains them the most."[30]

Mark Goodson, who would become the busiest and most successful quiz-show producer of all time, spoke up. "Most U.S. listeners with their love of sports competition and fascination with games find more drama in contests than in make-believe. But a quiz offers something beyond drama—it permits listeners to 'compete' in the game. While the spectator can only daydream of leaping onto the diamond of Yankee Stadium and saving the day for the home team, quiz contests offer him a chance to join the competition—even though he be thousands of miles from the studio."[31]

In March of 1949 the leading personality of morning radio, Arthur Godfrey, revealed to his CBS audience a plan by ABC to swamp him with quizzes like the network did on Sunday nights against Fred Allen and Edgar Bergen.

"So now I'm going to have to buck giveaways, huh?" Godfrey pondered. "Well, you're gonna have to think again, ABC, because I'll tell you something. The people who listen to us in the morning have got too doggone much sense to fool around there, sitting waiting for something which they'll never get. Right? Right! Nuts to your giveaways."[32]

It was a stance that Washington and its lottery-investigating regulatory agencies would assume, now that television had been successfully carried into America's living rooms.

› 13 ‹

Televox Pop

On June 25, 1948, a record-breaking audience in living rooms, taverns and hotels visually shared a major happening simultaneously. Nearly 10 million viewers watched the heavyweight boxing bout between title-holder Joe Louis and unsuccessful challenger Jersey Joe Walcott. The exciting and magical world of television was finally moving into the lives of a significant number of people after some 20 years of snail's-pace growth. The year 1948 would signal the spectacular rise of television and the irreversible decline of network radio, leaving little doubt that the small screen was destined to be the biggest form of entertainment in the second half of the twentieth century.

Coverage of pugilistic and gridiron battles sold truckloads of TV receivers. Nevertheless, it was vaudeville-rich variety shows that sparked an even greater avalanche of sales and, in turn, attracted big-budget advertisers and accelerated the completion of a chain of cross-country network stations and affiliates.

Less than a week before the telecast of the Louis-Walcott bout, a CBS program called *Toast of the Town* premiered. Hosted by newspaper columnist Ed Sullivan, this show on Sunday night presented eight acts, including Dean Martin and Jerry Lewis in their TV debut. The format filled a set owner's craving for a lively potpourri of comedy, song and dance. That same month, the *Texaco Star Theatre* burst onto the video tube with what was destined to be the most popular variety show in early TV history. With comedian Milton Berle as host, it scored an immediate sensation, introducing for the first time on the medium scores of established entertainers from radio, the stage and screen and earning Berle the sobriquet "Mr. Television."

But another telecast in June 1948 carried significant ramifications too. Network coverage of the Republican National Convention in Philadelphia provided millions of viewers with an admissions ticket to an American political ritual. The searching lenses of five cameras blanketed the auditorium, keeping abreast of the action as interest shifted from point to point and led to the nomination of Thomas E. Dewey as the party's presidential candidate. Certain veteran newspaper observers sensed that politics would never be the same with television in the convention hall and on the campaign trail.

"It represents an effective medium through which a political party may accomplish missionary work or confirm viewers in their opposition, retain adherents or lose them," wrote R. W. Stewart in the *New York Times*.[1] He also observed that people in the gallery were quick with candid opinions, and television seemed eager to pick them up. "A composite of the remarks," Stewart noted, "would indicate that greater consideration might be taken of the general public."

Television discovered a wide al fresco world, and virtually from its birth the medium beamed both the visage and the voice of the people. Unlike radio, which during its first 15 years generally kept the vox populi from its microphone, the video screen immediately sought out "the man in the street." By the very nature of its searching eye, television could not ignore the commonplace, the ordinary, the grass roots. The medium seemed destined both to capture the exciting glamour of show business and to focus on the everyday reality of the rank and file. Structured and programmed audience participation, of course, would figure prominently in the annals of television as it did in radio. Yet, from its beginning, video broadcasting projected a more proletarian picture than its auditory parent.

In actuality, the slow technical development of television transmission and reception, along with economic restraints, competitive rivalries, and wartime shortages, had held the medium in abeyance for more than a dozen years and delayed what broadcasters recognized as its vast potential as a commercial, social and cultural force.

In 1928 General Electric station WGY at Schenectady began experimental programs and soon aired the first TV drama, *The Queen's Messenger*. Attracted by the medium's possibilities, film pioneer D. W. Griffith traveled to the upstate New York studios to discuss with engineer Ernst F. W. Alexanderson the technical aspects of GE's mechanical scanning disk, which required a cluster of extremely bright lights, plus mirrors revolving on a drum, in order to project a picture onto a tiny screen. Griffith also participated in a telecast, describing television as "this last miracle of miracles."[2]

In 1930 NBC built an experimental station atop New York's New Amsterdam Theatre on 42nd Street. Uptown, GE briefly transmitted television pictures on a six-by-eight-foot screen at several RKO movie theaters. In Chicago, vaudevillian Ken Murray agreed to appear in a telecast test and tell a few jokes between his theater appearances. After five minutes on camera, the intense heat from the blinding TV lights virtually knocked him out.[3] A year later, in 1931 the West Coast Don Lee radio chain tried out its new equipment by beaming several experimental programs to the handful of set owners in the Los Angeles area.

CBS became the first New York broadcaster to start regularly scheduled telecasts.[4] On July 21, 1931, about 100 special guests in a room at 485 Madison Avenue watched a program from a nearby studio on screens about four inches square. M.C. Ted Husing introduced New York Mayor Jimmy Walker who officially opened the 500-watt TV station. The 45-minute inaugural featured CBS radio stars. Kate Smith sang her theme song, "When the Moon Comes Over the Mountain," and the Boswell Sisters harmonized on "Heebie-Jeebie Blues." Guest artist George Gershwin played "Liza." In all, a dozen performers endured the tedious application of heavy greasepaint and black lipstick, braved the banks of excruciatingly hot lights, and faced a disconcerting spinning disk mounted on a camera.[5]

Less than two years later, all broadcasts stopped, and television went back to the laboratory. Still looking like a distortion in an amusement park house of mirrors, TV's fuzzy, shadowy images needed a lot more fine tuning, as well as its own compatible sound system. Americans, too, were told that television remained beyond the reach of all but the rich. Moreover, radio still exuded an aura of newness and novelty. The business slump lingered for many enterprises but not for radio, and few broadcasters complained, pointing to network gross time sales in 1937 of a record $69 million. All signs pointed to even greater revenues, and radio chieftains were in no hurry to share the sponsor's largesse with an attention-grabbing visual upstart.

Nevertheless, mobile TV vans appeared on New York streets as part of RCA research and field testing. Its broadcast arm, NBC, traveled the city to experiment with outdoor pickups of parades, sports events, fires, airport arrivals and auto shows. Occasionally, its cameras focused on ice skaters at the Rockefeller Center rink in the very shadow of Radio City. Undoubtedly, while criss-crossing Manhattan, the NBC crew transmitted the very first wave of a hand as a camera lens scanned a cluster of anonymous bystanders.

RCA delayed no longer in acknowledging the feasibility of set manufacture and TV programming. Early in 1939 it announced the sale of receivers beginning on April 30. Would-be buyers, however, were reminded that television transmitters were located only in New York and Los Angeles, with reception still limited to a distance of 40 to 50 miles. DuMont Television, owned chiefly by Paramount Pictures, stressed the availability of sets with an 8-by-11-inch screen, slightly bigger than RCA's picture. DuMont, then CBS, hurried to beam programs from New York by June.

TV's first big step came with the opening of the 1939 New York World's Fair. NBC moved its cameras onto the fairgrounds to beam the inaugural ceremonies to the 400 or 500 set owners in the metropolitan area. At the same time, at department stores and radio shops, televiewers stood by to watch the dedication of the fair by Franklin D. Roosevelt, the first U.S. president to face a TV camera. In the minutes that followed, the images of New York Governor Herbert H. Lehman and Mayor La Guardia passed onto the screen, along with views of the large opening-day crowd.

Ten days earlier RCA had dedicated its own exhibit building at the fair where TV sets ranging in price from $199.50 to $600.00 were prominently displayed. Two patrolmen standing next to one of the exhibit's 13 large-size receivers were as enthusiastic as visitors. "It's quite the thing," one guard exclaimed. "Yeah," added his buddy, "it'll be wonderful for ball games and fights."[6] A fairgoer from Minneapolis expressed his amazement. "I read about it, but I never thought it would be like this. Why, it's beyond conception, and here it is!"[7]

The presidential smile of FDR was the cue for the curtain raiser of 30 hours per week of regularly scheduled—but, by FCC decree, unsponsored—programs.[8] New Yorkers soon sat comfortably at home and, with an acceptable degree of picture clarity, eyewitnessed numerous TV "firsts."

Vox Pop became one of the first telecasts of a complete network radio program when Parks Johnson and Wally Butterworth conducted all their interviews in front of the RCA NBC mobile unit at the World's Fair. Their televox pop exposure continued throughout the summer. Parks and Wally frequently loaded and smoked their pipes on camera, making sure tins of their radio sponsor's Kentucky Club Tobacco were in view.

On June 1 NBC broadcast the first boxing bout, an 11-round contest between Max Baer and Lou Nova, who kayoed his opponent in the 11th round. Sports editor Sam Taub handled the blow-by-blow commentary; announcer Ed Herlihy emphasized the marvels of RCA technology. New York appliance dealers with sets for sale stayed open late that night to provide viewing opportunities for would-be buyers.

Chair-bound onlookers experienced the first televised baseball game, a contest between Columbia and Princeton. Through the binocular-like telephoto lens, they soon watched basketball, hockey, bike races and track meets. Parades and political rallies, church services and circuses, beauty pageants and dance contests, appeared. Dramatic presentations, variety shows, audience-participation programs, quizzes and newscasts, grand opera and concerts, intrigued the pioneer viewers of 1939–40. Few, if any, realized that a typical studio-based TV show required more than 40 hours of rehearsal—three times as long as a comparable radio feature.[9]

As TV became less of a mirage and more of a reality, people living outside of New York and Los Angeles began to ask: "When will we have television? When will there be networks?" They were questions the industry seemed unable or unwilling to answer.

Yet after two years of breaking new ground, telecasters got the go-ahead from the FCC to move into commercial programming. At 7 P.M. on July 1, 1941, Lowell Thomas with the *Sunoco News* became the first sponsored feature on NBC. That evening *Uncle Jim's Question Bee* with host Bill Slater and announcer Dan Seymour, and sponsored by Lever Bros. and its Spry shortening, came on screen as the first commercial TV quiz program. It was, however, the first by only an hour or so. Ralph Edwards' *Truth or Consequences* (for Ivory Soap) followed later that night.[10]

Marred by the nonappearance of two previously announced guests, the *Question Bee* grabbed radio performer Allen Prescott and an artist's model to fill the gap. The model, viewers concluded, was apparently chosen for her photogenic features rather than any probable ability to contribute quiz answers. Commercials were instantaneous events, often with unpredictable results. The *Question Bee* dressed actress Edith Spencer as old Aunt Jenny to talk about her Spy-made chocolate layer cake. Gathered around a kitchen table the entire cast nibbled at the dessert as Spencer sold homemakers on the easy-to-prepare cake ingredient. When she licked the cake knife with her mouth and then cut slices with the same blade, *Variety* in its review added some sharply worded etiquette do's and don'ts.[11]

Times sales commenced to reward RCA for its past research expenditures totaling more than $25 million. NBC distributed a weekly listing of programs to the 5,000 or so set owners in the New York area. Included was a return card on which viewers could rate each program as excellent, good, fair or poor. The sum of the checks in each category measured TV sets in use as well as program interest. A three-city NBC network—New York, Philadelphia and Schenectady—came into place, and a handful of sponsors, including Bulova Watch, Botany Mills and Adam Hats, signed up.

CBS, which had placed most of its emphasis on the development of a color TV system, became New York's second commercial station in 1941 with a 15-hour-a-week schedule. Broadcasting from a pigeon-infested loft directly over Grand Central Station, WCBW bowed on July 2 with the first regularly scheduled game show on TV. Moderated and produced by Gil Fates, it bore the straightforward title, *The CBS Tele-*

vision Quiz. An hour in duration, this contest appeared weekly for 63 consecutive performances.

Within six months, CBS had transmitted some 300 hours of programs designed to satisfy a wide variety of the public's entertainment and educational interests. William Shirer, Norman Thomas, Patricia Bowman, Rex Stout, Paul Draper, George Fielding Eliot and Michael Strange were among the hundreds of celebrities who appeared before the network's cameras.

Naturalness, informality, and ease were found to be valuable assets for television. According to Gilbert Seldes, director of the CBS television program department and a noted critic and author, TV showed things as they really were. "Therefore, the simple and the unpretentious come over beautifully," he observed. "And everything that is faked is multiplied a hundred times. This means that informal shows, people being themselves, tend to be better than elaborate pretenses." [12]

At the close of a promising year for the "tube," the picture changed dramatically. The attack on Pearl Harbor by the Japanese and the declaration of war by Congress put a lid on TV expansion. Most television activities converted to government war work, including ultrasecret radar projects. After 1942, few new programs or innovations found their way onto the screen. Defense needs took priority, for example, as air-raid wardens received training by TV. [13]

An eager public waited for the reintroduction of television as part of the promised postwar dream world. Immediately after V-J Day, leaders of the industry began to hold out hopes that TV would assume big business proportions early in 1946. GE, Westinghouse, RCA, Philco and other manufacturers announced production of 500,000 receivers within the next 12 months chiefly in anticipation of the construction of new stations to add to transmitters already in place in New York, Philadelphia, Schenectady, Chicago and Los Angeles. NBC president Niles Trammell predicted new installations in Washington and Cleveland and "coast to coast network television made possible by automatic relay stations, coaxial cable and stratovision." [14]

But unforeseen reconversion hurdles, including material shortages and labor strife, quashed nearly all plans of accelerated expansion. The industry itself also shared in stymieing the new vehicle, evidenced by a long unresolved controversy between the introduction of color and its transmission over compatible black-and-white receivers. Factions fought each other over the issue of "color now" or "color in five years." Both sides accused the other of trying to snarl TV developments and, in turn, confusing the public.* Moreover, a sizable number of radio

---

*In early 1947 the FCC ruled to banish color television to the laboratory for further work.

stations sought to protect their interests from inevitable video competition by withdrawing or holding in abeyance their applications for TV transmitters. By the end of 1946 all signs pointed to still another year before TV became big.

Nevertheless, 22 more companies began making black-and-white sets in 1947, and sales augured well. Programming, however, failed to keep pace. Sport promoters, including the World Series club owners, eagerly threw open their gates to TV cameras, but labor unions—notably the American Federation of Musicians—stood on the sidelines undecided on a fee structure for its members. Without authority to broadcast "live" instrumental music, singers mouthed the words of their own records played from a behind-the-scenes machine. Television beefed up low-cost, easy-to-produce talk-show formats to fill the still-short broadcast day. Audience participation games and quizzes and panel question-and-answer sessions were economical as well as lively fillers for the video screen.

Stations beamed a handful of programs that had enjoyed success on radio and adjusted well to the addition of cameras. *The Missus-Goes-a-Shopping* was especially adaptable because its many stunts and gimmicks, such as a 250-pound truck driver trying to edge his frame into a girdle, provided more enjoyment when seen. M.C. John Reed King conducted the show like the game-show veteran he was. He quickly put his audience and contestants in a relaxed and jovial mood.[15] A large crowd always gathered in the supermarkets where the CBS traveling show originated, and there was no lack of shoppers to the glamorized cracker-barrel sessions. Yet the video "Missus" presented a problem or two that its radio counterpart never did. King and his crew constantly had to be on the lookout for people who came into the market and, not knowing what was going on, wandered in front of the cameras and blocked the lens.

In a similar vein, *Ladies Be Seated* made the transition with ease. Initially broadcast from Schenectady, it earned the highest audience rating of any show presented there by ABC up to that time. After DuMont opened its New York studios in the John Wanamaker Store in 1946, ABC borrowed space for this audience-participation feature. (It would be two years before the ABC network had its own New York station.) Sponsor B. T. Babbitt inaugurated the first premium giveaway; home viewers were invited to send in a Bab-O cleanser label and receive a genuine Egyptian scarab pin.[16]

ABC via DuMont repackaged its *Detect and Collect*. Chief attributes were the entertaining M.C. work of comedian Lew Lehr and the fact that the show, in the words of *Variety*, "doesn't go in for the sadistic treatment of the participants that have killed off other entries in the division."[17]

CBS's transplant from radio, *Consumer's Quiz*, with Fred Uttal, ignored the visual aspects of TV and soon lost viewers. Five women from the audience were asked questions on how best to shop for certain articles. Only when consumer expert Joan Barton elaborated on the correct answers by demonstrating visually a certain procedure did the show come somewhat alive.

Original quizzes popped up. In Chicago, WBKB mounted a quiz pitched for home viewers whereby questions in the form of charades were asked by telephone. Called *Telequizzicals*, it prominently displayed electrical appliances that tied neatly into the "plugs" for utility sponsor Commonwealth Edison.

In 1947 *Seven Arts Quiz* over NBC represented the closest that any TV question-and-answer show had yet come to emulating the sparkle and verve of a popular radio panel.[18] Using a group of experts to field the questions, director Fred Coe built this feature around a 1947 book on the arts by two New York radio publicity pros. Although no Clifton Fadiman, M.C. Bill Slater had a pleasant enough personality to begin a new career on the home screen.

Man-on-the-street programs brought spontaneity and individuality to the video screen. With a walkie-talkie strapped on his back, broadcasters took to the curb while TV cameras nosed through second-floor windows above him. Without prearrangement, crowds converged on these interviewers, eager to give their opinions on whatever question was asked. DuMont's Dan Peterson, for one, talked with passers-by five days a week on subjects such as what to do about Germany, whether Junior should monopolize the family car, and if husband or wife should handle the household finances. Cab drivers even slowed down to listen and then added a few short words of their own. Workers occasionally came up out of manholes to speak their mind on camera. As television matured, reporters gradually took over the man-on-the-street features, integrating them into their regular nightly newscasts.

During 1948 Joe Louis, Milton Berle, Ed Sullivan and a puppet named Howdy Doody began to change millions of American living rooms into small theaters. By midyear some 5,000 receivers—many selling as low as $250—were being hooked up to roof-top antennas every week.* More than 20 cities claimed at least one commercial station. New York led with five transmitters; both Washington, D.C., and Philadelphia boasted three, while on the West Coast only Los Angeles' two stations provided programs. At both ends of the country viewers were rediscovering an old party game that everyone said was a natural for the video tube.

---

*An effective stunt to sell television sets at an RCA exhibit in New York was "self-television," which enabled visitors to see themselves being televised.

The timeless charade, acted out by celebrities or a group of stock players, captured the attention of set owners who vicariously participated in the guessing game. Often home viewers contributed their ideas for skits and, in exchange, received a cash award or merchandise.

At New York's DuMont studios, Bill Slater presided over a panel for *Charade Quiz* that had 90 seconds to come up with the right answer to what was being enacted by a troupe of actors. If they missed, the contributor picked up an additional $15 to his basic $10 stipend. Some nights the show handed out $150, making it the most generous giveaway on TV in early 1948.

In Hollywood Mike Stokey already had created a diverting charade contest pitting two teams of movie personalities against each other, with each member of the "regulars" and the "challengers" entirely on his or her own when it came to acting out gag lines such as "Outside of a dog, a man's best friend is a book. Inside of a dog, it's too dark to read."

While a student at Los Angeles City College, Stokey had been active in the drama club. During rehearsal breaks, its members passed the time by playing charades. Once in 1939 at the local Don Lee station, he organized two school teams for a pantomime game for an experimental telecast. He soon joined NBC as an announcer, a job interrupted by wartime service in the air force. When KTLA commenced daily telecasts from the Paramount lot in 1947, Mike Stokey, now a member of its production staff, was suddenly caught without material to replace a cancelled show. He was given 36 hours to come up with a substitute. As he had done eight years earlier, he recruited a half-dozen drama students, this time from UCLA and the University of Southern California (USC), to play his *Pantomime Quiz*.

During the program, actor Roddy McDowell wandered into the studio to observe the proceedings. Fascinated by the contest, he asked if he might fill the empty chair on each team when a player moved to act out a puzzler. Stokey readily agreed. At the close of the highly animated game, McDowell looked at the camera and said, "If this is TV, it's a ball." To those Hollywood friends watching on their sets at home, he added: "Come on down and play this with me." [19]

At the end of the show, KTLA general manager Klaus Landsberg voiced overwhelming approval. "This is what TV is all about!" he exclaimed. [20]

"The second the game went off the air, we were swamped with calls for hours," recounted Stokey, who hosted the quiz. "Many movie stars phoned to ask if they could be included as participants in the challenging funfest. A dozen or so actually made their TV debuts with me— Jimmy Durante, Lucille Ball, Steve Allen, Danny Thomas. It was a busman's holiday for them." [21]

A contingent of familiar big-screen faces became "regulars": Jackie Coogan, Hans Conreid, Vincent Price, Beverly Garland, Dorothy Hart, John Barrymore, Jr., Robert Alda, Sebastian Cabot and Adele Jergens. Special guests ranged from Rudy Vallee and Eve Arden to Robert Morse and Buster Keaton. Their gestures and grimaces put a new twist to the centuries-old parlor game. Players screamed and weaved in their efforts to decipher the message. To speed up the proceedings, Stokey devised a number of shortcuts and symbols. For instance, a sawing motion and a twist of the arms came out to mean "was." The twist was a reverse symbol indicating that "saw" should be spelled backwards. Occasionally, a wag resorted to a highly unorthodox and perhaps off-color development of the text.

"Be the word," Stokey always urged his players. When Vincent Price had to act out the word "dog," he did so by getting down on the floor on his hands and knees, then "lifting" his long leg dog-style. But only the time-clock or a correct answer ever interrupted the gyrations of a player.

In January 1949 *Pantomime Quiz* won the very first Emmy as the medium's most popular show.[22] Later that year with coast-to-coast telecasts in place, the game went nationwide over CBS and won more awards for its popular host and energetic creator. Periodically, the show relocated to New York where Broadway favorites such as Bert Lahr, Nanette Fabray and Alice Ghostley teamed up against a Hollywood contingent. It continued to provide merriment through the 1950s and into the 1960s, when the quiz was retitled *Stump the Stars*. Stokey had no patent on TV charades, and other broadcasters presented similar entrants. *Act It Out, Let There Be Stars* and *Movietown R.S.V.P.* appeared briefly, but Stokey's sailed on year after year as both a live and a syndicated series.

Hollywood also provided grist for straightforward question-and-answer games. But identifying stars and films from still shots generated only mild audience interest. *Movieland Quiz* used ABC's Philadelphia outlet, WFIL-TV. The set depicted a film-theater entrance with M.C. Arthur Q. Bryan acting as M.C. and Patricia Bright serving as a combination receptionist and cashier. Movie-wise contestants picked up $5 and tickets to a nearby flick.

History, current events and famous photographs provided the basis for some contests. NBC's Ben Grauer hosted the prime-time *Americana Quiz*. Ben had had his hand into quizmastering since helping to spin the *Pot o' Gold* wheel. He later assisted Kay Kyser with his Kollege and even emceed a 1940 audience-participation quizzer, *What Would You Have Done?* His video game eight years later brought together a bright and attractive group of high school students to answer questions on American history, folklore and culture. The display of visible clues acknowledged the presence of the camera to what otherwise might have been a static panel quiz. A very recent radio feature, *Who Said That?* moved into TV with Robert Trout as chief quizzer of a panel of notables who tried to identify the sources of well-known quotations.

ABC's *Quizzing the News* attempted to test a panel's knowledge of stories from the day's headlines. Host Allan Prescott asked questions as cartoonist Albee Treider drew hints. The less-than-notable panel members didn't measure up as good guessers or bright bon moters. The show never came close to the hit class, and viewers were often distracted by Prescott's scratching various parts of his body while reading a script. "In radio," lectured *Variety*, "these things didn't matter, but it's not Emily Post on video."[23]

CBS's entry did not fare any better. Called *The Eyes Have It*, this panel show used newsreel clips as the basis for questions posed to a board of experts, including Paul Gallico, Charles MacArthur and Dale Carnegie. The film clips were a clever device for overcoming the narrow limits of the ordinary studio quiz, but the production came across as amateurish and inept. Repeatedly, the newsreel shots were out of synchronization with the questions or were too brief to absorb. CBS newsman Douglas Edwards, who pioneered the first nightly newscast on TV in 1948, expressed embarrassment over one production faux pas after another.

"It was a very early-on effort among quiz and game shows," Edwards remembered, "and ill-prepared and ultimately ill-fated. I did only one of the shows, and was pleased to be extricated from the shambles."[24]

With a mixed degree of success with original entries, networks in 1948 and 1949 turned to time-proven panels and games for their TV chain. Producer Martha Roundtree carried over her *Leave It to the Girls*, a discussion session by four prominent and outspoken women on career-girl questions submitted by the home audience. A male guest on each show spoke for his sex and tried to fend off the verbal onslaughts of articulate ladies such as Ilka Chase, Dorothy Kilgallen, Faye Emerson, Eloise McElhone and Robin Chandler. As on the radio version, the man came off second best in the encounter. But brave ones such as Bennett Cerf, Richard Kollmar, Ted Malone, Henry Morgan and Andre Baruch still managed to let go with some personal observations and insights about women that shook up the panel and viewers.

Gulf Oil, a sponsor of *We, the People* on radio, did little to dress up its show with an eye to a TV camera. On June 1, 1948, the human-interest program made claim as the first "simulcast"—a broadcast simultaneously over both mediums. Although CBS-TV cameras ranged all over the Empire Theatre on Broadway, host Dwight Weist was told by the producers to "play" to the much-larger radio audience. All remained intact—announcers, cue throwers, signals for studio applause and a cast wrestling with their scripts. With the single exception of a visual commercial midway, no attempt was made to give the show a greatly needed TV look. Spontaneity on the highly scripted program was forthcoming on but two occasions. Fred Allen demonstrated that he could be a natural for TV, using his script merely as a take-it-or-leave-it prop. The King Cole Trio with Nat King Cole relaxed when it performed the hit melody "Nature Boy" (whose composer, the bearded, hippielike Eden Ahbez, also appeared).[25]

Cameras were added to *Twenty Questions* to capture the spirited radio contest. This simulcast with M.C. Bill Slater reflected the dual nature of the dial-channel setup. It was originated by WOR-TV, New York, although carried by NBC-TV and aired on radio by Mutual. Seating the panel in two tiers allowed for a tight group show that fit the screen's dimensions and aptly registered the players' eagerness, disappointments and triumphs. Governor Alfred E. Driscoll of New Jersey joined the panel as guest to launch the video proceedings of a broadcast game that had had its nucleus in the New Jersey household of Fred and Florence Van Deventer.

The joke-telling session, *Can You Top This?* however, translated poorly to the screen. Essentially, it was the old radio show in front of a camera. Sightwise, viewers had a right to expect more and found panelists and their tales a static presentation. It lasted less than a season but returned in syndication in the 1970s when comedian Morey Amsterdam bought the rights and gathered a celebrity panel of gagmen that included Danny Thomas and Stu Gilliam.

Hardy perennial *It Pays to Be Ignorant* endured a similar fate, appearing only as a summer replacement in 1949 and 1951. The ultimate insult to viewers—the use of a script that required host Tom Howard and his panelists constantly to lower their heads in full view of the camera—took away most of the show's spontaneity. "The finished product seems cut and dried, not to mention very repetitious," noted the *New York Times*.[26]

The Quiz Kids, still shepherded by Joe Kelly in Chicago, proved that most of his charges had charm as well as brains when the show converted entirely to TV in mid-1949. Visual props to questions, ranging from a turn-of-the-century auto to a five-foot fox snake, proved at times more of a distraction than a quizzing aid. Frequently, the familiar academic robes were shed for costumes befitting a program theme, built around the settling of the West, U.S. neighbors south of the border, or the celebration of Halloween. Special guests appeared to ask questions related to their professions or occupations. When presidential hopeful Governor of Illinois Adlai Stevenson came on, he asked the kids if they would like to be President of the United States and why. Most replied affirmatively, adding that they wanted to stop wars, keep peace among countries and help poor people. Only eight-year-old Harvey Dytch voiced negative feelings, saying the job had "too many worries."[27]

The Kids' adult counterpart, *Information Please*, attempted to develop a following when it relocated to television. With Clifton Fadiman, regular panelists Adams and Kieran and two guest celebrities, it nevertheless faded after three months on CBS.

In 1956 Fadiman succeeded Kelly as question-popper for a 39-week run in the last, and lackluster, *Quiz Kids* classroom.

On the musical front, the opening of Kay Kyser's Kollege before millions of viewers earned scant praise. Basically straight radio, the hour-long show paraded a string of contestants to a microphone to answer absurdly simply questions. At the slightest hesitancy, Kyser rushed in to provide an excess of clues. As a result, there was no competition whatsoever and the "old professor" was left to his own devices of mugging and capering about. As a concession to the screen, he added questions in the form of charades. "A little bit of the parlor game goes a long way," observed *New York Times'* Jack Gould, "particularly when it is pitched to the nursery set."[28]

Even Kyser's announcer, Ben Grauer, failed to measure up. In Gould's eyes, he did "such a brusque and determined job as chaperon of the participants that the viewer might think he was escorting a group of fourth offenders to the Tombs." Contestants, he added, "should be led about with a little more tact and courtesy and not treated so obviously as stooges."[29]

Gould advised Kyser to reduce the show to a half-hour, accent the straight musical talents of his organization's vocalists Mike Douglas, Liza Palmer and Sue Bennett, ask sensible questions and not give the answers and, for his own part, relax. "Easy does it in television," Gould counseled.[30]

After two years on CBS radio, the Saturday night giveaway *Sing It Again* acquired sight as a full-hour simulcast. Network founder William Paley originally had thought of doing parodies of popular tunes and asked his chief of programming, Hubbell Robinson, to pursue the idea. Producer Lester Gottlieb received the assignment, quickly discovering that music publishers would not agree to a song parody unless the original was also performed so that the lyricists would gain performance credits for royalty payments. "This automatically gave us the inspiration that we would have to 'sing it again,' " Gottlieb remarked. "And that's how the program title came to mind."[31]

He gathered a cast of vocalists—Alan Dale, Patti Clayton, Bob Howard and the Riddlers quintet—backed by Ray Bloch's orchestra to perform a popular song or an old standard with the original lyrics. After the initial rendition, the soloist sang it again using humorous or offbeat lyrics specially written by professional songsmiths Hy Zaret, Albert Stillman, Irwin Drake, Bernie Hanghen or Bill Stein. Host Dan Seymour then telephoned a listener to ask the identity of the person, place or thing on the basis of clues furnished by the special rewording. If correct, a $100 check went in the mail and a chance followed at the "phantom voice" $1,000 jackpot.

Very rarely did masters of ceremonies encounter a contrary contestant . . . but Dan Seymour did on *Sing It Again*. A jackpot winner in Hartford, Connecticut, after giving the right answer, told him in no uncertain terms that he did not want the prize. "It will put me in a higher tax bracket. So don't tell me what I've won. I don't want it." The baffled Seymour—whose side of the conversation luckily was the only one broadcast—ignored the protests and spouted on how overjoyed the gentleman was with his windfall.[32]

Within its first year, *Sing It Again* increased the jackpot prize to $25,000 worth of merchandise. Rush Clarke, a sales engineer in Rochester, New York, walked off with that bonanza by naming swimmer Gertrude Ederle as the mystery voice. He immediately picked up another $25,000 in cash by giving the time, 14.5 hours, Ederle took to cross the English Channel in 1926. "That two-fisted windfall was about the biggest on the air in 1949," Lester Gottlieb recalled. "It was almost the equivalent of winning a state lottery today. No one ever thought New York State would have such a thing. Perish the thought back in 1949 or '50."[33]

Before ending its brief single season run on TV, the show established a minor "first." Pianist-singer Bob Howard, known as the "Jive Bomber," regularly played a solo number. On one particular program, the 320-pound entertainer came on stage and sat down on the piano bench. Just as he reached toward the keys, the seat collapsed tossing Howard onto the floor. Millions of viewers gasped as stagehands rushed out to lift the still smiling performer to his feet. "That's a first!" Howard joked. Offstage came the voice of the director: "And that's a last. Get him a double-duty bench."[34]

There were no doubts within the television industry that once ABC established its own flagship station in New York it would place on its network its two leading quiz shows: *Break the Bank* and *Stop the Music!* Bert Parks, a small-screen "natural," contributed tremendously to the high-stakes proceedings on both shows. *Break the Bank* added visual clues and a "television wishbowl" containing names of viewers asking to be selected for an appearance on the program, apparently satisfying most viewers who rated it high on their best program list.

Stop the Music! provided an opportunity for hopeful winners to see the many products just waiting for the right answer. The separate radio version, which continued on Sundays, naturally was limited to an ear-full recital of the long menu of prizes. Conductor Harry Salter gathered a visually attractive and well-costumed unit of singers (Betty Ann Grove, Jimmy Blaine, Estelle Loring) and dancers (Sonja and Courtney Van Horne, Don Little, Marina Palmer, Wayne Lamb). All fell neatly into the clue-giving format and, at the same time, gave out some straight entertainment. Only TV set owners were called as contestants; with still only eight or so million homes equipped with TV by 1949, the odds for the mystery melody jackpot were comparatively good for these pioneer viewers.

But radio still had a strong grip on the entertainment homefront. The FCC recognized this hold and aimed its big guns on the long-festering matter of lottery law violations.

› 14 ‹

No Answers

"It came awfully sudden, didn't it?" Bert Parks replied to a reporter asking his reaction to the Federal Communications Commission's intention to investigate "money shows" for violations of federal lottery laws. Reached at the Capitol Theatre on Broadway between stage-show versions of *Stop the Music!* the seemingly unperturbed Parks added that he had not heard from any of his listeners yet. "I just haven't had time to crystallize my thoughts."[1]

Bill Cullen, master of ceremonies on three CBS giveaways, said he expected to hear plenty from fans. "On the basis of our audience ratings, they are going to find the listeners are with us." He explained that plans were going ahead for him to M.C. still another quiz show on Mutual the following week.[2]

Bud Collyer, host of *Three for the Money*, thought some of the giveaway shows could be altered to meet limitations imposed by the FCC. Station WNEW, which had a new offbeat show entitled *You Can Lose Your Shirt*, was unruffled. "We're taking the money away from the contestants instead of us giving them any!"[3]

In August 1948 the FCC reminded Parks, Cullen and Collyer and fellow broadcasters of a section of the Federal Communications Act barring radio and television stations from offering prizes or gifts by means of a lottery or scheme. The commission said section 316 would prohibit programs where, as a condition to winning a prize, the winner furnished any money or other things of value or had in his possession any specified product of the sponsor or was required to give an answer previously announced by a station.[4]

Gearing up for the 1948–49 season, broadcasters pondered whether the FCC had issued a warning or proclaimed a fact.[5] Thrown into sudden chaos, the networks and independent stations turned to their lawyers and advisors to interpret the statement that apparently placed their lucrative game shows in jeopardy. Only NBC announced that it would not consider any new giveaway program. The other chains remained publicly silent while shoring up the 40 or so national giveaways aired each week.

The long-lingering question of what actually violated section 316 of the 1934 communications law stymied the industry. Broadcasters soon came to the conclusion that only the enforcement of explicit regulations declaring giveaway schemes, telephone quizzes and similar stunts not in the public interest could halt the "money show" spree.[6] Meanwhile, it was "deliver as usual."

Within the ranks of the American Federation of Radio Artists, however, hopes were high that the FCC would soon make good its threat. Its members believed a brake or a ban on giveaways could generate more jobs for actors and musicians, once the airwaves backed away from bank-night ballyhoo.[7] Others saw the bearing down on quiz shows as a sign that a laundry list of prizes would no longer be the be-all and end-all of a program, overrun elements of skill and knowledge or eclipse the performers. The cumulative complaints of radio's harsher critics, who argued for more substantial program fare and new ideas in programming, helped to spark interest in a proposed FCC rule directed toward the abolition of giveaways, including the telephone-centered *Stop the Music!* and *Sing It Again* as well as the stunt-oriented *Truth or Consequences* and *People Are Funny.*

Surveying a bonanza of approximately $2 million to $5 million distributed in money, goods and services to eager parties annually, the FCC decided to ignore the lotterylike hoopla no longer. In 1948 it initiated a study to bring in focus the problem of whether giveaways violated the statutory ban against the broadcasting of lotteries or were otherwise contrary to the public interest. The issue gained added attention that year when the telephone jackpot show *Dollars for Answers,* aired by Northern Virginia Broadcasters, Inc., over WARL Arlington, became the subject of an FCC inquiry. The commission quickly recognized its enormous task of delineating general rules to cover all variations of the giveaway theme. The WARL investigation brought forth a convoluted statement by the FCC acknowledging the complexity of lottery case law and, in a sense, admitting the gargantuan challenge ahead.

In the matter of the Virginia station, the commission stated: "The endless variations which have been engrafted upon gambling projects to relieve them of their statutory iniquity have necessitated the judicial evolution of lottery case law in compartmental panoramic form within the pattern of which there exists few cells of the precise dimension required to fit the measurements of subsequently arising cases."[8]

Both FCC counselors and broadcast lawyers spent months analyzing

the three cardinal elements of a lottery: prize, chance and consideration. No problem existed on the interpretation of what constituted a
prize. "Chance," however, generated a degree of dispute. A lottery
existed, if the scheme offered prizes dependent in whole or in part
upon lot or chance. An element of chance was deemed inherent in
every contest regardless of the skill involved but this did not result in
a lottery; rather it was the predominance of chance that determined the
existence of a lottery.[9] To circumvent this position, network legal advisors contended that those particular contests under fire undoubtedly
involved much "skill" and very little "chance."

A certain degree of skill certainly came into play on WARL's *Dollars
for Answers.* The intellectual challenge of answering over the telephone,
for example, the question, "By whom and in what year was deuterium
discovered?" surely demanded a highly specialized knowledge of
chemistry ("skill").[10] The FCC's examination of this program led to its
realization that the fortuitous or random selection of the person called,
as well as the absence of competitive conditions, were part of the complex problem.

The most difficult criterion—the element of consideration—had never
been interpreted by the courts since the enactment of the 1934 FCC
regulations. Now, 14 years later, the dilemma revived the unresolved
nature of what constituted consideration.[11] Doubtlessly, it was the fur-
nishing of money or a thing of value. But was it the purchase of the
radio or TV set itself? Was it just answering the telephone or writing a
letter? Or answering a question, the answer to which had been previously broadcast over the same station where emanated the giveaway
show? Could it be just listening to the program? The FCC proposed
that all, collectively or individually, were proof of consideration.

Looking back to the *Pot o' Gold* and a half-dozen other telephone
giveaways of 1939–40, network lawyers noted that these shows now
would be called lotteries under the new FCC outlook. In 1940 the FCC
sought to have them barred, but the Department of Justice had declined to prosecute the *Pot*—and gave no reasons. This decision ultimately gave the green light to more "money shows."

Eight years later, the FCC reverted to its original position and de-
creed *Dollars for Answers* illegal—a giveaway differing only slightly from
the 1940 *Dixie Treasure Chest*, whereby a person selected from a telephone directory was awarded $50 if he or she responded to a call and
correctly answered a question that, apparently, was always the same
until the right answer came forth. Seemingly, any rules forthcoming
from the FCC rested upon a weak legal base.[12] Definition of *consideration*, as well as of *chance*, generated confusion and uncertainty. Were
giveaways, indeed, outright lotteries?

Communications lawyers leaned to more solid ground to ban these shows. The broad jurisdictional power conferred on the FCC by Congress, they pointed out, could more easily outlaw giveaways. All they really had to do was to determine whether the overall program fare of a station was in the "public interest, convenience, and necessity." This was a legitimate power provided by the Radio Act of 1927 (the predecessor of the 1934 legislation).[13] Granting a broadcast license and the station's request for a renewal remained squarely in the hands of the FCC—and "public service" had been the primary criterion for issuing or continuing a license.

"If the Federal Communications Commission determines that giveaway programs over the air are contrary to the public interest," wrote former assistant to the general counsel of the FCC Leonard H. Marks in *The Georgetown Law Journal* in early 1949, "this decision can also be based upon the argument that giveaway programs consist of the same elements which have led legislators in the past to prohibit 'gambling activities.' Historically, the legislative ban has been placed on games of chance which induced people to 'gamble,' to 'substitute false standards for true,' to expect to profit by 'luck' instead of by work. Although the money giveaway show may not meet the tailored description of a lottery in the traditional sense, certainly the same appeal is made to the human desire 'to get something for nothing.' "[14]

"Although the fear of administrative abuse of power by federal agencies is omnipresent," Marks added, "the right of the Courts to reverse these actions when the exercise of power is arbitrary and capricious appears to be a reasonable safeguard for the protection of licenses and the public. Thus far, the actions of the Federal Communications Commission have been regarded by the courts and the public as within the realm of reasonable discretion."[15]

By its announcement of a study on the legality of giveaways, the FCC apparently hoped that radio and television would start to put its own house in order. To some degree, the commission expected broadcasters themselves to halt the contagious, runaway "money show"— and bring back a solid measure of talent and showmanship to draw audiences, not a jackpot of home appliances and gadgets. But at the start of the 1948–49 season, the networks and most individual stations pushed the thought aside and continued to capitalize on America's love of games of chance and reap the maximum benefits for sponsors and themselves.

Thus on August 19, 1949, the FCC added "teeth" to its earlier pronouncement; it now ruled that the broadcasting of giveaways was in violation of the U.S. Criminal Code. After October 1 it would not renew licenses nor grant construction permits to stations embracing this type of entertainment. "A scheme," it said, "involving award of prizes designed to induce persons to listen to the particular program certainly involves consideration furnished directly or indirectly by members of the public who are induced to listen."[16]

This time, the reaction among most broadcasters left no doubt as to the course of action: they would not relinquish this lucrative indulgence in jackpot shows without a fight to the finish.

Within days, both ABC and CBS sought a legal test and relief in the courts from the fast-approaching ban. CBS president Frank Stanton voiced the networks' position: "The authority and jurisdiction of the commission to impose an absolute prohibition upon a particular type of program is open to serious questions under the law which contemplates that broadcasters themselves shall determine what programs will be broadcast, consistent with the needs and desires of listeners."[17]

ABC eyed loss of existing airtime sales and new contracts. The network, with 13 major "money shows," added that the ruling was contrary to the First Amendment's guarantee of freedom of speech and also deprived the network of property without due process of law.* NBC similarly decried the extension of FCC authority. All three chains closed ranks and asked for a stay pending a decision in a court action that claimed the FCC lacked authority, and if it had authority, it had improperly interpreted the antilottery section. FCC rejected the stay, noting the courts should decide the scope of any temporary injunction.

By waiting a year until taking action on giveaways, the FCC now faced an even greater lineup of shows and found it harder to "stop the music" as it might have done in mid-1948. Some radio headliners, like Fred Allen, rooted for the FCC, believing that the ban would take radio away from the scavengers and give it back to the entertainers.

Actually, within the commission itself, the giveaway ruling represented the known position of only a minority of the seven-member group; the measure was carried by a vote of three commissioners to one. Oddly, chairman Wayne Coy had been attending international communications conferences in Europe during the final deliberation. Another absentee, Robert F. Jones, ill during the time of the decision, announced he had been preparing a dissent that would soon be filed.[18] Why the rules were rushed through by only four voting members on the specific day chosen was particularly difficult for broadcasters to understand since the FCC had been reviewing the giveaway matter for a full year. Seemingly, the commission had some explaining to do publicly. "Do 150,000,000 people wish to have their programs controlled by three people?" asked Congressman Richard Wigglesworth of Massachusetts.[19]

For their part, the three commissioners who approved the rules insisted that Congress already had enacted a law expressly forbidding

---

*ABC president Mark Woods joked whether he'd be permitted "to give away the bride" at his daughter Patricia's marriage on September 17, 1949. "Woods' Dilemma," *Variety*, August 24, 1949, p. 38.

the broadcasting of lotteries. Whether a broadcast license had violated such a statute, they claimed, was pertinent in determining one's qualifications to operate a station in the public interest.

No fan of giveaways, critic Jack Gould even took issue on the FCC maneuvers. "None of the FCC stipulations, of course, go to the heart of the giveaway issue, which is that such programs are bad for radio and attest to the industry's appalling lack of self-discipline. After all," he concluded, "it was the National Association of Broadcasters itself which decried 'buying' an audience instead of entertaining it, which is as succinct an indictment of the giveaways as had yet been written. If the broadcasters did their job, there would be no giveaway issue."[20]

The listening public liked the "money shows." A Gallup poll showed that 51 percent of those queried listened to giveaways "often or once in a while" and half of all interviewed wanted them to continue.[21]

Everyone admitted that the FCC faced a complex legal problem, compounded by the lack of a specific definition of what was a lottery on the air. In attempting to fill this legal void, the commission seemingly succumbed to the temptation not only to administer the law but also to write it.

Broadcasters faced the 1949–50 season with trepidation. The October 1 deadline drew nearer and nearer. Suddenly, on September 13, Judge Michael Igoe of the Federal District Court, acting on a suit filed by Radio Features, Inc., of Chicago, issued an order restraining the FCC from putting into effect its ban until his court could rule on its legality. A week later, Federal Judge Simon H. Rifkind came to the aid of the beleaguered networks and granted relief on their plea of financial damages and a denial of the lottery charge. At this point, an FCC lawyer candidly remarked that the commission fundamentally was more interested in improving program quality than in the lottery aspects of the case.[22] By late September the FCC backed down and suspended its new antigiveaway rules until at least 30 days after the decisions in the pending court tests.

The heat was off. The ultimate word, however, rested with the judicial system. Radio languished, television flourished, before the federal court spoke. In 1953 the FCC's long-pending rules were slapped down in a two-to-one decision which held that, for the most part, they misconstrued the lottery law and represented "censorship" in violation of the First Amendment.

Judge Vincent Leibell, in the majority opinion, wrote: "The act of listening to a broadcast of a giveaway program, or viewing it on television, does not constitute a 'price' or 'valuable consideration,' which is an essential element of a 'lottery.' "[23]

The court noted that the merits of jackpot shows were not an issue. When audiences tired of them, they will "make their exit."

A year later, the U.S. Supreme Court turned down an FCC appeal by an eight-to-zero ruling. The high court decision, written by Chief Justice Earl Warren, found that the commission exceeded its authority. The court solidly rejected the FCC argument that the listener's time was a valuable consideration comparable to money put up in a typical ticket lottery.[24]

By then, the number of giveaways and game shows had mushroomed to nearly 60 on radio and TV. Although the aggregate had increased, the size of the jackpots had substantially decreased. By early 1954, the top range stood between $5,000 to $10,000. The earlier days of the $30,000-to-$50,000 windfall in money and merchandise had apparently passed. Although the golden calf pulled in its horns, it was not put out to pasture.

›15‹

Vaudeo

By 1950 the public itself appeared to have beaten the government and critics to the draw in deflating the giveaway boom. Audiences knocked down a cluster of jackpot shows simply by not dialing them in. The giveaway craze peaked just as the FCC withdrew its ban.[1] The fall of *Stop the Music!* from 14th to 66th place in radio popularity gave pause to the networks. The monster giveaway on NBC, *Hollywood Calling*, now occupied the 104th slot in the Hooper ratings, which was about as far down as a show could go. Other major games, including *Hit the Jackpot* and *Quick as a Flash*, folded, and a handful were revamped to downplay the giveaway frenzy. Yet in spite of the audience tune-out, several new quiz programs made brave attempts to stem the tide.

ABC shoveled out gifts to both studio and home audiences on *Chance of a Lifetime*, emceed by the omnipresent John Reed King in an atmosphere of near-hysteria. He whipped up audiences with shouts, howls and a style of laughter that was usually heard on the mystery thriller *Inner Sanctum*. ABC also introduced a Monday-through-Friday morning session called *Pick a Date*. Host Buddy Rogers asked participants to give a memorable date in their lives and the reason for its selection in exchange for a heap of gifts and a crack at a $3,000-paying riddle. For Saturday nights, Mutual created *Meet Your Match* with jackpot questions emanating from a masked character called the Baron. But with once-hard-to-get autos and appliances now readily available, listeners found little appeal in dreaming of the day when a Bendix washing machine might come through the kitchen door.

Moreover, a popular new Jimmy Stewart movie called "The Jackpot" left 1950 audiences wondering whether a quiz-show windfall was really worth all it was touted to be. In that film, Stewart answers his telephone. The call is from a radio show quizmaster who asks him a handful of questions. Stewart's replies are correct and he wins a big jackpot. As the prizes pour into the home of this average, small-town bread-winner and his wife, played by Barbara Hale, their lives change. His favorite furniture is relegated to the garage, the house is decorated against his tastes, he has no place to keep the pony or the mountain of groceries delivered by the quiz show to his doorstep. Worst of all, Stewart finds the income tax people breathing down his neck. Then, he loses his job, makes a contact with a bookie and almost goes to jail. He quickly realizes that he is more content in a house devoid of super-fluous and bedeviling prizes.[2]

This biting satire on quiz programs, based on an article by John McNulty in *The New Yorker*, revealed an aspect of postjackpot life that disturbed, even repelled, many.

Increasingly, audiences switched back to comedy shows, agreeing that it was better fare than a run-through of a laundry list of loot. Co-medians, more than ever, stacked up as the most valuable commodity on the air. In the waning days of radio, these mainstays of mirth stood as the undisputed linchpins of prime time. No industry leader recog-nized the importance of radio comedy more than William Paley of CBS. Beginning in late 1948, he initiated a series of raids on the top-drawer comedy attractions of NBC. Paley aimed to build an in-house talent roster and peak ratings at the expense of his chief competitor. Some insiders claim it was his revenge against NBC for maneuvering the FCC to disapprove Columbia's advanced TV color system.[3]

By offering capital gains packages for the production companies owned and controlled by major performers—in contrast to highly taxed straight salaries and fees paid to the biggest stars—Paley lured a formidable lineup of top-rated talent to his studios. Meanwhile, NBC took the at-titude that "why should they buy something they already have" and refused to consider the purchase of stock in their valuable star-centered properties. Paley's tax-saving setups made good sense to most veteran comics. The venerable Amos 'n Andy switched from NBC to CBS in exchange for a lump sum. Then the indestructible Jack Benny entered its portals in a $3.2 million deal. Soon Burns and Allen, Red Skelton, Edgar Bergen and Charlie McCarthy, Phil Harris and Alice Faye and Ed Wynn followed, reaping sizable windfalls of their own. With many of its strongest attractions ensconced in the Columbia nest, NBC and ABC scurried to fill the talent gap. Most important, Paley now had a solid foothold to launch those kings of comedy onto his video chan-nels.

A flock of big-time air personalities, maneuvering for additional coin, were thrown into limbo as the networks began to bet on which artists would win top ratings on both radio and television.[4] Fanny Brice as a TV *Baby Snooks* attracted little interest, and she faced a stalemate in negotiations for a new radio contract. Ed Gardner's *Duffy's Tavern* waited to be "raided." Comedienne Joan Davis, dropped by Lever Bros. after a $17,500-a-week series, faced a sponsorless season. Briefly bankrolled by the Ford Dealers of America in his last season, Fred Allen signed an exclusive NBC contract, but ill health and the search for a new format delayed his return to radio and his debut on television.

At the same time, business slumped into a mild recession. Apprehension over the dip in car sales was just one signpost that tougher times seemed to be on the horizon. To add to the uncertainties, more and more of the mainstays of commercial radio—food, drugs and soap—were getting their feet wet in television and beginning to siphon off their radio expenditures. It soon became virtually impossible to interest a major sponsor in a radio program unless it had television possibilities or unless the star was being groomed for TV and was using radio as a means for a buildup.

For radio, the new battle cry was "sell," with many stations turning to accounts once frowned upon as undesirable, including mail order-type deals and spot commercials for liver pills and laxatives. NBC chairman Niles Trammell made it clear: 1950 was the year of the salesman. "In the year ahead," he emphasized, "we must use our ingenuity to sell to our advertisers, our talent, our stations and our public the positive aspects of all the busy things in which we're engaged in radio and television."[5]

Trammell realized the two mediums were now in competition for the home audience and for the advertising dollar. "Radio's roster of great entertainment stars," the NBC chief pointed out, "must be told more of the vastness and effectiveness of the medium to keep their enthusiasms keen and unflagging. At the same time more of our top stars should be persuaded to go into the arduous work of adapting themselves to television and joining in the development of this new medium with their customary vigor and creativeness. It's backbreaking work to carry water on both shoulders but that's the style for 1950 that has to be sold by those of us in the industry."[6]

Those exposed to a television set for the first time usually became converts overnight. Receivers "sold" themselves by merely flashing a picture on its screen. Once a TV set came into a living room, the radio, for the most part, was converted to an early morning wake-up device, transformed into a mealtime companion and positioned as a late-night slumber aid, while maintaining its position as a traveling mate in most cars. Meanwhile, TV viewers sought variety and comedy shows from the tube every night. "Vaudeo" became a new designation for the potpourri of comedy, music, dance and dramatic skits crowding the nighttime program lineup.[7] Milton Berle virtually owned Tuesday evenings with his pie-in-the-face hijinks and female impersonations on the *Tex-*

aco Star Theatre. Berle chalked up an unprecedented audience rating of 86.7—the highest ever for any radio or TV show.[8] Sid Caesar and Imogene Coca on the 90-minute *Your Show of Shows* and Ken Murray with his "blackouts" pastiche offered well-staged entertainment on Saturday. NBC's *Four Star Revue,* with rotating hosts Danny Thomas, Ed Wynn, Jimmy Durante and Jack Carson, and CBS's *Arthur Godfrey and His Friends* provided solid doses of vaudeville, nightclub and specialty routines on Wednesdays. But Sunday provided the biggest and brightest vaudeo night of the week. By the fall of 1950, ABC led off with the *Paul Whiteman Revue* and *Showtime U.S.A.,* featuring guests such as Frances Langford, Ethel Waters, Hal LeRoy, Jan Murray and Julie Wilson. From 8 to 9 o'clock, CBS and NBC created a dilemma for vaudevillephiles. Eddie Cantor (and rotating headliners Fred Allen and Martin and Lewis) starred on the *Colgate Comedy Hour,* while at the same hour, Ed Sullivan brought the *Toast of the Town* to viewers.

Vaudeo also encompassed game shows with joke-telling, cartoon-making or stunt-performing contests. Morey Amsterdam emceed *Stop Me If You've Heard This One* and Hal Block hosted *Tag the Gag,* both over NBC. Visual elements dominated *Draw Me a Laugh* at ABC. A kind of "can you top this?" with cartoons, it used comic-strip ideas and gag lines from viewers. Artist Mel Casson competed with a studio contestant in an attempt to draw a cartoon using the same punch line. A panel from the audience selected the funnier of the two. Between rounds, folksinger Oscar Brand performed ad-lib lyrics describing both the cartoons and prizes waiting for the winner. On *Draw to Win,* humorist Henry Morgan presided over a group of four cartoonists who tried to identify subjects drawn and sent in by home viewers. On a similar cartoon game called *Droodles,* celebrity guests tried to think of captions for line drawings submitted by home viewers or sketched on camera by host Roger Price.

These "drawing room" games were soon overshadowed by a contest that came straight out of an amusement park or circus with antics perfectly mated to a visual arena. *Beat the Clock* brought a jocular physical element to a game show—an aspect that could best come into play on a picture screen.

The Goodson-Todman partnership moved squarely into television with this CBS-based game that pitted contestants against a time clock. Fast-moving *Beat the Clock* gave a couple from the audience a chance to win several hundred dollars if they successfully completed a stunt or two on camera within a fixed number of seconds. A huge clock with an amplified tick dominated the set, sending players into high-speed antics to beat the allotted time frame. Stunts involving balloons, bean bags, blindfolds, seltzer bottles and crockery monopolized the weekly romp, which debuted in March 1950 and followed an 18-month run on radio where it initially was called *Time's a-Wastin'*.

A typical stunt had a participant stuff inflated balloons into his out-fit—an oversize set of long underwear—and not break any. A less physical contest had an individual arrange dingdong bells in correct ascending scale on a ladder, starting with do-re-mi. A messy stunt in-volved marshmallows buried in Jell-O. The contestant had to dig them out with a spoon in his mouth and deposit them on a nearby table. Each telecast featured a bonus stunt to tax the ultimate agility and co-ordination of the top winners of the show. This particular feat with big money riding on it became a weekly challenge until a contestant mas-tered it. Then a new one popped up the following week.

Sponsor Sylvania Electric made full use of its visually oriented prod-ucts, giving as prizes its television receivers and snapping pictures of contestants in the chaotic aftermath of their stunts with Sylvania flash-bulbs. On-the-set shutterbug and aide-de-stunt was an attractive blonde named Roxanne who became somewhat of a minicelebrity among TV fans.

Host Bud Collyer, although a veteran of radio quiz shows and soaps, seemed too much the gentleman to become involved in pie-throwing and egg-carrying frivolities. He had actually enjoyed the quiet anonym-ity of radio. "I could always ride on the subway and be unrecognized," he once said while comparing television with the older medium. "In TV, you've become a member of the audience's family. You're visiting in their living room every day. They're enthusiastic about seeing you."[9]

His grandfather, mother and sister—Dan, Carrie and June Collyer—had all been on the stage or in films, but Clayton (Bud) Collyer turned to law. A graduate of Williams College and Fordham Law School, he was eager to make a name as a lawyer. He started out as a clerk in a law firm dealing mainly in mortgages. At the end of two years with little to show for his labors, he returned to radio, capitalizing on the contacts made there while earning his way through Fordham. His stint at a microphone included singing part time over CBS. In his new career as an actor and announcer on as many as 25 shows a week, Bud was soon taking home as much in a month as he had made in a full year at law.

In 1938 Collyer assumed the role of Superman at WOR, an associa-tion that would last 14 years. Well before the man of steel melted into the ether in 1952—the year that TV network revenues ($137 million) surpassed radio network sales ($102 million) for the first time—he was already going strong with *Break the Bank, This Is the Missus* and *Winner Take All*. The newly created TV game intrigued Bud, and he agreed to jump into the fray of *Beat the Clock*. Goodson-Todman sized him up correctly as having a knack for taking even the most nervous contestants and putting them at ease. This paid off as energetic and determined contestants confronted the awesome, almost menacing, clock. Soon Bud was helping to dream up the show's stunts, along with the production team and writers. (At one point, they included future playwright Neil Simon and his brother Danny.[10]) Together, they prepared about 25 each week. Young, out-of-work actors usually tried out the stunts in front of the group who selected the five best for each half-hour show. Among the "testers" in the early 1950s was the then-unknown actor James Dean.

On *Beat the Clock*, which the amiable Bud emceed for its full ten-year run, he claimed he never met any contestant, win or lose, who was a bad sport. In general, he believed, women were more interested in the fun of playing a game; men put more emphasis on winning.

Couples occasionally brought their children to watch the antics from the sidelines. As the father of three youngsters and the longtime superintendent and teacher of a Sunday school in his home community, Greenwich, Connecticut, Collyer welcomed offspring and knew how to bring out their best side. He always asked the parents not to worry about what the child would do or say. "When a parent tells a child exactly what to do," Bud claimed, "the child begins to be self conscious and to retreat. Left to himself, he is apt to remain natural in spite of microphones and cameras and an audience out front. When a youngster is having a good time, he is usually making a good impression as well."[11]

Collyer recalled a little girl on *Beat the Clock* who simply went wild about the colored balloons used in a stunt her parents had to do. "She got hold of one and followed it back and forth across the stage in what looked like the most charming and graceful dance. If her mother had said anything to her, she would have remembered where she was. We all let her alone and it was a high point of the show."[12]

Thousands of couples, with or without their children, stood at Bud's side when he faced the *Beat the Clock* cameras during the 1950s. People marveled at the apparent ease of these contestants as he prepared to put them through the mill. But his public knew that Bud as the M.C. laughed with them, not at them. "I never tried to force people into impossible situations on the show," he stated.[13] His gentle bearing and jovial disposition took what might have been a forgettable short-lived game into a long-running, well-crafted series.

› 16 ‹

Heart Line

By 1947 Walter Framer had built up a reputation as a reliable, hard-working game-show innovator, producer and scriptmaker. His contributions to the success of *Break the Bank* were widely acknowledged among broadcasters and advertisers. When an ad agency suggested he come up with a new quiz for a major client, Framer began thinking about his Russian-born father.

Arriving in the United States with seven dollars in his pocket, Ben Framer had settled in Pittsburgh where he started making and selling cigars. Rising at 4 A.M. each morning, he loaded a horse-drawn wagon with boxes of cigars and peddled his wares until his supply was exhausted and then went back to his shop to work more hours to replenish his stock. America was the land of opportunity, and Ben did well. His shop grew into a small cigar factory. Neighbors and friends had helped him make a success of his business. In later years, he, in turn, gave a hand to others, many of whom were first-generation Americans like himself.

Walt never forgot his father's words of praise and gratitude over living in the greatest country in the world where people helped each other get ahead. He began devising a quiz show built around the idea of giving a boost to people who were down on their luck and in need of a bit of money to make a go of things. Framer decided to stress the theme "the show with a heart" and gave it the working title "We're in the Money."[1]

One evening he mentioned to his wife that plans for the new show were moving ahead, but the name didn't quite fit.

"You've got to think what this show will do for a contestant," she pointed out. "People are telling listeners why they need to have some money—why they want to strike it rich."

"Wait a minute! What did you just say?"

"They want to strike it rich."

"That's it! That's the title of my show—*Strike It Rich*."[2]

In the spring of 1947 Framer prepared a demo disk with the thought that Mutual might add it to its schedule. Meanwhile, Framer picked up a copy of *Radio Daily* and read that *Take It or Leave It* was leaving CBS. Convinced that *Strike It Rich* could replace this popular program, he telephoned CBS and got through to Bill Paley. While explaining the merits of his show, Framer was suddenly interrupted by Paley.

"Are you the son of Ben Framer of Pittsburgh?" he asked. "If you are, then your father and my father were both in the cigar business in Pennsylvania and worked together in the early years. If you're Benny Framer's boy, come in and tell me about your program."[3]

They met the next day and a deal was mapped out for a late Sunday afternoon place on the dial. Luden's Cough Drops signed on as sponsor; Todd Russell, as M.C.

From the very first show, Framer encouraged would-be contestants to write telling him why they needed help. Bags of mail began to arrive at his office each week. He and several secretaries dug into the mound of letters to come up with provocative candidates. Some 20 of the best were asked to appear each Sunday at the CBS Playhouse to tell their story directly to Framer and his staff. A half-dozen were picked with an eye toward contrast and overall audience appeal. One or two candidates also came out of the studio audience before each broadcast. Framer then briefly rehearsed them by explaining what to say and what not to say on the air.

Borrowing elements of *Queen for a Day* and *Take It or Leave It*, Framer's brainchild provided a platform for a contestant in dire straits to tell his story and then play a game whereby he could win up to $800 by answering easy general knowledge questions from five or so categories. A participant might risk anywhere from $5 to his entire capital on each question.

But it was the *Strike It Rich* Heart Line—in the form of a strategically placed telephone with calls from the off-stage voice of Framer—that really paid off for most contestants whether or not he or she won any cash from the questions. This dramatic device allowed listeners (and after 1951, viewers) across the country to phone in help in the form of money, goods, services, even jobs for the down and out. For sailor Jackie Mendoza, whose six-year-old son needed an operation for a clubfoot, $800 was phoned in from a California listener, as was an offer of free medical services from a Florida hospital.

On another broadcast, a young violin-playing prodigy told about the loss of his instrument and the need to strike it rich for $300 or $400 to replace it. After the lad finished his story and played a selection on a borrowed violin, the telephone rang in the control booth.

"Mr. Framer," the operator said, "Mr. Fritz Kreisler wants to talk with you."

"Put him on."

"Mr. Framer, I am at my New York apartment recuperating from a broken leg and watching your show. I want the little fellow to have my 3/4-size Stradivarius."

Framer immediately interrupted the program. "This is the Heart Line calling," his voice announced to millions of viewers. "Bring back on stage the young violinist. I want him to know that the famous virtuoso Fritz Kreisler has just called and would like to give him a Stradivarius to replace his stolen violin."[4]

Not too many calls were as spontaneous as Kreisler's generous offer. Most Helping Hand assistance was mapped out days, even weeks, in advance. "Calls were preset," explained Framer in a 1985 interview. "We'd arrange with donors to phone in gifts for a particular contestant. If a widow with six children came on to explain the pressing need for a new roof for her house, we would contact ahead of time a roofer to set up a donation of his services. He got a 'plug' for his company, and if the woman had won some money, well, it was there for other necessities. If someone told about needing a sewing machine in order to take in work as a dressmaker, a firm like Singer might donate a machine—if it had been called in advance of the contestant's appearance."[5]

After the program added television to its schedule—on TV it ran as both a daytime and a weekly prime-time show—Framer and sponsor Colgate-Palmolive introduced the Helping Hand celebrity. In exchange for a chance to say a few words about a new movie, play, book, song or other accomplishment, a well-known personality answered questions as a "helping hand" for a nonplaying needy contestant. Eddie Cantor, Jackie Gleason, Merle Oberon, Burt Lancaster, George Jessel, Ronald Reagan and countless other notables pitched in to help with the answers.

For the downtrodden with a sob story, it became a no-lose situation. No one went away empty-handed. People everywhere vied to gain a berth on *Strike It Rich*. Television added to its drawing power, and a new M.C. augmented the heart-tugging aspects of this wildly successful series.

Warren Hull had first met Framer when the Warner Bros. actor came to Pittsburgh to promote a picture. A capable player in more than 35 "B" movies in the days of double features, Hull also worked as a radio announcer in the 1930s. He appeared on *Your Hit Parade,* the *Bea Lillie Show* and *Good News of 1939.* In 1941 he won the job as cointerviewer with Parks Johnson on *Vox Pop,* traveling around the country putting on shows before servicemen. He had just finished a stint on *Spin to*

Win for Goodson-Todman Productions when Walt Framer ran into him on Madison Avenue.

"I need an M.C. to replace Todd Russell. Are you interested, Warren?"

From a Quaker background, Hull had looked upon the program as one of radio's few public service efforts that came to the aid of the despondent and problem-ladened.

"I love the 'help your neighbor' idea," he replied. "I'd do it for scale."[6]

Hull found a show that suited both his talents and his own beliefs. It gave him an inward feeling of satisfaction to help the less fortunate. Often tearful as he coaxed participants to tell their stories, Hull genuinely seemed to understand how hard life could be at times and the difficulty some people had in getting back on their feet. "And those radiant bedroom eyes of his," recalled announcer and fill-in M.C. Ralph Paul, "added to the intensity he brought to the show."[7] Later, as *Strike It Rich* encountered a period of complaints and criticisms, it was especially hard for Hull to fathom such attacks on what he saw as doing good deeds in full view of a vast audience.

Soon after the program reached nighttime TV and more than 7 million homes, Jack Gould took a contemptuous dislike to the proceedings, writing that it "callously exploits human anxiety to sell the products of a soap manufacturer and does it with a saccharine solicitude that hits the jackpot in bad taste." He termed it "a giveaway warped beyond belief" and "an instance of commercial television gone beserk."[8]

His denunciation was chiefly based on the tale of a young mother—deserted by her husband—who said she was going to give up her baby for adoption unless she quickly got some money. Moreover, the woman had recently undergone an operation. "I just have to make it. I'm just hoping God's with me."

Gould criticized the buildup of suspense. Would she be able to answer the questions and get the money so desperately needed? Or would she fail and face continued misery?

The woman struggled through the quiz questions, answering four correct for a cash award of $500. A moist-eyed Warren Hull wiped away a tear. Then a commercial with a glamorous movie star for a deodorant interrupted the vignette of human emotions.

Offers of help arrived, including one from the studio audience. A man volunteered a $40 monthly stipend until the young mother found another husband. "Is this entertainment?" Gould asked. "The crises that occur in the lives of individuals must not become grist for the morbid mill of TV."[9]

A feud developed between Gould and Framer over what the *Times* writer called TV's most miserable misery show. "I ran into him one day," Framer remembered, "and asked him a very pertinent question.

"Jack, on what page of the paper does your column appear?"

"Why do you ask?"

"On that page and on the front page, too, you have a lot of misery stories. Doesn't the *Times* sell papers out of misery? What is most news? Few good things appear on the front page."

"But that's different, Walt. You're directly making money out of hard luck."

"Listen, Jack. Your salary is being paid out of misery news."[10]

Framer claimed that every time Gould wrote a scathing column on *Strike It Rich* the ratings went up.*

But the fast-talking producer had no reply to a troublesome incident that made national headlines. A young disheveled man filled out an audience-participation card, stating that he wanted to win some money to bring his family to New York from Texas where he had had some problems. He hoped to make a fresh start in the city. Framer chose him to tell the story of hardships faced by his wife and four children.

With $165 of winnings in his pocket, the contestant lost little time in leaving the CBS theater. A few days later the program was repeated on an Austin, Texas, station. A local sheriff saw the show and recognized the fellow as an ex-convict who had been indicted for theft and embezzlement and then had fled the state. Framer was immediately called to explain how a fugitive got on the program. Meanwhile, a 13-state alarm went out. Police traced the Texan to Pennsylvania and two weeks later nabbed him in upstate New York.[11]

"The newspapers had a field day with that episode," remembered Framer. "When I faced this guy after his arrest, I said to him, 'you knew the minute you went on the air, the authorities would be on your tail.' He replied, 'Yeah, but I had to take the chance.' Well, at least, he got his family all together for a short time."[12]

The incident was grist for the mill of high-placed critics. The Travelers Aid Society now complained that *Strike It Rich* was luring prospective contestants to New York.[13] The society noted that ever since Major Bowes' *Original Amateur Hour* of the 1930s persons had been coming to the organization for help returning home.

Would-be—and destitute—contestants from around the country were arriving in New York and ending up on relief. The city's Department of Welfare decided to crack down, denouncing the show as an unlicensed "welfare agency" for the public solicitation of money. It or-

---

*After the quiz scandals killed off nearly all game shows, Gould called to say that he thought it wasn't fair to include Framer's programs. "You've been had," he concluded. Interview with Walt Framer, April 24, 1985.

dered an examination of Framer's books and records and called on him
to stop luring people who later go on some sort of welfare. Framer
denied the allegation, saying that all contributions were voluntary, and
therefore, the Welfare Department had no jurisdiction. The program
would continue even without official approval, he declared.[14] Framer
also wondered why the department objected to people already on welfare going on the show when it might offer a way for them to find a
job.[15]

Welfare Commissioner Henry L. McCarthy asserted that 55 families
had come to New York in search of easy money from the program and
had ended up on the dole within the first nine months of 1953. "To
dramatize his claim," Framer said, "he arranged for a destitute family
of hopefuls to arrive at the bus terminal in the middle of the night.
Reporters and photographers were alerted by his office. This couple
and their nine children were then warned by McCarthy that his people
would no longer "be responsible for any indigent fortune seekers."[16]

"He wanted to run for mayor," according to Framer. "McCarthy
thought the publicity would strengthen his chance. He took us to court
where Warren Hull and I were charged with fundraising without a
license."[17]

Strike It Rich was found guilty of the violation, but the Manhattan
Court ruled that local authorities had no jurisdiction over the relation-
ship between the show and its nationwide TV audience. The magis-
trate stated that if the program wasn't aired before a studio audience
he would have dismissed the charge. Framer agreed to two of the Welfare Department's demands: to investigate the background of each and
every contestant and to warn the home audience not to come to New
York unless specifically invited to do so by the program. In effect, the
show eliminated contestants chosen from a studio audience, as well as
"helping hands."[18]

"And once again, this agitation helped the ratings," Framer added.[19]

The flareup set off by the charges sparked a state legislative inquiry
and a congressional review. Albany gave the show a clean bill of health.
In Washington, however, Representative Katherine St. George of New
York introduced a bill to require station licensees to investigate persons
and organizations on whose behalf contributions were solicited on radio and TV programs.[20] Mrs. St. George also criticized what she said
was the practice of placing U.S. armed forces personnel on *Strike It
Rich*. "Our servicemen are well taken care of," she noted, "and do not
need the type of help solicited by the show."[21]

In the midst of the fray, the Providence *Journal-Bulletin* announced
that it was dropping *Strike It Rich* from its radio-TV listings because of
public attention called to "certain radio and television broadcasts which
deliberately exploit human want and misery for commercial gain."[22]

The Rhode Island paper also dropped two other so-called "agony programs": NBC Radio's Chicago-based *Welcome Travelers* and NBC-TV's daytime series *On Your Account*.* Framer protested the move, charging news censorship, despite the disavowal of such intent by the newspaper.

Strike It Rich with all its merits and faults continued high in popularity almost to the end of its 11-year run. After many battles and barbs, Framer preferred to remember the hundreds of needy people given a boost. The paraplegic war veteran using his winnings and offers of kitchenware to open a diner he called Strike It Rich. The father seeking money to pay for an expensive drug to treat his young son's leukemia. The widowed mother of five made fatherless by a hit-and-run driver receiving a special check from the program's Heart Line fund. The choir of blind Negro gospel singers gaining a helping hand for a traveling van for concert tours.

More than 2,000 individuals, Framer estimated, were helped from 1947 to 1958. After prime-time quizzes left the air, he, his wife and seven children settled in Miami. There, he went into real estate and tourist development. But to the end of his life he never gave up his interest in game shows. In the 1970s he tried to interest the city fathers in airing "Make It Big," whereby a contestant nominated the "big" person in his or her life, and "The Great Escape," with all-expense trips to couples who answered world travel questions.[23]

Walter Framer, who died in Miami in 1988, even thought about doing a new helping-hand series, bringing back many of the contestants of the 1940s and 1950s to give an update on their lives since striking it rich. "Wouldn't that provide a new chapter in the great American book of dreams!" he often exclaimed.

On Your Account contestants related their hard-luck tales to a panel that picked the most deserving participant.

›17‹

"The One, The Only—Groucho"

That Groucho Marx, the wittiest and most outspoken of the zany Marx Brothers, had failed to link up with radio in a big way by the 1940s seemed incomprehensible. Nearly every major comedian of vaudeville, Broadway and the movies took to the microphone like a duck to water. Only Groucho was relegated to guest appearances and was never able to land his own show, particularly after the celebrated brother act of Groucho, Harpo and Chico wound up its MGM contract with "The Big Store" in 1941. In due course, Groucho's efforts as a single performer happily would lead to a radio show—an outstanding series that also transferred readily to television and cast aside more industry barriers and social taboos than possibly any other program at the time.

Fifty-five year old Groucho had mastered nearly every form of entertainment, yet faltered on the air. Then in the mid-1940s, several skits on the Rudy Vallee *Sealtest Show* brought the promise of a new start. Pabst Beer signed him for a program with tenor Kenny Baker and actress Virginia O'Brien, but it did not catch fire and was dropped. By the spring of 1947, Groucho, with time to spare, eagerly signed for a two-hour all-star special emceed by Bob Hope. "We were to do a sketch in which Hope was running a radio station in the middle of the Sahara," Marx wrote in his autobiography *The Secret Word Is GROUCHO*, "and I would be playing a traveling salesman."[1]

On the broadcast, Hope read from the script: "Why Groucho Marx! What are you doing out here in the Sahara Desert?"

"Desert, hell," he extemporized. "I've been standing in a drafty corridor for 45 minutes."

This broke up the audience, as well as Hope, who in his laughter dropped the entire script. Groucho casually stepped on it.[2]

The two comics proceeded to ad-lib, and before anyone could stop them, they made an absolute shambles of the carefully prepared show.

"Can you ad-lib like that all the time?" radio producer John Guedel asked after the broadcast.

"I've ad-libbed a whole Broadway show many a time."

"You're so much better ad-libbing than trading scripted gags with a stooge," the cocreator of *People Are Funny* observed. "It gives you more credibility. You ought to work with real people."[3]

Marx neglected to tell Guedel that he had already been approached to succeed Phil Baker on *Take It or Leave It.* Five others also were sounded out and auditioned. Groucho's performance was well received, but Eddie Cantor got the nod.

Guedel and Bernie Smith, the West Coast producer for *We, the People,* then thought about a game format where the free-spirited comic of "A Night at the Opera" and "Duck Soup" could ad-lib with contestants. Groucho was lukewarm to a game show. In the early 1930s he and his brothers had performed in an original radio comedy, *Flywheel, Shyster and Flywheel.* One of the funniest series of the season, it nevertheless was dropped by sponsor Esso gasoline after 26 weeks. Groucho resented the action.[4] Fifteen years later, his standards on what he would and would not do remained high.

Guedel convinced him to cut an audition disc for the quiz. As a result they became partners, each putting up $125 to make the recording. Groucho made the decision to appear in his own character, playing himself and not a clown. Bernie Smith asked him to wear his characteristic swallowtail coat and fake mustache. Groucho refused. Smith explained that the public, and particularly the studio audience, wouldn't know who he was without his familiar movie artifacts. The coat stayed in the closet, but Groucho agreed to grow a mustache.[5]

For the audition a handful of contestants faced Groucho, his questions and his barbs. Pleased with the results, Guedel took the program, which he called *You Bet Your Life,* to the networks. All turned it down, so he decided to sell it directly to a client. In *Daily Variety,* he spotted an item announcing that the president of Elgin-American Compact Company was coming to Hollywood to sign Phil Baker for the new quiz *Everybody Wins.* Guedel called the Elgin executive on his arrival at the Beverly Hills Hotel and urged him to listen to a record of Groucho's show. Elgin's president heard the disc and bought the idea.* Guedel then took the package to ABC, which agreed to air *You Bet Your Life,* beginning October 27, 1947.[6]

---

*Suddenly without a sponsor, Phil Baker fired his press agent for placing the item in the trade columns before the deal with Elgin was actually signed.

Not unlike *Take It or Leave It*, the format was simple. A pair of players tried to answer a group of questions in a category of their choice; if the duo were the biggest winners of the three couples on the half-hour program, they got a chance at a jackpot question. A "secret word" gimmick, thrown in at the last minute on the audition disc, became an inspired piece of plotting and a chance for players to split an extra $100. If a contestant inadvertently said the secret word—"something you see every day"—a toy duck suddenly dropped down from the ceiling to interrupt the proceedings.

On the day before the initial broadcast, director Robert Dwan first learned that Groucho would be prerecorded on large acetate discs. Apparently, somebody in the network hierarchy had gotten nervous over his notorious ad-libs and salty asides. By prerecording, cuts and edits could be made to satisfy any station censor.[7]

You Bet Your Life went over the air from 33 ⅓ rpm platters spun on turntables. Before the close of the 1947–48 season, Bing Crosby's staff at ABC switched to newly introduced audiotape for his prerecorded Philco series. Groucho followed suit, and soon all major shows of ABC went onto reels.

Groucho's bow was far from an overnight sensation. Most listeners felt his genuine comic talent was underused in a show that never really came off. Only occasionally did his explosive banter register several notches above the level of the average quizmaster and carry a quality of freshness about it. It remained a rather unoriginal quiz with a run of uninspired participants. One day, the critics noted, Groucho happily will get a break over the air: he will be assigned to a program without a stylized format, and his comedy will be truly integrated into radio.[8]

If, in the fall of 1947, a clairvoyant had proclaimed that Marx would develop into one of the snappiest quizmasters, win an Emmy as the Most Outstanding Personality of 1950 and figure as the focal point of a weekly half-hour of classic proportions, this seer would have been given the unending task to find—in the words of the then-current catchphrase—"the key to open Richard's door." Nonetheless, Guedel and his team wasted no time in revamping the readily apparent weak spots. They quickly found out that the audience wanted the quiz section to be more seriously conducted. The contestants might be taken over ego-shattering coals only minutes before, but when as much as $1,000 or more was at stake, the game segment had to get down to business.[9]

Initially, Guedel wanted Groucho to meet the contestants before airtime. That procedure, however, diluted the show's unpredictability. Instead, participants were interviewed at length and coached by Guedel's assistants. Briefed with overview of a contestant's age, occupation and hometown, Groucho, assisted by several jokewriters, prepared his lines, drawing upon his innate wit and a 40-year inventory of impertinent retorts and sharp quips.

Yet it was the choice—and combination—of contestants that provided the fuel for Groucho's sure-fire response. Hollywood itself seemed to attract adventuresome and colorful people, and Guedel capitalized on their easy availability. Later, he would scout the country for offbeat players. On a single show, he would team up a spinster and a bachelor, a librarian and a wrestler, a man with 13 children and a female Gallup pollster, a druggist and a gravedigger's wife. The team members generally had opposite tastes, vocations or quirks, and this allowed for a wide latitude of vocal trickery by the nimble Marx.

When a contestant on a particular program developed mike fright and was unable to speak, Groucho said, "Either this man is dead, or my watch is stopped." Interviewing a tree surgeon, he asked, "Have you ever fallen out of any of your patients?" When a contestant gave her age as "approaching 40," he quipped, "From which direction?" Another participant said he had gone to school at San Francisco State. "Was that a college or a reformatory?" he remarked.

From time to time, Groucho was guilty of a few rough cracks. He'd rib a druggist for charging $2 for a prescription that cost 20 cents, and draw from a wrestler a denial that matches were fixed. "It was all done in the spirit of levity, however," reassured *Variety*, "and none but the hyper-critical could take umbrage." [10]

During the first season, Groucho became a special favorite of both intellectuals and children and never fell out of favor with them. His popularity with academics led to the presentation of the prestigious Peabody Award, given by the University of Georgia School of Journalism in 1948.

At the end of the customary 39-week run that spring, both Guedel and Smith faced the traditional summer break whereby a "replacement" held the reins for the star and his time slot for some three months. They worried over having to build the show up again in the fall once it left the dial. Since the series had been recorded, it occurred to them they could take the 13 best broadcasts and run them again instead of a summer fill-in. ABC agreed after some fast talking by Guedel who made up a claim that the average listener hears a series only once of every 3.4 times that it is on. Thus *You Bet Your Life* successfully inaugurated the concept of the "rerun." [11]

In June 1949, at the end of the second season, Guedel realized that he had a potentially long-running property. But he said to Groucho one day, "It's never going to be a total smash unless we move it from ABC to one of the two other major networks. We're going to want to sell the show to TV, but it's not moving there unless the ratings are even higher." [12]

In October 1949, Groucho switched to CBS and a Wednesday night berth. Within a month, the show shot up to sixth place in the ratings and stayed at that level. At the end of the year, DeSoto-Plymouth auto dealers became sponsors, allocating a reputed $27 out of every car sale to pay for the program. "Tell 'em Groucho sent you" now became a familiar signoff of the DeSoto-backed shows. As the quiz ended its third season in 1950, it prepared for its television debut—and still another network, NBC, as home base.

The transition required few changes. The basic stage platform and drapes remained. Director Robert Dwan proudly called the show the most static TV program ever produced. It certainly didn't bother viewers. Even critic Jack Gould welcomed it. "To Mr. Marx' credit, this is probably the first radio show that without material change holds interest on television." [13]

Guedel also convinced DeSoto to carry on with the radio version by using the sound track from the television show. NBC radio now aired Groucho on Wednesday night, and 24 hours later, NBC-TV played the video. [14] In other words, on Wednesday a listener heard all the gags; on Thursday the picture came. The duplication indicated that NBC had conceded publicly that a prime-time televiewer by 1950 was not apt to turn on his radio.

In a period when the overwhelming majority of television shows were live, John Guedel made his own rules. He not only filmed his half-hour series but used for the first time in television production a multi-camera 35mm system. This prevideotape setup allowed continuous run of the cameras, each of which contained only a ten-minute reel of film. A pair of cameras was pointed at Groucho; another two, at contestants; a third pair moved or panned from Groucho to each contestant; and still another two shot all three participants. Each set of cameras would shoot one and a half hours in all, providing plenty of good visual choices. [15]

You Bet Your Life played a significant part in breaking down the prevalent barriers of segregation between Negro and white musicians. Musical director Jerry Fielding (who replaced then-unknown Billy May after the first season) complained that Los Angeles had two musicians unions: one for blacks and another for Caucasians. Few blacks played network shows on the West Coast; most were paid less, and all had fewer union benefits. Fielding felt Groucho should hire them if they met his musical needs. He agreed. When Fielding met resistance from NBC, Groucho and Guedel backed him. An amalgamation between the two unions soon occurred, while, in the workplace, the Groucho team was already bringing all musicians together. [16]

Members of most minority groups also gained significant exposure on television—many for the first time—through the efforts of Guedel and his coworkers. "I realized the audience was made up of a whole lot of minorities," Bernie Smith explained. "We're all minority groups," he added. Coming from a Smith, that was quite a concession! He made sure some ethnic group was represented on nearly every show. Within a year, he covered practically everybody and always tried to put them in a sympathetic situation.[17]

Along with minorities, famous Americans and would-be celebrities faced the cameras—although many well-known individuals did not want to match wits and risk a public put-down by "the one, the only—Groucho." General Omar Bradley made a memorable appearance out of uniform and was paired with a soldier from the audience. (Groucho had the GI tell him everything that was bad about the army.) In 1957 comedienne Phyllis Diller made her first TV appearance with Groucho and baritone John Charles Thomas came out of retirement to play *You Bet Your Life*. Future novelist William Peter Blatty split a $10,000 jackpot in 1960 and then quit his job to write books. A dozen years later, he achieved fame as author of *The Exorcist*. A young Californian named John A. Ford caused a stir. BBD&O, DeSoto's ad agency, said Guedel could not have a Ford on a DeSoto show, so they changed his name. Ford was the son of a Los Angeles County supervisor, and the different moniker did not sit well with many local viewers.

The person Groucho most wanted to have on his show was the character actress Margaret Dumont, the haughty dowager and long-suffering comic foil in many Marx Brothers films. But she wouldn't do it unless Guedel paid her a fee, and the show did not pay celebrity contestants—the only money changing hands came from what they won, along with a reimbursement for any air fare.[18]

Groucho fans, as well as everyone connected with the show, remember contestant Ramiro Gonzalez Gonzalez, a clever but uneducated Mexican with hopes for a movie career. A low-paid TV crew worker at WOAI in San Antonio, he found himself in a position to do a comedy routine, including a dancing bit with the statuesque and sexy Dagmar of late night TV, on a local telethon hosted by Walter O'Keefe. M.C. O'Keefe urged Gonzalez Gonzalez to go to California to try to break into show business. He also told Groucho about the incredibly funny Mexican. *You Bet Your Life* sent him carfare to come to Hollywood and do a show.[19]

During the broadcast, Groucho made great sport of Gonzalez' double name.

"What does your wife call you—Ramiro or Gonzalez?"

"She call me Pedro."

"Where are you from, Mr. Gonzalez Gonzalez—Walla Walla?"

"San Antonio, Te-has."

Then Gonzalez showed how he could dance, grabbing at his teammate, an attractive young girl. As he danced, he sang the tune's lyrics in a meld of Spanish and broken English.

During the quiz, Gonzalez kept looking up, trying to get the toy duck with the secret word to come down. After answering the third question, he asked if he could stop; the money won so far could buy lots of beans and tortillas for his wife and three kids. The audience broke into helpless laughter.

Overnight, the country took him to its heart. Groucho described him as the most naturally funny person who ever appeared on his show. Others tagged him the Mexican Jerry Lewis. He signed a personal contract with John Wayne and made several westerns and performed at rodeos and county fairs. His contribution to better Mexican-American relations was so appreciated that San Antonio named a municipal park after him.

By the mid-1950s, the combined radio-TV audience of *You Bet Your Life* numbered some 40 million people. Occasionally, sight gags that didn't play on radio would be cut from the radio tape but were kept on television. The radio version was the last prime-time commercial quiz carry-over of network radio. For several seasons, the show ran neck and neck with top-rated *I Love Lucy* and *Dragnet*, justifying Groucho's NBC contract guaranteeing him $760,000 annually over a ten-year period, plus $4,800 weekly for the 39 weeks the program was on the air. Guedel, too, gained handsomely. He pulled in some $300,000 a year and 13 percent on the net profits.[20]

Groucho's announcer George Fenneman relished his long stint as straight man and scorekeeper on *You Bet Your Life*. "I pinched myself regularly," he said of this association, "to make sure that a kid who planned to be a schoolteacher could find himself on the same stage with one of the master wits of all time."[21] The debonair, knowledgeable Fenneman won a large following of his own and briefly emceed his own TV quiz, *Anybody Can Play*, for Guedel and Salem Cigarettes.

Guedel weathered the quiz scandals and investigations and even outlasted DeSoto when auto production ceased for that Chrysler division in December 1960. New sponsors, Toni Home Permanents and Old Gold Cigarettes, stepped in. Ratings, however, had dropped to a low point: fewer than 10 million homes were tuned in to *You Bet Your Life*. The season limped to an end. With no renewals in sight, the last show, number 528, aired on June 29, 1961.

That fall, Guedel created for Groucho a new type of audience-participation vehicle during which contestants appeared to talk about some problem. *Tell It to Groucho* lasted 20 shows. Then NBC decided to rerun selected shows from the late 1950s, calling them *The Best of Groucho*. But the effort floundered. Next followed a spinoff version in England, but Groucho failed to register with the British. Most of the time, they hadn't the foggiest notion of what he was talking about.[22]

In the early 1970s Groucho tried to interest NBC in syndicating the show. The network, however, considered the program too slow and old-fashioned. Besides, it was filmed in black and white, and most TV audiences had become color conscious. A year or so later, NBC called Guedel to tell him they were going to destroy the prints from all 11 years of *You Bet Your Life* because they needed the storage space. Would he like a set for old-time sake, they asked.

"Stop! Right now! Send them all to me," he shouted. Two hundred thirty-five negatives and 1,600 prints arrived by air express from New York to Guedel's garage. Eventually, Guedel persuaded a friend, John Reynolds, manager of KTLA in Los Angeles, to take a chance and air them. The station agreed to pay $54.88 a broadcast. These reruns for late-night viewers drew encouraging ratings, and Guedel and Groucho leased the rights from NBC and put the series into national syndication. Stations near and far picked up the vintage telecasts, and a new Groucho cult emerged. Soon the old partners were splitting more than $50,000 a year from frequent airings of the golden age quiz. A dozen people shared in residuals, including George Fenneman who collected nearly $20,000 a year, or seven times the original salary he made starting out with Groucho.[23]

At the time Groucho Marx died in August 1977 at age 86, he had not appeared on a TV series in 15 years nor played a movie role in 25 years. Yet his outrageous, improbable humor preserved on celluloid and rerun again and again lured and captivated both old and new fans. The one-time radio dropout remained a timeless hit.

› 18 ‹

High Comedy, Low Stakes

The good fortune of Groucho with *You Bet Your Life* encouraged co-medians, searching for a place in television, to consider a role as quiz-master. "The one, the only" Groucho Marx made the job look like child's play. Others attempted to emulate his success. Fred Allen tried with *Judge for Yourself.* His show selected three persons from the audience to rate professional acts that performed during the half-hour program. A second panel of judges from the entertainment world also rated the acts. The amateur critic who rated them in the same order as the show business pros won a thousand dollars; if the outcome was a tie, the prize was divided. But the program failed to catch fire for this veteran comic and lasted only through the 1953–54 season.

Humorist Herb Shriner had better luck. His *Two for the Money* made the grade. It had not been easy for producers to classify Shriner. He was part comedian and part musician, a combination of humorist Will Rogers, buffoon Bob Burns and harmonica virtuoso Borah Minnevitch.

Raised in Indiana, Shriner first performed in a Fort Wayne amateur show while he was in high school. A radio producer heard the teen-ager and invited him to make his broadcast bow on a program called *Hoosier Hop*, which CBS beamed to many parts of the country. Herb soon gathered a half-dozen friends, taught them all how to play the harmonica and became the proud leader of the "Harmaniacs."

After a year of radio work and personal appearances in Indiana and Ohio, the act broke up. But Shriner went out as a solo performer, add-ing his own homespun comedy between the musical numbers. Book-ings on the West Coast led to a radio spot on the popular *Camel Cara-van* in 1942. When the show was revamped a year later, Herb became a sidekick to M.C. Jack Carson. On his own, he was featured on the *Chesterfield Supper Club* and the Philip Morris program, *Johnny Presents.*

But Shriner never fully captivated radio audiences. A daily postwar stint, *Herb Shriner Time*, with Raymond Scott and his quintet, failed to lead to prime time. Television held greater promise.

While Shriner was wondering if video might revitalize his career, Goodson-Todman were making plans to mount a quiz similar to Groucho's. In 1952 they took a look at Shriner and then signed him to a Groucho-like post for Old Gold's *Two for the Money*, getting double exposure for their vehicle by simulcasting it over NBC radio and television. A sidekick was needed. The producers decided to bring in one far removed from show business. A Harvard Ph.D. and professor of philosophy at Rutgers University named Mason Gross met their requirements as a quiz moderator and subject-matter authority. Not a complete greenhorn, he had been the host of the short-lived ABC-TV quiz *Think Fast* a few seasons earlier. The pedagogic-looking Dr. Gross was well cast and gained wide recognition far from his campus. Later, when his video days came to an end, he assumed the presidency of Rutgers, and a decade later, the presidency of the Guggenheim Foundation.

Herb Shriner found his comic quiz niche with Old Gold, his fourth association with a cigarette sponsor. He injected his own down-home Hoosier wit, drawn upon personal observation and a vivid imagination—with the help of scriptwriters. In retrospect, his television career was much too brief. He left *Two for the Money* in 1956 and was succeeded by Dennis James and finally by Sam Levenson, a schoolteacher-turned-comic.

By 1955 Edgar Bergen stood as the last top-billed comedian of prime-time network radio still not on a television series. After nearly 20 years at a microphone and facing a dwindling choice of national sponsors, ventriloquist Bergen and his alter ego Charlie McCarthy had to either retire from the air or regroup on the video screen. Bergen opted for the latter and a comedy vehicle called *Do You Trust Your Wife?* The game was played by two competing married couples, each of whom had to decide if the husband or wife would try to answer a particular question asked by Bergen. To what extent the husband "trusted" his wife to take the question added an element of suspense and tomfoolery. The player who wrote down the correct answer first scored points.

A latecomer among television comedy quizzes, Bergen apparently lost interest in the show after a year on CBS. The series, however, departed in a blaze of publicity and prize money. The final contestants tallied up a 23-week string of wins. All in all, Erik Gude, an engineer from Southern California, and his wife, Helena, chalked up total winnings of $120,800.* This windfall was then placed by the producers in

*The prize money and notoriety led to a near-kidnapping of their three-year-old daughter. Interview with Karl-Erik Gude, December 5, 1990.

a Bank of America trust fund paying them an ongoing prize of $100 a week for the next 23 years.[1]

The series, retitled *Who Do You Trust?* returned after a six-month hiatus with a new comedian-host. Revamped with comic questions, off-beat contestants and lower stakes, it afforded M.C. Johnny Carson an opportunity to display his taunting, glib humor. Abetted by a relatively unknown announcer from Philadelphia named Ed McMahon, Carson attracted a large following, especially among teenagers, for his afternoon game session. Aired from ABC in New York, it was for Carson and McMahon a stepping stone to the *Tonight Show* and a record-breaking association with insomniacs.

Earlier in the decade, another future *Tonight Show* host tried out his hosting skills as quizmaster. Comedian Jack Paar held the reins on two short-lived programs: a current events quiz called *Up to Paar* and a movie-inspired game tagged *Bank on the Stars.*

The fact that certain verbal-oriented quizzes worked on television did not go unnoticed. Quiz producers sized up early TV audiences and readily found a high degree of acceptance for basic word games and straightforward panel shows without much visual input. The mere presence of celebrity players as contestants, panelists or mystery guests, as well as a number of offbeat quizmasters, fascinated viewers of the 1950s. The first generation of TV fans became a party to what, in retrospect, were the halcyon days of video panels.

"I never cease to marvel that I am paid money for this at all," exclaimed one avocational quizmaster at the height of the panel show popularity.[2] Bergen Evans, a university lecturer, former Rhodes Scholar and author, referred to his extracurricular job as a quiz host for *Down You Go,* a word game devised by Louis Cowan as an adaptation of the old parlor game, "Hang the Butcher." Cowan selected the Northwestern University professor of English for his erudition, wit and authoritativeness. Like Mason Gross, Evans seemed an anomaly in show business. But he had actually appeared as a regular panelist on Mike Wallace's show, *Majority Rule,* in Chicago in the late 1940s.

As *Down You Go* quizmaster, Evans deftly conjured up his own sprightly clues for questions on book and song titles, quotations and expressions, for which his panelists—Robert Breen, Francis Coughlan, Carmelita Pope and Toni Gilman—were provided only blank lines on a blackboard, indicating the number of words and letters in them. The requirements for clues were exacting. Although they had to be factually true, hints were purposely distorted and confusing. Evans played his role with a scholarly bent and a flair for showmanship.

In 20 years as a teacher, he had spent a lot of time delving into the evolution of words and phrases and the background of subject matters that many years later would become quiz-question sources.

"Something that's been around a lot," was his first clue for "used car." Later, he added another clue. "This is a rattling good buy . . . . this is what comes of having been driven too far. You may go for this, but it's not certain whether it will do the same for you." Then he noted that there used to be quite a lively business in used coaches and chariots, quoting passages from Sterne's *A Sentimental Journey*.[3]

Sponsored by the ubiquitous Old Gold cigarette over the DuMont chain, Bergen Evans admitted that he did not envy out-and-out hucksters on television. "Some unhappy masters of ceremonies on top of all this have to eat cheese and crackers, drink soup, or deodorize themselves, interlarding their cues, clues, and quips with rapturous dithyrambs in praise of the product. These," he concluded, "are the prices of the profession."[4] Before he lit his last Old Gold on the series, the profession honored him with a Peabody Award for excellence in broadcasting.

By 1951, the year of the debut of Dr. Evans and *Down You Go*, tens of thousands of ex-servicemen of World War II had recently completed their studies for degrees under the GI Bill. Great literature, uncommon quotations, odd phrases and esoteric words now fell upon the ears of a larger and more responsive audience. The exposure to higher education by many Americans, who, in the past, would not have had an opportunity to dwell in halls of ivy, ostensibly contributed to the broad interest in panel games and the rise in a handful of intelligent and diverting shows.

Newscaster John K. M. McCaffrey moderated *Take a Guess*, whereby guests competed with Ernie Kovacs and three other panelists in trying to figure out words and sayings. *What's in a Word?* gave Clifton Fadiman the task of supplying a series of one-word clues to identify a mystery word. Players such as Faye Emerson, Mike Wallace and Audrey Meadows participated. John Daly, as moderator of *Who Said That?* tested the current events knowledge of the likes of Bob Considine, Wally Cox and Pat Carroll on the identification of authors of quotations taken from each week's news.

In the shadow of academia, *Answer Me This* proved a unique break from the commercially based word quizzes. Aired by WNHC-TV in New Haven, Connecticut, it was as close to the old *Information Please* as was possible to get. A completely gimmickless regional program with no prizes and a cavalier concern over scores, *Answer Me This* featured host Tom Romano of the station staff and panelists such as Fred Rodell, professor at the Yale Law School; James Egan, a Hartford attorney; Dick Banks of the Yale News Bureau; and Irma Thomas, a professional ice skater. Exceedingly good questions, augmented by spritely banter among the panel on subjects ranging from Broadway plays and eighteenth-century poetry to comic-strip heroes and song hits, provided, in the words of critic Jack Gould, "warm, civilized television—not spectacular, not 'bigtime,' just real."[5]

Another Ivy League environment contributed to the acceptance of a learned question-and-answer format. The University of Pennsylvania and CBS station WCAU of Philadelphia produced *What in the World?* The program employed popular quiz elements, with experts being called upon to identify items in the university's museum—an Indian mask, an old warrior's helmet, a whalebone spear, a male skull, and a ceremonial axe. Produced by Edythe J. Meserand—one of the earliest woman pioneers of broadcasting—this series combined game playing with learning. *What in the World?* held the interest of its audience light years before the establishment of public television channels, and its educational value was self-apparent.

Jack Gould and other media critics wondered if network television was perhaps overlooking a prime source of program material and participants. Throughout the country, they noted, there were plenty of cultural institutions as well as intelligent people who could add much to many types of quiz, panel and game shows.[6] Not untypically, the network centers held other firm ideas. To them, there was no business like show business—and from that field, they would virtually cultivate and harvest all the moderators, panelists and guests ever needed to stock a series.

Deft comedian Morey Amsterdam summed up the feelings of the army of performers and celebrities who found a permanent or temporary anchorage on panel and quiz shows. "Appearing on a game show is good fun, easy work, and great exposure. Besides, it pays well. Shows such as *Hollywood Squares* and *The Match Game* have been stimulating and informative to those of us playing the game as well as to viewers. Moreover, it's an ad-libber's heaven."[7]

Besides, many personalities close to that career zone best termed "over the hill" gained a reprieve because of panel assignments. Frequent visibility often brought a variety of lucrative "fringe" rewards: movie roles, commercial spots, summer stock leads, and public appearance opportunities. Panel work upped one's credit standing with the performers' guild as well as at the local bank.

For established stars and people of stature in other fields, fees were generally unimportant. Academy Award winners, state governors, major league ball players, symphony conductors, best-selling authors and college presidents, for the most part, cared little about the $500 or $600 stipend. Not infrequently they donated it to charity. They came aboard to plug themselves, to hype something of concern to them or simply to reaffirm the fact of their ongoing importance. Some words of promotion for a new film or book, a statement on the need to support an educational or scientific institution, or a reminder to vote in an upcoming election led many well-known figures to match their wits and skills on camera, as did many earlier on radio.

In the case of one particular game, it gave the guest celebrity an opportunity to dress up in full disguise and try to outwit a panel. *Masquerade Party* outfitted notables in elaborate costumes and heavy makeup and then paraded them before a quartet of questioners comprised of Ogden Nash, Ilka Chase, Buff Cobb and Peter Donald or perhaps Sam Levenson, Betsy Palmer, Jonathan Winters and Faye Emerson. Panelists were given clues by the costumes themselves as to the mystery guest's identity.

Hollywood's Jeanette MacDonald and husband Gene Raymond appeared as two old farmers wearing jeans. America's most famous bachelor girl of the early 1950s, Margaret Truman, came garbed as Dickens' spinster, Miss Havisham of *Great Expectations*. Costar of the song-filled Broadway success "South Pacific," Ezio Pinza, who introduced "Some Enchanted Evening," dressed as Santa Claus, representing Christmas and the most "enchanted eve" of all. Actress sisters Joan and Constance Bennett disguised themselves as the well-known Smith Bros., the bearded "Trade" and "Mark" of cough drop packages.[8]

Masquerade Party, first packaged by Ed Wolfe's "Break the Bank" shop, began as a summer replacement with host Bud Collyer in 1952. It returned for two subsequent summers before going on full time. The second master of ceremonies came from the CBS newsroom. Douglas Edwards considered exposure on *Masquerade Party* as complementary to the *Evening News*, which he anchored during those years.

"One night," Edwards recalled years later, "the actor Eddie Bracken appeared dressed as a rat—a visual reference to his Broadway and film role in 'Brother Rat.' During the course of the guessing, I became involved in a dispute with panelist Peter Donald over whether rats have short or long tails. He prevailed with the proper identity, reminding millions of viewers that rats, indeed, have long tails and mice, short ones."[9]

Edwards enjoyed emceeing this diverting interlude in the formative days of television. "But after two summers, CBS News decided it was not good policy for correspondents to host or appear on quiz shows, or in any way endorse a product."[10] Edwards did manage one final bow—in the guise of a mystery guest. He came on stage as a handsomely garbed King Edward, and the panel failed to identify their well-hidden former quiz liege.

By far the most pleasantly spontaneous panel show of the decade came into view in 1950, the same year as Groucho and *Beat the Clock*. *What's My Line?* outlasted both those programs and virtually every other series of early television. It broadcast live over CBS, becoming a Sunday-night fixture for 17 years. Ultimately, more than 2,000 half-hour

broadcasts of this occupation guessing game aired, spanning the pre–
Korean War days of the Truman administration to the Vietnam turmoil
of the LBJ White House.

The premise of *What's My Line?* was very simple. The game was played
before a studio audience by a panel of four bright, witty individuals, a
contestant with an interesting occupation, and a moderator. The occupation was revealed to everybody, but the panelists, who then, by asking only questions that can be answered with a "yes or "no," tried to
determine what the occupation was. The panel won by identifying the
occupation before ten "nos" were accumulated. In addition each program featured a mystery guest, a famous person whom everyone was
supposed to recognize at sight. The panelists were blindfolded before
playing this segment of the show.

In print, it sounded easy. In practice, it took a bit of doing to make
it work and thrive. The game evolved from an idea for a program called
Stop the Camera, which was the suggestion of Goodson-Todman's Bob
Bach. Sprinkled among the studio audience of this show were three or
four celebrities. The moderators placed a telephone call to a viewer
who was asked to watch the TV screen as a camera panned the audience. As soon as the contestant saw a familiar face, he would yell "Stop
the camera!" and then for a prize identify the celebrity in the closeup.
Sort of a visual "Stop the Music," it didn't really jell.[11]

Bach and his assistants then suggested seating a group of people
with different occupations on the stage and, as the camera panned the
lineup, let a contestant at home guess their jobs—more proletarian perhaps, but still off-target. Next, Mark Goodson came on the scene. He
mulled over the idea for weeks and finally boiled it down from a lineup
to a single individual. This person would come before a panel of four
questioners who would try to guess the contestant's occupation or
profession. After a number of informal run-throughs using various
members of the Goodson-Todman staff, the show with host John Daly
took shape in time for its first broadcast early in 1950 at CBS.

Producer Gil Fates remembered the first *What's My Line?* and wondered why CBS encouraged him to do a second. "John Daly was un-
comfortable, the panel was inept and unfunny, the direction was uncertain, and the set was lighted like a police line-up."[12]

After all the testing and tryouts, the panel on the premiere turned
out to be a very mixed bag: gossip columnist Dorothy Kilgallen, former
Governor of New Jersey Harold G. Hoffman, Park Avenue neuropsy-
chiatrist Richard Hoffman and poet-anthologist Louis Untermeyer.
Certainly not an all-star lineup. The mystery guest was Phil Rizzuto,
outstanding shortstop of the New York Yankees.

Critics had little to say about the opener, other than remark that
there was so little visual appeal about it that it might as well be on

radio. (In fact, a separate radio version did land on the dial two years later.) Some fast changes were made for a show that Goodson admitted many years later, had, at best, a chance of running six weeks.[13]

Governor Hoffman—later to have had a secret "line" as an embezzler—departed after two shows and was replaced in a stroke of superb casting by veteran game-show performer Arlene Francis. Doctor Hoffman quickly followed Governor Hoffman to the exit and soon was in the news as a party in a sticky lawsuit involving a rich female patient. Comedian Hal Block occupied his seat.

In the fall of 1950, *What's My Line*—now sponsored by a spray-on deodorant product called Stopette—moved to a permanent spot on Sunday nights and into the top ten programs of television. The following year, Louis Untermeyer unjustly fell under the stigma of McCarthy-inspired "red channels" hysteria and, after many boycott threats from various quarters, reluctantly agreed to relinquish his place on the panel. Publisher and author Bennett Cerf took his place.

Bennett Cerf developed into a real panel pro. A self-admitted "ham," he brought a touch of humor, an openness and a *joie de vie*. He already had a certain amount of radio and TV experience; in 1949 he appeared with John Daly on a CBS Sunday night quiz called *Riddle Me This*, which, lacking spark and pep, missed the mark by a considerable margin.[14] Being a man who sought a platform for his witty remarks and droll puns, he grabbed the chance to appear on *Line*, which, in turn, benefited from his laughter-provoking flashes. His contribution to the show was solid, although he claimed "no illusions" about himself. "John Daly is *What's My Line*," Cerf believed. "As for me, well, they could find two hundred and fifty people in two weeks who could replace me."[15] Goodson-Todman knew a great panelist when they had one; Cerf stayed until the end of the long run and even participated in a syndicated version that continued to air many months after his death in August 1971. By the end of the second season, the lineup of Cerf, Francis and Kilgallen became the video-age equivalent of radio's Kieran, Adams and Levant.

Other "regulars" in the early days were comedian-musician Steve Allen, who left in 1954 to start NBC's *Tonight Show*, and his replacement, Fred Allen, who played the game for 18 months and then suddenly collapsed from a fatal heart attack on a sidewalk one March night in 1956.* His vacant berth became the seat for a different guest panelist each week, and during the late 1950s and 1960s, they ranged from Errol Flynn, Elsa Maxwell and Ronald Reagan to Ernie Kovacs, Jane Powell and John Lindsay.

---

*Ironically, the producers of his antagonist *Stop the Music!* became his employers in TV where he ended his long career on one of their game shows.

The most amusing and unpredictable part of this twenty questions-like format came in the comparison of the inquiries with the actual occupation, of which the audience was told in advance. Gil Fates did admit, however, that before airtime the production staff, unbeknownst to John Daly, would suggest a line of questioning to one of the bright comedians on the panel that night. The comedian was never told the occupation. All he knew was that if he followed the suggested line of questioning he would get his laughs and a no answer at the end.[16] In the wake of the quiz scandals, the practice was dropped, even though there was a top prize of only $50 to each contestant and the staffers gave misinformation rather than legitimate information to the panelists.

Week after week, the production team faced great pressure to book specific people as regular contestants or mystery guests. Offers of cash, gifts and favors in exchange for inviting on the show certain celebrities or VIPs led Goodson-Todman to preclude the problem of payola by separating the functions of contestant finding and contestant booking.[17] From a list of potential candidates, producer Fates made the final selection on the basis of putting together the most entertaining and effective program possible that week.

Both completely unknown individuals and the most widely recognized personalities were amazed by the impact of a single brief appearance on What's My Line? Leading stage and screen actor Frederic March was stopped on the street so often in the days following his guest spot that he requested to see the kinescope of his appearance and figure out what was so special about it. When the producer of the film colossus "Around the World in 80 Days," Mike Todd, appeared, 30 million viewers had a special bonus; he brought along his bride of two weeks, Elizabeth Taylor. Architect Frank Lloyd Wright gave his candid opinion of the Big Apple in answer to panelist Faye Emerson's question, "Mr. Wright, what do you think of New York City?" Said "live" coast to coast: "Miss Emerson, I never think of New York City."[18] Both Gerald Ford and Jimmy Carter appeared on the syndicated run in 1969 and 1973, respectively. Congressman Ford stumped the panel. Carter, then governor of Georgia, was identified by Gene Shalit after the seventh no answer, and in Fates' cryptic program notes on that particular show, Carter was described as a "very charming man. Good interview. Good spot."[19]

For no planned or apparent reason, two comedians tied the all-time record for mystery guest appearances. Milton Berle and Art Carney claimed seven apiece. Occasionally, much humor came from noncomedians. Actress Marilyn Maxwell gave the network a jolt when asked by Bennett Cerf, "Are you a girl?" In a high-pitched voice, she answered, "Last time I looked."[20]

Several incidents involving black guests and panelists reminded Goodson-Todman that pockets of racial prejudice remained. When Arlene Francis kissed mystery guest Ella Fitzgerald on January 21, 1962, there was a "murderous" outcry.[21] Earlier in June 1961, panelist Harry Belafonte, seated between Arlene and Dorothy Kilgallen, caused such a stir that a dozen southern stations dropped the show for several months.[22]

Of the 2,500 occupations presented to the panel, one of the more interesting was uncovered in the summer of 1955. The job of elephant keeper for the Jones Beach, Long Island, Marine Amphitheatre musical "Arabian Nights" was a pip. Jim Mitchell easily stumped the panel. But a viewer in Detroit recognized him under the guise of a different occupation. He was the man who had stolen his car and was now sought by the Michigan police. The next day, the FBI arrived at the Goodson-Todman office and soon tracked down Mitchell. His $50 check for outwitting the panel was sent in care of his jail cell.[23]

By the mid-1960s, *What's My Line?* had slipped in popularity. A major blow struck the show in November 1965. The irrepressible Dorothy Kilgallen died in her sleep. A skilled and determined player, she had gained a legion of fans as well as a host of belittlers. Nevertheless, she was a drawing card who had worked hard on 712 shows.

A dip in ratings soon disturbed *Line*. In the words of Fates: "A dose of relaxant, an occasional injection of surprise, would have relieved the creative constipation from which the program suffered."[24] But John Daly refused to give an inch to all the suggested invigorating changes. Daly wanted to ride out the series in low gear, and no one pushed too hard the experienced, proficient M.C. and perhaps the dean of all TV panel moderators.

What's My Line? quietly slipped off live television on September 3, 1967—but not before siring a small stable of other Goodson-Todman thoroughbreds and *Line* lookalikes: *The Name's the Same, I've Got a Secret* and *To Tell the Truth*.

Practically a dead ringer for the Daly-led panel show, *The Name's the Same* brought forth a succession of individuals bearing the same names as celebrities and historical figures. A panel had a total of 30 or so chances to guess a contestant's identity through yes or no answers. Bowing in December 1951, the show featured Robert Q. Lewis as M.C. He readily copied the mannerisms and inflections of *Line's* John Daly, mimicking the nodding head, hesitant reply, and raised eyebrow.[25]

After a season or two, the scope of participants was extended to the relatives of the famous (Jack Benny's daughter; Pee-Wee Reese's wife) and to individuals with an "unusual action name" (Mrs. Will Tickle). Occasionally, a person with a name "as same as a thing" was subjected to cross-examination. When Mrs. A. Husband of Wilkes-Barre, Pennsylvania, came in front of the panel, radio-TV actress Joan Alexander asked, "Is it something good to have around the house?" Believing the name was a piece of furniture, she then queried, "If you don't take care of them, will they sag in the middle?" Encouraged by a positive response, she asked, "Could you re-stuff them?" The laughs were long and loud.[26]

Guest stars appeared with a "special wish," usually an inane whim. Hollywood's Rhonda Fleming came with the wish to give Bob and Ray a good luck kiss on their becoming the show's comoderators in 1955. In the same vein, Van Johnson, then in New York shooting the film "Miracle in the Rain" with Jane Wyman, "wished Bob and Ray wore their hair differently."[27] From time to time, individuals with the same name as a panelist, such as Laraine Day, Roger Price and Audrey Meadows, provided a twist, albeit feeble. Time ran out for *The Name's the Same* after a four-year run and a course, in the words of moderators Bob and Ray, of "moderating moderately."[28]

Another Goodson-Todman lookalike, *To Tell the Truth* focused on a trio of guests, each of whom claimed to be the same person. The story of the real claimant was read aloud, and a panel of such wide-awake and astute players as Kitty Carlisle, Peggy Cass, Tom Poston and Orson Bean quizzed each of the guests. Two imposters were free to lie, but the real individual was sworn "to tell the truth." At the conclusion of the questioning, each panelist voted separately. The identity of each of the three guests was revealed after the real claimant stood up. Since the identity of the genuine contestant was not revealed until the end of the questions, home audiences were able to play the game—one of the few opportunities they had to test their skills while chair-bound in front of a TV set.[29] Reputedly, a number of home viewers even bet among themselves on the outcome of each game segment.

A latecomer into the arena of panel programs, *To Tell the Truth* first appeared on CBS in December 1956. M.C. Bud Collyer and the panel soon discovered that there was absolutely no foolproof system for separating the two imposters from the genuine article. "Actually, I'm like a referee at a tennis match," Bud said. "I watch the ball go back and forth. I have the fun of playing the game but it's the panel that has to do the work."[30]

Anyone who liked *What's My Line?* went for its chief copycat, *I've Got a Secret*, because about the only difference was the panelists and host. Initially a summer filler for 1952, it introduced guests harboring a "secret," often a far-fetched one. Developed by struggling comedy writers Allan Sherman and Howard Merrill, the game seemed more an attempt to cash in on existing successful money-making formats than to create a genuinely original property. After watching *Line* and the howling responses of the audience over guessing the job of a mattress salesman, Merrill asked his buddy, "What is even more personal than a person's occupation?"[31]

Sherman, who would in the 1960s gain much fame for his recorded song parodies entitled "My Son, the Folksinger," replied: "Secrets. Everybody has terrible, guilty secrets that they are ashamed to tell to anybody else."[32]

"Exactly!" Merrill exclaimed. "Now—all we have to do is get these guilt-ridden, shame-filled people to tell these awful secrets to twenty-five million other people every week, and we are rich."[33]

Allan and Howard played a mockup of their brainchild and then took it to CBS and the offices of Goodson-Todman Productions. After a thorough once-over by Goodson, the idea met approval. "Think of the enormous range of things about a person, besides just guessing their job," Sherman reminded Goodson, who, in turn, pointed out that they had no intention of stealing from their own property, What's My Line? Sherman replied that if they didn't start copying this show, somebody else would. Goodson acquiesced.[34]

The team of Sherman and Merrill signed an agreement with Goodson-Todman that would bring a weekly royalty and, for the former, the job of associate producer. Constant run-throughs, day after day for months, honed the show into a solid, well-crafted program that bowed with host Garry Moore and a panel consisting of Louise Allbritton, Orson Bean, Laura Z. Hobson and Melville Cooper. The opener used a judge and jury theme with each contestant becoming a "witness." This misconceived courtroom basis was scrapped after the first show and in came the basic panel-show props: two tables and six chairs.

Producer Gil Fates described "I've Got a Secret as "omnivorous," opening up a new world of possibilities from the realm of human accomplishment. "It was all embracing," he noted, "so embracing that it even took in occupations that heretofore were the exclusive property of the mother show."[35]

Mail from would-be participants was prodigious. Thousands of letters arrived for Sherman's attention. He bought a zany quality to the game until the day he was fired four years later because of his intransigence on scheduling certain distasteful and poorly executed demonstrations that tied in to "secrets." On the brink of sponsor cancellations and audience repercussions, the prográm was rescued by Goodson-Todman producer Chester Feldman.

Secret never ceased to amuse and startle. The flaccid-appearing character actor Mischa Auer surprised observers with the unlikely secret: "I used to be a lifeguard."[36] A "trick" secret devised for David Niven became "I'm sitting on a keg of ice." The secret of another guest was:

"I have a live snake in my pocket." Other contestants ranged from the man who figured out Einstein's income tax to the person who had a library book 19 years overdue.

Big-name celebrities came on the program mainly because it became so popular (and by 1954 placed sixth, and ahead of *Line*, in the top ten) and undoubtedly was the "in" show to do. "It had occurred to me that celebrities should not have secrets in the same way the regular contestants had them," Sherman wrote in his autobiography, *A Gift of Laughter*. "Celebrities have real secrets, but they sure as hell don't get on a television show and reveal them. I kept saying to Goodson and Todman that reality was the great secret of their success; that this entire genre of show was successful because it had the fresh smell of actuality—it was *happening* right there before your eyes." [37]

This sense of "live" tension and excitement as a cross-section of real people was subjected to a form of "human analysis" by a well-balanced group of engaging and bright personalities made *I've Got a Secret* and other panel games into TV perennials. Viewers tuned in, less for the stimulation of the competition than for the weekly encounter with a gang of old friends. For almost all of its 15 years the *Secret* panelists remained the same—Bess Myerson, Henry Morgan, Betsy Palmer and Bill Cullen. Inveterate fans of this and other panels considered them cronies and knew all their personality quirks and many details of their private lives. The weekly banter often touched upon the latest accomplishment of their offspring, a recent vacation trip, a new film or stage role, or a relative visiting from out of town. Thus a clublike "fixed" or "stacked" panel evolved quickly. In the classic days of panel shows, hosts and panelists were changed with great care and caution. In 1964, when Garry Moore left *Secret*, only Steve Allen or a moderator of his ilk could take over and maintain the long-standing loyalty of an audience.

Nevertheless, when CBS decided to switch the show to Monday night from its old berth on Wednesday, *Secret's* ratings declined, and all too many viewers drifted away. The axe fell on *Secret* just a few months before a similar fate met *Line* and *To Tell the Truth*. The cast's farewells on April 3, 1967, were lighthearted and brief. "I've had fun," concluded Henry Morgan as the program quietly went off like the flick of a light switch.

The panels of early TV were bright, hard hitting and winsome. Often the games differed little from one to another, but it was the well-known, friendly lineup of faces presided over by a skilled and engaging moderator that drew viewers week after week and insured the survival of these shows while the scandal-scarred, big-money games fell like duckpins from the force of a high-powered missile.

›19‹

Cash Pyramid

On a clear January morning in 1955, Louis Cowan sauntered from the dining room of his Park Avenue duplex apartment to his study. Dressed in pajamas and dressing gown, the tall, dark-haired producer fell into an easy chair to read the daily newspapers. Later at his desk he made a few telephone calls and completed some correspondence. At 10 A.M. he pushed aside the paperwork and unplugged the telephone. It was time to think about the creation of a new program for television.

Cowan and his assistants had been drafting formulas for a major game show for several years. His company already had acquired the rights to *Take It or Leave It* but had been stymied in trying to mold a visual idea from that radio show. The recent scaling of Mt. Everest had led him to an idea for a game that had elements of a tortuous ascent and final triumph. Periodically, the image of a mountain climber became superimposed on a picture of a quiz contestant struggling up a pyramid of increasingly difficult questions.[1]

Fifteen years earlier, Cowan had thought up the idea of the *Quiz Kids*, a show that opened up his career in broadcasting, brought him wide acclaim and added to his already sizable family fortune. A similar blockbuster on the video screen had eluded the one-time Chicago press agent. The TV version of *Quiz Kids* proved a modest success but never equaled the appeal of the radio edition. Cowan had produced *Stop the Music!* which crossed over to television and maintained good ratings. His word game *Down You Go*, packaged for TV in the early 1950s, found a niche but drew only a limited audience.

His mind once again began to run down the track of game shows in search of a program that would arouse and hold the interest of a large audience . . . a format that would be dramatic and newsworthy . . . a vehicle that would be immediate yet suspenseful . . . a contest that

would test intelligence, offer a considerable reward and provide participants with broad recognition.

He mulled over the formula whereby audience identification and em-
pathy might build and pull in a wide spectrum of Americans. A creator, too, of documentaries and dramas on TV, he felt that there was
very little reality on television. The greatest things, he thought, were
the real things one sees—baseball, football, political conventions—where
the unexpected was ahead of you. "I wanted," he observed later that
year, "to set up an event where people would be tremendously interested, would care what happened and not know until it happened what
was going to happen."[2]

His old friend Bob Hawk, who had just retired after 15 years as a
leading quizmaster, often reminded Cowan that people who were no-
bodies had a lot more knowledge than people gave them credit for
knowing.[3] Recognizing that fact, he again turned to the well-established $64-question format as a way to display a contestant's expertise
in a certain field. The time-tested *Take It or Leave It* had left the air in
1950 without raising its jackpot from its original 1940 level.* Cowan
realized that a $64 prize on TV would not excite viewers or make news.
Nor would $640 or even $6,400. But $64,000—that was in the realm of
the dramatic, the nearly impossible.

In the waning hour of that January morning, Cowan remembered
being assailed by a perceptible euphoria. "Once I had that," he later
remarked in a somewhat apocryphal account, "I knew just what was
going to happen."[4] That afternoon he discussed the framework of his
idea with his office staff. A few weeks later they began filming a dry
run in preparation for a polished and well-packaged pilot. Ultimately,
as *The $64,000 Question*, it became an immediate hit and the bellwether
of an unprecedented wave of quiz shows and, eventually, an influence
on the entire spectrum of future TV games.

In March 1955 Cowan announced the new series and the biggest
jackpot ever offered. A modest-sized cosmetics company called Revlon
took the reins as sponsor. Apparently, it involved a good deal of prod-
ding from adman Walter Craig of Norman, Craig & Kummel for the
firm to sign a contract. At first, Revlon boss Charles Revson resisted
his agency's pitch. His lipstick and nail-enamel business sold on the
basis of colors; the TV picture was still overwhelmingly black and white.
Moreover, this hands-on chief executive could control print ads much

---

*When the sponsor of *Take It or Leave It* suggested changing the $64 question to $6,400,
M.C. Garry Moore refused to have any part of this scheme. "When the stakes are too
high," he declared, "the game isn't fun any more. The losers go away mad." Quoted in
Harriet Van Horne's "Dishwashers and Diamonds for Cinderella," *The Story of Our Time:
Encyclopedia Yearbook 1949* (New York: The Grolier Society and J. A. Richards Publishing
Co., 1949), p. 390.

better than live TV commercials. Yet television was selling cosmetics. Competitor Hazel Bishop had boosted sales with the sponsorship of Ralph Edwards' *This Is Your Life*. Revson agreed to bring his products to television, but insisted on the right to pull out of Cowan's program after 13 weeks.[5]

Revson probably didn't know at the time that the new quiz had been turned down by Helena Rubenstein ("only poor people watch those awful machines," she remarked), Chrysler (they were afraid of giving away huge sums of money while fighting pennies-an-hour wage increases) and Lewyt Vacuum Cleaner (whose president felt the mass appeal of TV was better suited to selling inexpensive impulse items). Weeks before the first show on June 7, 1955, Revson still felt the proceedings were not conducive to the emotional aura and surroundings in which he really wanted to see his beauty-care products.[6]

One structural element that Cowan insisted upon: no contestant could win a top prize above $8,000 in one evening. A successful player must appear and answer the 17 questions over a period of weeks to build continuity and suspense. With so much money at stake, contestants must be shut off from the studio audience in a soundproof isolation booth to eliminate the chance of prompting from the audience.

The selection of contestants took on the mantle of a significant aspect of quiz-show production. Because individuals with specialized knowledge were to be "tested," it became necessary to seek them out far in advance. Scouting and correspondence, followed by interviews, preceded the appearance of virtually every contestant picked to display his or her expertise. Before bringing a potential contestant from outside the New York metropolitan area, Cowan's staff made a check in the would-be player's hometown to make certain that the individual wasn't a "professional" quiz contestant. The days when a person seated in a studio audience might be picked as a contestant just before airtime were passing. "Whether the new show will start another giveaway trend," wondered *New York Times* reporter Val Adams, "remains to be seen."[7]

The results of the initial broadcast on June 7, 1955, were nothing short of sensational. "I expected that it would either be very popular or nothing," Cowan candidly admitted.[8] But he never visualized such an overwhelming hit. *The $64,000 Question* scored a home run the very first time at bat. (It replaced the CBS dramatic anthology *Danger*—a prophetic title to bump for those who dealt in omens.) On an average Tuesday night at 10 o'clock, a resounding 82 percent of the television sets around the country were focused on M.C. Hal March, the dramatically positioned glass isolation booth and the locked and closely guarded strongbox containing top money questions.

Hal March was an inspired choice of casting. The slender, dark-haired Californian had been a moderately successful performer. At a station in San Francisco in the early 1940s, he met Bob Sweeney, then a staff announcer. Their act, Sweeney & March, ran on radio for years, ending up as a disc jockey duo. Hal also worked as a single with Burns and Allen, Jack Benny, Perry Como, Jackie Gleason and Bob Hope. He did *Sam Spade* and other suspense shows, as well as a dozen movies. When he began Cowan's show, the 35 year old March was doing a comedy series called *The Soldiers* with Tom Andrea.

March brought to *The $64,000 Question* all the requisite qualities expected of a game host: good nature, quick wit, sympathetic bearing, intelligence and respect. In essence, he was a personable, all-round nice guy. Jack Gould singled him out for his agreeableness. "He is as human a master of ceremonies as there is on the air, and it is refreshing indeed to see one TV host behave as might any ordinary mortal in the same spot. Mr. March's humanness and naturalness are a tonic amid all of TV's super-slick perfectionism."[9]

Unquestionably, the real stars of this mental gymnasium were the carefully selected contestants. They had to be individuals the audience could identify with, whether it be an extroverted shoemaker or an introverted sea captain. The producers avoided mental freaks and sought, instead, unusual people, most of whom were intelligent hobbyists in a particular field. For the premiere, only two contestants appeared: a New Jersey housewife with a keen knowledge of the movies who was stopped on the eighth question, lost all her winnings, yet drove away with the not-inconsiderable consolation prize of a Cadillac convertible; and a policeman from Staten Island with a remarkable recall of Shakespeare. Redmond O'Hanlon built up his winnings to $8,000 when time ran out and by doing so won the attention and respect of millions of Americans. As prearranged, he would return the following Tuesday to announce whether he would take his cash bounty or try for more.

The 39-year-old Shakespearean enthusiast had heard about Cowan's new quiz in March and wrote a letter asking to go on the show. A cop versed in the Bard was too good to pass by. Contestant O'Hanlon became the first major winner, stopping at $16,000—a sum equal to about three years' pay on the police force. In bowing out of the contest, O'Hanlon gained the admiration of many when he said, "I am placing the conservation of a father of five children above the egotism of the scholar."[10] His valedictory was widely quoted, appearing in scores of newspapers with his photograph. In the years ahead, O'Hanlon remained on the police force while engaging in a Shakespeare consultation service and pursuing a Ph.D. at New York University. In 1956 he picked up another $16,000 on a Cowan spinoff quiz.[11]

If O'Hanlon represented the young, ambitious and education minded, Catherine Kreitzer symbolized the hardworking, middle-aged, all-American mother. Bringing to the screen an in-depth familiarity of the

Bible, this 54-year-old homemaker with six sons generated intense audience interest. A civilian typist for the navy, she, with her carpenter-husband in Camp Hill, Pennsylvania, together earned less than $8,000 a year. The night she went into the stuffy, unventilated isolation booth to try for $32,000, March thought that what was happening might put an end to the show.

"Actually the question should have been a pushover," he recalled. "I had asked her to name the Disciples of Christ, and she breezed through seven, not realizing she had left out John. This put me in a spot. I knew she had just been careless. I also knew that she and her husband needed the money. I looked her in the eye and said, 'Mrs. Kreitzer, I want you to forget everything you just told me and give me those names once more.' "[12]

That's when a sense of terror struck March. Mrs. Kreitzer's right eye began to twitch uncontrollably as the syncopated clocklike "think music" signaled the fleeting seconds. Her forehead broke out in a clammy sweat. Her face turned an ashen gray and she weaved like a boxer. March thought she must be having a heart attack. But she pulled herself together and rattled off the list again, with John the second name out of her mouth.

With $32,000 in hand, Catherine Kreitzer stopped, citing the biblical phrase, "Let your moderation be known unto all men." The country embraced this refreshing outlook. At once, she was the "toast of the town" as Ed Sullivan introduced her to read biblical verse to his Sunday TV audience. The requests for loans and aid were so frequent in the weeks that followed that she remarked, "I didn't even have time to get the ironing done."[13]

Americans everywhere tuned in the absorbing contests and its latest captivating players. Who knows? One of these weeks there just had to be a winner for the giant $64,000 jackpot. Meanwhile, the show dipped into the proverbial American melting pot and came up with an Italian immigrant with a comprehensive knowledge of opera. Gino Prato, a shoe cobbler from the Bronx, came on the program on the basis of a letter sent by his daughter Lorraine, a vocal student with hopes of an operatic career. She told of his youth in Genova, his departure for New York at age 21 and the decades of hard work in his shoe-repair shop. But he loved to sing as he labored over his bench. A special treat were the performances at the Metropolitan Opera where he climbed six floors to the top balcony to stand and listen. Lorraine described just the kind of contestant Cowan's office sought. A staff member paid a scouting visit to Prato's shop. There was nothing to distinguish it from the many shoemaker shops throughout the city—nothing but the radio that stayed tuned to classical music and nothing but the sunny disposition of Gino.

His first appearance as a contestant proved frustrating. Time ran out just as he started toward the cameras. His second appearance was a little longer. He was still identifying opera characters when the time-keeper called a halt and March asked him back. He soon reached the first "rung" and, to Gino, the lofty sum of $512. An enterprising wire-service editor sent the story of Gino's win to Italy, where he soon became a folk hero. He also remarked on TV that he hoped to visit his homeland and his 92-year-old father, whom he had not seen in 23 years.

Week after week Prato moved up the ladder toward the $64,000. Newspapers printed his picture, TV critics wrote about his charm, people stopped him on the street. New customers began dropping into his shop. Everyone wanted to know if he would go for the $64,000 question.

The strain was apparent. When he came before the cameras to decide on pursuing the $16,000 question, his voice was hoarse. "I sing so many arias I lose my voice," he whispered. The question proved an easy one for Gino. He identified the opera Puccini never completed as "Turandot" and also gave the name of the man who finished it—Franco Alfano. By that time, it seemed as though all America and a sizable part of the rest of the world had discovered Prato and waited for his return on August 9 for a possible try on the next to the last question.

Gino settled the matter by responding correctly to the question: "Name the opera, the country where young Toscanini conducted it, the city in which it had its world premiere, and give the eve of what holiday it occurred."

Gino ticked off the answers: " 'Aida,' Brazil, Cairo, Christmas Eve." For good measure, he added, "December 24, 1871."

For his final appearance a week later, Gino paused to explain to Hal March that he had received a cable from his father in Italy. He translated the message. In English, it read: "Stop wherever you are, and that's enough this way. Regards Papa." Noting that he had always followed paternal advice, the 54-year-old cobbler understandably bowed out.[14] There were disappointments in many quarters, especially the producer's. For practical purposes, they wondered, would the program become "The $32,000 Question?"

Gino Prato undoubtedly had the largest summer audience ever to watch a TV show, and happenings beyond his wildest dreams rapidly came his way. He accepted a new job at a $10,000-a-year salary to act as a national spokesman for Biltrite Rubber Company, a large manufacturer of shoemaker supplies, while still keeping his own shop. Rudolph Bing, manager of the Met, let him know his standing days were over; he sent two season tickets, eighth row center. RCA Victor shipped a complete library of opera recordings for what he had done to popularize opera. Managers of summer-concert series invited him and his family as special guests to performances throughout the metropolitan area. When he visited his father in Italy, an audience with the pope was on the itinerary, and daughter Lorraine got a chance to audition for the New York City Opera.

Prato came back for an encore of sorts early in 1956. He teamed up with another cobbler and opera sage, Michael Della Rocca of Long Island. As the "expert" now permitted by *The $64,000 Question* to assist a contestant on the homestretch, Gino helped his fellow tradesman win the jackpot. Della Rocca's winnings went toward underwriting a small amateur opera company and the staging of productions at a local high school in Baldwin, New York.

On the night of Prato's own big success, a controversy over the fairness of the show's questions developed.* A housewife in Woodbury, Connecticut, Jean Thompson, felt unfairly disqualified on the question about the Mona Lisa portrait. The question on which Thompson was faulted in seeking $8,000 read: "Who was the lady who sat for the portrait?"

Thompson said she did not know, and Hal March said it was Madonna Lisa, the wife of Francesco di Partolommeo del Giocondo. After the broadcast, Alfred M. Frankfurter, editor of *Art News,* said that the identity actually was a matter of legend or presumption, not an established fact. He suggested that the Connecticut homemaker should have received the benefit of the doubt or the question should have been more carefully worded.[15]

The dispute over the Mona Lisa was quickly dispatched as a very young and engaging new contestant reached the launching pad. Not only was Gloria Lockerman of Baltimore a mere 12 years old but she was black.

Little Gloria displayed her expertise as a champion speller and captivated viewers with her skill with words. She parlayed her spelling-bee talent into a $16,000 bankroll, stopped only by her grandmother's decision to call it a day. Gloria was the first black to make an impact on a major quiz show. With a child leading the way, barriers against blacks as contestants on high-stakes giveaways fell. When Frances De Berry, a 74-year-old widow from Louisville, appeared a year later with a knowledge of Shakespeare and walked off with $16,000, the novelty of an intelligent and poised black participant struck fewer and fewer as extraordinary.

During that first season there were no people like no-show business people. Real unglamorized folk on *The $64,000 Question* fascinated viewers. Television, more than ever before, was holding a mirror up to life and reflecting an obvious and seemingly inexhaustible supply of

---

*The questions in about 40 categories were prepared by a staff of ten, headed by university professor Dr. Bergen Evans, whom Cowan had chosen on the basis of their association in presenting *Down You Go.*

material: genuine people. The medium was making its own celebrities from individuals off the street.[16]

In England, the BBC was considering doing its own devalued variation on Cowan's creation. To catch the fancy of the owners of Britain's 5 million sets, officials turned to the show's formula to compete with the opening of the country's first commercial channel. BBC gave thought to a quiz that would have a jackpot of 500 pounds, or $1,400. The corporation, however, faced the ticklish policy question about the use of public funds and backed off. As it turned out, commercial British TV presented a version of the $64,000 Question called *Double Your Money* with a top prize of one thousand pounds ($2,800).[17]

Meanwhile, to pull in whatever nonvideo areas were left in the United States, CBS simulcast *The $64,000 Question*. The move proved effective in reaching for the million or so remaining prime-time radio listeners.

By mid-August 1955 everyone connected with Cowan's new show, as well as multitudes of viewers, were eager to see a contestant go all the way to $64,000. A strong candidate came into play that month—in fact, an ideal choice to capture the top prize. He was a 28-year-old marine, a veteran of service in both World War II and Korea and the father of three children. Moreover, his hobby was food and cooking. Captain Robert McCutchen seemed destined to "go for broke." By his fourth appearance, the lean, attractive officer correctly described five types of desserts and their countries of origin to gain a chance at the highest plateau. He would return to decide whether to take his $32,000 or try for more.

To prepare for the finale, three books on cookery—including volume 23 of *The Encyclopaedia Britannica* (covering vegetables, vitamins and wines)—were given him by the program directors. McCutchen studied these daily, memorizing innumerable statistics, figures and menus. He had acquired an interest in food from his father, a retired Navy captain and an amateur chef. "All my relatives cook well," he pointed out. "My father, my mother-in-law, everybody."[18] Like most Navy families, the McCutchens lived in many parts of the world. In each country they made it a point to eat and learn to prepare the native dishes.

When on September 13 Hal March asked McCutchen if he planned to try for the big prize, he replied:

"I've known my decision for a long time. I belong to a very proud organization, and the answer is—go!"[19]

The confident marine knocked off a tremendously complicated question about a state dinner given at Buckingham Palace on March 21, 1939, for the president of France. Helped by his "food expert" father, McCutchen named and described the seven courses, plus the two wines served on that occasion 16 years earlier. The studio audience squirmed with anxiety as he gave his detailed answers. Gasps of relief could be heard as he overcame each barrier to the prize.

Just before he answered the last part of the question, Captain Mc-Cutchen asked if he could have a minute on the final puzzler. He conferred briefly with his father as they stood in the soundproof booth. Father and son came up with a full description of the two wines—and correctly completed the answer. There was a roar from the audience and then an ovation. For the final touch, the studio orchestra struck up "The Marines' Hymn."

As well-wishers, reporters and photographers clustered about him, McCutchen announced his $64,000, less some $32,000 in taxes, would go into the bank, and he would remain in the Marine Corps.

After three and a half months on the air, the CBS show touted its first winner of the most fabulous prize in the history of radio and television. Before the end of 1955, the quiz would have its second jackpot champion. Joyce Brothers, a 28-year-old psychologist, won by answering questions on boxing. Brothers went on the show to bring in some money to help her husband, an intern at Mount Sinai Hospital. Her answers became a race with the clock on December 6 as the program's end neared. In a rare move, CBS allowed the show to run 30 seconds overtime and then cut it off just as Hal March screamed: "You're right for $64,000!"[20]

Triumphant contestants of 1955–56 included Myrtle Power, a 70-year-old grandmother from Georgia and a baseball fan who batted in $32,000; Steven Frohlich, a Czech immigrant-seed salesman who built up $32,000 from a knowledge of American history; the Rev. Alvin Kershaw, a jazz-loving minister in Oxford, Ohio; Thomas Kane, a taxi driver with a command of the English language; Mabel Morris, a welfare recipient and former schoolteacher, who refrained from going beyond the $32,000 mark with her category of Charles Dickens because her physician felt the excitement would be too much. There also were mailman-poet Roscoe Wright, who stopped at $16,000 to buy a much-needed organ for his church; Hartford lawyers James and William Egan, who answered a potpourri of questions in 11 categories and split $32,000; and Tennessee minister Stoney Jackson, who gained $16,000 from "great love stories."

Not every contestant on the high plateau left with a check. Robert Edward Bennett, a store clerk from Georgia with a large stock of Abraham Lincoln lore, struck out on the $64,000 question, becoming the first loser at that level.[21] Nevertheless, he left town in his consolation prize, a 1956 Cadillac.

With large sums regularly paid to players, audiences looked on *The $64,000 Question* as a costly show to produce. Actually, the weekly expenses, including prize money—which averaged only $14,000 per show—was $27,000 (about half what it cost Hazel Bishop to produce *This Is Your Life*). Another $40,000 went for the half-hour of network broadcast time. In total, Revlon aired some three minutes of commercial time and picked up inestimable press coverage for less than $70,000 a week.[22] Cadillac received much publicity by handing out the keys to a car about once a month.

The show raised Revlon sales, profits and consumer awareness dramatically. Some of the Revlon products featured in commercials delivered by actresses Wendy Barrie and Barbara Britton experienced 300 percent and 500 percent sales increases within weeks of their airing. One particular item, Living Lipstick, sold out in ten days. Overall sales shot up 54 percent in 1955 and profits tripled. Six months after the quiz bowed, Revlon went public at $12 a share. It quickly hit $30 and the following year split two-for-one. Those who bought Revlon stock in the public offering realized a 1,000 percent gain in just four years.[23]

In the meantime, Louis Cowan achieved the post to which he apparently had long aspired: a CBS vice presidency and a shot at the top job of TV network head. He had stayed with the *Question* until it was successfully launched and then turned over the reins of his company to Harry Fleischman and production control of his top-rated show to Steve Carlin. Whether Cowan had fully relinquished his part of *The $64,000 Question* remained unclear, more so in the wake of the future quiz probe.

But in late 1955 no one really wondered about Cowan's "arrangement" with CBS. Audiences were hungry for more supercash quizzes, and networks and producers geared up to satisfy their appetite.

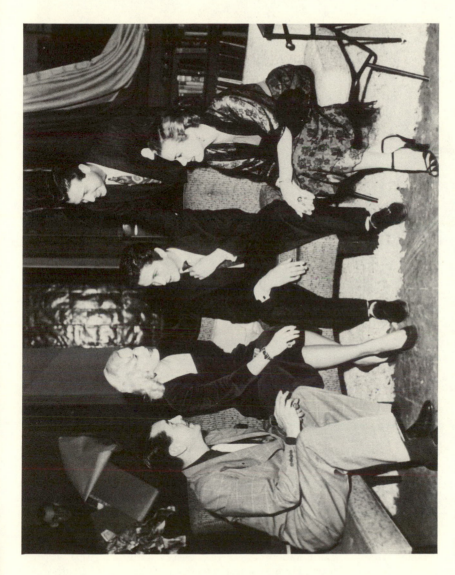

Mike Stokey (standing) created and hosted the pioneer television game *Pantomime Quiz*. Hollywood players in 1952 included (left to right) Reginald Gardiner, Jean Wallace, John Barrymore, Jr., and Gale Storm. (Courtesy Mike Stokey.)

Walt Framer (right), creator and producer of "misery show" *Strike It Rich*, handles the telephone Heart Line with guest celebrity Burt Lancaster. (Author's collection.)

Medicine taster Shirley Morabito (left) meets *What's My Line?* host John Charles Daly (right) and panel. Her unusual job stumped Keenan Wynn, Arlene Francis and Bennett Cerf in 1959. (Courtesy Shirley D. Morabito.)

Since the 1940s Mark Goodson has produced an unparalleled string of innovative and durable game shows, including *Winner Take All, What's My Line?, Beat the Clock, To Tell the Truth* and *The Price Is Right.* (Courtesy Mark Goodson Productions.)

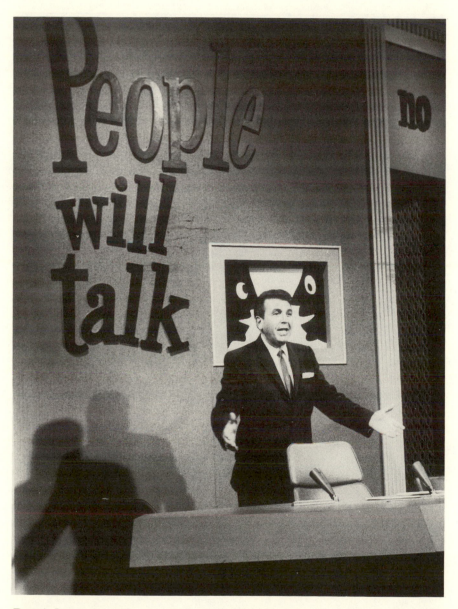

Dennis James emceed many audience-participation shows, starting in the earliest video days. His *People Will Talk*, a celebrity game, ran on NBC in 1963. (Courtesy Dennis James.)

Amiable and erudite *College Bowl* M.C. Allen Ludden presided over the weekly intercollegiate contests on radio and television from 1953 to 1962. (Courtesy College Bowl, Inc.)

Ethel Park Richardson sings a folk song as part of a complex multi-part question posed by Jack Barry on *The Big Surprise*. Seventy-two-year-old Richardson was the first contestant to win $100,000 on the big-money shows of the 1950s. (Courtesy Jonathan Guyot Smith.)

The popular, erudite Charles Van Doren kayoed major contender Herbert Stempel on *Twenty-One* and went on to topple many opponents in 1957. Van Doren later admitted his participation in the rigged big-money series. (Courtesy Studio N.)

Bob Barker became the host of long-running *The Price Is Right* in 1972. Models Dian, Holly and Janice helped display the merchandise prizes on the daily full-hour game. (Courtesy Phillip Wayne—Mark Goodson Productions.)

Chuck Woolery was representative of the new wave of virile, well-groomed quiz-masters in the 1970s and '80s. His popular shows included *Wheel of Fortune*, *Scrabble*, and *Love Connection*. (Courtesy Reg Grundy Productions.)

Navy pilot Thom McKee won an unprecedented 88 games on *Tic Tac Dough* in 1980. For nine weeks, M.C. Wink Martindale quizzed the 24-year-old service-man, one of the biggest and most popular winners on televison. (Courtesy Wink Martindale.)

›20‹

Champions and Challengers

Some 15,000 Americans wrote letters to CBS every week asking for a chance to go on *The $64,000 Question.* Its staff was besieged by would-be contestants with claims of extensive knowledge and recall. Many told of a desperate need for money. All were confident that they could hit the jackpot.

To most people, a slice of $64,000 loomed as a princely sum in 1955, and to many even a small portion represented a total paycheck for a year or two. Machinists earning $80 a week imagined being handed a five-figure check from Charles Revson. Stenographers struggling on $55 a week dreamed of meeting an eligible big winner. Every wage earner and spouse envisioned a windfall that would buy a $14,000 three-bed-room split-level home in Bethpage, Long Island, and a new $2,000 Ford automobile. With all-wool tropical suits at Bloomingdale's selling for $69, two front-row seats at the Broadway musical "Fanny" going for $15 and charcoal-broiled steaks at Howard Johnson's listing for $1.95, even low-plateau winnings could create an upswing in life-style.

These were days of peace, prosperity and high hopes. Two years earlier, President Eisenhower had kept his campaign promise to end the war in Korea. The economy reacted by steaming ahead to new highs in employment and production and in wages and profits. By mid-1955 32 million homes had TV sets, and every Tuesday at 10 o'clock the overwhelming majority were tuned to CBS and its *$64,000 Question.*

Rival networks struggled to compete. Without a TV transmitter, Mu-tual reacted to television's giant game by formulating plans for a super radio prize of $250,000. The coast-to-coast chain announced that it was preparing a daily two-hour quiz. A listener would first qualify by writ-ing an award-winning letter on "What I Would Do if I Won $250,000." Then 40 letter writers each week would have an opportunity to win anywhere from $100 to the top prize by answering a seven-part question over the telephone.[1]

ABC auditioned several giant jackpot quizzes, including a show that would give a contestant a stake in a working oil well. Another program idea called "Security for Life," took a long-range point of view. It would give away approximately $250 a month for life.[2]

NBC came on to more solid ground by copying the CBS blockbuster. In announcing The $100,000 Big Surprise, its producer, Louis Cowan, Inc., merely added $36,000 to the top prize and hired an easygoing, talk-show moderator cut from the same cloth as Hal March. Jack Barry, with ten years' experience handling both juveniles and octogenarians, got the job as M.C., and NBC placed the quiz on its Saturday evening lineup, making certain that soap-opera suspense surfaced on the initial broadcast in October 1955. In selecting contestants, the show required an extra fillip: a participant had to have performed a "worthy deed." In addition, an IBM "magic typewriter" spelled out the big-money questions, which were written by well-known figures in the particular category chosen.[3]

Echoing the Revlon giveaway, the program recruited its first contestant from the ranks of law enforcers. The producers chose Brooklyn detective Barney Arluck who had recently played a role in freeing a man wrongfully imprisoned on a murder charge. Sgt. Arluck, a part-time law student hoping to pass the bar exams upon retirement from the police force, picked a category tied to his future career. He won $10,000 on the show's premiere, returned three more Saturdays to build up his winnings and departed with $50,000.

A month later, a Pennsylvania housewife who once battled Germans at Leningrad as a backup lieutenant in the Russian infantry displayed an uncanny knowledge of war and weapons. The former sharpshooter, Kyra Petrovskaya Shirk, proceeded to move with assurance toward the biggest prize on television. For $50,000, she first identified four American rifles and then from an array of bullets matched each one with the proper weapon. To complete the question, she lifted the rifle, pulled the trigger, and fired the blank round above the heads of a startled studio audience.[4] Shirk returned to try for $100,000. Her question, reputedly prepared by Admiral Chester Nimitz and Field Marshall Montgomery, was a complicated one on World War II battles. She failed to answer correctly. But after weeks as a video celebrity, she would not leave empty-handed. The show allowed her to keep $25,000, a consolation prize that far outstripped the value of The $64,000 Question's Cadillac.

Big Surprise producer Steve Carlin had his first star-quality contestant in the form of a 72-year-old great-grandmother who had had a career as a folksinger, musicologist and educator. Living in a makeshift trailer in Los Angeles, Ethel Park Richardson wrote a letter explaining her qualifications and enclosing a photograph of herself taken in a mountaineer costume. Someone remembered her early radio appearances as a singer, actress and writer on *The Cabin Door, Heart Throbs of the Hills* and *The Wayside Cottage.* The production staff was intrigued over locating a pioneering broadcaster who long ago had retired to California and had fallen into obscurity.[5]

The sprightly folksong expert drove her prewar car cross-country to appear on the New York show. Her recall of Americana, buoyed by responses in the form of singing little-known lyrics, took her to high ground. On December 10, 1955, Richardson answered a six-part catchall question on folklore and music. Although it was clear that she knew her stuff right from the start, observed Richard F. Shepard of *The New York Times*, "she faltered in singing the first stanza of 'The Streets of Laredo,' and went on to answer the other questions, then returned to the song in a quavering tremolo."[6]

The hushed audience waited open-mouthed as Richardson pitched the final right answer to Barry in slow-ball fashion, becoming the first quiz contestant ever to tote away a $100,000 jackpot.

Richardson's appearances had become nerve-wracking cliffhangers. On one particular show, she had slipped on a question but was brought back into the game by a complicated procedure that required someone who looked like her to answer another question on another subject. Critics complained over this confusing mishmash of rules, a number of which changed frequently. Besides introducing a "rescuer" to answer a substitute question (and receive 10 percent of the regular player's winnings), there was a period when a contestant could be asked easy or hard questions, thus varying his cash rewards, and a time when he might answer two insurance questions, guaranteeing all the money won up to that point.

Less than two months after Ethel Park Richardson struck gold, a 14-year-old high school freshman from New York talked and sang his way to $100,000 by identifying the song "Me and My Shadow" and rendering a chorus of this hit of the 1920s. George L. Wright and his family immediately began plans to move from their Third Avenue walkup apartment to a home in the suburbs. Television now had its youngest jackpot winner . . . but others were in the wings.[7]

Teenage contestants periodically boosted audience interest. But Jack Barry took much of the blame for the game's erratic ratings, being described by one critic as having "as much warmth as a head waiter someone forgot to tip."[8] A rising TV personality out of Chicago named Mike Wallace replaced him in March 1956.

Born in Brookline, Massachusetts, Myron Wallace entered the University of Michigan at age 16 and planned to teach college-level English. In his sophomore year, he developed an interest in dramatics and did some acting in school plays. Swayed toward broadcasting by speech professor Waldo Abbot, he was also influenced by Ann Arbor classmates Arthur Miller, a budding playwright; Robert Q. Lewis, a soon-to-be host of quiz shows on radio and TV; and Peter Arnell, a future TV producer for Wallace's daytime panel show *I'll Buy That*. As a senior, Wallace taught radio production at the Interlochen, Michigan, summer camp and after graduation won an audition over 75 hopefuls for an announcer's job at Station WOOD in Grand Rapids. In 1940 he moved to WXYZ in Detroit and, a year later, to Chicago as an announcer, actor and newscaster. After three years of Navy service in World War II, Mike Wallace hosted an interview show, *Famous Names*, over WGN. Not long after, CBS offered Wallace a job in New York as the M.C. of *All Around the Town*, a TV potpourri of places and people. His wife, actress Buff Cobb, joined him on the series, which evolved into the *Mike and Buff* show, a lively afternoon discussion session. A capable jack-of-all-assignments, including a role on Broadway, Mike emerged as an early TV personality and managed to convey a compelling visual presence.[9]

Wallace's mettle was soon tested by a ten-year-old whiz kid from Los Angeles. Leonard Ross had attracted national attention by passing a federal examination for a ham radio operator's license at age seven. His mother enjoyed being a stage mother for her precocious son and entered him in the pool of contestants for *The Big Surprise*. Leonard's category, the stock market, and his remarkable grasp of Wall Street won him the top prize.

Widely acclaimed as a child prodigy, Ross entered Oregon's Reed College four years later, at age 14. At 21 he completed Yale Law School. A brilliant but troubled man, Ross faced a life bedeviled by despair and frustration amidst singularly praiseworthy accomplishments.[10]

Other big winners that season were a Chinese-American, Maisie Chen, with a wealth of baseball information, and Rear Admiral Redfield Mason of the Brooklyn Navy Yard, who displayed a profound familiarity with Greek mythology.

Notwithstanding folksingers and admirals, Revlon's Tuesday giveaway still topped the quiz-field ratings. On that night, movie theaters complained of poor attendance and restaurants worried over lack of business. The crime rate dropped as did the number of long-distance telephone calls. Now dominating the cosmetics business, as well as the video ratings, Charles Revson looked for a spinoff to capitalize on his vast audience of 50 or more million. So Cowan's team came up with *The $64,000 Challenge*.

This sister show gave viewers an opportunity to see their favorite quiz champions back in action. Now familiar faces, they returned to the spotlight, giving their fans more vicarious thrills as they struggled and sweated through a round of weekly contests. A new twist was adopted: established players and fledgling challengers would be pitted against each other with identical questions piped into twin isolation booths. The game continued until one of them missed, making the other the winner.[11]

In their apparent haste to launch a second blockbuster, Cowan, Inc., and CBS chose the 31-year-old host of a Sunday children's program called *Let's Take a Trip*. From the very first telecast on April 8, 1956, Sonny Fox committed verbal *faux pas* and seemed slightly unsure of himself.[12] He fluffed his lines and lost his objectivity. At several crucial moments, he also let slip the answer to a question, causing a flood of complaints and, thus, periodic rematches. After four months, Fox was fired for committing one "blooper" too many. Perhaps the task of two diverse shows on the same day (Sunday) proved too much for the intelligent and good-humored M.C.

The producers brought in a relatively unknown but experienced broadcaster from Station KNX in Los Angeles. Ralph Story had been offered *The $64,000 Question* but thought Cowan's initial quiz idea insane.[13] He recommended his friend Hal March, who secured the job and briefly commuted from Hollywood to New York every week. Cowan again called. The forthcoming *Challenge* was his if he wanted to pull up stakes for New York. Story didn't believe a spinoff would succeed. So when Cowan approached him for the *third* time, he agreed to M.C. the latest big-money contest and sever his ties with the West Coast.

Ralph Story had started in radio as a disc jockey and announcer in Kalamazoo and Grand Rapids. In the early 1940s he joined WGR and the Buffalo Broadcasting Company. After the war, when the station's Bob Smith became NBC's New York wake-up man and needed a writer for his Howdy Doody TV series, Story decided to try his luck at Radio City. He also landed the job as director for WOR's early-morning program, *The John Gambling Show*—strong competitor to "Buffalo Bob" Smith and CBS's new replacement for Arthur Godfrey, Jack Sterling. That led to KNX and to the dual job of early-morning director and host for CBS. In the process, his name was changed from Ralph Sneider to Ralph Story. On CBS television he substituted for Linkletter on *House Party* and hosted the quiz *What Do You Have in Common?* during the summer of 1954.

The recollection of his first appearance as *Challenge* M.C. made him shudder for years afterward. "I figured I had only gone to TV school for 13 weeks on that summer show, and no one learns much in 13 weeks. So I had to depend on the staff and crew to teach me."[14]

Coworkers believed it was his very slowness, his courtesy and his willingness to learn that saved him from being replaced. By the second program, the crew had enough confidence in Story to kid him during rehearsal. They ribbed him about the time he asked a girl stand-in, "What do you do?" and she replied, "Nothing," and Story said, "How did you prepare for it?"[15]

During the next two years, *The $64,000 Challenge* refilled the pockets of many past big winners through contests between champion and challenger. Leonard Ross competed. So did Redmond O'Hanlon and Myrt Power. Tennessee preacher Stoney Jackson bested another Tennessean, Doll Goosetree. Dr. Joyce Brothers returned, upping her winnings to $135,000 in a contest on boxing against a team of ring veterans, including Two-Ton Tony Galento, Tiger Jones and Tommy Loughran.

Before the close of the first year of giveaway contests, producers realized the drawing power of full-fledged celebrities. Why not regularly bring on a famous individual with specialized knowledge of a subject, preferably outside of his professional field? With the choice of uniquely interesting candidates from off the street somewhat diminished and ratings a bit sluggish, game recruiters turned to movie studios, city halls, sports arenas, bandstands, art galleries and even pulpits. The zealousness of packagers to transform the quiz platform into a celebrity hall of fame ultimately contributed to the desuetude of the big-buck bonanzas.

Yet at the beginning, a who's who of notables intrigued and often enlightened viewers. Hadn't Charlie Revson said to his lieutenants, "Get me some famous faces and make them smart."[16]

In a brilliant stroke of "casting," *The $64,000 Challenge* matched Edward G. Robinson against his fellow actor Vincent Price. Both art experts and collectors, they tied at $64,000 after six appearances and split the prize. The contest reputedly brought about increased attendance at museums throughout the country and a rise in the sale of art books.

What was exciting, beyond the tension of the contest, observed noted art critic Aline B. Saarinen, was the two actors' attitude about their subject and the fact that a vast audience inescapably learned that art was something significant and enriching and within the reach of everyone. "For in the time before their answers and their display of nuggets of knowledge which each had acquired from earnest cramming, both contestants forcibly communicated their own feelings about art."[17]

Robinson and Price referred to their barrel of mail as evidence of a stirring interest in art. Among the letters, Price pointed out, were ones that showed how many people were prevented from buying art only by fear and by ignorance of the possibilities. This got him thinking about lecturing on art and bringing modest-priced works of art to many Americans through mass merchandisers such as Sears, Roebuck.[18]

The world of art received another solid boost when Vincent Price as challenger vied with the well-known jockey and art enthusiast Billy Pearson. The 35-year-old rider had qualified for the *Challenge* by winning $64,000 on the *Question*. Before that windfall, Groucho Marx had had him on *You Bet Your Life*. He wanted art as a category, but Groucho's producer John Guedel figured it had a limited appeal. Pearson chose "explorers," and he and his partner lost. So confident of success, he had placed bets with jockeys Eddie Arcaro and Willie Shoemaker and then ended up spending $1,140 out of pocket to pay them off.

By 1956 Pearson was flat broke, his race track earnings totally spent. A friend urged him to write a letter to *The $64,000 Question* about how he had become interested in art while working as a jockey for movie director John Huston. A questionnaire from the program soon came in the mail. To go to New York for an interview, Pearson withdrew the last of his savings—a slim $461. He was among 30 interviewed in a single day. Producer Joe Cates asked him to be on the next show.

Pearson spent his dwindling resources on the purchase of art books and studied them day and night in his hotel room. It paid off. He quickly advanced to the $8,000 plateau and gained his first exposure inside the isolation booth. He described the experience in his autobiography *Never Look Back:* "The door of the booth closed behind me with a thud. There was no sense or feeling of motion and activity around me. The powerful lights blinded me, and it was dead silence—just like a tomb. It was hot in there with the powerful lights. I was used to sweatboxes; I'd spent half my life in one reducing to ride horses." [19]

To bone up further on his category, he borrowed money to buy $600 worth of art books and to hire an art tutor and to bring his wife to New York. Again, it paid off—this time to the amount of $32,000. With this in hand, he decided to come back the following Tuesday and tell Hal March that because of a promise to his wife, he'd bow out. He realized, too, that he could only gain another four or five thousand dollars after taxes if he nailed down the jackpot. Why risk $32,000 for a few more grand? But by lunchtime the day before the show, Pearson secretly changed his mind; he'd give the $64,000 a try.

"I respected Pearson's guts," Hal March once replied to a reporter's question on the contestant whose courage he admired the most. "He promised his wife and friends he would quit. But there was the gambler in him. On the show, he spontaneously looked toward his wife and said, 'I'm sorry, kid, I lied to you. I have to go on.'" [20]

Pearson spent a grueling 18 minutes in the booth while replying to his final question. Just as airtime ran out, he figured out the last part of the $64,000 puzzler. From his appearances, widespread interest in art and artists grew. Certainly, for the down-and-out jockey, his ordeal proved rewarding and led to his opening an art gallery in California.

The famous and near-famous—including a few down on their uppers—faced the TV cameras. One-time swashbuckling actor Errol Flynn was a winner on questions about ships and the sea. Author Randolph Churchill, son of Sir Winston, made a special trip from London. His chosen category was the English language. At the $128 level, he could not remember the derivation of the word *boycott*. Churchill rubbed his hands and looked thoroughly pensive but he could not recall that the word stemmed from the action of C. C. Boycott, a British Army officer. Churchill was mercifully cut off by the lack of airtime. Asked to return the following week, he replied: "I have no business trying to become a quiz kid at 45."[21]

From Hollywood, early cinema idol Francis X. Bushman fared much better, picking up $30,000 on *The Big Surprise*. Ex-mayor George Dempster of Knoxville—inventor of the widely used Dempster Dumpster refuse remover—agreed to play *The $64,000 Question*, but only if his winnings could be given to some member of the television audience. Former Quiz Kid Joel Kupperman, now 21, won $8,000 by defeating a headwaiter from Philadelphia whose hobby was classical music.

Bandleader Xavier Cugat competed against singer Lillian Roth in a battle over Tin Pan Alley knowledge. Movie cowboy Tim McCoy vied against rodeo performer May Colett in the category of Wild West lore. Actor Peter Ustinov battled a Los Angeles truck driver, Al Einfrank. Old-time vaudevillians Pat Rooney and Carter DeHaven came as experts on turn-of-the-century show business. Vintage screen stars Lila Lee and Jackie Coogan displayed recall of their profession.

The creative brains behind the *Challenge* even sought as contestants such diverse public personalities as J. Edgar Hoover, Bishop Fulton J. Sheen, Perle Mesta, Gen. Curtis LeMay and Senator Wayne Morse.[22]

The ultimate celebrity booking brought Jack Benny to *The $64,000 Question*. True to his stage character, he stopped after pocketing $64 on the first question. (A dozen years earlier, to the delight of his radio fans, Benny had "performed" the same stunt on *Take It or Leave It*.)

Turning to celebrities as contestants—especially those connected with the movie business—kept program interest high. It also accelerated the shift of prime-time television fare to Hollywood from New York. History repeated itself. Radio had had its start chiefly in the East and made Manhattan the main network center. But as radio's top comedians, actors, and musical headliners entered the movies, California became home base. The site of their weekly shows switched from Radio City to Sunset and Vine. Now it was happening again with television.[23]

With networks recruiting more and more personnel and artists from film, television, once and for all, went where the talent lived. Moreover, by the mid-1950s, a growing percentage of programs had switched from "live" to filmed productions. Hollywood-developed series such as *I Love Lucy*, *Private Secretary*, *Dragnet* and *Topper* went on film for initial network presentations and then were syndicated for sales on a station-by-station basis. In the future, even quiz shows would follow their lead.

The proverbial covered wagons containing much New York-created TV content were rapidly moving west to stake new claims. The broad popularity of an ABC Western series called *Cheyenne* accented the necessity to make California the primary production center. Derived from a quickly forgotten feature of Warner Bros. as an opportunity to beef up ABC's perennial last-place choice among viewers, *Cheyenne* required outdoor location shooting that only movie knowhow, terrain and talent could offer.[24]

Cheyenne's success signaled the entrance of major studios into TV production after being at arm's length from its chief competition for a decade. By mid-1957 there would be dozens of carbon copies of this Hollywood-made trendsetter: *Wagon Train, Sugarfoot, Maverick, Colt .45, Zorro, Wyatt Earp, The Lawman, Rawhide, Bonanza*. Except for news presentations, soap operas, quiz shows and occasional special programs—all predominantly live—New York was losing its grip as the video showplace. To offset the growing dominance of the West Coast, quiz creators and producers augmented the lineup of big money games and upped the stakes. Their response quickly became a no-holds-barred race toward greater publicity and bigger procurements.

›21‹

High Stakes Heroics

Bill Todman, the sales-oriented half of the Goodson-Todman production team, when questioned by a TV columnist about possible new quiz shows on the drawing board for 1957, admitted that he and his partner planned its own big-money contest. "It's called 'Cash on the Line,' and the big prize is $300,000. It would be completely different, though," he added while declining to spell out any details.[1]

The Goodson-Todman top-dollar entry fell by the wayside in early run-throughs, and it was hardly missed. By mid-1958 there was at least one big-money quiz in prime time every night of the week, and the quizzes were quickly filling up the daytime schedules. Soon there would be only six half-hour periods from 10 A.M. until 6 P.M. when no giveaway was being telecast. All told, the jackpot was boiling up to a total of 49 hours of games per week.[2]

Many early staples among video quizzes reacted to the magic of money too. New heights were scaled by *Break the Bank* as it upped its giveaway assets to become *Break the $250,000 Bank*. Winning the grand prize now meant answering questions of greater difficulty over a period of 20 weeks. In place of an isolation booth, a contestant entered a hallowed area called the "Hall of Knowledge." Although not a celebrity game, notables sometimes appeared to introduce a contestant. Ballplayer Enos Slaughter, on an early telecast of the revamped *Bank*, introduced a girl from his hometown who was an authority on football.

Bert Parks, still the *Bank*'s M.C., appeared more subdued than he normally was on the TV screen. "But his reserve is understandable," a critic noted. "One should expect some dignity from a man who—in theory, at least—may some night hand out a quarter of a million bucks."[3] But Parks never got to hand over more than $50,000, and the *Bank* failed completely some six months after it tried to compete with the big-money operators.

Beat the Clock offered players a chance at a grand prize with an ever-rising cash value by undertaking a special and highly challenging stunt. For 25 weeks, contestants attempted—and failed—a 30-second test of physical agility. Contestant number 54, Gabriel Fontana, a printer from Washington, D.C., succeeded. Wearing a football helmet to the front of which was taped a salad bowl with its flat bottom facing outward, he tilted his head back, then manipulated a fishing rod and line so that a flat-ended baton attached to it would balance upright on the bottom of the bowl.[4]

Name That Tune responded to the greater rewards. In 1955 its stakes escalated to $25,000 from a modest $1,600. This musical quiz show grew out of *Stop the Music!* which folded in 1953 after people apparently got tired of waiting for their telephone to ring. Conductor Harry Salter created a new vehicle from the old. Many called *Name That Tune* a better musical game than its frantically staged predecessor.

Salter's updated game lined up two agile contestants who were outfitted in sneakers. When either one—or both—recognized the name of a tune being played, the contestant ran 25 feet to be the first to pull a cord that rang a bell and thus be positioned for the musical puzzler. Salter and M.C. Red Benson found players who had stage presence and were not above providing some musical entertainment. Children as well as adults competed and often vocalized on the tune in question. It was during an appearance as a contestant that 14-year-old Leslie Uggams was spotted by Mitch Miller for his TV *Sing Along*.

To add some measure of difficulty to the game, the songs were frequently sung in a foreign language. Featured vocalist Vicki Mills had audiences wondering if she had spent most of her formative years at Berlitz. In truth, Mills was Carmella Melillo of Danbury, Connecticut, a former student at the New England Conservatory of Music. She first came to New York to audition for Arthur Godfrey's *Talent Scouts*. On that very day she and her father entered an elevator at CBS and began chatting over the chances of winning. Fellow passenger Harry Salter overheard the conversation and introduced himself.

"When you're through with Godfrey," he added, "come to audition for my new show."[5]

Nineteen-year-old Vicki Mills spent four years on *Name That Tune*, singing 30 languages phonetically. Viewers, thinking her fluent in each of them, wrote letters in their native script—nearly everything from Arabic to Zulu. But only once did she get a chance to finish a song. "On a Thanksgiving broadcast," she recalled, "Salter let me do the verse and chorus of 'Bless This House.'"[6]

On most programs, Mills and announcer-vocalist Bob Kennedy sang a "golden medley" sent in by a viewer who shared the winnings of the contestant who attempted to name all the tunes in 30 seconds. M.C. Bill Cullen, who replaced Red Benson in 1954, provided lots of clues on the identity of a song. On one particular telecast, his coaching brought down the house.

In trying to elicit the title of the tune "Christopher Columbus," Cullen asked a young woman, "Now, Rose, you think of an Italian man who did something very, very important. In fact, if he hadn't done what he did, you wouldn't be here tonight. Who is this Italian man?"

Without hesitating, Rose replied: "My father!"

After a half-minute of solid laughter and applause, Cullen observed: "It's pretty hard to call an answer like that wrong."[7]

Later, on the very same program, the orchestra played a snippet of "Under a Blanket of Blue," but the contestant was stumped. Cullen gave a clue. "If it was a girl baby, you could tell because she would be under a blanket of pink. Therefore, if it was a boy baby, how could you tell?"

"By looking under its diaper," replied the contestant.[8]

By 1955 a new host, George DeWitt, shared the stage with an increasing array of celebrity guests. Ezio Pinza, Hank Bauer, Kirk Douglas, Jimmy and Tommy Dorsey, Joe Louis, Peggy Wood and Roy Campanella helped to identify tunes and, in most cases, won some money for a favorite charity. A new twist—people in teams—characterized this phase of *Name That Tune*.

One of the most engaging team players was a Marine major who had just become the first man to pilot a jet coast-to-coast at supersonic speed. On July 16, 1957, John Glenn pushed his needle-nosed Navy F8U Crusader from Los Angeles to Brooklyn in the breathtaking speed of three hours and twenty-three minutes. It was a spectacular achievement, and TV news shows were quick to leap at an opportunity of interviewing America's new jet-age idol.

Harry Salter observed one of the TV interviews and commented to his staff that Glenn had that mysterious, elusive personality ingredient called "projection." A day or so later, Glenn and his son David went shopping in Macy's. The affable supersonic hero was wearing his uniform when a representative from Salter's program recognized him and invited him to try out for the show.

"I cleared the invitation with the Marine Corps, and researched the show because I was not familiar with it," Glenn explained in 1985. "My only preparation for the program was my musical background—as a member of glee clubs and as a trumpet player in my high school band and college orchestra. Our family was also musically inclined; my wife Annie was a music major, having been offered a partial scholarship to

Juilliard, and family sing-a-longs had been a favorite activity in our home."[9]

As Glenn was being readied for his appearance, a Salter scout discovered a red-haired, goggle-eyed youngster from Mississippi. This unabashed music-loving boy named Eddie Hodges wanted to be a Baptist preacher like his granddaddy. Polite and articulate, he was teamed up with John Glenn. Their good humor, jokes and bantering, along with frequent harmonizing on the *Tune* answers, made this duo the talk of the country. While chipping away at the jackpot, they put on a terrific show—a contest Hodges called "fantabulous." Audiences were sad to see them leave, although they were thrilled by their success over a period of five weeks in the fall of 1957.

Hodges and Glenn split the $25,000 grand prize. The marine put his share—approximately $7,500 after taxes—into a college fund for his children. Hodges placed his winnings not in trust for divinity school but in an effort to launch a show-business career. After his third appearance, he auditioned for a key role in "The Music Man" and soon achieved success in that Broadway show and later in films and television. As an adult, he pursued an interest in clinical psychology, working in the field of alcohol and drug-abuse prevention.[10]

Five years later, Lt. Col. John Glenn was back in the news. One of the country's pioneer astronauts, he orbited the earth aboard Friendship 7. TV audiences remembered the modest, winsome contestant of the 1950s and took a measure of pride in his latest achievement. Following his legendary space mission, Glenn went into politics, eventually winning a landslide election to the U.S. Senate from Ohio in 1974.

The wave of big-money games not only deposited stacks of dollar bills at the feet of contestants but provided mountains of merchandise to lucky players. *The Big Payoff,* a generous giveaway even before *The $64,000 Question,* added more stylish apparel and accessories, in addition to the ongoing grand prize of a $2,000 mink coat and an overseas vacation. The durable daytime series brought together as contestants a deserving woman and her husband, father, son or a male close enough to attest to her good works or character. While the lady sat on a queenlike throne, he answered three questions from M.C. Randy Merriman, a Minneapolis broadcaster chosen by Walt Framer for the job.

The Big Payoff was basically a fashion show with music. It showcased major label clothes and led to promotional spinoffs such as Big Payoff dinnerware and dolls.[11]

"The giveaway really wanted you to win every prize," recalled Paul Bennett of Cleveland, a contestant in January 1958 with his wife, Sally, a young songwriter. "There were no trick questions, but I looked for one on the second question about the world's largest desert. I bypassed the obvious answer 'Sahara,' " Bennett ruefully remembered, "and replied 'Gobi.' Nevertheless, for our brief moment of fame we won a closetful of dresses, luggage and jewelry."[12]

The chief fashion model was a former Miss America, Bess Myerson, whom producer Walt Framer had heard speak at a Jewish Anti-Defamation League gathering. "He was moved by what I said," explained Myerson. "Some time later, he called me to co-host his new show 'The Big Payoff,' because, he said I was beautiful, talented and could speak well and because I was Jewish."[13] The mink coat giveaway was "the start of my own big payoff," stated Myerson who became commissioner of cultural affairs for New York City in the 1980s and then fell from high positions in political and corporate circles when she figured in a conspiracy to rig the divorce of her lover. Ultimately, scandal enmeshed her as it did a number of her quiz-genre contemporaries of the 1950s.

ABC's *Treasure Hunt* gave winners a chance to open one of 30 or so boxes. The contents ranged from $25,000 in cash to a head of lettuce. Originated, produced and emceed by comedian Jan Murray, the daytime show added drama through the mechanism of choice. But before a treasure chest was opened, Murray, who was one of the very few stand-up comics to host a game show, gave the player an alternative. He could play it safe by drawing a card and settling for the amount of money shown on its face.[14]

Murray had to "marry" a good game with comedy. "Quizzes were the most alien type of program for me. If a game is good, audiences don't want some clown interfering with the proceedings." *Songs for Sale* at CBS provided a vehicle for Murray's successful entry into broadcasting in 1950. He never thought the series would last. "I was convinced that it would run out of competing would-be songwriters, but it became a great and long-lasting show, bringing in people with songs from all walks of life."[15]

Later with *Treasure Hunt*, Murray formed his own merchandise-gathering outfit called Ceilward Enterprises. By 1956 this show and many of the other big giveaways had their own companies to procure prizes. Giveaway merchandisers or "contest consultants" collected so many extra refrigerators, boats and fur coats that periodically they sold off a warehouseful to discount dealers. Thus a number of such middlemen fared very well. Norman King, after some ten years as a prize coordinator, managed to acquire investments such as a small factory and several apartment houses. "The television prize business has been very good to me," he understatedly boasted to a *Broadcasting* magazine reporter in 1959.[16]

Some moderately successful producers on the sidelines attempted to enter the big-game field. Jack Barry and partner Dan Enright searched for a quiz after their *Life Begins at Eighty* panel was dropped and *Can*

Do, a celebrity stunt feature with host Robert Alda, failed. Barry-Enright then adapted the game of blackjack to video. The first player to score 21 points—at $500 a point—without missing any quiz questions earned the right to return indefinitely until a contestant defeated him. Theoretically, there was no limit to the amount of money anybody could win. Questions came from categories over which the players had no control, and during a match, a contestant could halt play if he thought he was ahead after the second question was asked.[17]

On the first show, a policeman once again scored high, taking home $12,500. Yet during the first two months, *Twenty-One* failed to catch on. Many viewers complained about the lack of dazzle as well as the overly complex rules; others tuned out because of its midweek 10:30 P.M. time slot. Pundits remarked that *Twenty-One* needed a dose of the sponsor's products, Geritol and Serutan. Then Enright made what seemed a suicidal move; it placed the NBC show opposite *I Love Lucy* on Monday nights.

Enright and M.C. Jack Barry knew it had a chance to pull away some of Lucy's audience if it could line up some personable contestants like Gino Prato, Redmond O'Hanlon, Myrt Power and Capt. McCutcheon. Enright's staff found their star attraction only a few miles from their office. In the last weeks of 1956 it brought to viewers a good-looking and affable 30-year-old English professor from Columbia University. Charles Van Doren, whose interests ranged from sports to music, was teaching literature at a salary of $4,400 a year. With the approval of his father, Pulitzer Prize poet Mark Van Doren, and his mother, author-editor Dorothy Van Doren, Charles entered the contest. It would turn out to be a 14-week game and the most eagerly watched duel of wits of the 1950s.

Van Doren faced a part-time, and not-so-young, college student, Herbert Stempel. He had written to the show after its second telecast, requesting a chance to appear. He passed the program's standard three-hour screening test, scoring a very high grade. Enright's first major winner, Stempel was cast as an ex-GI struggling to get through City College. A complacent, arrogant contestant, he struck viewers as the know-it-all "heavy," while readily winning $48,000 in a half-dozen broadcasts. The boyish Ivy Leaguer Van Doren was brought in to knock off the overbearing Stempel. The well-bred challenger quickly kayoed the smug champion.[18]

By mid-January 1957 Van Doren, with an amazing knowledge of many varied subjects, had built up his winnings to $99,000. On January 21 he crossed the hundred-grand mark, outscoring a former college president, Edgar Cummings. His popularity surpassed all previous game-show contestants. His mail ran to 500 letters a week, and his telephone rang so often, day and night, that he had to request an unlisted number. Hollywood offered film roles and *Time* magazine made plans for a cover story. Proposals of marriage to the handsome bachelor poured in. Meanwhile, Lucy's ratings at CBS dropped measurably.

On February 11 Van Doren built up his bank roll to $138,000 by answering questions on George Washington, musical shows, European queens, and bodies of water. He won by outscoring John Kieran, Jr., son of the *Information Please* panelist, and Dr. Hall Griffith, a writer. A week later, he fended off Kenneth Gould, editor-in-chief of *Scholastic* magazine, to add $5,000 to his winnings. The second challenger of the evening, an attractive lawyer, gave indications that the champion might be in trouble. Vivienne Nearing, whose husband, Victor, had unsuccessfully competed with Van Doren in January, battled him to a tie before time ran out. On February 25 a determined Nearing, who admitted she was out to avenge her spouse's loss, again tied the most famous English instructor in America. Van Doren, now breaking out in cold sweats as he stammered and struggled for answers from within his isolation booth, reached for another record-making bundle of cash. On the third appearance together, Nearing and Van Doren again tied. On March 11 the long-running battle of the booths neared a climax.* Was a fourth tie in the cards? Another closely fought contest kept viewers on the edge of their chairs. On the first question, Van Doren failed to name Baudoin as the king of Belgium. Nearing already had supplied the correct answer. On the next category, "animals," she added seven to her point score of ten. Van Doren trailed with ten. Nearing decided to stop, thus deposing the popular professor.[19]

Twenty-One crowned a new champion who, in the weeks ahead, followed in the same tracks as her illustrious predecessor.

Charles Van Doren's charm and intelligence seemed to herald a new day for academe. Students and their parents expressed great pride and pleasure that a campus in the 1950s could produce an all-around, likeable "Mr. Chips." Many youngsters, inspired by Van Doren, took a greater interest in school work. He was too important a symbol to fade back into the halls of ivy. Van Doren signed a lucrative contract with NBC as a frequent guest on Steve Allen's show, guest host on the *Today Show*, and a regular panelist on NBC radio's *Conversation*. His days of obscurity and frugality seemed over.

Barry-Enright, too, was on a roll. During 1957 they added four new shows to day and prime time. *Dough Re Mi*, a musical game, had a contestant try to identify songs after listening to a handful of notes. *High-Low* was an adaptation of poker in which a contestant competing against a panel had the choice of bucking the panelist with the highest

---

*On March 4, in spite of widespread protests by viewers, *Twenty-One* was preempted by a special *Producers' Showcase* presentation of "Romeo and Juliet."

number of answers with the one with the lowest number within a multiple-answer question. The bright and affable panel for the premiere consisted of Burl Ives, Patricia Medina and John Van Doren, who was described as "a chip off brother Charles' block." Jack Barry added this Ford-sponsored show to his host assignments, keeping a firm and pleasant hand on this new money game.[20]

Tic Tac Dough, an NBC noontime giveaway, branched out as an evening series. Quizmaster Jay Jackson presided over the game board of squares, divided into various categories and questions, which, if answered correctly, entitled the player to cross or circle. A surprise nonplaying guest on the initial prime time version was Charles Van Doren, who plugged his upcoming stint on NBC's *Wide Wide World*.[21]

M.C. Win Elliot, who took over *Tic Tac Dough*, soon created his own quiz, *Win with a Winner*, based on the concept of horse racing and track betting. Five players, each at a numbered post, advanced according to their ability to answer odd-lot questions. The contestant with the most points won the race. Home audiences got into the race by sending in postcards with their calculation of the exact winning order. "It was something like picking the Daily Double," Elliot explains.[22]

As producer, he auditioned a dozen M.C.s, including the relatively unknown Ed McMahon. NBC leaned toward Sandy Becker, a kids' show host. He got the assignment but flopped on the first show. "He just couldn't handle the race track format," Elliot declared. "The show fell apart, and I had to step in and take over as M.C. We survived the opener and ran until the fall of 1958."[23]

Vying with the 1957–58 entries of Elliot and Barry-Enright were presentations such as the Goodson-Todman *Play Your Hunch* with Merv Griffin; *For Love or Money* from Walter Framer's shop and featuring Bill Nimmo; *Lucky Partners*, a Martin and Allen Stone offering with M.C. Carl Cordell; *Bid 'n' Buy*, a summer replacement for *The $64,000 Question* starring old giveaway hand Bert Parks; *Top Dollar*, produced for CBS by Merrill Heatter and introducing radio personality Toby Reed.

Producer Joe Cates placed his *Haggis Baggis* across the board at NBC Monday through Friday. Disc jockey Fred Robbins emceed the daily telecasts, while twenty-year-old Jack Linkletter, the son of Art, handled the Monday night edition. "Like father, the son appears destined to enshrine himself among vacationing out-of-town contestants in search of giveaway iceboxes and washer-dryers," concluded *Variety*. "In addition to the closing plug for the airline carrying contestants, there's now a payoff credit to a moving van for hauling the loot home to winners."[24]

Tic Tac Dough was one of the first quizzes to air in color. Quiz shows generally received low priority for color telecasts, although by late 1956 NBC increased its evening schedule of color TV programming by 50 percent. Variety shows, dramatic presentations, and special events attracted those advertisers who insisted on color. But by 1958 game shows were sharing more of the NBC peacock and its rainbow-hued equivalent at CBS.

Videotape, too, had made an impact. Ampex introduced its efficient recording system and its pristine clear picture in 1956, and the first application of video tape and the machine was CBS's broadcast on November 30 of *Douglas Edwards and the News*.[25] The network outlet in Hollywood recorded the feed and replayed it three hours later. Taped programs licked the troublesome conflict between sun speed, signal speed, clock time and human habit. "The advantage," wrote Helen Bolstad in *TV-Radio Mirror*, "is obvious to any viewer who, because of his location, has been offered a major drama just when he wanted to eat dinner, or, at late night, had had the weird experience of watching the second half of the Jack Paar show 'live' before the kinescoped first half could be delivered to his screen by his local station."[26]

Game-show producers welcomed tape and its superiority over film and kinescope because it could be played back immediately, erased and purchased more cheaply. It now allowed them regularly to stockpile a supply of programs for network airing and syndication. "Live" quizzes, however, still dominated the evening hours, and color remained an unnecessary frill. Producers were still more concerned with jackpots.

In the wake of Van Doren's coup on *Twenty-One*, *The $64,000 Question* and its sister show opened the gates to winnings in the quarter-million-dollar plateau. Hardly a week passed without some $100,000 passing to a winner on one of these games or from its closest competitors. The pressure grew to discover engaging and bright players to fill the home screen nearly every night of the week. Television games not only found and presented these new folk heroes but created and shaped them. The saga of Horatio Alger had taken on an aspect undreamed of in the traditional rags-to-riches optimism.

Once again, New York quizmakers turned to local city schools for a potential young hero. In the fifth grade of P.S. 26 in the Bronx, Revlon found a ten-year-old youngster with an uncanny knowledge of science and math. In March 1957 Robert Strom began a meteoric financial rise as he answered a string of interminable complex questions week after week. He soon doubled his $64,000 winnings by unraveling complicated electronics formulas and intricate mathematical questions. Strom, whose father taught electricity at a vocational high school, became interested in science at age seven, after starting to read and write at three. Outwardly, he seemed untouched by the turmoil attendant on his celebrity status. The strain was on his parents who put an end to his winning streak at the unparalleled level of $192,000—triple the $64,000 prize of a year earlier. To save taxes for the Stroms and other such winners, Revlon worked out a special deal. Money would be paid in three annual installments. At one point in the contest, Hal March quipped to Strom, "If you get married this year, you can save $28,000 in taxes."[27]

In July Strom was back in action. The science whiz picked up $32,000 from a tie with eleven-year-old David Junchen of Sherrard, Illinois, on *The $64,000 Challenge*.

Mere $64,000 winners became almost footnotes. When Comdr. Edward Peary Stafford, a Navy pilot and grandson of the Arctic explorer Robert E. Peary, won for his knowledge of American literature, he was overshadowed by the growing $100,000-plus contingent.

As Robert Strom moved into the winner's circle, a $70-a-week stockroom clerk from St. Louis was found by the *Challenge*. Forty-seven year old Teddy Nadler was poorly educated but gifted with a photographic memory. In a multisubject category he defeated four college professors on classical music, geography and history and outscored notables such as restauranteur Toots Shor on baseball facts and figures. The tense, ordinary-looking savant parlayed his ability to dredge up obscure information to $252,000—the largest individual cash prize ever awarded in the history of U.S. broadcasting.[28] Like Leonard Ross, his fortune and notoriety later became a mixed blessing and, at times, an ordeal for himself and his family. Yet in 1957 and 1958 Teddy Nadler was the pride of St. Louis and the envy of millions of brainy but unaccomplished ne'er-do-wells.

Millions more—including many undergraduates and professors on college campuses—began suffering from acute inferiority complexes as a result of the multitude of genius-appearing quiz winners. Leading academicians reassured those worried over not being able to store up facts, names and dates. Astounding memories for such data were not really the best type of brain to possess, they were told. Princeton's new president, Dr. Robert F. Goheen, agreed. "There is more to a liberal education than a meticulous storing up of facts about everything under the sun. The important thing is to know what to do with the facts and the ability to think objectively."[29]

"Relief at Last," headlined the Philadelphia *Bulletin* in an editorial that concluded a bit tongue-in-cheek: "That settles a problem that had been gnawing at the nation's very social fabric."[30]

But another kind of problem was gnawing inside those who had been contestants on some of the big-money games. Several participants felt manipulated and cheated and now were about to do something about their displeasure and vexation.

›22‹

The Chips Fall

Standby contestant Edward Hilgemeier, Jr., waited outside the CBS studio broadcasting a new daytime quiz. A would-be actor and part-time bartender and butler, he had supplemented his income by appearances on game shows. Now, on May 20, 1958, he sat in a backstage room with two contestants already selected to play *Dotto*, a test of connecting dots that formed a famous face. Each face contained 50 dots, and two competing players were given the choice of answering five-, eight- or ten-dot questions. A correct answer connected the corresponding dots. When the well-known face was identified, each unconnected dot was worth $20 to the lucky contestant. To young Hilgemeier, every dollar culled from this children's game would help pay room and board as he struggled with a career on the fringes of show business.

As he waited to be called by program producer Edward Jurist, *Dotto* challenger Yeffe Kimball and another contestant were herded away for last-minute instructions for the opening repartee with M.C. Jack Narz. Hilgemeier was left alone with current *Dotto* champion Marie Winn. He observed her writing in a small notebook. Soon everybody was led off to another area. Hilgemeier was struck by the unusual camaraderie between Winn and the staff of *Dotto*.[1]

The show that morning pitted Winn against Kimball, who was quickly defeated. As Hilgemeier watched from the wings, he felt Winn's answers were at the tip of her tongue before the question was completed. He sauntered back to the standby area and picked up Winn's abandoned notebook. There he found a page with names written on—names that he had just heard Marie Winn give as answers. He ripped out the page and returned to the *Dotto* studio where he met the unsuccessful Yeffe Kimball going off.

"This is a fixed show," he said to her. "I've got proof in my pocket."[2]

Both sought legal counsel. Together, they confronted producer Ed Jurist who acted appalled by their accusations. When shown a copy of the notebook page, Jurist offered Hilgemeier an appearance on *Dotto* if he remained silent. He refused and left. Soon lawyers on both sides attempted to settle the matter. Offers of cash were made and turned down. Kimball accepted a $4,000 settlement, but Hilgemeier, who had never actually appeared on camera, was offered only $1,500. Now called a blackmailer by *Dotto* program supervisor Sy Fischer, Hilgemeier finally agreed to that amount after Fischer threatened to call the police.[3]

Nevertheless, the disparity between Kimball's settlement and his smaller cash sum annoyed the unemployed actor. He already had told his friend Jack O'Grady, a reporter at the *New York Post,* the full story. With his encouragement, he retained a lawyer to draw up an affidavit describing everything that had happened in connection with the quiz, including his acceptance of the hush money. On July 31, O'Grady delivered a copy of this document to the office of the Federal Communications Commission. Another copy was deposited at the advertising department of *Dotto* sponsor, Colgate-Palmolive.

Within days, talk of behind-the-scene investigations, coverups and payoffs spread through the quiz empires. Rumors flew back and forth between Radio City and Madison Avenue, Wall Street and Publishers Row. The shock waves actually had been building up for three years. The bold question, "Are quiz shows rigged?" had been asked journalistically from time to time.[4] But never had this issue been taken too seriously by the press or the public. Every now and then panel show producers slipped questions to panelists that were calculated to draw laughs. A few might have passed along an answer or two. Big-money quizzes, producers realized, provided sponsors with free newspaper space when an ongoing contestant climbed up the money pyramid and won. Ratings increased weekly from such contests, and a sponsor had only ill will to reap from the defeat of a public favorite.

At the peak of the big-money craze in December 1957, writer Gordon Cotler compared quiz proceedings to wrestling or a Western: "A television play always ends the way it ought to end. Why not a quiz show? How long would wrestling have lasted on television without scripts?" Turning to the Western as an analogy, Cotler wrote that when a man works his way up to the $64,000 question, the viewer wants him to answer it as surely as he wants the sheriff to outdraw the heavy. "The fact is, of fourteen contestants who have gone for the $64,000 question, only two have missed."[5]

Yet after two and a half years since the bow of *The $64,000 Question,* nobody had turned up evidence that a fix was in on any quizzes. Cotler surmised that the only method of favoring a contestant would be to ask him questions to which he knew the answers. On the other hand, knocking out an undesirable player was easy. A very hard or ambiguous question usually did the job. (One of the early radio quizzes used this one on contestants it didn't like: "If the new tubular lights are called fluorescent, what are the old-style electric lights called?" Seven out of ten didn't know that the answer was "incandescent."[6])

Both Dan Enright and Steve Carlin, who between them produced the three quizzes offering the largest cash prizes in 1958, regularly denied that they even knew enough about what a contestant knew to weigh the question for or against an individual. "Some people have said our contestants are too good to be true," Carlin said. "Well, the typical American has many facets, and those who doubt it show little faith in the American way."[7]

Was it un-American to doubt the honesty of the big-money TV quizzes? Weren't games on network radio a bit seasoned with scripted responses? Hadn't television just followed and built upon the ways of the older medium?

Producer Earle McGill had included a section on audience-participation shows in his 1940 textbook *Radio Directing*. The CBS executive explained that it was best to rig a program to prevent tie scores (unless the players were to return for a subsequent rematch): "When contest programs end in a tie . . . there is a note of uselessness about the whole program. By rigging the program, it is not suggested that dishonest methods be used to make sure that there is a winner, but when the scorer has passed on the information that there is likelihood of a tie, by judicious framing of a question, the M.C. can reduce the possibility of there being one."[8]

A little manipulation for the sake of entertainment was accepted. Television took this premise several steps further—to the point where prebroadcast coaching and advance feeding of information had become par for many a quiz course. But some of those individuals "manipulated" soon would cry "foul."

Behind the scenes, Herbert Stempel had been fuming over his loss to Van Doren. "Now we have a clean-cut intellectual as champion instead of a freak with a sponge memory," he overheard someone say backstage after leaving *Twenty-One* with a hefty $49,500.[9] Stempel departed with more than a sockful of money; he left with the knowledge that he had participated in a fix. Enright had instructed him to miss a question that called for identifying the Oscar-winning picture of 1955, "Marty," which was one of Stempel's favorite films. To soothe his pride, Barry and Enright held out the possibility of future employment as a research consultant.

Before his final appearance on *Twenty-One*, Stempel told several friends including reporter Dave Gelman of the *New York Post* of his forthcoming "dive."[10] None apparently took him very seriously. But early in 1957, having gambled away or been swindled out of most of his winnings, he started to haunt Enright's office, voicing threats of exposure unless he was given money or a job. To combat what he sized up as a blackmail attempt, Enright persuaded Stempel to sign a document that he had not received any aid whatsoever. Temporarily appeased with the lure of a panelist slot on a future program after his college graduation, Stempel nevertheless railed against the overnight acclaim and lucrative offers falling into the lap of one-time rival Van Doren.

In June 1957 the promised job fell through. Enright explained that all his shows—*Twenty-One*, *Tic Tac Dough*, *Dough Re Mi* and *Concentration*—had been sold to NBC, and thus he was unable to do any hiring. An angry Stempel again turned to the press—this time, the *New York Journal-American*. The paper investigated his accusations. Reporters met with the *Twenty-One* production team and NBC, but lacking significant corroborating evidence, the paper declined to print any story.

Meanwhile, a contestant on *The Big Surprise* sued the producers for $103,000, claiming a deliberate "sacking." Dale Logue had missed her question at the $10,000 plateau. She claimed it was the same question as the one she had missed in a warmup session before going on camera. Logue's lawyer brought the little publicized case to the attention of the Federal Trade Commission (FTC). The FTC initiated an investigation at the lower staff levels, which proceeded to get ex parte statements from the producers as well as their assurances that the quiz was not false and deceptive. The complaint never reached the high levels of the commission, and the inquiry was closed in May 1958, a year or so after the program had left the air.[11]

Another incident at the height of the big-money games would remain hushed up. In late 1957 a winner of $16,000 on *The $64,000 Question*, the Rev. Charles "Stoney" Jackson appeared on the sister show. A couple of days before the broadcast, he was interviewed and quizzed on his field of interest—great love stories—and given a number of definite questions and answers. When Jackson stood in his isolation booth, the same question given him in the interview was given to his opponent, who missed it. When Jackson received the same question, he reluctantly answered correctly, winning the round and ending the match.

Although he took his $4,000 in winnings, Jackson was upset enough to send a telegram to *Time* magazine saying that he had been given an answer on the quiz. The magazine ignored it. Even his hometown paper in Nashville declined to publish his story. He told his parishioners of the deceit and then gave up trying to convince anybody of the TV fraud.[12]

The public remained unaware of the deceptions until Ed Hilgemeier held in his hand solid documentation of rigging. Hilgemeier filed a complaint with the New York District Attorney's office. Meanwhile, CBS promptly terminated *Dotto* without explanation and moved into its place a daytime version of *Top Dollar* with Warren Hull. (The prime-time *Dotto* was similarly dropped by NBC.) Several days later the D.A.'s investigation began. Nonetheless, other top-rated quizzes continued their run. They were still very cheap to produce and built up sponsor identification quickly. That summer, a handful of new games had emerged with gimmicks, such as extra sensory perception of contestants *(E.S.P.)* and auctions of off-beat prizes *(Bid 'n' Buy)*.

"Through all these gimmicks, most quizzes earned adequate, if not spectacular, ratings while waiting for the next public hero to appear," media historians Harry Castleman and Walter Podrazik have observed. "No matter how many variations were devised, audience identification with contestants was the most important element of success."[13]

Nonetheless, by the middle of 1958 the big-money quizzes were running out of steam. Their ratings had declined. Viewers tired of the all-too-similar formats. Soon *The $64,000 Challenge* would be canceled, then *Twenty-One*, and finally, the prototype of all such programs, *The $64,000 Question*. The networks claimed poor ratings for the departures, not the many charges being leveled from all directions.

That August the *Journal-American* finally ran Stempel's story on the *Twenty-One* fix. On August 25, 1958 (the morning after Teddy Nadler set the all-time quiz prize record of $252,000 on *Challenge*) D.A. Frank Hogan announced that his office was looking into a complaint of quiz fixing. Hogan soon widened the inquiry to include a full-fledged grand jury investigation.

The grand jury, under the aegis of assistant district attorney Joseph Stone, began hearing witnesses in September. Scores of ex-contestants were called, as well as program producers, staff supervisors, and sponsor representatives. Nine months later, in June 1959, after 59 sessions and 200 witnesses, the grand jury finally finished its assignment and handed over a report to Judge Mitchell D. Schweitzer. Its findings did not constitute an indictment but rather a presentment, calling attention to corrupt practices within the television industry without holding specific people responsible. Because no trial would result from the report, Schweitzer declared that the document would damage those named in it by not providing an opportunity for them to publicly clear their names. He promptly sealed and impounded the presentment.[14]

Most of the summer was spent debating whether the report should be made public or not. Judge Schweitzer finally agreed to provide the minutes of the proceedings to Congressman Oren D. Harris, the chairman of the House Committee on Interstate and Foreign Commerce, who had announced that his Subcommittee on Legislative Oversight would hold public hearings on the quiz-show matter that fall.

Congressional investigators were unable to uncover any law that game producers might have broken. A breakthrough took place when witness Dan Enright acknowledged that "controls" had been standard operating procedure for years on his and other quiz shows. He said that the whole point of rigging was to insure a dramatic flow of events while making certain that characters who appealed to the public became the returning champions. Other witnesses came forward to voice similar revelations and feelings.

Then on November 9 into the witness chair came the most famous contestant of all. A subpoenaed Charles Van Doren, after having denied before the grand jury any advance help and wrongdoing in connection with his appearances on *Twenty-One*, confessed that he accepted help before each broadcast. The deeply troubled Van Doren revealed that producer Albert Freedman had coached him in both answers and demeanor. Freedman told the college teacher that quiz programs were only mass entertainment and giving help to contestants was a common practice. Besides, it enhanced the acquisition of knowledge and the pursuit of teaching careers. Van Doren felt that he was promoting "the intellectual life" to the youth of the country. Later, he conceded that he had been "living in dread for almost three years."[15]

Following his startling disclosure, other contestants revealed the various ways and measures that they had been a party to in order to rig a game. Even 13-year-old Patty Duke, who had gone on to Broadway as Helen Keller in "The Miracle Worker" after an appearance on the *Challenge*, admitted that she had been coached and "screened" by assistant producer Shirley Bernstein. At a press conference that week, President Eisenhower voiced his dismay over the spreading scandal, comparing it to the 1919 Black Sox World Series baseball fix. He ordered the Justice Department to determine whether new laws were needed to crack down on quiz shows. While network executives denied knowing that the shows were "plotted" and no one was directly implicated, a number of game producers and quizmasters fell into disrepute, including Dan Enright, Jack Barry, Hal March and Louis Cowan.

All in all, the scandal led more to a comprehensive self-examination and self-policing than to the passage of laws. The networks assumed greater control over programming, trusting less to ad agencies and sponsors. Legislation was eventually enacted, but it was limited to the area of making it a crime to fix a quiz contest.[16]

Critic-historian Les Brown wrote in his *Encyclopedia of Television* that the episode ruptured the public and the government's trust in the integrity of commercial broadcasting. "Coupled with the concurrent payola revelations in radio (involving disc jockey payoffs, likened to commercial bribery), the episode led to amendments to the Communications Act in 1960. One amendment made illegal the presentation of programs purporting to be contests of skill or knowledge where the result is in any way prearranged, another made more explicit a station's obligation to make known on the air when money or other consideration is received for broadcast material."[17]

Despite the FCC's support for tighter regulations, the agency sought to prevent excessive government control of the industry. In a speech to the National Association of Broadcasters in April 1960, FCC Chairman Frederick Ford said broadcasters could prevent government interference by "adherence to the Television Code by all stations rather than risk the imposition of restrictive measures which can only result in destroying originality and initiative."[18]

Within the television industry, many pointed out that quiz shows were no different from any other type of video entertainment. Dan Enright admitted that contestants were selected on the basis of admiration or distaste. "People tuned in to see someone unpleasant defeated," he stated in 1987. "The press played a part in making contestants celebrities. One reason for the subsequent outcry was because newspapers felt deceived, cheated and foolish. Their professional standards had been tarnished." But Enright candidly admitted, "We did something wrong and had to pay for it."[19]

Albert Freedman, the producer of *Twenty-One*, insisted that programming be recognized and judged as entertainment and entertainment only. The real crime, in his estimation, was the attempt to convince the public that the shows were not approximations of reality, but living breathing reality itself. "Our only error was that we were too successful," he said at the time. "The stakes were too high, and the quiz winners fused themselves into the home life and the hopes and aspirations of the viewers."[20]

Jack Narz, M.C. of *Dotto*, believed that the producers should have admitted that they "scripted" the show in order to make contestants sound better and advance as big winners. "I thought the show would last a long time," he observed in 1987, "but it went off in six months. Colgate kept me under contract after *Dotto* was pulled. They realized it was not my fault and didn't want me to suffer."[21] *Dotto* was his first network show as an M.C., and he had given up announcer and sportscaster assignments in California to come East for the quiz. The brother of Tom Kennedy (who changed his name when he went into the announcing and emceeing business to avoid a sponsor conflict if Jack were selling an auto or shampoo and he had a chance to work for a competitor), the *Dotto* host overcame the rigging stigma and went on to fill the quizmaster job on *Top Dollar*, *The Price Is Right*, *Video Village*, *Beat the Clock*, and *Concentration*.

The dean of audience-participation shows, Dennis James believed that every contestant needed direction.* "I told them to prepare, bone up, act excited, sweat a little. They direct Gregory Peck in a movie don't they, so why can't we direct contestants in order to create a show?" he said some 25 years after hosting *High Finance, People Will Talk* and *Name That Tune*. "I'm a firm believer in control and not being a mere traffic cop. That's showmanship. But that doesn't mean one gives the answers—absolutely not!"[22]

CBS president Frank Stanton accepted both blame and responsibility and thus diffused much of the antipathy felt toward the networks. Taking bold action, he canceled the only three big money quizzes left on CBS: *Name That Tune, Top Dollar* and *The Big Payoff*.[23] The latter's producer, Walt Framer, heard about the end of his show from a telephone call from Stanton.

"Walt, we're taking off all shows that give away more than $100."

"Mr. Stanton, how do you determine whether there's honesty or dishonesty on the basis of a $100, one way or the other?"

"That's an interesting point. And I really don't know that answer."[24]

Viewers, too, were bewildered over the scandals. Some were downright angry over the deception. Others wanted to forgive the sins of contestants and those who took part in the sham that fooled tens of millions of Americans. A straw poll conducted by the *Miami Herald* hardly condemned the quiz hoaxes. Most Miamians wanted the shows back, regardless of all that had taken place. Crooked or straight, most loved them. "Everything on TV is somewhat of a lie," one such individual observed, "but it's still entertainment."[25]

None of the "coached" players or the "coaches" themselves met punishment for their participation in the duplicity that became one of the top ten news stories of the year (along with Soviet Premier Khrushchev's visit to the United States, Russia's successful moon rockets and Eisenhower's year-end tour of Europe and Asia). A handful pleaded guilty to charges of second degree perjury in Special Sessions Court in New York. They admitted that they had lied earlier to a grand jury. All drew suspended sentences and were given no jail terms, no fines. Judge Edward A. Breslin even spared them the pain of probation. Their long humiliation, he said, had been punishment enough.[26]

Most of these sullied TV game-created figures made concentrated efforts to stay clear of the limelight and rapidly passed into comparative obscurity. Of the many notable contestants, Joyce Brothers emerged virtually "clean" and parlayed her TV exposure into a successful career as a television talk-show hostess and author of a syndicated column on

---

*James began appearing on DuMont's experimental TV station in New York in 1938. When that company began regular network telecasts in 1946, he hosted the pioneer video quiz *Cash and Carry* and daytime variety program *Okay, Mother*.

psychological problems. Reputedly, she was one of the few players that producers could not nudge out of the winner's circle. Her comprehensive and keen knowledge of boxing outmaneuvered the quiz masters.[27]

Panic-stricken, Charles Van Doren, however, handled himself very badly, at first protesting his innocence to NBC, to his own lawyer, to the audience of the *Today Show*, to the grand jury and to the Senate investigating committee. His escalating association with television and academe came to a decisive end. The deceit ended both careers, as he was fired from NBC and dismissed from Columbia University. He took to writing books under a pseudonym and later editing works under the auspices of the *Encyclopaedia Britannica*. By the mid-1980s he was an author under his own name, yet far removed from academia and the media limelight.

Variety covered in great detail the medium's troubled times. Somewhat introspective and self-laudatory, it paused to remind readers of the merits of the industry. "TV, for all its worth, for all the enjoyment it had brought millions, for all its contributions to education and other worthwhile endeavors, has had its growing pains. It is young, but it's not a juvenile delinquent. It's learned a lesson."[28]

›23‹

Viands and Popcorn

In an address before the National Association of Broadcasters in the spring of 1961, the new Kennedy-appointed FCC chairman viewed television in contrasting terms. Newton Minow first spoke of the industry with words of admiration, calling broadcasting a most honorable profession. It had given broadcasters a profit, he noted, of more than $243 million in 1960—a return of 19.2 percent. "For your investors the price has indeed been right."[1] But he described the achievements of the medium as few and far between. Finally, he invited the convention delegates to sit down in front of a TV set for a full day. "I can assure you that you will observe a vast wasteland. You will see a procession of game shows, violence, audience participation shows, formula comedies about totally unbelievable families, blood and thunder, mayhem, violence, sadism, murder, western badmen, western good men, private eyes, gangsters, more violence, and cartoons."[2]

Chairman Minow called for an accounting with broadcasting's beneficiaries, the American audience. "Never have so few owed so much to so many." He called for the industry to offer more substance and quality in return for using public property.[3] The big-money quizzes especially had polluted the video environment in Minow's estimation. Like a cloud of smog, the offensiveness still hung over Minow's "wasteland," a reminder of the sorry state into which the industry had very recently fallen.

Network housecleaning of games cleared prime time of the genre, sparing only the tried and true celebrity panel and charade shows, Groucho Marx and *The Price Is Right*. Some of the void left by the "hard" quizzes was filled by news and public affairs programming. Yet overall television still beamed most of its prime-time fare to those viewers geared toward comedy, action-adventure or dramatic series. On the other hand, the daytime schedules took on more commercial significance as stations salvaged their existing untarnished low-stake games and developed new question-and-answer formats for the morning and afternoon viewer. In one form or another the quizzes, the panels, and all the programs that came under the loosely knit grouping of "bringing audiences into the act" showed no sign of totally disappearing from the home screen. In fact, by 1961 audience-participation shows occupied 37 weekly hours of network television.[4]

Whereas CBS had eliminated many of its quizzes, NBC acted more selectively. One program it kept in place was a highly successful game purchased from Barry-Enright in a lucrative prescandal arrangement. *Concentration* first appeared with host Jack Barry as a temporary replacement for *Twenty-One* in the fall of 1958. Named after and based on the children's card game in which two players alternately uncover two cards at a time from a deck spread out face down until one player collects the greater number of pairs to win, the contest added a puzzle, called a rebus, with prizes described on the face of two matched card squares. Winning contestants could continue to play until they were unseated or until they won 20 games in a row.

Concentration became an immediate hit, helped in part by avoiding the usual series of mind-boggling questions that by 1958 had begun to bore audiences. Hugh Downs, the TV sidekick of Jack Paar on *The Tonight Show* and a debonair and well-read broadcaster, agreed to act as host for the daytime version just as the quiz-show scandals started to rock the industry. "We made the game virtually rig-proof," Downs said, "and thank God, the public trusted us."[5] Before joining the program, Downs made it clear that he would not be part of a contest that could survive only with controls. He noted: "Those vestiges of showmanship that *Concentration* displays are neither a threat to its acceptance as an honest broadcast, nor are they considered essential to interest on the part of the viewer. They are part of a tradition that does not need to be discarded immediately for the sake of avoiding an appearance."[6]

Downs remained as host of the well-crafted game for more than a decade, until his daily appearance on *Concentration* as well as the early morning *Today Show* made impossible demands on him physically. Before his departure in 1969 he won an Emmy for his role on the show, which briefly surfaced as a nighttime summer replacement. The series ran into the 1970s and then was purchased by Goodson-Todman for syndication, bringing the engrossing contest to a new generation of game fans.

The relatively low-key handling of quiz programs brought well-deserved attention (and an Emmy) to a straightforward high-level quiz called *College Bowl*. Originated and produced by Don Reid—first on radio in the early 1950s—it graduated to CBS television in 1959. The upscale contest was structured like a basketball game, complete with tossup and bonus questions. "I had a feeling that there was a need for a sport that utilized mental abilities on wide-ranging subjects, just as there were physical contests for undergraduates," Reid explained.[7] A *College Bowl* team had a coach and four members, each specializing in a different area of knowledge. Any member of the team could try to answer, but he had to be right or the question passed to the other team.

Schools vied to field teams for the weekly Sunday competition. Lesser-known colleges often topped the academic heavyweights. Student participants fought for the glory of their alma mater. The college represented by the winning team received $1,500 for its scholarship fund from longtime sponsor General Electric. The runner-up institution was awarded $500. When the series ended in 1970—routed by televised Sunday football games and other opponents—there were nearly 1,500 institutions on a waiting list.

Another benefit stemmed from a team's appearance on the collegiate contest. Between "halves" each team was permitted to show a short promotional film extolling the virtues of its school, a maneuver that frequently boosted that college's alumni fund campaign. When the University of Notre Dame defeated rival Georgetown, the school's team members were welcomed back to the campus by the mayor of South Bend, Indiana, a band and a cheering section.

College Bowl's best-known host was a highly educated Phi Beta Kappa graduate of the University of Texas. Allen Ludden took to the job naturally. Professorial in horn-rimmed glasses and boyish crewcut, he brought a sparkling and cordial demeanor to the collegiate proceedings. Ludden was soon in demand to handle another game whose players needed mental agility.

Password bowed in late 1961 as a daily CBS game and within months expanded into an evening feature with Ludden as the series' host for its long run. A simple but engaging game, it was based on word association. Two teams played against each other. During a round, one member of each team was given the secret word and then, either by synonym or wild suggestion, tried to cue his partner by guessing the word. Each team consisted of a member of the studio audience and a celebrity. This arrangement—the first successful pairing of celebrities with civilians—proved to be unusually popular and allowed a wide spectrum of players whose free-association responses were often clever, offbeat or witty and occasionally Freudian.[8]

From its start, the country became hooked on the game. Some viewers were virtually addicts—to the degree that they purchased and played the Password board game at home. Annual tournaments were a highlight of this Goodson-Todman production, whose staff, including originator Bob Stewart, producer Frank Wayne and M.C. Allen Ludden, reportedly played it compulsively backstage and at home.[9]

Jack Benny's appearance on the show (with his daughter Joan) remains a classic. When he was given the secret word *miser*, his first clue to his partner was "me."

An equally attractive no-frills game began a long run in the mid-1960s. Created by a former game-show host, Merv Griffin (*Play Your Hunch* and *Keep Talking*), *Jeopardy!* reversed the usual procedure of question and answer to "answer and question." The elementary format had an almost bewitching appeal as three players competed for comparatively modest cash prizes by supplying correct questions to answers uncovered on a board of 30 squares, containing five answers in each of six categories. The program's last round, the suspense-filled Final Jeopardy question, allowed contestants to wager as much of their winnings as they dared on an "answer" question.

Presided over by the gentlemanly Art Fleming, the contest attracted all ages. College students were among its biggest fans, and they often cut classes to tune in the daytime show. Many of their professors admitted it was their favorite game too. A home version of *Jeopardy!* went through a dozen editions and honed the skills of countless future contestants. The series enjoyed a decade of tremendous popularity and then, after a three-year hiatus, emerged in a new syndicated version with a *Super Jeopardy* board and higher stakes. Few TV games ever stimulated the audience's thinking process while generating a modicum of humor and surprise.

Although the decade hatched a number of classic games, it introduced its share of desultory mishmashes. NBC showcased "Mr. Television" Milton Berle with a contest of physical dexterity. *Jackpot Bowling* combined rolling bowling balls with comedy relief in an attempt to attract viewers besides sports fans. Audience mail for the series rapidly fell into two categories: (1) "How dare bowlers take up so much time?" and (2) "What do we need Berle for?"[10]

Each Monday at 10:30 P.M. two professional bowlers competed in a nine-frame match in which only strikes counted. The winner received $1,000, with bonuses for successive strikes. The odds against one's rolling five or six straight strikes, for example, were astronomical; yet less than a month after its debut, Frank Clause hit paydirt picking up a six-strike jackpot of $40,000.

As a spectator sport, the pastime failed to excite viewers. Berle's nine-minute repartee fell short of attracting a diverse audience. Sports fans, accustomed to more animated and dramatic events in larger arenas, tuned out. This "TV turkey" lasted 26 weeks. Steve Allen, asked by Berle at the time why he wasn't hosting a game show, answered: "It isn't because I haven't got the talent. I haven't got the guts."[11]

The 1960s also brought to audiences the shortest-lived game in the

history of the medium. In an effort to keep their in-house star comedian Jackie Gleason on the home screen, CBS tossed together a guessing game, à la *What's My Line?* On the first and only telecast of *You're
in the Picture,* a guest panel of four celebrities stood behind a flat of
headless bodies, poking their heads through holes above each torso.
The contest revolved around them guessing what the picture formed
might be.

Within the opening minutes of the game, everyone sensed the makings of a monumental flop. Gleason knew it was doomed, and neither
he nor his panel was funny or engaging. "The show was such a disas-
ter that I draw a blank every time I try to explain the format," he said
later. "It had something to do with identifying celebrities' pictures. The
only good show was the second one, in which I apologized for the first
one."[12]

A far more visually and logistically angled game aired on location as
America's first daily outdoor TV show. *Treasure Isle* originated from a
large four-foot-deep concrete lagoon, constructed for the video treasure
hunt by multimillionaire John D. MacArthur at his Colonnades Beach
Hotel near Palm Beach. The series began on December 18, 1967, with
the on-camera blessing of Florida Governor Claude Kirk after Mac-
Arthur's dog reportedly bit through the main broadcast cable, delaying
the premiere several days.

In the first round of each game, a married couple in bathing suits
paddled around in a rubber raft, picking up pieces of a giant foam
rubber jigsaw puzzle floating in the lagoon. In round two, they landed
on Puzzle Island to assemble the pieces. The number of pieces they
collected and the number they assembled spelled out a riddle and determined how much time they had to dig in the sand for hidden bounty
on Treasure Isle, once they navigated through hazards, like whirlpools
and coral reefs.

Contestants had to pass an unusual test for a game show. "These
people," explained producer-director Paul Alter on the eve of the first
telecast, "must have some familiarity with the water." Chosen so that
they wouldn't drown, they also had to be "personable people who
enjoy being outgoing and sparkling—the kind of people you'd like in
your home."[13]

Hosted by a onetime high school English teacher, John Bartholomew
Tucker, the complicated game encountered rough sailing. Audience interest paled after a few weeks of rather repetitious racing and tedious
digging. A unique, albeit exhausting format without predecessors, the
show sunk by the end of the tourist season. MacArthur had hoped
Treasure Isle would revive business at his oceanfront hotel. But the contest only proved to be another unsuccessful gimmick to shore up sag-
ging revenues at his seaside digs.

MacArthur, Berle and Gleason had no monopoly on game failures.

David Susskind produced *Supermarket Sweep,* a race against the clock to see which shopper could tally up the highest grocery bill. Red Rowe hosted *Face the Facts,* a daytime game on which contestants tried to predict the outcome of previously filmed dramatizations of criminal trials. *The Family Game* with Bob Barker gathered parents and their children in a game of what answers came from which offspring. A similarly mounted entry, *The Generation Gap,* saw a team of adults face a team of juveniles, with predictions on who would answer what. The gambling game *Beat the Odds* with M.C. Johnny Gilbert just didn't.

The new programs of the 1960s steered clear of big-money prizes and superluxury jackpots. Together with vigorous controls by the networks over contestants' participation, quiz shows were called game shows and avoided the red flag of giant dollar signs. But after four years' distance from the scandals, the executives at ABC decided that the turmoil had been forgotten. The network that came out unblemished in the earlier investigations chose to enter the field of big jackpots in the fall of 1963.

Producer Robert Stivers went back and tore apart all the other shows of the 1950s to see what caused them to be rigged and how they were rigged and then announced his absolutely unriggable *100 Grand.* The game pitted an amateur expert against five professionals in a chosen field. If the fledgling downed the pros (selected by chambers of commerce) and then answered five questions submitted by viewers, he won $100,000.

Widely publicized as the incorruptible big-money game that would bring back honest "hard" quizzes, *100 Grand* even had players write their own questions while encased in large, bubble-shaped isolation booths.[14] The number of deadly dull obstacles between the contestant and the big prize became evident on the first telecast. The public looked but wasn't interested. The Sunday night show with host Jack Clark had three outings before its cancellation. ABC had better success with low-stakes formulas such as *Camouflage* and *Play Your Hunch.*

It seemed clear that prize money had become less of a riveting attraction to viewers and contestants alike. For the thousands who lined up at a game show studio with the hope of being selected as a contestant, it was less the promise of dollars and merchandise. The lure was television itself. The payoff came from the exposure on screen and the memories of a day in show biz.

Chuck Barris capitalized on this allure. He had floated from jobs as a promoter, management trainee and salesman to the head of ABC's West Coast daytime programming department. There were few pre-evening ABC shows beamed from Los Angeles in the early 1960s, but for Barris, the weather was great, the girls were tanned and pretty and the setup was ripe for a saleable TV game show. He soon created, packaged and sold a 1960's version of the popular wartime *Blind Date* program. The premise was the same old idea with a few contemporary twists and dialogue. A young, attractive woman asked questions of three eligible bachelors hidden on the side of the stage by a high partition. Then, on the basis of their answers, she chose one for a dream date. The girl's only basis for choosing a suitable escort was her instinct, grounded on how the guys responded to her inquiries. But before she was allowed to meet the bachelor she had picked, she was forced to face the two she had ruled out. When girl met boy, in front of millions of viewers, she and he would suffer some form of traumatic reaction, either one of extreme disappointment or ecstasy.

The low-budgeted contest, everyone agreed, fell far short of good taste and was inherently dangerous. The first seven or eight taped shows contained so much sexual double entendre and innuendo that they were totally unfit for broadcast. "Spontaneous shows give birth to spontaneous asides," wrote Barris in his autobiography, *Confessions of a Dangerous Mind*, "and—depending upon the intelligence of the performer—the asides may not always be within the bounds of acceptability."[15] He recalled those early tapings when contestants were getting a kick out of being flagrant on coast-to-coast television. "Angelic little girls and seemingly benign gentlemen were metamorphosing into garbage pails in front of our very noses—and there didn't seem to be anything we could do about it."[16] In near desperation, Barris brought in an actor who posed as an FCC agent. Backstage, he portrayed a character whose job was to scare contestants with threats regarding their use of foul language on the show. It solved the question of downright crudity. Nevertheless, *The Dating Game* jiggled with a full measure of "tits and ass" humor that made the proceedings—with host Jim Lange—a salacious put-on.

It was only a step more for Chuck Barris Productions to add an equally suggestive whoopee-prone show called *The Newlywed Game*. All it needed was four couples married less than a year. The program's premise—how well newly married husbands and wives know, or don't know, each other—was primal and highly identifiable. The wives would first be asked a set of questions and then their husbands would be brought on-stage and asked the same set of questions. A couple was awarded points when their answers matched. The duo with the most points would win a prize. Bowing with M.C. Bob Eubanks less than a year after its sister show, it had undeniable mass appeal, although the tasteless fluff was totally lambasted by critics.

"I concluded that 'The Dating Game' and 'The Newlywed Game' were hits because the television audience could identify with the contestant," explained Barris.[17] "Almost everybody had, at one time or another, dated, and many were married. And if they weren't already married, they had parents who were, and who knew what marriage was all about." He observed that everyone could relate to what the contestants were going through: the discomfort, the embarrassment, the relief, the anger, the humor. Both shows had the "fork-stopping ingredients television viewers loved: spontaneity, drama, titillating sexual innuendo, identifiability."[18] By 1969 Barris claimed he was producing more network television shows than any other company in the world: 22 half-hours a week of national TV.

ABC, if not for these two games, might have fallen into the hands of the acquisitive Howard Hughes. He made two attempts to purchase the network. He abandoned the first in July 1968 because he did not want to appear personally before the FCC; the second in March 1969 after watching these two Barris shows back to back one Saturday evening. "These two game shows represent the largest single collection of poor taste I have ever seen," Hughes was quoted as saying. "Let's forget about ABC."[19]

Barris's parodies and putdowns basically reflected the raison d'être of some of the reigning series of the 1960s (*Beverly Hillbillies, Petticoat Junction, My Favorite Martian, The Addams Family*) and resulted in still another banal display of off-the-wall peculiar habits and proclivities. In 1976 he launched *The Gong Show*, a nongame amateur hour-type contest for anyone who aspired to perform on television, whether gifted or totally talentless. First hosted by Gary Owens and then by Barris himself, it became the most outrageous show on the tube with a melange of acts from singing farmers to acrobatic Eskimos. Such was the instant whirling dervish appeal that clubs and groups across the country began staging their own "gong shows" and periodically fed their lunatic fringe "winners" to the Hollywood-based paterfamilias.

Barris's zany creation—he once called all his shows "popcorn for the mind"—was apparently inspired by an earlier show in "human motivation."[20] Monty Hall's *Let's Make a Deal* welcomed a studio audience to play the old pea and shell game of choices and deals. But very soon would-be players came to broadcasts outfitted in bizarre and outlandish costumes and props. All hoped to attract attention and be selected on the basis of their colorful, unusual garb and items to trade with ebullient Hall. The exchange of one prize of known value for a mystery prize stimulated America's gambling urge. Should one stick with a box that may be empty or go for an object in back of a screen? Hall dangled several tension-building choices before each contestant—sometimes a chance to win a car if the key fit versus a color TV set already in hand. A pure-and-simple gambling show, it became the only program to compete successfully on Sunday evenings with the *Ed Sullivan Show* and *The FBI*. It was said to be the best deal NBC ever made, running in prime time and daytime for years.[21]

Although plain folk off the street may have dominated the daytime home screen, celebrities received a big boost during the 1960s from the introduction of a highly engaging and well-packaged contest called *Hollywood Squares*. Developed by former script and comedy writers Merrill Heatter and Robert Quigley, it grew out of an earlier format, *Celebrity Game*, with Carl Reiner. Using a tic-tac-toe stage set, with celebrities seated in the three-tiered box, the game's civilian contestants earned their Xs and Os by stating whether a selected Hollywood Square had correctly answered a question. Straightman Peter Marshall of the comedy team of (Tommy) Noonan and Marshall proved to be apt casting for M.C. His interacting regulars included many a comedian's comedian—Morey Amsterdam, Jonathan Winters, Wally Cox, Cliff Arquette, George Gobel and Paul Lynde (who occupied the center square for years).

With squares for nine players, the show hired an array of show business notables who eagerly sought a well-paying square to showcase their charm and wit. Both Marshall and Paul Lynde won Emmys for their work, and the program itself gained several Emmys as the year's Outstanding Game or Audience-Participation Show.

On New Year's Eve 1962, NBC introduced a Goodson-Todman contest with two celebrities and four contestants called *The Match Game*. Based on the concept of asking people to write down something to fill in the blank in a sentence and seeing if the answers matched, this word show generated many humorous replies and sometimes downright risque responses. Two panels competed under the guidance of M.C. Gene Rayburn. An actor-comedian (who started at NBC as a page) and a mainstay of Steve Allen's *Tonight Show*, he had branched into games as host for *The Sky's the Limit* and later the popular daytime musical quiz *Dough Re Mi*.

The Match Game flourished throughout the 1960s. After a four-year hiatus, it resurfaced from Los Angeles with more celebrities and fewer civilians and increasingly provocative lines of questioning like "The Burbank Fire Department doesn't have a hose, so when there's a fire, the men stand in line and blank on it."[22] Still hosted by the genial Rayburn, the proceedings built up an even bigger following during its second run and soon went into a syndicated edition as well. For one season it combined with *Hollywood Squares* into a 60-minute show, bringing the top scorers of *Match* into the second half-hour to play out the X and O grid.

Heatter-Quigley, Monty Hall, Chuck Barris, Merv Griffin and other game-show producers and developers nibbled away at television time and clearly demonstrated that games were back in ample number, especially on daytime schedules. By the fall of 1969, there were 16 game shows on the networks between the daytime hours of 10 and 3 o'clock.[23]

But head and shoulders above all quiz and game packagers and promoters stood the company that had had its roots in radio, introduced
enduring TV panel shows and weathered the storms stirred up by the
fixing scam. Goodson-Todman dominated the game-show business with
a steady stream of old favorites and new entries. Mark Goodson emerged
as both eloquent defender and statesman of the genre.

In 1938 at age 23, Mark Goodson had entered radio to make some
money but not as a contestant. He had studied economics at the University of California at Berkeley, had been elected to Phi Beta Kappa,
and intended to pursue a law career. The plan fell through. A job as a
disc jockey in San Francisco provided an immediate livelihood and radio itself an intriguing challenge. His assignments as a record spinner
and announcer led to work on a regional quiz program called *Quiz of
Two Cities*. The proceedings vied San Francisco against Los Angeles in
a battle of wits and barbs between a team representing each metropo-
lis. A foursome from each city, usually from a particular occupation or
profession, answered the same questions. Each team played the game
from a studio in the home city and were blocked from hearing the
questions and answers of their opponents situated in another studio
hundreds of miles away. Only listeners picked up both sides of the
match, which resulted in $2 for each correct answer and $12 to the
winning team.

The show gave Mark Goodson his first exposure to handling quiz-
show contestants. The spontaneity and unpredictability were still unique
to radio, and he was fascinated by the possibilities of combining people
off the street in a game situation. Goodson soon created his own show,
Pop the Question, for San Francisco listeners. Broadcast from the basement of a theater, it positioned contestants in front of a dart board
covered with balloons. When a player popped a balloon of a certain
color, a question of predetermined difficulty and prize value was asked.
He soon realized his attempts at ad-libs and jokes would be no threat
to the networks' then-popular Bob Hawk.

Late in 1941, Goodson came to New York where he got into directing
radio programs. Assignments on *Portia Faces Life*, *Appointment with Life*
and dramatic segments on the *Kate Smith Show*—which he also wrote—
kept him busy. His work showed promise. His experience with *Quiz of
Two Cities* was not wasted either. He took on the job as announcer for
the New York version of the game, which vied the city's five counties
against each other in a contest called *Battle of the Boroughs*. But it was
his attempt at creating a radio game show called *Winner Take All* that
gradually opened up a new direction to his activities.

Winner Take All brought two contestants to the microphone at the
same time—a significant departure for quiz programs of that time. A
question was posed to them, and the first to answer correctly won

points. If he outscored his opponent, he went on to play another round. The winner was often "carried over" to the next show, thus building suspense, not unlike the closing moments of a soap opera. Goodson also introduced an electronic signal device called the "lock out."[24] This gadget determined which of the two contestants pushed his answer button first. A fraction of a second was crucial when both contestants simultaneously signaled an answer. The device solved the dilemma. An audition of *Winner Take All* had failed to interest broadcasters in San Francisco. Goodson, however, had made a recording of the pilot and brought it to New York.

Not long after his arrival, Goodson met radio writer-producer William Todman. A recent graduate of The Johns Hopkins University, he had freelanced before joining the CBS flagship station in New York. Goodson told his new friend about the audition disc for *Winner Take All* and his hope to sell the program. Bill Todman listened to the show and liked it.

"I'm a pretty good salesman," he said to Goodson.

"Fine. You're welcome to take the idea and sell it," Goodson replied.[25]

Todman made the rounds of agencies and networks but to little avail. Year after year, he continued to tote the idea. Finally, in 1946 as the postwar giveaway craze took off, CBS added the show as a daytime sustainer with Bill Cullen as M.C. It gained an audience, and a partnership between Goodson and Todman was formed.

Next came *Stop the Music!* In spite of a barrage of criticism over the almost constant and time-consuming spiel of prizes offered and won, the show topped its competition. A year after its radio bow, it reached television as millions now saw the array of prizes while waiting to hear their telephone ring. The program spawned imitations, including Goodson-Todman's own offshoot, *Hit the Jackpot*.

This spinoff attempted to ride on the coattails of *Stop the Music!* The quiz solicited cards by mail from radio listeners, who were randomly selected, called and quizzed. It featured Bill Cullen, Al Goodman and his orchestra and the Ray Charles Singers. Prizes occasionally ran over $25,000 and often included a car from sponsor DeSoto. Lasting only the 1948–49 season, *Hit the Jackpot* gained some attention among book lovers. The jackpot included $1,000 worth of books representing several hundred titles from publisher Rinehart & Co. This solid stack of hardcovers was intended to add dignity to the giveaway proceedings. Bill Todman, in particular, had become sensitive to the charge flung by the press that giveaways were "a form of lunacy for which giveaway producers will be held accountable on the day of judgment."[26]

Columnist John Crosby was bemused by the prize. "The printed page," he noted, "is a competitive medium and, while it has been consistently losing ground to the blandishments of radio, it still seems to me a risky proposition to expose a radio listener to $1,000 worth of books. The sheer bulk of which," he wrote, "is sufficient to keep him entertained for a couple of years without any assistance from the radio." [27]

Now deeply entrenched in game shows, Goodson-Todman drew upon the vast untapped competitive and acquisitive nature of the growing new television audience. A 20-questions format with a panel of celebrities, *What's My Line?* became a Sunday night viewing habit and the second longest-running show on TV—only Ed Sullivan topped this record in the first quarter-century of the medium. [28]

The decade of the 1950s augured well for Goodson-Todman. Viewers readily embraced their shows *Beat the Clock, I've Got a Secret, To Tell the Truth* and *The Price Is Right.* In an interview 30 years after the introduction of these programs, Mark Goodson noted that these were "golden" shows—original, unique and popular. "Such big ones come along infrequently. These heavyweights appear on the average of once in five years." [29] Goodson-Todman apparently defied the odds. They had a half-dozen emerge in the space of five or six years.

"Good ideas create the public mood, not anticipate it," he explains. "The formula comes first; then we see if the public goes along with it. Creating a game show is like inventing a new sport, or a new card game. And how often does that happen? A blockbuster has got to be as compelling as a football game." [30]

Like major team sports, the chief ingredient is people. Bill Todman often remarked that his shows were "people" shows on both sides of the camera. "People are in them and people like them." [31]

Like every game-show shop, Goodson-Todman turned out a string of misses on radio and television: *Judge for Yourself, Get the Message, Spin to Win, What's Going On? Number Please* and *Split Personality.*

In Goodson's view, only about 25 people in the entire country have an instinct for dreaming up games that are good. His own all-time favorite is *To Tell the Truth,* which he calls a "textbook of a great game" with its well-balanced combination of verbal fencing between a panel of questioning celebrities and a trio of responding contestants. [32]

Goodson-Todman made it a rule to focus attention on the "people factor" in all their game endeavors. The widespread criticism of *Stop the Music!* taught them a lesson in avoiding heavy-handed merchandise spiels—although *The Price Is Right* by its very nature emphasizes prize merchandise. In their shop, prizes have been important but certainly could not make a weak show well; prizes, they acknowledge, often do make a solid show a bigger and more important event. *What's My Line?* Goodson frequently pointed out, gave a top prize of only $50—a nominal cash award by most standards.

The most important aspect of an audience-participation show is the desire to be seen or heard, according to Goodson. Recognition is what attracts an individual to the game-show spotlight. "Of course, a contestant wants to win something and make money by hitting the jackpot. But people who don't win a dime are thrilled anyway. Losers always say they had a wonderful time. They've had their day in the sun, and at the moment that's all that matters."[33]

One of the significant changes during Goodson-Todman's long involvement in games—together with the move of operations from New York to Hollywood in the 1970s—has been the switch from live to taped shows. In the days of instantaneous television broadcasts, there was greater excitement and tension, especially among the cast and production staff. Contingency planning formed a part of the proceedings. If a guest did not show up, for example, there had to be a backup. *What's My Line?* designated Bill Todman or John Daly as an alternate mystery guest. The very nature of live television took away the concept of full censorship. Spontaneous answers, observations and ad-libs on quiz shows had no prior review. Anything approaching a complete script was impossible by the very nature of the show.

"Live TV was like a car without brakes, a pencil without an eraser," Goodson observed in an interview in 1984. "Tape is easier, but you lose something that those earlier shows had."[34]

By the 1980s, his shop had supplied a dozen games to television overseas, including *The Price Is Right, I've Got a Secret, Family Feud* and *Beat the Clock.* London's *Daily Mail* has called Mark Goodson "king of the games" for good reason.[35] No other creator of game shows, British or American, comes close to equaling the output of Goodson-Todman (and since the mid-1980s, Mark Goodson Productions) in the United Kingdom. Around the world, too, their game shows have been repackaged with local hosts, be it Holland or Australia, Trinidad or Italy.

Bill Todman's selling stick-to-it-iveness helped to build an empire that became the biggest, richest and oldest supplier of TV games. By the time he died in 1979, his multimillion-dollar partnership with Goodson had expanded into other fields, such as newspaper publishing, real estate and film production. During the 33-year collaboration, more than 30 games—a remarkably high percentage for a single outfit—came to life through the golden touch of Goodson-Todman.

›24‹

Play's the Thing

"Come on down! You're the next contestant on 'The Price Is Right!' " was the call that propelled jubilant contestants down the aisles year-in, year-out. The audible trademark of *The Price Is Right*, it has reverberated over the air longer than any other quiz catchphrase—undeniable proof of the popularity of the longest-running network game of television. *The Price Is Right* bowed during the height of the big-money quizzes, survived the postscandals crackdown, gained in audience appeal, revamped its pricing games and expanded its broadcast time period. A generation later, it was as fresh and exciting as it had been when it first appeared in 1956.

A gambler's dream, this game of guessing the retail price of merchandise integrated elements of blackjack, or 21. A winner had to come close to naming the price without going over the top. "If you do, you're broke," creator Mark Goodson explains. "It's the essence of danger."[1]

Goodson claimed *The Price Is Right* came about when he and Bennett and Phyllis Cerf played it at home, trying to guess the value of a dress, a piano, a table. Not an original concept among this game-conscious trio, the format had been aired by radio personality and program developer Maurice Dreicer over WOR in the 1940s as *What's It Worth?* Early television attempted a prototype called *Auction-Aire* in which contestants bid on canned goods.

During the troubled days of quiz shows, the program stood as a paragon of what a TV game could and should be. *Price* was a game that literally anyone could play. "By rewarding shrewd bidding on small grocery items as well as on lavish showcases," Maxene Fabe points out, "it made a virtue of being a thrifty, knowledgeable shopper. Everyone in the audience became a vociferous consumer expert."[2]

Everyone who managed to secure one of the 320 tickets for a broadcast of *The Price Is Right* had a chance to be picked as contestant. Just before each show, as the audience lined up outside the doors of the studio, the selection was secretly made.

"One of the things that contributes to the success of 'Price' is that contestants don't know that they've been chosen until their names are called out over the air from the stage," explains Phil Wayne, who joined the production staff as a "go-fer" at age 18 in the 1960s. "When I find someone I think is suitable I use a code word, and my assistants make a note of it."[3] Of the nine chosen for each show, the majority are women because daytime audiences, both at home and in the studio, tend to be largely female. The staff looks for natural enthusiasm and extroverted attitude in their selection. But looks play a significant part too.

"Often there is a year's wait for tickets," says Phil's father, Frank Wayne, the executive producer. "But the network gives special attention to out-of-town requests."[4]

Host of the series since its reintroduction in 1972 (after a hiatus of three years), Bob Barker believes that *Price* has a bigger cross-section of America than any other show in television with people from more far-flung parts of the country and varied walks of life.[5] Barker, who helped revitalize *Truth or Consequences* in the late 1950s, gained inestimable skills in dealing with audiences on that Ralph Edwards madhouse. In the 1970s the high-tech *Price* became the only game to air each day for a full hour in many areas and in the process augmented its games to six per show from an inventory of some 50 contests.

Of the thousands of contestants that have "come down," Barker individually remembers very few. He does recall the woman who suddenly fainted, falling dead away over backwards. "All I could do was step over her and say to announcer Johnny Olson, 'Who's our next player?'" At another taping, during a commercial break, a woman began to give birth to a baby. Barker asked the ushers to help her out. But she didn't want to leave.

"You might call my name," she exclaimed.

"We're not calling any names until you get out of here," Barker replied.[6]

The most imperishable incident involved a young woman in a very low-cut tank top. Olson called her name as the first contestant to come on down. She stood up and began to jump up and down wildly. In her joy, both of her breasts popped out and she ran undraped onto the stage. The audience went crazy. Barker was behind the set, ready to be introduced. "When I came on camera, the audience was out of its mind," he recalls, "and I thought it was all for me. I kept turning around, gradually realizing something more was going on. I turned to Johnny and asked what happened."

"Bob Barker, this girl has just given her all for you."[7]

Bill Cullen, M.C. for the first nine years of *Price*, usually implied that conducting a game show was as easy as it looked. But not so for *Price*. There, you had to know exactly where you were to be at every moment. "It's a complicated show mechanically. You could break your neck if you didn't know where to stand." A host, he explained, had to know how to steer the game so that it broke right for commercials, end on the second and handle difficult contestants, whether they be frozen by nerves or loquacious to the point of distraction, and not overshadow the format.[8]

Cullen's work on *Price* helped make him one of the most sought-after hosts on television. He called himself a "natural upwinder" on the set. But off-camera he talked much less, especially about himself. By the 1980s he tried to retire but producers continually came along with new ideas, proposals and offers. For one who started in radio at $25 a week, it was hard to turn them down, Cullen admitted.[9] He kept busy, hardly concerned if the latest series ran for 13 weeks or 13 years. His quick wit had made him a major personality, even though producers were hesitant to hire him for his first television game *Give and Take* because he had a pronounced limp, left over from a childhood case of polio.

Meanwhile, radio never totally abandoned the quiz format. Although it chiefly aired news, disc jockeys and talk shows after 1960, when the last of its daily soap operas was scrubbed, promotional giveaways and competitive gimmicks never disappeared. They gained attention and lent an atmosphere of excitement for regional stations.

Some of the most dramatic proof of sales effectiveness for advertisers, national and local, was demonstrated by many stations using on-the-air promotion and quiz features to stimulate listener interest. The contests were as varied as the sponsors that joined in the giveaways. Sure Way Super Markets in Green Bay, Wisconsin, for one, moved into first place in retail grocery sales by broadcasting a daily telephone quiz. KWIZ in Santa Ana, California, offered *Kwiz Magic Numbers* with local merchants providing prizes, including autos, pianos and food products. WSB Atlanta hosted a weekly quiz whereby each contestant received $25 worth of air time for each correct answer. The prize was paid off in spot announcements for the civic organization or charity the player represented.

A group of five New England stations carried *Women's Quiz Bowl* with two five-woman panels competing on current events, theater and art questions. Winnings went to United Fund agencies. A Hempstead, Long Island, FM station asked listeners to submit a list of "joywords" to be eligible for prize drawings. Nearby WBLI gave away thousands of gallons of gasoline in prizes. To win, a listener had to call the station after his license plate number was broadcast.[10]

The "hard" quiz format maintained a hold on radio. KDKA Pittsburgh broadcast a 16-week science students quiz. Some 60 high school panelists competed for scholarships at Carnegie Tech and Pittsburgh University. The similarly structured *College Bowl* periodically reappeared, both regionally and nationally. *Texaco Opera Quiz* continued to flourish during Saturday afternoon intermissions of the Met Opera broadcasts. Producer Geraldine Souvaine pointed out that the quiz was the best known of the regular intermission features and generated many of the 10,000 letters received during a Met season. The quiz gathered a panel of experts or opera enthusiasts who tried to answer questions sent in by listeners. Prizes included opera books and recordings and radios.[11]

Another durable format based on the parlor game of animal, mineral or vegetable was *The Man Says Yes*. First beamed from KMPC Hollywood by staff announcer Bob Shannon in 1947, it combined studio players and call-in contestants. Some 30 years later Shannon revived the show, claiming it to be the only "live" radio quiz in Los Angeles.[12] As late as 1989 a syndicated lineup of 12 three-minute games was being bought by stations for call-in contests. Producer Mark Richards who popped *The Radio Game Show* questions at KENO-AM Las Vegas licensed the idea for other outlets aiming to gain higher ratings and greater attention.

For daytime and early evening television viewers it became almost impossible not to tune in a game show, especially after the 1970s. The FCC unknowingly contributed to the lineup. The agency, concerned about increasing domination of local television by the networks, ruled that stations in the 50 top markets must fill at least one of their four nightly prime-time hours with independently produced material. Stations were no longer allowed to use network reruns or previously broadcast movies. The rule was designed to promote competitive development of alternate sources of television programs.[13]

This so-called access time rule represented the most far-reaching effort by the FCC to stimulate diversity in TV programming through economic regulation. The National Association of Broadcasters, however, called it "an unwarranted intrusion in the internal affairs of our industry."[14] Other dissenters rightly predicted that the substitute programming would generate more games and more M.C. talk shows.

By the fall of 1975 quiz shows, indeed, dominated the prime-time access slot—7:30 to 8:00 P.M.—on the networks, Monday through Friday evenings. Exemptions were made for network news, public affairs and children's programming. Thus from 7:00 to 7:30 P.M., the networks maintained their usual newscasts while meeting the one-hour stipulation.

To fill the half-hour weekday slot, stations decided to avoid the high cost of putting together their own shows and readily turned to outside producers, mainly syndicators, to find vehicles to adhere to the FCC rule. Broadcast executives pointed to what they called the high audience acceptance, namely, high ratings, of game shows and lighter forms of entertainment, compared to documentaries and children's shows.

An array of recycled old favorites and unproven new entries poured from the syndication houses. Fleeting games such as *Anything You Can Do, Jackpot Bingo* and *On the Money* vied with established formats, including *Name That Tune, It Pays to Be Ignorant* and *The Dating Game*. The increased output of games also brought a new wave of hosts to audiences—more sophisticated, debonaire, movie-star handsome and wardrobe-conscious than many of the earlier TV M.C.s. The group included disc jockey Wink Martindale *(Gambit)*, singer Jim Perry *(Card Sharks)* and newscaster Alex Trebek *(High Rollers)*.

Chuck Woolery, for one, put aside his country music songwriting and singing to join a new NBC game in 1975. Called *Wheel of Fortune*, it gave players a chance to solve a mystery word or phrase and earn money to go shopping. All it took was the spinning of a roulette wheel and guessing correct letters. The Kentucky native and navy veteran helped build the initial high ratings for the daytime program. He parlayed his smooth style and keen gregariousness—and knack of cajoling contestants into self-revelation—into another show called *Love Connection*. An updated syndicated version of *The Dating Game*, it added a new twist—a couple returned to the show to report on the outcome of their first date.

Then in 1984 Woolery augmented his assignments when Reg Grundy Productions adapted the classic board game Scrabble into a fast-paced visual contest. Not an intellectual show, *Scrabble*, nonetheless, appealed more to households that had a greater familiarity with the word game that sold some 100 million sets by the mid-1980s. Actually, *Scrabble* resembled less the board game than it did a newspaper crossword puzzle. But it had the capacity to involve the viewer in competition with the players, "which is always an asset," *Variety* noted.[15]

Woolery's smooth colloquy combined a hearty zest and a natural response in handling players. "I'm not worried about making mistakes," he pointed out. "They're part of life." Looking back to his start in the early 1970s in the game-show genre (with a rudimentary *Wheel of Fortune* pilot called *Shoppers Bazaar*), he once observed: "Being a game host back then was like aspiring to be a used car salesman."[16]

TV dance party host Dick Clark, who had built a teenage following in the 1950s, brought his warmth and even-handedness—and grownup fans—to the game-show set. In 1973 he expanded from producing movies and music-related TV programs to hosting *The $10,000 Pyramid*. The ultimate professional who is always in control, he appealed to a broad spectrum of viewers who often commented on his appropriate compassion for those not quick enough to make the grade. As the *Pyramid* upped its kitty to $25,000, $50,000 and $100,000, the genial Clark never lost his enthusiasm for the Emmy-winning series that between 1973 and 1986 used more than 500 miles of words typed on index cards.[17]

A Broadway musical lead, Bert Convy seemed an unlikely candidate for a game host. The good-looking pop singer and serious actor—and one-time baseball player—was well established in his field. But with the growth of talk shows in the early 1970s, the chipper and glib performer discovered an affinity to hosting. He began his own show, *Tattletales*, on which three celebrity couples competed. A not untypical Goodson-Todman game of matching responses correctly, it won Convy an Emmy and, in the 1980s, the reins of *Super Password*. In 1987 he took another step when he created, together with Burt Reynolds, a spirited celebrity game titled *Win, Lose or Draw*. This sketch-pad charade game combined the aura of Hollywood at play with the intrigue of visual clues.

Members of minority groups, however, were slow to come into place as M.C.s. The game show stood as the last bastion to fall. Women as quizmasters (or mistresses) had made little headway. Blacks, too, were virtually ignored by network television game producers. Radio as well had only offered sporadic opportunities. Those few who broke the barriers had to demonstrate again and again their audience appeal at every step.

A radio actress in the 1930s, Arlene Francis, more than any other broadcaster of her sex, proved that a woman had a place at the reins of a quiz show. In March 1938 she joined Budd Hulick as cohost on a Mutual audience game that capitalized on her acting talents. This quiz, *What's My Name?* was built around the identification of celebrities, past and present. The main clues consisted of impersonations by Frances (of Dolly Madison, Eleanor Roosevelt, Martha Raye) and Hulick (of Fred Allen, Walt Disney), with frequent musical assistance from Ray Bloch's orchestra. "In general, show was smooth and smartly handled," *Variety* concluded. "Miss Francis perhaps a trifle too jolly. More easygoing approach might be better."[18]

Francis remembered the program as her first experience at ad-libbing and saying things not on a written script. It was important training for her future assignments on talk, panel and interview shows.

Her ability to handle herself as an M.C. brought her a show of her very own. *Blind Date* began as a summer replacement for Fanny Brice during World War II and matched servicemen and "glamor girls" for a date at New York's swanky Stork Club. The girl chose the G.I. who impressed her most favorably. Francis' polished professionalism in bringing together three couples for the evening won praise. *Variety* had only one criticism; "She lets herself appear too bright for her guests."[19] She later took the program to television. By 1952 she expanded her game-show chores as the so-called femcee of *That Reminds Me* and ever-present panelist on *What's My Line?* Perhaps the secret of her popularity and longevity is, as a friend describes it, "because she is the only person I know who acts as though life were the best party she ever attended."[20]

Radio groomed few quiz ladies as capable as Arlene Francis. Old-time musical comedy star Julia Sanderson was a good-natured cohost with her husband, Frank Crumit, on *Battle of the Sexes* at the end of their singing careers. But she acknowledged that her talents alone could not carry a game show. When Crumit died suddenly in 1943, she immediately retired and the *Battle of the Sexes* format came into the hands of men such as J. C. Flippen and Walter O'Keefe.

Film actress Wendy Barrie first gained recognition over the air from cohosting *Detect and Collect* during the war years. It gave away merchandise hidden behind stage curtains. Five clues were provided to detect it and collect it, together with cash prizes and a carton of Old Gold cigarettes. This radio exposure later help to launch a TV career. Her telecasts, usually talk shows, were very informal with little preparation other than lining up the guests. She was seen frequently sitting on the floor as she spoke to viewers, a tactic definitely considered a radical departure, even for the new medium. Barrie was seldom dull, which put her in "a rather exclusive class as far as daytime video is concerned," observed critic Jack Gould in 1955.[21]

Apparently, it also took an entrepreneurial-type performer to prove women could handle a quiz format. Singer and scriptwriter Irene Beasley sold the Ted Bates agency on a daily 15-minute musical quiz with questions submitted by listeners who, in turn, competed with studio contestants for 90 items of merchandise a week. Beasley agreed "to plan, build, assemble, provide, furnish, produce and broadcast" as a complete unit and package *Grand Slam* on behalf of the Continental Baking Company. She also supplied all the scripts, announcer, pianist, organist, director, stage director and prize supervisor for $2,100 a week in 1946 (an extra $600 was allocated for prizes).[22]

"She auditioned and hired me and all the staff," announcer Dwight Weist explains. "As the owner and producer of the series, Irene was totally in control. She was impetuous and brooked no backtalk. To her credit, *Grand Slam* ran for seven years on CBS."[23] When it ended, it was 14th in daytime radio ratings; 10,761 people chosen by Beasley played the game and carried off a share of some 35,000 prizes.

In Maxene Fabe's book *TV Game Shows*, Mark Goodson replies to the question of why so few women ever got to M.C. games. "Finding the right woman is very difficult for societal reasons," he says. "So far it's been tough to get a woman who has the necessary control who can say 'all *right*, that's enough fun, let's *play*' without sounding like a third-grade teacher or a gym coach. Often, if you get a woman who's soft and pretty and feminine, she comes over as mousy or saccharine or like a B-girl."[24]

It was Goodson who helped break down reservations against distaff M.C.s. In 1977 for *The Better Sex* he chose Sarah Purcell as the first woman to preside over a game show since Arlene Francis. With the girl-next-door good looks and a sense of humor, she had begun in TV as a local weather girl and movie host and then worked on a Los Angeles talk show before joining *Real People* for a five-year run. But not untypically, Purcell joined the new daytime (and short-lived) game as a cohost with Bill Anderson in a contest between teams of all male and all female contestants. Not until the 1980s did women make firmer strides. Betty White, a regular panelist on *Match Game* and *Liar's Club*, became the M.C. of *Just Men*. But the Emmy-winning endeavor lasted only three months. Actress Elaine Joyce soon took over *The All New Dating Game*, a syndicated remake of the original series, and actress-singer Vicki Lawrence presided over *Win, Lose or Draw*, a charade and drawing game. Yet it was a giant step from the days of radio when critics complained over the "handicap" of the female voice. One such commentator wrote in 1944: "Were it possible to pitch it several notes lower on the scale or slow up the speed of delivery, the program *Listen, the Women* would gain much in clarity and force."[25]

Blacks had an even higher and nearly insurmountable wall to climb. Beyond sports events, musical segments and comedy bits, very few were heard on radio or later seen on early television. Behind the scenes, too, they were virtually nonexistent. In the mid-1950s television quizzes made a concentrated and successful effort to bring blacks to the fore-front as contestants. A handful were recruited, and of them, a few became TV-created big-money winners. Celebrity contestants, such as Ethel Waters, Joe Louis and Geoffrey Holder, also appeared and won thousands of dollars. Earlier, radio had failed to use both the emceeing talents of black performers and the drawing power of black contestants—with one briefly aired exception.

In 1941 at the peak of the big-band era, producer Doug Storer came up with the idea of a black "Kollege of Musical Knowledge." Cast in the role of quizmaster-conductor in the manner of Kay Kyser was Cab Calloway. Billed as Harlem's own idea of what a musical quiz should be, *Quizzical* was basically a road show for Cab and his band. Contestants were picked from his audience and rolled dice. The dice gave the numbers of the question they were to answer. All the questions were about songs or musicians or musicals, but much of the fun was the clowning that went on by several vaudeville characters who were created by members of the band. In performance, the ethnic angle gave the show an extra boost. The contestants, too, were more diverting and uninhibited than most players, and brought a sense of fun and bubbling good humor rarely, if ever, heard over a major station.

But sponsors were nowhere to be found. "We auditioned dozens of backers," Calloway explained, "but it was impossible for Negroes to get a regular commercial sponsor in those days. . . . It was all right if we came on as entertainers on a white show, but we couldn't have a show of our own." [26]

Variety sized up that obstacle at the very start, along with biases. "Hard to predict how such an intangible will work out," the journal stated, "but there's no logical reason why the program shouldn't go nationally and commercially, possibly even in the south." [27] To Calloway's and Storer's credit, *Quizzical* jumped from WOR to NBC's Blue Network and lasted nearly a year as a sustainer.

Not until some 35 years later did a black M.C. return. Singer Adam Wade became the first black to host a network game show, *Musical Chairs*, at CBS. But the overly hip daytime game was short-lived, and the idea of a black Dick Clark or Dennis James had yet to get off the ground. Although blacks made tremendous gains before and behind the camera in the news and sports field, in situation comedies, soaps and made-for-TV movies, the game show seemed the last genre to welcome their presence.*

In the 1970s the doors opened wider to black contestants and indeed to members of all minority and ethnic groups. Although the welcome mat attracted all comers, once inside, they came under greater scrutiny. Potential players were rigorously screened and tested. If picked, on the day of their appearance they were rigorously sequestered. Kept apart from network employees, studio audiences and program guests, contestants were cloistered for long hours under the watchful eye of station standards and practices personnel. Until their moment on camera, they could never be certain of their ultimate selection.

With shows usually taped four or five back-to-back in a single day, the ordeal of waiting backstage took some of the glamour off the experience. A number of contestants who had gone through the process, from initial interview to player's platform, wrote of their trials and reactions to the amusement and enlightenment of would-be competitors.

Lois Lowry, a freelance writer who faced M.C. Art Fleming on *Jeopardy!* described her experience as impersonal and "no worse than having a baby." [28] Frank Giordano, an actor between jobs, claimed he had fewer auditions for a David Merrick show than he did for NBC's *Win-*

---

*In the mid-1980s black comedians Nipsey Russell and Flip Wilson briefly hosted *Your Number's Up* and *People Are Funny*, respectively.

ning Streak. "Six of us were ushered into a room to play the game. We were given specific instructions: answer enthusiastically, applaud yourself when you get a correct answer, and kiss your opponent regardless of who is victorious." For Giordano, the actual game was over in three minutes. "Bill Cullen thanked me for being on the show, and I was quickly led backstage to sign a release for my consolation prizes. I had won two bumper guards and a case of Veg-All."[29]

Yet players who came out on top reaped rewards that were soon to equal and, on a few programs, surpass the bounty of the late 1950s. Big-money shows crept back into fashion. *Sale of the Century,* a general knowledge game, held out the promise of $50,000 windfalls. A series of *Pyramid* word-association contests gave contestants a chance at $10,000, upped it to $25,000 and inflated the prize to $100,000 in the 1980s. *50 Grand Slam* had a top prize living up to its name. *Super Password* maintained an all-cash jackpot ranging from $45,000 to well over $100,000. The durable radio feature *Chance of a Lifetime* became *The $1,000,000 Chance of a Lifetime* with married couples vying for the biggest prize ever on television. When in 1976 Viacom Enterprises brought back the syndicated revival of *The $64,000 Question,* it faced inflation straight on. Viacom president Henry Gillespie stated that the prize money had been doubled and the title changed to *The $128,000 Question.* "Times have changed; we wish to change with them. We feel $128,000 is a proper reward for extraordinary knowledge."[30]

Other shows reflected such presentments. *Tic Tac Dough,* after a hiatus of 19 years, resurfaced in 1978 in network and syndicated versions with a seemingly unlimited treasure-trove of cash and luxury merchandise. A young contestant tested its capacity in 1980. Navy Lt. Thom McKee, a pilot based in San Diego, passed a 75-question exam and an interview to get a chance to play this nine-category trivia-question game patterned closely after the children's pastime of placing Xs and Os in a grid. "If you're in uniform, I think you have a bit of an advantage," he remarked of his selection.[31]

That spring twenty-four-year-old McKee began a nine-week winning streak of 88 games. The upstate New Yorker defeated 20 opponents and raked in $312,700 in cash and prizes, including 8 autos, 3 sailboats and 16 vacation trips. His winnings made him the all-time single top ace on a game-show series. (Runner-up Teddy Nadler in the 1950s had collected $252,000 from *The $64,000 Question* and its sister show.) "I never did count how many trips I actually won. Close to 20 I think. They had to be taken within a year, so most of them went by the board because I was on active duty."[32]

Ratings for *Tic Tac Dough* soared with McKee's unprecedented streak of luck. After 57 straight matches, he faced computer analyst Erik Kraepelien. M.C. Wink Martindale asked the champion: "What leading actress appeared both in "The Wind and the Lion" and "Starting Over?" McKee, an avid reader of almanacs, encyclopedias and *National Geographic*, could not think of the right answer (Candice Bergen). "Actually I wasn't too unhappy after two months of competition that I lost to Erik. He did very well himself, winning $66,000."[33]

Executive producer Jack Barry viewed McKee and his attractive wife as the all-American dream couple. "He's a grad of the U.S. Naval Academy—she's the daughter of a Navy man. He's tall and blond and blue-eyed. If 'Tic Tac Dough' had gone out and hunted for an all-American couple, they couldn't have come up with anyone better than the McKees."[34]

Jack Barry, as did *Tic Tac Dough,* had reemerged after a lengthy banishment. Blackballed by the industry, along with his partner Dan Enright, he once said to John Guedel—when he was coping with a drinking problem—"I took the rap. You guys got away with it. You guys were just as dirty." Barry later apologized. Guedel's shows, Barry subsequently realized, had been investigated and given a clean bill of goods.[35]

Unemployed and forced to move his family seven or eight times during the 1960s, Barry struggled to regain a foothold. His exile ended when the FCC approved his application for part ownership of a small FM radio station. With that base he began to create new game shows. In 1972 he brought to CBS *The Joker's Wild*, a game in which two players took turns spinning devices that resembled casino slot machines.

Enright, too, was hurt by his being part of the rigging syndrome of the 1950s. Only Screen Gems gave him a break. It hired him to develop games in Canada. Enright worked his way back into the business and rejoined Barry in the early 1970s. Soon Barry-Enright's *Joker's Wild* and *Tic Tac Dough* were very popular on the networks and in syndication.

But a Goodson-Todman game proved the most successful new entry of the 1970s. Based on the premise of second guessing, this contest between two five-member teams matched players' responses to those given previously by a nationwide group of 100 people. Called *Family Feud*, it had begun as a parlor game in Goodson's own home. "The concept evolved from the asking of a question with an answer that does not exist in a book," he once explained. "The answers were compiled from the group poll; contestants to win had to match their answers with the earlier feedback."[36]

Players were recruited from family groups, adding a concept only occasionally tapped by producers. Goodson expected to tape the new show in New York, where many diverse ethnic groups live. But Los Angeles proved an equally fertile ground for such families. The family element later was extended to professional and social groups and on special occasions to soap-opera "families."

Family Feud jelled at the onset from the deadpan barbs and distaff kissing by an unconventional M.C. British-born Richard Dawson, an actor and comedian, had played a six-year role on *Hogan's Heroes* and had gained a berth on *Match Game*. Dawson's agent asked for an audition for his client when *Feud* was announced. *Match Game*'s premise was not unlike that of *Family Feud* in that a player had to answer a question as someone else would. When Dawson signed a contract for the series in 1976, he decided to M.C. by his own rules. The practice of bussing each female family member began on the very first show. The gesture produced a storm of protest from some viewers. Dawson refused to back down. He took his case to his audience. The mail response came up prokiss by a margin of 40 to 1. "I'm just trying to be nice to someone else," he maintained.[37]

His insults and remarks caused more waves. He inspired a tide of critical mail by saying of Henry Kissinger: "He's the man who declared 'Peace is at hand' and then put the world on hold while another 17,000 guys died.' Sponsors complained vehemently. ABC ordered him to excise such anti-Nixon remarks. He, in turn, threatened to quit, and the network backed off.[38]

Richard Dawson and *Family Feud* built up the largest game audience of the 1970s. In 1977 it won an Emmy, and the following year, impish, incorrigible Dawson received one as program host. The proceedings enjoyed nearly a decade of daily airings before the cheeky king of tart remarks moved back into acting. Such was his typecasting that his first movie assignment was the role of a smug and vicious game-show M.C. in Arnold Schwarzenegger's "The Running Man."

No game of the next decade, the 1980s, achieved greater audience popularity, critical approbation or media attention than *Wheel of Fortune*. Some 42 million people viewed the show every day, making it one of the most successful programs ever on television and by far the biggest game show in history. Not since *The $64,000 Question* had there been such interest in a high-stakes phenomenon. Each evening *Wheel* gave away more than $20,000 in prizes such as jewelry, autos and trips and another $10,000 on the daytime series.

Wheel started on daytime television with Chuck Woolery in 1975. Created by Merv Griffin out of an idea from his childhood when he and his sister played hangman, the show allowed the audience at home to play along and share in the vicarious thrill of a shopping spree. Contestants on screen spun a big wheel, bought missing letters and tried to solve word puzzles. (Players won money only for guessing consonants, not vowels.)

The series never really caught fire until 1983 when Griffin decided to sell distribution rights to the original daytime episodes to local stations for early evening broadcast. Distributor King World Productions soon launched a syndicated nighttime version. In its new form and time slot—with Pat Sajak, a former TV weatherman and radio disc jockey, replacing Woolery—the prize-heavy, glitz-filled game immediately captured the attention of a broad spectrum of viewers who began to tune in religiously night after night. At the close of its second season in syndication, Michael King, president of King World, commented on its unprecedented success. "First-run game shows tend to have a run of seven years. But the way it's going, *Wheel* has unchartered borders. We're still a baby."[39]

Host Sajak's whimsical geniality greatly contributed to the game's popularity. But for many viewers, the star of the *Wheel* remained blond, blue-eyed Vanna White, a former model who enthusiastically turned the letters on the puzzle board. Dressed in modish outfits that looked like part-cheerleader and part-Miss America, she won a loyal following and generated a pop-icon status—all by smiling, flipping letter cards, applauding for players, bantering with Sajak and waving to the audience.

Into the 1990s Pat and Vanna and the long-spinning *Wheel of Fortune* continued to dominate the preprime-time hours on more than 185 stations and on affiliates of all three major networks. "You can track it around the nation," Howard Stringer of CBS News remarked in the mid-1980s as the *Wheel* brought a degree of havoc to his news program schedules. "'You find yourself stumbling over its impact wherever you look."[40]

›25‹

Flavor of the Common Man

Profit-rich staples of the air, game shows continue among the oldest, ongoing program formats, as much as the newscast, soap opera and sports events. Survivors of devastating accusations and harsh criticism, they flourish in daytime and access time, while periodically nudging into prime time, and add up to more than 50 hours a week in most viewing markets. Short of a monumental scandal or federal legislation, the game show remains solidly entrenched.

Viewers treat such contests as a necessary part of their daily TV menu. Like snack food, they can be nibbled or devoured. As with a favorite dish, they increase the appetite for more tantalizing helpings. Sometimes they get to be downright habit-forming.

The opportunity to become involved, to play along, to test oneself, approaches a sports contest. Matched vicariously with—or against—a player, a viewer experiences a measure of both complacency and impunity, victory and defeat. "So like the theoretical horseplayer, with his infallible system," journalist Milton Bracker once wrote, "the viewer gets no cash but has the soothing feeling that he could have cleaned up. At the same time—tieless, shoeless and as relaxed as he likes—he can miss the answer with impunity. He gets credit for what he knows without suffering for what he doesn't. In a double sense, he can't lose."[1]

But he no longer is relegated to passivity. Computer technology already is turning home viewers into armchair participants. Cable television services have introduced systems that allow viewers to play along with quiz shows by using small computer terminals. Two-way TV is giving viewers a chance to compete for prizes against other viewers, with scores tallied at the end of a show and compared. Called interactive television, the system combines telephone lines and computer equipment to permit audiences to compete with on-screen contestants, whether on *Jeopardy! Name That Tune* or a regional version of bingo.[2]

In content, the quiz show generally puts a premium on facts and trivia, but above all it must entertain. People are unlikely to stay with a program unless they are diverted and amused, as well as have a better than even chance of competing successfully with contestants. A quest for information seems not to have much to do with the appeal or success of a show. Nonetheless, the game show may act as a teaching tool, especially for children. *Family Feud* can serve as a good example of how the family decision-making process works. *Let's Make a Deal* emphasizes the necessity for creativity and imagination during competition. Perhaps no show has taught cooperation and teamwork—not to mention the importance of a good vocabulary—better than *Password*.

"All quiz shows educate the public in one degree or another," observes Joseph N. Kane, architect of thousands of quiz questions.[3] Question-and-answer, skill-testing programs, indeed, stimulate many people to think, to probe, to recollect, even to read.

Apart from the classic quiz offerings, there are inane and grotesque games. Some virtually celebrate the theater of cruelty and humiliation amidst frantic commercial hype. *Time* magazine has described them thusly: "Masochistic contestants meet fourth-rate Hollywood celebrities in a neon-lit orgy of product plugola, group hysteria and psychological mayhem."[4]

Networks have never slackened their tight security systems for contestants. Legislation that made it illegal to manipulate the outcome of a game remains on the books. For celebrity players, the controls are a bit relaxed. On their behalf, some game shows shuffle make-believe and actuality in the name of audience enjoyment and entertainment. Mark Goodson has raised this point, noting the disclaimers flashed on TV screens after a game. For *Celebrity Sweepstakes* and *Hollywood Squares*, he observed, celebrities have been furnished with comic answers, as well as with some of the questions and answers. In essence, jokes and one-liners were supplied ahead of time. "It's a show business truism that audiences respond differently—indeed, far more generously—to extemporaneous ripostes than to jokes they know have been prepared in advance by comedy writers."[5]

Game-show producers, for network, syndication, cable or satellite, continue to mine the ore that has fueled past audience ratings. Updated versions of *Match Game, To Tell the Truth* and *Quiz Kids* periodically reappear on schedules. The ever-green field of popular board games regularly yields entries such as *Monopoly* and *Trivia Trap*, and the perennials *The Price Is Right, Let's Make a Deal* and *Concentration* still flourish.

For contestants, quiz and game shows remain a part of a new Horatio Alger story: get on a show and strike it rich. For the middle class, it's a chance to get something for nothing or close to it. "It may be harder than ever to make a living these days," Tom Buckley writes, "but game shows continue to reflect the American dream of easy money and a free frost-free refrigerator in every home.[6]

In the past, particularly for radio, most contestants were picked by lot from a studio audience just before air time; today, they are sought and "packaged" far in advance. Classified ads for "energetic contestants," "fun-loving couples," "talkative and outgoing brother and sister teams," fill newspaper columns, especially in Los Angeles. An opportunity to win money and merchandise draws hundreds of calls a day. Each year more than 10,000 players compete for a grand total of more than $30 million on the top dozen or so games. Only state and local lotteries vie as a way to carry home a windfall. But equally alluring is the on-screen chance to be seen and recognized and achieve a bit of glory and immortality.

Where would game shows be without people and what social scientist Max Lerner has said is the "flavor of the common man."[7] Earlier in television's growth an Everett, Massachusetts, viewer wrote: "The appeal of the quiz show is that the lonely American wants to meet real people whom he feels he can know and trust."[8] Game shows draw upon a vast common-man population—a self-replenishing wave of faces. Whereas other types of television programs ultimately devour its performers and material, more and more TV entertainment is being provided by the people who watch it. In the 1990s a grass-roots glimpse of the average Joe and Jill called *America's Funniest Home Videos* opened up the opportunity for nearly everyone to have his proverbial "15 minutes of fame." Candid camcorder contests and game shows are places where real people—the vox pop—even your neighbors can go on and be themselves or close to it. "What's the big deal about Mr. Ed's talking horse when we can see a real woman fall off of one?" asks humorist Erma Bombeck.[9]

Instant entertainment and prizes distinguish the quiz show, say, from a routine schoolroom exam. Without these elements in solid measure, quiz and game shows would wither on the video vine. A show-business atmosphere apparently insures ecstatic winners, happy runners-up and even smiling losers. An audience of more than 70 million viewers from coast to coast identifies with middle-America people as they compete on TV game shows. Real people with real emotion, these contestants are individuals whom viewers can briefly know and interact with, as they both pursue the deeply ingrained dream to strike it rich, break the bank, hit the jackpot.

Appendix: Program Data

Only radio (R) and television (TV) quiz and game shows in the text are listed, with their initial network and/or station of origin, broadcast dates and M.C.s. Announcer (An.) and musical director (Mus.) or bandleader (Bandl.) are included if they played a key role in the format. (Data for syndicated or cable versions have been omitted.)

ACT IT OUT (aka *SAY IT WITH ACTING*) (TV), 1950–52, NBC, NY; M.C.: Ben Grauer, Maggi McNellis, Bud Collyer

AMERICANA QUIZ (TV), 1947–49, NBC, NY; M.C.: John Mason Brown, Ben Grauer

ANSWER AUCTION (R), 1940, KNX, LA; M.C.: Tom Breneman

ANSWER MAN (R) 1936–50, WICC, Bridgeport, CT, WOR-Mutual, NY; M.C.: Albert Mitchell

ANSWER ME THIS (TV), 1954, WNHC, New Haven, CT; M.C.: Tom Romano

ANSWERS BY THE DANCERS (R), 1939, NBC, NY; M.C./Bandl.: Horace Heidt

ANYBODY CAN PLAY (TV), 1958, ABC, LA; M.C.: George Fenneman

ASK-IT-BASKET (R), 1938–41, CBS, NY; M.C.: Jim McWilliams, Ed East

AUCTION-AIRE (TV), 1945–50, ABC, NY; M.C.: Jack Gregson

BANK ON THE STARS (TV), 1953–54, CBS, NY; M.C.: Jack Paar, Bill Cullen, Jimmy Nelson

BATTLE OF THE BOROUGHS (see *QUIZ OF TWO CITIES*)

BATTLE OF THE BUREAUS (R), 1943–44, WTOP, Washington, DC; M.C.: Lee Vickers; Mus.: Johnny Salb

BATTLE OF THE SEXES (R), 1938–44, NBC, NY; M.C.: Frank Crumit, Julia Sanderson, Walter O'Keefe, J. C. Flippen

BEAT THE BAND (R), 1940–44, NBC, Chicago; M.C.: Garry Moore, Hildegarde; Bandl.: Ted Weems, Bob Grant, Harry Sosnik

BEAT THE CLOCK (aka *TIME'S A-WASTIN'*) (R-TV), 1948–61, CBS, NY; M.C.: Bud Collyer

BETTER HALF (R), 1943–44, WOR-Mutual, NY; M.C.: Tom Slater, Tiny Ruffner

BETTER SEX (TV), 1977–78, ABC, LA; M.C.: Bill Anderson, Sarah Purcell

BID 'N' BUY (TV), 1958, CBS, NY; M.C.: Bert Parks

BIG PAYOFF (TV), 1951–59, NBC, NY; M.C.: Randy Merriman, Bess Myerson, Robert Paige, Mort Lawrence, Bobby Sherwood, Bert Parks; Mus.: Burt Buhrman

BLIND DATE (R-TV), 1943–46/1949–53, ABC, NY; M.C.: Arlene Francis, Melvyn Douglas, Jan Murray; An.: Ken Roberts; Bandl.: Glenn Osser, Ray Bloch

BRAINS TRUST (aka *ANY QUESTIONS?*) (R), 1943, BBC, London, WNEW, NY; M.C.: G. McCullough

BREAK THE BANK (R-TV), 1945–57/1976, Mutual, NY; M.C.: John Reed King, Bert Parks, Bud Collyer, Tom Kennedy; Bandl.: Hank Sylvern, Peter Van Steeden

BREAKFAST IN HOLLYWOOD (R), 1945–49, ABC, LA; M.C.: Tom Breneman, Garry Moore

BRIDE AND GROOM (R-TV), 1945–58, ABC, NY; M.C.: John Nelson, Robert Paige, Byron Palmer, Frank Parker

BRUNSWICK HOUR MUSICAL MEMORY CONTEST (R), 1924–25, WJZ, NY

CAMOUFLAGE (TV), 1961–62, ABC, NY; M.C.: Don Morrow

CAN YOU TOP THIS? (R-TV), 1940–54, WOR, NY, NBC, NY; M.C.: Roger Bower, Ward Wilson

CARD SHARKS (TV), 1978–81/1986–89, NBC, LA; M.C.: Jim Perry, Bob Eubanks

CASH AND CARRY (TV), 1946–47, DuMont, NY; M.C.: Dennis James

CATCH ME IF YOU CAN (R), 1948, CBS, NY; M.C.: Bill Cullen

CBS TELEVISION QUIZ (TV), 1941–42, WCBW, NY; M.C.: Gil Fates

CELEBRITY GAME (TV), 1964–65, CBS, LA; M.C.: Carl Reiner

CELEBRITY SWEEPSTAKES (TV), 1974–76, NBC, LA; M.C.: Jim McKrell

CHANCE OF A LIFETIME (R-TV), 1949–51, ABC, NY; M.C.: John Reed King

CHARADE QUIZ (TV), 1947–49, DuMont, NY; M.C.: Bill Slater

CHILDREN'S RECESS (R), 1937, WHEC, Rochester, NY; M.C.: Charlotte Edwards

COLLEGE BOWL (R-TV), 1953–70, NBC, NY; M.C.: Allen Ludden, Robert Earle

CONCENTRATION (TV), 1958–73, NBC, NY; M.C.: Hugh Downs, Jack Barry, Bob Clayton, Ed McMahon

CONSUMER'S QUIZ (R-TV), 1946, CBS, NY; M.C.: Fred Uttal

COUNTY FAIR (R-TV), 1945–59, CBS, NY; M.C.: Jack Bailey, Win Elliot, Bert Parks; Bandl.: Bill Gale

DATING GAME (TV), 1965–73, ABC, LA; M.C.: Jim Lange

DETECT AND COLLECT (R-TV), 1945–46, CBS, NY; M.C.: Fred Uttal, Wendy Barrie, Lew Lehr; Bandl.: Ted Rapf

DOLLAR A SECOND (TV), 1953–57, DuMont, NY; M.C.: Jan Murray

DOTTO (TV), 1958, CBS, NY; M.C.: Jack Narz

DOUBLE OR NOTHING (R-TV), 1940–53, WOL, Washington, D.C., Mutual, NY; M.C.: Walter Compton, Todd Russell, Walter O'Keefe, Bert Parks; Bandl.: Elliott Jacoby

DOUGH RE MI (TV), 1958–60, NBC, NY; M.C.: Gene Rayburn; Bandl.: Paul Taubman

DOWN YOU GO (TV), 1951–56, DuMont, Chicago; M.C.: Bergen Evans, Bill Cullen

DO YOU TRUST YOUR WIFE? (TV), 1956–57, CBS, LA; Edgar Bergen with Charlie McCarthy; Mus.: Frank DeVol

DR. I.Q. (R-TV), 1935–50/1953–54/1958–59, KTRH, Houston, NBC; M.C.: Ted Nabors, Jim Crocker, Lew Valentine, Jimmy McClain, Jay Owen, Tom Kennedy

DRAW ME A LAUGH (TV), 1949, ABC, NY; M.C.: Walter Herlihy, Patricia Bright

DRAW TO WIN (TV), 1952, CBS, NY; M.C.: Henry Morgan

DROODLES (TV), 1954, NBC, NY; M.C.: Roger Price

E.S.P. (TV), 1958, ABC, LA; M.C.: Vincent Price

EARN YOUR VACATION (R), 1949, CBS, NY; M.C.: Jay C. Flippen

EVERYBODY WINS (R), 1948, CBS, NY; M.C.: Phil Baker; An.: Ken Roberts

EYES HAVE IT (TV), 1948–49, NBC, Washington, D.C.; M.C.: Ralph McNair

FACE THE FACTS (TV), 1961, CBS, NY; M.C.: Red Rowe

FAMILY FEUD (TV), 1976–85, ABC, LA; M.C.: Richard Dawson; An.: Gene Wood

FAMILY GAME (TV), 1967, ABC, LA; M.C.: Bob Barker

50 GRAND SLAM (TV), 1976, NBC, LA; M.C.: Tom Kennedy

FISH POND (R), 1944, ABC, NY; M.C.: Win Elliot

FOR LOVE OR MONEY (TV), 1958–59, CBS, NY; M.C.: Bill Nimmo

FUN IN PRINT (R), 1940, CBS, NY; M.C.: Sigmund Spaeth

FUNNY SIDE UP (R), 1959, CBS, NY; M.C.: Bert Parks

GAMBIT (TV), 1972–81, CBS, LA; M.C.: Wink Martindale

GANGPLANK (R), 1937, WMCA, NY; M.C.: Frankie Basch, Martin Starr

GENERATION GAP (TV), 1969, ABC, LA; M.C.: Dennis Wholey, Jack Barry

GET RICH QUICK (R), 1948, ABC, NY; M.C.: Johnny Olson; An.: Jimmy Blaine

GILLETTE COMMUNITY SING (R), 1936–37, CBS, NY/Philadelphia; M.C.: Milton Berle, Wendell Hall, Billy Jones and Ernie Hare

GIVE AND TAKE (R-TV), 1945–52; CBS, NY; M.C.: John Reed King, Bill Cullen

GO FOR THE HOUSE (R), 1948–49, ABC, NY; M.C.: John Reed King

GONG SHOW (TV), 1976–78, NBC, LA; M.C.: Gary Owens, Chuck Barris; Mus.: Milton DeLugg

GRAND SLAM (R), 1946–53, CBS, NY; M.C.: Irene Beasley; An.: Dwight Weist

GUESS WHERE (R), 1939, Mutual, NY; M.C.: Budd Hulick, Shirley Booth, Charles Cantor; Bandl.: Johnny Green

HAGEN'S SPELLING BEE (R), 1936–37, CBS, NY; M.C.: Harry Hagen

HAGGIS BAGGIS (TV), 1958–59, NBC, NY; M.C.: Fred Robbins, Jack Linkletter, Dennis James

HAVE YOU GOT IT? (R), 1941, WWSW, Pittsburgh; M.C.: Walt Framer; An.: Bill Cullen

HIGH FINANCE (TV), 1956, CBS, NY; M.C.: Dennis James

HIGH LOW (TV), 1957, NBC, NY; M.C.: Jack Barry

HIGH ROLLERS (TV), 1974–76/1978–80, NBC, LA; M.C.: Alex Trebek

HIT THE JACKPOT (R), 1948–50, CBS, NY; M.C.: Bill Cullen; Bandl.: Al Goodman

HOLLYWOOD CALLING (R), 1949–50, NBC, LA; M.C.: George Murphy, Jack McCoy, George Jessel

HOLLYWOOD SQUARES (TV), 1966–80, NBC, LA; M.C.: Peter Marshall

HOUSE PARTY (R-TV), 1944–69, CBS, LA; M.C.: Art Linkletter; An.: Jack Slattery

HOW'M I DOIN'? (R), 1942, CBS, NY; M.C.: Bob Hawk; An.: Bert Parks; Bandl.: Vaughn Monroe

I'LL BUY THAT (TV), 1953–54, CBS, NY; M.C.: Mike Wallace

INFORMATION PLEASE (R-TV), 1938–48/1950–52, NBC, NY; M.C.: Clifton Fadiman; An.: Milton Cross

INTERESTING NEIGHBORS (R), 1937, WGY, Schenectady, NY; M.C.: Jerry Belcher

IT COULD BE YOU (TV), 1956–61, NBC, LA; M.C.: Bill Leyden; An.: Wendell Niles; Mus.: Ivan Ditmars

IT PAYS TO BE IGNORANT (R-TV), 1942–51, WOR, NY, CBS, NY; M.C.: Tom Howard; An.: Ken Roberts, Dick Stark

I'VE GOT A SECRET (TV), 1952–67/1976, CBS, NY; M.C.: Garry Moore, Steve Allen, Bill Cullen; Mus.: Norman Paris, Leroy Anderson

JACKPOT BOWLING (TV), 1959–61, NBC, LA; M.C.: Leo Durocher, Mel Allen, Bud Palmer, Chuck Hearn, Milton Berle

JEOPARDY! (TV), 1964–1975/1978–79, NBC, LA; M.C.: Art Fleming; An.: Don Pardo

JOKER'S WILD (TV), 1972–75, CBS, LA; M.C.: Jack Barry

JUDGE FOR YOURSELF (TV), 1953–54, NBC, NY; M.C.: Fred Allen; Mus.: Milton DeLugg

JUST MEN! (TV), 1983, NBC, LA; M.C.: Betty White

JUVENILE JURY (R-TV), 1946–54, WOR, NY, Mutual, NY; M.C.: Jack Barry

KEEP TALKING (TV), 1958–60, CBS, NY; M.C.: Monty Hall, Carl Reiner, Merv Griffin

KID WIZARDS (R), 1941, WHN, NY; M.C.: Louis L. Wolff

KOLLEGE OF MUSICAL KNOWLEDGE (R-TV), 1937–50/1954, WGN, Chicago, Mutual, NY; M.C./Bandl.: Kay Kyser; M.C.: Tennessee Ernie Ford; An.: Ben Grauer; Bandl.: Frank DeVol

LADIES BE SEATED (R-TV), 1944–49, ABC, NY; M.C.: Johnny and Penny Olson, Tom Moore; Mus.: Buddy Weed

LAWYER Q (R), 1947, Mutual, NY; M.C.: Karl Swenson; An.: Dennis James

LEAVE IT TO THE GIRLS (R-TV), 1945–54, Mutual, NY; M.C.: Paula Stone, Maggi McNellis

LET'S MAKE A DEAL (TV), 1963–76, NBC, LA; M.C.: Monty Hall; Mus.: Ivan Ditmars

LIAR'S CLUB (TV), 1969, KTTV, LA; M.C.: Rod Serling

LITTLE RED SCHOOL HOUSE (R), 1940, WGY, Schenectady, NY; M.C.: Eddie Flynn

LUCKY PARTNERS (TV), 1958, NBC, NY; M.C.: Carl Cordell

MAJORITY RULES (TV), 1949–50, ABC, Chicago; M.C.: Ed Prentiss, Tom Moore, Mike Wallace

MAN IN YOUR NEIGHBORHOOD (R), 1937, WSAI, Cincinnati; M.C.: Red Barber

MAN SAYS YES (R-TV), 1947–53/1982–88; KMPC, LA; M.C.: Bob Shannon

MASQUERADE PARTY (TV), 1952–60, CBS, NY; M.C.: Bud Collyer, Douglas Edwards, Peter Donald, Eddie Bracken, Robert Q. Lewis, Bert Parks

MATCH GAME (TV), 1962–69/1973–79, NBC, NY; M.C.: Gene Rayburn; An.: Johnny Olson

MATCH GAME-HOLLYWOOD SQUARES HOUR (TV), 1983–84, NBC, LA; M.C.: Gene Rayburn, Jon Bauman

MEET YOUR MATCH (R-TV), 1949–53, Mutual, NY; M.C.: Tom Moore, Jan Murray

MELODY PUZZLES (R), 1937, WOR, NY, NBC, NY; M.C.: Fred Uttal; An.: Ed Herlihy; Bandl.: Richard Himber, Harry Salter

MISSUS GOES A-SHOPPING (R-TV), 1941–48, WABC, NY, CBS, NY; M.C.: John Reed King

MONOPOLY (TV), 1990, ABC, LA; M.C.: Mike Riley

MOVIE QUIZ (R), 1945, ABC, NY; M.C.: Jack Bailey

MOVIELAND QUIZ (TV), 1948, ABC,. Philadelphia; M.C.: Arthur Q. Bryan, Patricia Bright, Ralph Dumke

MOVIETOWN R.S.V.P. (TV), 1947, KTLA, LA; M.C.: Dick Lane

MUSICAL CHAIRS (TV), 1975, CBS, NY; M.C.: Adam Wade; Mus.: Derek Smith

MUSICAL MOCK TRIAL (R), 1940, CBS, NY; M.C./Bandl.: Ben Bernie; M.C.: Lew Lehr; An.: Ernest Chappell, Dan Seymour

MUSICAL TREASURE HUNT (R), 1940–43, NBC, NY; M.C./Bandl.: Horace Heidt

NAME THAT TUNE (TV), 1953–59/1974–75/1977, NBC, NY; M.C.: Red Benson, Bill Cullen, George DeWitt, Tom Kennedy, Dennis James; Bandl.: Harry Salter, Ted Rapf, Bob Alberti, Tommy Oliver, Stan Worth

NAME THREE (R), 1939–40, Mutual, NY; M.C.: Bob Hawk

NAME'S THE SAME (TV), 1951–55, ABC, NY; M.C.: Robert Q. Lewis, Dennis James, Bob Elliott and Ray Goulding, Clifton Fadiman

NEWLYWED GAME (TV), 1966–71/1984, ABC, LA; M.C.: Bob Eubanks, Jim Lange

NUMBER PLEASE (TV), 1961, ABC, NY; M.C.: Bud Collyer

ON YOUR ACCOUNT (TV), 1953–56, NBC, NY; M.C.: Win Elliot, Dennis James

100 GRAND (TV), 1963, ABC, NY; M.C.: Jack Clark; An.: Bill Wendell; Mus.: Milton DeLugg

$100,000 BIG SURPRISE (TV), 1955–57, NBC, NY; M.C.: Jack Barry, Mike Wallace; An.: Jack Clark; Mus.: Jimmy Leyden

ORIGINAL AMATEUR HOUR (R-TV), 1934–70, WHN, NY, NBC, NY; M.C.: Major Edward Bowes, Ted Mack; An. Ralph Edwards

PALMOLIVE COMMUNITY SING (R), 1936, CBS, NY; M.C.: Homer Rodeheaver, Tiny Ruffner

PANTOMIME QUIZ (TV), 1947–59, KTLA, LA, CBS, LA; M.C.: Mike Stokey

PASSWORD (TV), 1961–67/1971–75, CBS, NY; M.C.: Allen Ludden

PASSWORD PLUS (TV), 1979–82, NBC, LA; M.C.: Allen Ludden, Tom Kennedy

PEOPLE ARE FUNNY (R-TV), 1942–61/1984, NBC, LA; M.C.: Art Baker, Art Linkletter, Flip Wilson

PEOPLE WILL TALK (TV), 1963, NBC, LA; M.C.: Dennis James

PICK A DATE (R), 1949, ABC, NY; M.C.: Buddy Rogers

PLAY YOUR HUNCH (TV), 1958–62, CBS, NY; M.C.: Merv Griffin, Richard Hayes, Gene Rayburn, Robert Q. Lewis

POT O' GOLD (R), 1939–41/1946–47, NBC, NY; M.C./Bandl.: Horace Heidt; An.: Ben Grauer; M.C.: Happy Felton; Bandl.: Harry Salter

POP QUESTION GAME (R), 1923–26, WJZ, NY; M.C.: Briton Hadden, Roy Larsen

POP THE QUESTION (R), 1941, KFRC, San Francisco; M.C.: Mark Goodson

POPSICLE PETE'S MONEY BOX (R), 1940, WOAL, San Antonio, TX

PRICE IS RIGHT (TV), 1956–64/1972– , NBC, NY; M.C.: Bill Cullen, Bob Barker; An.: Johnny Olson, Gene Wood, Rod Roddy

PROFESSOR QUIZ (R), 1936–41, WJSV, Washington, CBS, NY; M.C.: Jim McWilliams, Craig Earl; An.: Arthur Godfrey, Robert Trout

PULL OVER, NEIGHBOR (aka ALL ABOARD) (R), 1938; M.C.: Art Baker

QUEEN FOR A DAY (R-TV), 1945–64, Mutual, NY; M.C.: Dud Williamson, Jack Bailey

QUICK AS A FLASH (R-TV), 1944–51/1953–54, Mutual, NY; M.C.: Kenneth Roberts, Win Elliot, Bobby Sherwood, Bud Collyer; An.: Frank Gallop, Cy Harrice; Bandl.: Ray Bloch

QUICKSILVER (R), 1939, NBC, Chicago

QUIZ KIDS (R-TV), 1940–53/1956, NBC, Chicago; M.C.: Joe Kelly, Clifton Fadiman

QUIZ OF TWO CITIES (R), 1940, KFBC, San Francisco, KHJ, LA, WTIC, Hartford, etc.; M.C.: Bruce Kern, Mark Goodson, Reed Kilpatrick, Maurice Fitzmaurice, Durwood Kirby

QUIXIE DOODLE (R), 1939–41, Mutual, NY; M.C.: Bob Hawk, F. Chase Taylor

QUIZZER BASEBALL (R), 1941, NBC, NY; M.C.: Harry Von Zell; Bandl.: Peter Van Steeden

QUIZZICAL (R), 1941–42, WOR, NY, NBC, NY; M.C./Bandl.: Cab Calloway

QUIZZING THE NEWS (TV), 1948–49, ABC, NY; M.C.: Allan Prescott

RADIO SCHOOLHOUSE (R), 1939, WXYZ, Detroit; M.C.: Dick Osgood

RECESS TIME (R), 1938, WSCH, Portland, ME; M.C.: Harry Botwick

RHYMO (R), 1940, CBS, NY; M.C./Bandl.: Johnny Green

RIDDLE ME THIS (TV), 1948–49, CBS, NY; M.C.: Douglas Edwards, Paul Gallico, Conrad Nagel

RIGHT DOWN YOUR ALLEY (R), 1946, ABC, NY; M.C.: Bill Slater, Don Gardner

SALE OF THE CENTURY (TV), 1969–73/1988–89, NBC, NY; M.C.: Jack Kelly, Joe Garagiola, Jim Perry; An.: Bill Wendell, Jay Stewart

SCRABBLE (TV), 1984–90, NBC, LA; M.C.: Chuck Woolery; An.: Charlie Tuna

SCRAMBY AMBY (R), 1940–46, WLW, Cincinnati, NBC, LA; M.C.: Perry Ward, Ray Shannon; An.: Larry Keating; Bandl.: Paul Martin, Charles Dant

SCRIPTEASERS (R), 1937, NBC, LA; M.C.: Buddy Rogers, Benny Rubin

SECOND HONEYMOON (R), 1946–48, WAAT, Newark, NJ, ABC, NY; M.C.: Bert Parks, Dick Todd; An.: Mort Lawrence; Mus.: Rosa Rio

SERVICE WITH A SMILE (R), 1941–42, NBC, NY; M.C.: Garry Moore; An.: Ben Grauer

SEVEN ARTS QUIZ (TV), 1947, NBC, NY; M.C.: Bill Slater

SEZ WHO! (R), 1957, CBS, NY; M.C.: Henry Morgan

SIDEWALK QUESTION BOX (R), 1937, WBT, Charlotte, NC; M.C.: Lee Kirby

SING IT AGAIN (R-TV), 1948–51, CBS, NY; M.C.: Dan Seymour, Jan Murray; Bandl.: Ray Bloch

$64,000 CHALLENGE (TV), 1956–58, CBS, NY; M.C.: Sonny Fox, Ralph Story; Mus.: Norman Leyden

$64,000 QUESTION (TV-R), 1955–58, CBS, NY: M.C.: Hal March; Mus.: Norman Leyden

SKY'S THE LIMIT (TV), 1954–56, NBC, NY; M.C.: Gene Rayburn, Monty Hall

SO YOU THINK YOU KNOW MUSIC (R), 1938–46, WNYC, NY, CBS, NY; M.C.: Ted Cott; An.: John Reed King; Bandl.: Allen Roth, Hank Sylvern

SO YOU WANT TO LEAD A BAND? (R-TV), 1938–55, NBC, NY; M.C./Bandl.: Sammy Kaye

SONGS FOR SALE (TV), 1950–52, CBS, NY; M.C.: Jan Murray, Steve Allen; Bandl.: Ray Bloch

SPELL-A-BEE (R), 1940, WAPI, Birmingham, AL; M.C.: Douglas Hunt

SPELLING BEE (R), 1937–40, NBC, NY; M.C.: Paul Wing

SPELLING BEE PARTY (R), 1937, WICC, Bridgeport, CT; M.C.: George A. Patridge, Joseph Lopez

SPIN TO WIN (R), 1949, CBS, NY; M.C.: Warren Hull

SPLIT PERSONALITY (TV), 1959–60, NBC, NY; M.C.: Tom Poston

STOOPEROOS (R), 1943, CBS, NY; M.C.: F. Chase Taylor; An: Ken Roberts

STOP ME IF YOU'VE HEARD THIS ONE (R-TV), 1939–49; M.C.: Milton Berle, Roger Bower, Ted Brown, Leon Janney; Bandl.: Horace Heidt, Joe Rines

STOP OR GO (R), 1943–45, KNX, LA, ABC, LA; M.C.: Ken Murray, Joe E. Brown

STOP THE MUSIC! (R-TV), 1948–52/1954–56, ABC, NY; M.C.: Bert Parks, Dennis James; An.: Doug Browning; Bandl.: Harry Salter

STRIKE IT RICH (R-TV), 1947–58, CBS, NY; M.C.: Todd Russell, Warren Hull; An.: Ralph Paul

STUMP THE AUTHORS (R), 1946, ABC, NY: M.C.: Sidney Mason

STUMP THE STARS (aka *PANTOMIME QUIZ*) (TV), 1962–63, CBS, LA; M.C.: Pat Harrington, Jr., Mike Stokey

SUPER PASSWORD (TV), 1984–89, NBC, LA; M.C.: Bert Convy

SUPERMARKET SWEEP (TV), 1965–67, ABC, NY; M.C.: Bill Malone

TAG THE GAG (TV), 1951, NBC, NY; M.C.: Hal Block

TAKE-A-CARD (R), 1943, Mutual, NY: M.C.: Lew Lehr, Wally Butterworth; An.: Jimmy Wallington

TAKE A GUESS (TV), 1953, CBS, NY; M.C.: John K. M. McCaffrey

TAKE A WORD (R), 1946, WOR, NY: M.C.: George Hogan, Carlton Warren

TAKE IT OR LEAVE IT (R), 1940–50, CBS, NY; M.C.: Bob Hawk, Phil Baker, Garry Moore, Eddie Cantor, Jack Paar; An.: Ken Niles; Bandl.: Ray Bloch, Jacques Renard, Cookie Fairchild

TATTLETALES (TV), 1974–78/1982–84, CBS, LA; M.C.: Bert Convy

TELEPHONE INTERVIEWS (R), 1937, WEVA, Richmond, VA; M.C.: Irv Abel-off

TELEQUIZZICALS (TV), 1946, WBKB, Chicago; M.C.: Bill Anson, Meg Haum

TELL IT TO GROUCHO (TV), 1962, CBS, LA; M.C.: Groucho Marx; An.: George Fenneman

$10,000 PYRAMID (aka *$20,000, $25,000, $50,000* and *$100,000 PYRAMID*) (TV), 1973–80/1982–89, CBS, LA; M.C.: Dick Clark

TEXACO OPERA QUIZ (R), 1940–, NBC, NY; M.C.: Milton Cross, Edward Downes

THANKS TO THE YANKS (aka *THE BOB HAWK SHOW*) (R), 1942–53, CBS, NY; M.C.: Bob Hawk

THAT REMINDS ME (TV), 1952, NBC, NY; M.C.: Arlene Francis

THINK FAST (TV), 1949–50, ABC, NY; M.C.: Mason Gross, Gypsy Rose Lee; Bandl.: David Broekman

THIS IS FORT DIX (R), 1940–44, Mutual, NY; M.C.: Tom Slater

THIS IS THE MISSUS (TV), 1948–49, CBS, NY; M.C.: Bud Collyer, Warren Hull

THIS IS YOUR LIFE (R-TV), 1948–61, NBC, LA; M.C.: Ralph Edwards

TIC TAC DOUGH (TV), 1956–59/1978, NBC, NY; M.C.: Jack Barry, Bill Wendell, Jay Jackson, Win Elliot, Wink Martindale

TO TELL THE TRUTH (TV), 1956–68, CBS, NY; M.C.: Bud Collyer; An.: Johnny Olson

TOP DOLLAR (TV), 1958–59, CBS, NY; M.C.: Toby Reed, Warren Hull, Jack Narz, Bergen Evans

TRANSATLANTIC QUIZ (R), 1944, NBC, NY, BBC, London; M.C.: Alistair Cooke, Lionel Hale

TREASURE HUNT (R), 1938, KSD, St. Louis; M.C.: Frank Eschen, Tom Reid

TREASURE HUNT (TV), 1956–59, ABC, NY; M.C.: Jan Murray; Mus.: Milton DeLugg

TREASURE ISLE (TV), 1967–68, ABC, Palm Beach, FL; M.C.: John Bartholomew Tucker

TRIVIA TRAP (TV), 1984–85, ABC, LA; M.C.: Bob Eubanks

TRUE OR FALSE (R), 1938–51, Mutual, NY; M.C.: Harry Hagen, Eddie Dunn, Bill Slater

TRUTH OR CONSEQUENCES (R-TV), 1940–51/1954–65, CBS, NY; M.C.: Ralph Edwards, Jack Bailey, Steve Dunne, Bob Barker; An.: Mel Allen

TWENTY-ONE (TV), 1956–58, NBC, NY; M.C.: Jack Barry

TWENTY QUESTIONS (R-TV), 1946–55, Mutual, NY; M.C.: Bill Slater, Jay Jackson; An.: John Gregson, Frank Waldecker

TWO FOR THE MONEY (TV-R), 1952–57, CBS, NY; M.C.: Herb Shriner, Walter O'Keefe, Sam Levenson; Mus.: Milton DeLugg

UNCLE JIM'S QUESTION BEE (R), 1936–41, NBC, NY; M.C.: Jim McWilliams, Bill Slater

UP TO PAAR (TV), 1952, NBC, NY; M.C.: Jack Paar

VIDEO VILLAGE (TV), 1960–62, CBS, LA; M.C.: Jack Narz, Red Rowe, Monty Hall; An.: Kenny Williams

VOX POP (aka *SIDEWALK INTERVIEWS*) (R), 1932–48, KTRH, Houston, NBC, NY; M.C.: Parks Johnson, Jerry Belcher, Wally Butterworth, Warren Hull

WE, THE PEOPLE (R-TV), 1936–52, NBC, NY; M.C.: Gabriel Heatter, Milo Boulton, Dwight Weist, Eddie Dowling, Burgess Meredith, Dan Seymour; Bandl.: Mark Warnow, Oscar Bradley

WELCOME, TRAVELERS (R), 1947–54, ABC, Chicago; M.C.: Tommy Bartlett

WHAT DO YOU HAVE IN COMMON? (TV), 1954, CBS, LA; M.C.: Ralph Story

WHAT IN THE WORLD? (TV), 1951–55, CBS, Philadelphia; M.C.: Ralph Linton, Froelich Rainey

WHAT WOULD YOU HAVE DONE? (R), 1940, NBC, NY; M.C.: Ben Grauer

WHAT'S GOING ON? (TV), 1954, ABC, NY; M.C.: Lee Bowman; An.: Jimmy Blaine

WHAT'S IN A WORD? (TV), 1954, CBS, NY; M.C.: Clifton Fadiman

WHAT'S IT WORTH? (R), ca. 1940, WOR, NY; M.C.: Maurice Dreicer

WHAT'S MY LINE? (TV-R), 1950–67, CBS, NY; M.C.: John Daly

WHAT'S MY NAME? (R), 1938–42, Mutual, NY; M.C.: Budd Hulick, Arlene Francis, John Reed King

WHAT'S MY NAME? (TV), 1950–53, NBC, NY; M.C.: Paul Winchell with Jerry Mahoney; An.: Ted Brown; Bandl.: John Gart, Milton DeLugg

WHAT'S THE NAME OF THAT SONG? (R), 1944–48, Mutual, LA; M.C.: Bill Gwinn, Dud Williamson; Bandl.: Harry Zimmerman

WHAT'S YOUR OPINION? (R), 1937, WJBK, Detroit; M.C.: Billy Morell

WHEEL OF FORTUNE (TV), 1975–, NBC, LA; M.C.: Chuck Woolery, Susan Stafford, Pat Sajak, Vanna White

WHICH IS WHICH? (R), 1944–45, CBS, LA; M.C.: Ken Murray; Bandl.: Richard Humber

WHO DO YOU TRUST? (aka *DO YOU TRUST YOUR WIFE?*) (TV), 1957–63, ABC, NY; M.C.: Johnny Carson, Woody Woodbury; An.: Bill Nimmo, Ed McMahon, Del Sharbutt

WHO SAID THAT? (R-TV), 1948–55, NBC, NY; M.C.: Robert Trout, Walter Kiernan, John Daly

WHODUNIT? (R), 1940, KFRC, San Francisco; M.C.: Mel Venter

WHO'S DANCING TONIGHT? (R), 1939, KSFO, San Francisco; M.C.: Art Linkletter

WIN, LOSE OR DRAW (TV), 1987–90, NBC, LA; M.C.: Vicki Lawrence

WIN WITH A WINNER (TV), 1958, NBC, NY; M.C.: Sandy Becker, Win Elliot; An.: Bill Wendell

WINNER TAKE ALL (R-TV), 1946–52, CBS, NY; M.C.: Bill Cullen, Bud Collyer, Barry Gray

WINNING STREAK (TV), 1974–75, NBC, LA; M.C.: Bill Cullen

WOMEN'S QUIZ BOWL (R), 1962–63, WESX, Salem, MA; M.C.: Steve Stavis

WORD GAME (R), 1938, CBS, NY; M.C.: Franklin P. Adams

YANKEE DOODLE QUIZ (R), 1943–44, ABC, NY; M.C.: Verlia and Ted Malone

YOU BET YOUR LIFE (R-TV), 1947–61, ABC, LA; M.C.: Groucho Marx; An.: George Fenneman; Bandl.: Billy May, Stan Myersand, Jerry Fielding

YOUR NUMBER'S UP (TV), 1985, LA; M.C.: Nipsey Russell

YOU'RE IN THE PICTURE (TV), 1961, CBS, NY; M.C.: Jackie Gleason

YOUTH VS. AGE (R), 1939, NBC, NY; M.C.: Cal Tinney

Notes

CHAPTER 1: QUIZ ROOTS

1. William and Mary Morris, *Morris Dictionary of Word and Phrase Origins* (New York: Harper & Row, 1977), pp. 474–475.
2. Ibid.
3. Don Abarbanel, "America's Most Popular Pastime: Crossword Puzzles," *MD* Magazine, November 1983, p. 209.
4. Ibid., p. 210.
5. Herbert Mitgang, "Margaret Farrar, 87, Editor of Crossword Puzzles, Dies," *New York Times,* June 12, 1984, p. IV-27. The mid-1920s puzzle mania also led Guy Lombardo and his brothers to write "Crossword Puzzle Crazy" for their newly formed orchestra, Guy Lombardo, with Jack Altshul, *Auld Acquaintance* (Garden City, NY: Doubleday, 1975), p. 72.
6. John Scarne, *Encyclopedia of Games* (New York: Harper & Row, 1973), pp. 579–587.
7. Ibid., p. 6.
8. "Giveaways vs. Horatio Alger," *Variety,* February 7, 1940, p. 26.

CHAPTER 2: DIFFERENT WAVELENGTHS

1. George H. Douglas, *The Early Days of Radio Broadcasting* (Jefferson, NC: McFarland & Co., 1987), pp. 4–11.
2. Ibid., pp. 154–155.
3. Ibid., pp. 44–46.
4. Erik Barnouw, *A Tower in Babel* (New York: Oxford University Press, 1966), pp. 67–70.
5. Douglas, *Early Days.*
6. William Peck Banning, *Commercial Broadcasting Pioneer: The WEAF Experiment* (Cambridge, MA: Harvard University Press, 1946), p. 90.

7. Robert T. Elson, *Time Inc.: The Intimate History of a Publishing Enterprise, 1923–1941* (New York: Atheneum, 1968), pp. 98–100.

8. "Brunswick Music Memory Contest," *New York Times*, January 14, 1925, p. 7.

9. Harrison B. Summers, ed., *A Thirty-Year History of Programs Carried on National Radio Networks in the United States, 1926–1956* (New York: Arno Press and the New York Times, 1971), pp. 15–18.

10. Ibid., pp. 25–36.

11. Orrin E. Dunlap, "Now the Audience Joins the Broadcast," *New York Times Magazine*, April 23, 1933, p. VI-9.

12. Arthur Frank Wertheim, *Radio Comedy* (New York: Oxford University Press, 1979), pp. 93–96.

13. Interview with Ted Malone (Alden Russell), May 29, 1985.

14. Ibid.; see also Thomas A. DeLong, "ABC's 60-Year Roots Spread Throughout Area," *Bridgeport Sunday Post* (CT), September 6, 1981, p. B-1.

15. Interview with Ireene Wicker, February 28, 1974.

16. Douglas, *Early Days*, pp. 95–97.

17. " 'Those Audition Blues' Sad Lament Of Those Who Can't Crash Radio," *Variety*, December 12, 1931, p. 33.

18. McAlister Coleman, "Hopes and Heartaches," *Stage*, May 1935, pp. 53–55.

19. "Radio Reviews," *Variety*, November 16, 1938, p. 28.

20. Coleman, "Hopes," p. 54.

CHAPTER 3: VOX POPULI

1. "Had Your Say Yet?" *New York Times*, November 2, 1941, p. IX-10.

2. "Radio Reviews," *Variety*, July 10, 1935, p. 52.

3. Ibid.

4. "Thursday's Highlights," *Radio Mirror*, July 1940, p. 48.

5. "Radio Reviews," *Variety*, November 3, 1937, p. 35.

6. Parks Johnson, Notes prepared for an advertising agency presentation (unpublished), 1947.

7. Letter from Dick Joy, West Coast announcer, June 23, 1987.

8. "Radio Reviews," *Variety*, November 3, 1937, p. 34.

9. "Radio Reviews," *Variety*, September 3, 1937, p. 36.

10. "Suicide's Vox Pop," *Variety*, December 16, 1936, p. 39.

11. Interview with Walt Framer, April 24, 1985.

12. Ibid.

13. "Radio Reviews," *Variety*, November 8, 1937, p. 35.

14. "Vox Pop by Phone Worries Utility," *Variety*, December 15, 1936, p. 39.

15. Fred Sammis, "The Program on which You are the star," *Radio Mirror*, October 1935, pp. 79–80.

16. "Paul Wing's Spelling-Bee Begins New Series," *Radio Guide*, September 24, 1938, p. 16.

17. "Radio Reviews," *Variety*, November 3, 1937, p. 34.

18. "Tuesday's Highlights," *Radio Mirror*, December 1939, p. 44.

19. Ibid.

20. "Tuesday's Highlights," *Radio Mirror*, January 1941, p. 40.

21. Interview with Dwight Weist, January 31, 1985.

22. Ibid.

23. Ibid.

24. "Radio Reviews," *Variety*, July 15, 1936, p. 64.

25. "Radio Reviews," *Variety*, March 17, 1937, p. 32.

26. "CBS Decides to Forego Royalty Claim as 'Prof. Quiz' Show Goes to NBC," *Variety*, September 23, 1936, p. 31.

27. "Tuesday's Highlights," *Radio Mirror*, November 1940, p. 40.

CHAPTER 4: QUIZ CRAZE

1. "Monday's Highlights," *Radio Mirror*, September 1940, p. 45.

2. "Some Dr. I.Q. Broadcast Oddities," *Variety*, June 25, 1940, p. 45.

3. Ibid.

4. Ibid.

5. "Portland, Me., Audience Sour on Dr. I.Q.," *Variety*, February 7, 1940, p. 26.

6. "Radio Games Increase," *Variety*, May 25, 1938, p. 25.

7. Ibid.

8. "Monday's Highlights, *Radio Mirror*, July 1939, p. 43.

9. "Friday's Highlights," *Radio Mirror*, June 1939, p. 52.

10. "Radio Reviews," *Variety*, October 25, 1939, p. 36.

11. "Radio Reviews," *Variety*, February 16, 1938, p. 32.

12. "Quiz Programs Too Successful as Mail Lure; Handling is an Embarrassment," *Variety*, May 21, 1940, p. 34.

13. Charles Oppenheim, "Accent on the Answer," *New York Times*, June 10, 1945, p. II-5.

14. Ibid.

15. Ibid.

16. Sally Ashley, *F.P.A.: The Life and Times of Franklin Pearce Adams* (New York: Beaufort Books, 1986), pp. 208–209.

17. Dan Golenpaul, Oral History Project interview, Columbia University, 1964.

18. Ibid.

19. Interview with Clifton Fadiman, August 1, 1984; "Clifton Fadiman," *Current Biography, 1941* (New York: Wilson Co., 1942), p. 190; "Clifton Fadiman," *Current Biography, 1955* (New York: Wilson Co., 1955), pp. 266–267.

20. Robert Landry, "Radio Reviews," *Variety*, June 1, 1938, p. 34.

21. Orrin E. Dunlap, "Stumping the Experts," *New York Times*, June 19, 1938, p. IX-10.

22. "Radio: Shindig," *Time*, November 27, 1939, p. 39.

23. Fadiman.

24. John Kieran, *Not Under Oath* (Boston: Houghton Mifflin, 1964), pp. 60–61.

25. Fadiman.

26. Kiernan, *Not Under Oath*, p. 66.

27. Henry Morton Robinson, "Information Please," *Reader's Digest*, January 1939, p. 68.

28. Fadiman.

29. "Farley Stars as Guest on 'Information Please,' " *New York Times*, November 15, 1939, p. 9.

30. "Maverick Is Stumped by La Guardia's Query," *New York Times*, July 26, 1939, p. 20.

31. Letter from Joseph Kahn, January 25, 1986.

32. Ibid.

33. Ibid.

34. Ashley, *F.P.A.*, pp. 214–215.

35. "Any Questions?" *LIFE*, May 17, 1943, pp. 31–32.

36. Vincent Terrace, *Radio's Golden Years* (San Diego: A. S. Barnes, 1981), p. 272.

37. Ashley, *F.P.A.*, p. 217.

38. Interview with Emerson Foote, advertising executive, August 4, 1986.

39. Fadiman.

40. Ibid.

41. Ibid.

CHAPTER 5: "HOLD IT, HORACE!"

1. Interview with Horace Heidt, April 22, 1984.

2. Interview with Harold Hackett, April 23, 1984.

3. Ibid.

4. Fred Lowery, *Whistling in the Dark* (Gretna, La.: Pelican Publishing Co., 1983), pp. 179–181.

5. Heidt.

6. Ibid.

7. Ibid.

8. "Silver & Gold: Lewis-Howe Starts Two New Shows," *TIDE*, July 15, 1939, pp. 42–43.

9. Ibid.

10. "Tuesday's Highlights," *Radio Mirror*, February 1940, p. 46.

11. Heidt.

12. Ibid.

13. NBC radio broadcast, *Pot o' Gold*, November 28, 1939 (Los Angeles: Pacific Pioneer Broadcasters).

14. Heidt.

15. Ibid.

16. Hackett.

17. Lowery, *Whistling*, p. 216.

18. Heidt.

19. "Should Tums Decide to Take a Hint (and a Walk) NBC Won't Be Unhappy," *Variety*, January 30, 1940, p. 29.

20. " 'Pot o' Gold' Inspires Another," *Variety*, April 2, 1940, p. 31.

21. "Should Tums Decide," p. 29.

22. Heidt.

23. "Won't Prosecute 'Pot o' Gold,' " *New York Times*, April 13, 1940, p. 18.

24. Ray Tucker, "Uncle Sam Probes Pot o' Gold," *Movie & Radio Guide*, February 24–March 1, 1940, p. 5.

25. "The 'Pot o' Gold' Runs into Trouble" (Part I), *Movie & Radio Guide*, February 17–23, 1940, p. 5.

26. Ibid.

27. "Peeking in on a 'Pot o' Gold,' " *Movie & Radio Guide*, January 12, 1940, p. 20.

28. "The 'Pot o' Gold' Runs into Trouble" (Part II), *Movie & Radio Guide*, March 9–15, 1940, p. 10.

29. "Disgruntled Almost-Winner Ties Up Coin of Tums Company in Albany," *Variety*, March 6, 1940, p. 29.

30. "Man Who Said 'Pot o' Gold' Didn't Play Fair Dies," *Variety*, December 17, 1940, p. 28.

31. "WWJ Cancels 'Pot of Gold,' " *Variety*, March 20, 1940, p. 27.

32. Heidt.

33. Hackett.

34. Howard Barnes, "On the Screen: 'Pot o' Gold'—Roxy," *New York Herald Tribune*, April 5, 1941, p. 8.

35. "U.S. Tax Court Ruling on 'Pot o' Gold,' " *New York Times*, January 5, 1946, p. 15.

36. Hackett.

CHAPTER 6: WUNDERKINDER

1. Robert Lindsey, "School Is Back in Session for 'The Quiz Kids,' " *New York Times*, April 13, 1980, p. II-37.

2. Fred Ferretti, "Fleeting Fame: When Quiz Kids Grow Up," *New York Times*, December 26, 1982, p. 63.

3. Ruth Duskin Feldman, *Whatever Happened to the Quiz Kids?* (Chicago: Chicago Review Press, 1982), p. 10.

4. Louis Cowan, Oral History Project interview, Columbia University, 1967.

5. Feldman, *Quiz Kids*, p. 9.

6. Cowan.

7. Ibid.

8. "Radio Reviews," *Variety*, July 3, 1940, p. 32.

9. "Kelly of 'Quiz Kids' Shoots Burglar Dead," *New York Times*, April 22, 1947, p. 33; "Cleared in Killing Thief," *New York Times*, April 23, 1947, p. 27.

10. "Joe Kelly," *Current Biography, 1945* (New York: Wilson Co., 1946), p. 320.

11. J. P. McEvoy, "The Quiz Kids," *Reader's Digest*, October 1940, p. 24.

12. Ibid.

13. "Joe Kelly," p. 321.

14. Eliza Merrill Hickok, *The Quiz Kids* (Boston: Houghton Mifflin, 1947), p. 32.

15. Feldman, *Quiz Kids*, p. 16.

16. Ibid., p. 347.

17. Ibid., p. x.

18. Ibid.

19. CBS television broadcast, *The Quiz Kids*, January 13, 1952 (New York: Museum of Television and Radio).

20. "Radio Reviews," *Variety*, April 9, 1941, p. 30.
21. "Radio Reviews," *Variety*, December 18, 1940, p. 38.
22. Cowan.
23. Feldman, *Quiz Kids*, pp. 353–354.
24. Ferretti, "Fleeting Fame," p. 63.
25. Feldman, *Quiz Kids*, p. 96.

CHAPTER 7: "AREN'T WE DEVILS?"

1. Ralph Edwards, "The Truth about Truth or Consequences," *Radio & Television Mirror*, January 1949, pp. 24–25.
2. Ibid., p. 86.
3. Ibid.
4. "Radio Reviews," *Variety*, March 27, 1940, p. 28. See also "Saturday's Highlights," *Radio & Television Mirror*, September 1940, p. 52.
5. Frank Buxton and Bill Owen, *The Big Broadcast: 1920–1950* (New York: Viking Press, 1972), p. 244.
6. "Ralph L. Edwards," *Current Biography*, *1943* (New York: Wilson Co., 1944), p. 193.
7. Ralph Edwards, "To the Defense of 'Truth or Consequences,' " *New York Times*, November 8, 1942, p. VIII-12.
8. "Radio Insanity," *LIFE*, April 2, 1945, pp. 118–120.
9. Ralph Edwards, "The Quiz Program Operates as a Modern Business Organization," *Variety*, January 8, 1941, p. 103.
10. "Radio Quiz Tells Guest Where $1,000 Is, Holyoke Listeners Beat Train, Dig It Up," *New York Times*, November 6, 1944, p. 21.
11. "Radio Error Starts a Shower of Pennies That Turn to Mail Deluge in Staten Island," *New York Times*, January 26, 1943, p. 38; "Mail Flood Gives Radio Quiz Loser No Rest as Truckloads of Gifts Begin to Arrive," *New York Times*, January 28, 1943, p. 17.
12. "Cause of It All Turns Up," *New York Times*, January 31, 1943, p. 26.
13. John K. Hutchens, "Money in the Mail," *New York Times*, February 7, 1943, p. II-9.
14. "Radio Reviews," *Variety*, July 10, 1940, p. 25.
15. Interview with John Guedel, May 5, 1987.
16. Interview with Art Linkletter, May 7, 1987.
17. Ibid.
18. Guedel.
19. Ibid.
20. John Dunning, *Tune in Yesterday* (Englewood Cliffs, NJ: Prentice-Hall, 1976), p. 473.
21. Linkletter.
22. Ibid.
23. Ibid.
24. Promotional material, Ralph Edwards Productions, 1984.
25. Guedel.
26. John Crosby, *Out of the Blue* (New York: Simon & Schuster, 1952), pp. 158–160.

27. Interview with Robert Jensen, NBC engineer, April 23, 1984.

28. Linkletter.

29. Jack Gould, "Jack Benny or Jackpot?" *New York Times Magazine*, August 15, 1948, p. 41. Edwards appealed directly to newspaper columnists not to print the answer to the payoff questions. "In as much as this charity is one of the most worthy and least financed, we would like the contest to last long enough to give the mental health drive funds time to do a real job." Edwards quoted in "News of TV and Radio," *New York Times*, October 10, 1948, p. X-11.

30. Promotional material, Ralph Edwards Productions, 1976.

31. Promotional material, Ralph Edwards Productions, 1971.

32. "Saturday's Highlights," *Radio Mirror*, December 1939, p. 48.

33. "Radio Reviews," *Variety*, October 11, 1939, p. 37.

34. "Radio Reviews," *Variety*, December 11, 1940, p. 39.

35. Diana Gibbings, "Distaff Humor," *New York Times*, August 19, 1945, p. II-5. See also "Thanks to Joe Miller," *Tune In*, November 1944, pp. 40–41.

36. Ted Shane, "Misinformation Please," *Liberty*, September 9, 1944, p. 13.

37. Moreover, producers realized it was the style of the storytellers, and not the content, that mattered. The shortlived WJZ-Blue Network program *That's a Good One* proved that old jokes fell flat if delivered "straight." John K. Hutchens, "Radio Notebook," *New York Times*, September 19, 1943, p. II-7.

38. "Radio Reviews: Follow-up Comment," *Variety*, December 2, 1942, p. 32.

CHAPTER 8: SMOKE RINGS MUSICAL KNOWLEDGE

1. "Today on the Radio," *New York Times*, May 23, 1940, p. 28.

2. Quin Ryan, WGN manager, dictated manuscript, Broadcast Pioneers History Project, Washington, D.C., undated, p. 12.

3. Ibid.; see also "Kay Kyser," in George T. Simon, *The Big Bands* (New York: Macmillan, 1967), pp. 312–313.

4. Louis Cowan, Oral History Project interview, Columbia University, 1967.

5. Eliza Merrill Hickok, *The Quiz Kids* (Boston: Houghton Mifflin, 1947), pp. 194–195.

6. George T. Simon, *The Big Bands* (New York: Macmillan, 1967), p. 312; "A Salute to Kay Kyser: The First Ten Years," *Radio Mirror*, March 1948, pp. 48–49.

7. NBC radio broadcast, "Kay Kyser's Kollege of Musical Knowledge," December 10, 1941 (New York: Museum of Television and Radio).

8. Cowan.

9. Interview with Harry Babbitt, May 8, 1987.

10. Liz Lucas, "Bandleader Kay Kyser Dead at 79," *The Chapel Hill Newspaper*, July 24, 1985, p. 1A.

11. Martin Tolchin, "On Centennial, Truman Recalled in Washington," *New York Times*, May 9, 1984, p. A-18.

12. Orville B. Campbell, "So Long, Mr. Kay Kyser, You Gave Living a Lift," *The Chapel Hill Newspaper*, July 24, 1985, p. 14A.

13. "Kay Kyser's Confession," *New York Times*, October 12, 1979, p. II-5.

14. "A Salute to Kay Kyser," p. 104.

15. See "George Washington Hill: Industrial Tornado," in *Biography of an*

idea: Memoirs of Public Relations Counsel Edward L. Bernays (New York: Simon & Schuster, 1965).

16. Interview with Ward Byron, producer-writer, December 12, 1989.

17. Ibid.

18. Interview with Sammy Kaye, May 14, 1985.

19. See "Sammy Kaye," in Simon, *The Big Bands*, pp. 283–284.

20. Kaye.

21. Ibid.

22. Ibid.; "Television Reviews," *Variety*, March 30, 1949, p. 31.

23. "Radio Reviews," *Variety*, April 17, 1940, p. 32.

24. Interview with John Green, May 8, 1987. Another 1940 summer filler was *On the Spot* with quizmaster Henry Morgan; it aired with various bands from Manhattan Beach, N.Y.

25. NBC radio broadcast, "Beat the Band," February 18, 1940 (Los Angeles: Pacific Pioneer Broadcasters).

26. Souvenir Programme, "Milwaukee Welcomes Incomparable Hildegarde," September 18, 1948, p. 10.

27. "Radio Reviews," *Variety*, June 23, 1943, p. 46.

28. "Radio Reviews," *Variety*, June 21, 1944, p. 34.

29. Ted Cott, Oral History Project interview, Columbia University, 1960.

30. Ibid.

31. Victor Rosen, "The Show They Couldn't Kill," *Movie & Radio Guide*, May 18–24, 1940, p. 51.

32. Ibid.; WOR's *The Treasure Hour*, starring world opera figures such as Licia Albanese and Jan Peerce, instituted listener-participation musical contests in 1946.

33. Rosen, "The Show They Couldn't Kill," p. 51.

34. In 1946 Cott briefly aired over WNEW, *So You Think You Know People*, an audience-participation show that explored weighty topics and permitted amateur thinkers to test the validity of their grasp of a subject against that of an expert, such as psychologist Ernest Dichter.

35. "Parlor Games on the Ether," *The New Republic*, September 28, 1938, Vol. 86, No. 1243, p. 202.

CHAPTER 9: RIGHT, WITH EVERSHARP

1. Milton H. Biow, *Butting in . . . An Adman Speaks Out* (Garden City, NY: Doubleday, 1964), p. 112.

2. Ibid.; "Sunday's Highlights," *Radio Mirror*, June 1940, p. 44.

3. Interview with Peter G. Cranford, January 16, 1985.

4. Ibid.

5. Ibid.

6. Ibid.

7. "Quiz Show Originator's Million-Dollar Idea," AP release in *Miami Herald*, January 4, 1960.

8. Cranford.

9. Biow, *Butting in*, p. 112.

10. "Right, with Eversharp," *Sponsor*, December 1946, p. 11.

11. "He's Doin' Fine, Thanks . . . ," *Radio Mirror*, April 1942, p. 43.

12. "Radio Followup," *Variety*, August 28, 1940, p. 31.

13. Cranford.

14. John Dunning, *Tune in Yesterday* (Englewood Cliffs, NJ: Prentice-Hall, 1976), pp. 85–86.

15. "Of the Melancholy Phil," *New York Times*, March 3, 1946, p. II-7.

16. "Phil Baker," *Current Biography, 1946* (New York: Wilson Co., 1947), p. 25.

17. Ibid.

18. "Inside Stuff-Radio," *Variety*, September 2, 1942, p. 41.

19. Biow, *Butting in*, p. 112.

20. CBS radio broadcast, *Take It or Leave It*, November 8, 1942 (Los Angeles: Pacific Pioneer Broadcasters).

CHAPTER 10: SERVICE WITH A SMILE

1. "Whodunits, Quizzes Head Escapist Scripts Offered Nets by Outsiders," *Variety*, April 21, 1943, p. 31.

2. "Quiz Shows Blitz Actors, *Variety*, July 10, 1940, p. 1.

3. Jack W. Harris and Edward M. Kirby (who served as chief, Allied Radio Network, Supreme Headquarters, Allied Expeditionary Forces, 1941–45) cover quiz and audience-participation shows and the war effort in *Star-Spangled Radio* (Chicago: Ziff-Davis, 1948).

4. "Sunday's Highlights," *Radio Mirror*, March 1941, p. 44.

5. MBS radio broadcast, *Double or Nothing*, May 3, 1942 (Los Angeles: Pacific Pioneer Broadcasters).

6. Ibid.; Interview with James B. Taylor III, January 25, 1985.

7. "Spokane's Three Alerts," *Variety*, December 17, 1941, p. 41.

8. "From the Office of Wartime Radio Censorship," *Variety*, January 21, 1942, p. 25.

9. Ibid.

10. Ibid.

11. "Quiz Programs Can Easily Meet Government Wartime Precautions and Retain Values, Admen Think," *Variety*, January 21, 1942, p. 24.

12. "Censorship Strikes Hard at Types of Program Dear to Local Stations," *Variety*, January 21, 1942, p. 24.

13. "War Regulations," *Variety*, December 24, 1941, p. 32; "NBC Hires 100 Guards," *Variety*, December 17, 1941, p. 41.

14. John K. Hutchens, "Visiting 'Vox Pop,' " *New York Times*, December 5, 1943, p. II-13.

15. "Vox Pop: The Story of 'The Show That Travels America,' " CBS promotional brochure, 1945.

16. Letter from Bill Johnson, son of Parks Johnson, July 21, 1987.

17. "A Salute to Kay Kyser: The First Ten Years," *Radio Mirror*, March 1948, p. 104.

18. Orville B. Campbell, "So Long, Mr. Kay Kyser, You Gave Living a Lift," *The Chapel Hill Newspaper*, July 14, 1985, p. 14A.

19. Eliza Merrill Hickok, *The Quiz Kids* (Boston: Houghton Mifflin, 1947), pp. 92–93.

20. "Hub Reaction to 'Info Please' Bond Date Indicates $50,000,000 Tour Total," *Variety*, December 2, 1942, p. 28.

21. " 'Another Versailles' Scorned by Wallace," *New York Times*, September 28, 1943, p. 6.

22. Ralph Edwards, "Truth and the Consequences of a Cross-Country Tour for Uncle Sam," *Variety*, July 14, 1943, p. 52.

23. Ibid.

24. "Phil Baker," *Current Biography, 1946* (New York: Wilson Co., 1947), p. 25.

25. NBC radio broadcast, "Battle of the Sexes," November 1943 (exact date unknown) (Los Angeles: Pacific Pioneer Broadcasters).

26. John Dunning, *Tune in Yesterday* (Englewood Cliffs, NJ: Prentice-Hall, 1976), p. 535.

27. Ibid., p. 646.

28. "Radio Reviews," *Variety*, November 1, 1944, p. 32; Interview with Ken Murray, April 26, 1984.

CHAPTER 11: PRIZED EVENTS

1. John Kieran, *Not Under Oath* (Boston: Houghton Mifflin, 1954), p. 176.

2. Interview with Win Elliot, May 28, 1985.

3. Ibid.

4. Ibid.

5. "Radio Reviews," *Variety*, July 5, 1944, p. 29.

6. Elliot.

7. Ibid.

8. Ibid.

9. Interview with Johnny Olson, April 25, 1984.

10. Bart Andrews with Brad Dunning, *The Worst TV Shows Ever* (New York: Dutton, 1980), pp. 142–145.

11. "Reigns of Queens for a Day Span 15 Years with 3,921 Rulers, Mostly Crowned by Bailey," *Los Angeles Times*, May 1, 1960, p. 3.

12. Ibid.

13. "Radio Reviews," *Variety*, October 1, 1947, p. 24.

14. Ibid.

15. Interview with Walter O'Keefe, May 15, 1982.

16. Ibid.

17. NBC radio broadcast, *Double or Nothing*, October 15, 1948 (Los Angeles: SPERDVAC).

18. Thea Traum, "Twenty Questions," *Radio & Television Mirror*, July 1948, pp. 40–41.

19. Bobby (McGuire) Van Deventer, Old-Time Radio Convention panel, Newark, NJ, October 24, 1987. Van Deventer said his mother joined the program because daytime commentator Mary Margaret McBride proved unavailable.

20. Traum, "Twenty Questions," p. 96.

21. Ibid., p. 97.

22. "Radio Reviews," *Variety*, October 24, 1945, p. 38.

23. Interview with Joseph Nathan Kane, November 28, 1984. Kane also wrote a guidebook for contestants, *How to Win on Quiz Shows* (New York: Bartholomew House, 1956).

24. Jack and Edith Weiss, "We Broke the Bank," *Radio Mirror*, January 1947, p. 66.

25. Letter from Jack Weiss, April 8, 1985.

26. Weiss, "We Broke the Bank," p. 67.

CHAPTER 12: THE WHOLE SEARS, ROEBUCK CATALOG

1. Joseph C. Goulden, *The Best Years: 1945–1950* (New York: Atheneum, 1976), p. 107.

2. Harriet Van Horne, "Dishwashers and Diamonds for Cinderella," *The Story of Our Time: Encyclopedia Yearbook, 1949* (New York: The Grolier Society and J. A. Richards Publishing Co., 1949), p. 390.

3. "Give-Aways: They're a big business," *Sponsor*, May 1948, p. 34. See also "Radio's $7,000,000 'Bank Night,' " *Variety*, June 2, 1948, p. 1.

4. Ibid., p. 32.

5. Sidney Lohman, "Concerning Radio," *New York Times*, January 30, 1949, p. II-10.

6. "Radio News," *New York Times*, June 10, 1949, p. 50.

7. "Winner Gets 49,000 $1 Bills," *New York Times*, May 25, 1949, p. 31.

8. Interview with Harry Salter, October 7, 1975.

9. John Brooks, *Telephone: The First Hundred Years* (New York: Harper & Row, 1976), p. 214.

10. Louis Cowan, Oral History Project interview, Columbia University, 1967.

11. Letter from Richard Osk, network publicist, February 23, 1985.

12. Ibid.

13. Interview with Kay Armen, December 7, 1982.

14. Cowan.

15. "Radio Reviews," *Variety*, March 24, 1948, p. 34.

16. Jack Gould, "Programs in Review," *New York Times*, April 4, 1948, p. II-9.

17. Cowan.

18. Osk. NBC's movie quiz, *Hollywood Calling*, similarly tipped off the press with answers. Host George Murphy (and future U.S. senator) refused to be a party to the leaks and insisted on leaving the listener-phoning show. The network tried to hold him to his contract. But when Murphy said he would disclose the reason for his departure, it backed down and hired Jack McCoy and George Jessel as M.C.s. Interview with George Murphy, April 15, 1986.

19. Osk.

20. Van Horne, "Dishwashers and Diamonds," p. 390.

21. Robert Taylor, *Fred Allen: His Life and Wit* (Boston: Little, Brown, 1989), pp. 280–281.

22. Fred Allen, *Treadmill to Oblivion* (Boston: Little Brown-Atlantic Monthly Press, 1954), pp. 217–218.

23. Osk.

24. Cowan.

25. Ben Gross, *I Looked and I Listened* (New York: Random House, 1954), p. 153.

26. Jack Gould, "Give Away Curse," *New York Times*, May 16, 1948, p. II-9.

27. "Phone Starts Dispute Over Contest Prize," *Los Angeles Times*, December 23, 1950, p. I-2.

28. "Loss of $24,000 Laid to Phone Call Cutoff," *Los Angeles Times*, December 8, 1948, p. I-28.

29. Bob Hawk, "This Quiz Business," *Radio & Television Mirror*, March 1949, p. 30.

30. Mark Goodson, "Confessions of a Quizo-Phrenic," *Variety*, January 5, 1949, p. 101.

31. Mark Goodson, "Giveaway Defense," *New York Times*, July 11, 1948, p. II-7.

32. "Godfrey: 'Nuts to Giveaways,' " *Variety*, April 6, 1949, p. 27.

CHAPTER 13: TELEVOX POP

1. R. W. Stewart, "The Convention Via Video," *New York Times*, June 27, 1948, p. X-9.

2. Richard Schickel, *D. W. Griffith: An American Life* (New York: Touchstone Book, 1984), pp. 548–549.

3. Interview with Ken Murray, April 26, 1984.

4. Eugene Pitts III and Walter I. Siegal, "Fifty Years of TV," *Audio*, July 1981, p. 28.

5. Ibid., pp. 28–32.

6. "Thousands See Pageantry by Television," *New York Herald-Tribune*, May 1, 1939, p. 4.

7. Ibid.

8. Joseph H. Udelson, *The Great Television Race* (University: University of Alabama Press, 1982), p. 131.

9. "Incubator Baby," *TIDE*, May 1, 1939, p. 17.

10. "Television's Pioneer Sponsors, *Variety*, July 9, 1941, p. 30.

11. Ibid.

12. Will Marcus, "Reporting on Television," *Radio Mirror*, February 1942, p. 3.

13. Erik Barnouw, *The Golden Web* (New York: Oxford University Press, 1968), p. 128.

14. John P. Callahan, "Aims of Television Set High for 1946," *New York Times*, December 23, 1945, p. III-5.

15. "Television Reviews," *Variety*, August 9, 1944, p. 28.

16. "Television Followup," *Variety*, September 25, 1946, p. 46.

17. "Television Reviews," *Variety*, October 2, 1946, p. 34.

18. "Television Reviews," *Variety*, October 15, 1947, p. 29.

19. Interview with Mike Stokey, October 3, 1990.

20. Ibid.

21. Ibid.; see also Richard F. Shepard, "A Handy Man Hangs On," *New York Times*, July 29, 1956, p. II-9.

22. Alex McNeil, *Total Television*, 2d ed. (New York: Penquin Books, 1984), p. 819.

23. "Television Reviews," *Variety*, August 25, 1948, p. 32.

24. Letter from Douglas Edwards, April 4, 1985.

25. "Television Reviews," *Variety*, June 9, 1948, p. 28.

26. Jack Gould, "Television in Review," *New York Times*, June 26, 1949, p. II-7.

27. CBS television broadcast, *Quiz Kids*, January 13, 1952 (New York: Museum of Television and Radio).

28. Jack Gould, "Television in Review," *New York Times*, December 11, 1949, p. II-11.

29. Ibid.

30. Ibid.

31. Interview with Lester Gottlieb, February 6, 1975.

32. Interview with Dan Seymour, January 30, 1975.

33. Gottlieb.

34. Interview with Bob Howard, August 6, 1985.

CHAPTER 14: NO ANSWERS

1. Robert W. Glasgow, "N.B.C. Forbids New Give-Away Shows on Radio," *New York Herald-Tribune*, August 7, 1948, p. 21.

2. Ibid.

3. Ibid.

4. "Here's What the FCC Says," *Variety*, August 11, 1948, p. 30. For an overview, see Jack Gould, "Jack Benny or Jackpot?" *New York Times Magazine*, August 15, 1948.

5. George Rosen, "FCC to Give Way on Giveaways?" *Variety*, August 11, 1948, p. 25.

6. Ibid.

7. Ibid., p. 30.

8. Leonard H. Marks, "Legality of Radio Giveaway Programs," *The Georgetown Law Journal*, Vol. 37, 1948–1949, p. 323.

9. Ibid., pp. 324–325.

10. Ibid., p. 320.

11. Ibid., pp. 328–329.

12. Ibid., pp. 332–333.

13. Ibid., pp. 334–335.

14. Ibid., p. 340.

15. Ibid.

16. "FCC Finds 'T'aint Easy Trying to Give Away a Giveaway Ruling," *Variety*, August 24, 1949, p. 38. See also Thomas F. Hagan, "Give-Away Shows to Be Banned from Air by FCC after October 1," *New York Times*, August 20, 1949, p. 1.

17. "CBS Network to Seek Legal Test of FCC Order Outlawing Give-Away Shows," *New York Times*, August 23, 1949, p. 46.

18. "2d Dissent Ready on Give-Away Ban," *New York Times*, August 31, 1949, p. 46.

19. Ibid.

20. Jack Gould, "Give-Away' Issue," *New York Times*, August 28, 1949, p. X-7.

21. "Giveaways on Radio Hold Public Favor," *Los Angeles Times*, Septembre 28, 1949, p. I-13.

22. "Giveaways to Get Court Aid," *New York Times*, September 20, 1949, p. 31.

23. "The First 50 Years of Broadcasting: 1953," *Broadcasting*, March 23, 1981, Vol. 100, No. 12, p. 104.

24. "The First 50 Years of Broadcasting: 1954," *Broadcasting*, March 30, 1981, Vol. 100, No. 13, p. 78.

CHAPTER 15: VAUDEO

1. "Public Apathy Dooming Radio Giveaway Shows," *Los Angeles Times*, December 5, 1949, p. I-6.

2. Tony Thomas and Aubrey Solomon, *The Films of 20th Century-Fox: A Pictorial History* (Secaucus, NJ: Citadel Press, 1979), p. 211.

3. Robert Metz, *CBS: Reflections in a Bloodshot Eye* (New York: Playboy Press, 1975), pp. 137–145. See also William S. Paley's *As It Happened: A Memoir* (Garden City, NY: Doubleday, 1979).

4. "Availabilities—1949–'50," *Variety*, May 25, 1949, p. 23.

5. Niles Trammell, "1950: Year of the Salesman," *Variety*, January 4, 1950, p. 100.

6. Ibid.

7. George Rosen, "46% of TV Viewers Prefer Vaudeo; Snub News, Kid, Quiz, Musical Shows," *Variety*, November 17, 1948, p. 29.

8. "Texaco's 86.7 All-Time High," *Variety*, November 17, 1948, p. 29.

9. Harold Bender, "Bud Collyer Recalls the Vintage Years on TV," *New York Journal-American Pictorial TView*, May 7, 1961, p. 14.

10. Maxene Fabe, *TV Game Shows* (Garden City, NY: Dolphin, 1979), p. 139.

11. Frances Kish, "Bud Collyer—For Real," *TV-Radio Mirror*, September 1958, p. 70.

12. Ibid.

13. Corinne Swift, "Bud Collyer—Man with an Open Mind," *Radio-TV Mirror*, June 1953, p. 60.

CHAPTER 16: HEART LINE

1. Interview with Walt Framer, April 24, 1985.

2. Ibid.

3. Ibid.

4. Ibid.

5. Ibid.

6. Ibid.

7. Interview with Ralph Paul, announcer, July 29, 1985.

8. Jack Gould, "Radio and Television," *New York Times*, November 9, 1951,

p. 34. See also Gould's "TV's Misery Shows," *New York Times*, February 7, 1954, p. II-11.

9. Gould, "Radio and Television," p. 34.

10. Framer.

11. "Ex-Convict Strikes It Rich Briefly on TV, but Fame Proves a Give-Away to Police," *New York Times*, January 27, 1954, p. 19.

12. Framer.

13. "Charity Load Linked to Give-Away Shows," *New York Times*, February 5, 1954, p. 21.

14. "City Puts Curb on 'Strike It Rich'; Calls TV-Radio Show Solicitation," *New York Times*, February 4, 1954, pp. 1, 34.

15. Framer.

16. Ibid.; "Family of 11 Fails to 'Strike It Rich,' " *New York Times*, March 9, 1954, p. 29.

17. " 'Strike It Rich' Loses," *New York Times*, May 4, 1954, p. 41.

18. "Court Sets Curb on 'Strike It Rich,' " *New York Times*, December 29, 1954, p. 25.

19. Framer.

20. " 'Strike It Rich' Still Makes News," *Broadcasting Telecasting*, March 8, 1954, p. 50.

21. "Rep. St. George Enters 'Strike It Rich' Fray," *Broadcasting Telecasting*, February 22, 1954, p. 54.

22. " 'Strike It Rich' Stricken," *Broadcasting Telecasting*, February 22, 1954, p. 54.

23. Jack Anderson, "Quiz Show Vet Eyes New Show," *Miami Herald*, June 8, 1974, p. 7-C.

CHAPTER 17: "THE ONE, THE ONLY—GROUCHO"

1. Groucho Marx, *The Secret Word Is Groucho* (New York: G. P. Putnam's Sons, 1976), p. 18.

2. Ibid.

3. Ibid., p. 19.

4. Arthur Frank Wertheim, *Radio Comedy* (New York: Oxford University Press, 1979), p. 123.

5. Marx, *Secret Word*, p. 27.

6. Interview with John Guedel, May 5, 1987.

7. Marx, *Secret Word*, p. 29.

8. "Radio Reviews," *Variety*, October 29, 1947, p. 28; "G. Marx," *New York Times*, December 7, 1947, p. II-13.

9. Marx, *Secret Word*, p. 35.

10. "Radio Reviews," *Variety*, October 12, 1949, p. 28.

11. Marx, *Secret Word*, p. 46.

12. Ibid., p. 47.

13. Jack Gould, "TV Debut Is Made by Groucho Marx," *New York Times*, October 6, 1950, p. 50.

14. Ibid.

15. Marx, *Secret Word*, pp. 55–56.

16. Ibid., pp. 58–59.
17. Interview with Bernie Smith, codirector and producer, May 6, 1987.
18. Guedel.
19. Marx, *Secret Word*, pp. 74–82.
20. Ibid., p. 52.
21. Interview with George Fenneman, announcer, May 5, 1987.
22. Marx, *Secret Word*, pp. 140–141.
23. Lee Demart, "Groucho's 1950's Quiz Show is a Hit All Over Again," *New York Times*, March 9, 1975, pp. II-1, II-31.

CHAPTER 18: HIGH COMEDY, LOW STAKES

1. Maxene Fabe, *TV Game Shows* (Garden City, NY: Dolphin Books, 1979), p. 171.
2. Larry Wolters, "Television's Rhodes Scholar," *New York Times*, August 10, 1952, p. II-11.
3. Ibid.
4. Ibid.
5. Jack Gould, "A TV Hit for $250," *New York Times*, February 14, 1954, p. II-11.
6. Jack Gould, "2 New TV Debuts Foster Education," *New York Times*, April 11, 1951, p. 42.
7. Interview with Morey Amsterdam, April 24, 1984.
8. Allen Sherman, *A Gift of Laughter* (New York: Atheneum, 1965), p. 184.
9. Letter from Douglas Edwards, April 4, 1985.
10. Ibid. Walter Cronkite had moderated a CBS-TV panel titled *It's News to Me*. His services later were sought by Goodson-Todman for *Nothing but the Truth*, but CBS policy against its newsmen on entertainment shows prevailed.
11. Gil Fates, *What's My Line?* (Englewood Cliffs, NJ: Prentice-Hall, 1978), p. 4.
12. Ibid., p. 7.
13. Ibid., p. 8.
14. Jack Gould, "The Radio Essay," *New York Times*, January 2, 1949, p. X-9.
15. Bernard Kalb, "Bennett Cerf: He Also Works in Video," *New York Times*, August 2, 1953, p. II-9.
16. Fates, *Line*, p. 24.
17. Ibid., p. 50.
18. Ibid., p. 67.
19. Ibid., p. 65.
20. Ibid., p. 94.
21. Mark Goodson, "The Anatomy of a Game," Seminar, The Museum of Television and Radio, October 9, 1985.
22. Ibid.
23. Fates, *Line*, p. 26.
24. Ibid., p. 118.
25. Jack Gould, "Radio & TV," *New York Times*, December 14, 1951, p. 43.

26. ABC television broadcast, *The Name's the Same*, May 1955 (exact date unknown) (New York: Museum of Television and Radio).

27. Ibid.

28. ABC television broadcast, *The Name's the Same*, April 11, 1955 (New York: Museum of Television and Radio).

29. Fabe, *TV Game Shows*, pp. 171–173.

30. Frances Kish, "Bud Collyer—For Real," *TV-Radio Mirror*, September 1958, p. 20.

31. Sherman, *Gift*, p. 125.

32. Ibid.

33. Ibid.

34. Ibid., pp. 126–127.

35. Fates, *Line*, p. 71.

36. Val Adams, "Radio and Television," *New York Times*, August 29, 1952, p. 20.

37. Sherman, *Gift*, pp. 134–135.

CHAPTER 19: CASH PYRAMID

1. Gilbert Millstein, "Its Creator Explains the $64,000 Appeal," *New York Times Magazine*, August 21, 1955, p. 36.

2. Ibid.

3. Louis Cowan, Oral History Project interview, Columbia University, 1967.

4. Millstein, "Creator Explains," p. 36.

5. Andrew Tobias, *Fire and Ice* (New York: Warner Books, 1977), pp. 155–156.

6. Ibid.

7. Val Adams, "TV Ready To Pose $64,000 Question," *New York Times*, March 9, 1955, p. 35.

8. Cowan.

9. Jack Gould, "TV: A Word for Hal March," *New York Times*, October 12, 1955, p. 63.

10. J. P. Shanley, "TV: Whew! He Stopped at $16,000," *New York Times*, June 22, 1955, p. 59.

11. Interview with Stephen O'Hanlon, July 17, 1985.

12. "Bird in the Hand Is Worth $32,000," *New York Times*, July 13, 1955, p. 53.

13. Ibid.

14. Jack Gould, "TV: Father Knows Best," *New York Times*, August 10, 1955, p. 51.

15. Ibid.

16. Jack Gould, "Man in the Street," *New York Times*, August 14, 1955, p. II-11.

17. "More Capsule British Com'l TV Reviews," *Variety*, October 19, 1955, p. 36.

18. June Owen, "Marine Officer Who's an Expert on Food Got His 'Basic Training' the World Over," *New York Times*, September 9, 1955, p. 20.

19. J. P. Shanley, "Marine Wins $64,000 TV Quiz, Aided by Father in Food Queries," *New York Times*, September 14, 1955, p. 1.

20. "Boxing Fan Wins $64,000 Decision," *New York Times*, December 7, 1955, p. 79.

21. "Question on Money Costs Clerk $64,000," *New York Times*, March 21, 1956, p. 75.

22. Tobias, *Fire*, p. 159.

23. Ibid., pp. 58, 113.

CHAPTER 20: CHAMPIONS AND CHALLENGERS

1. Kent Anderson, *Television Fraud* (Westport, CT: Greenwood Press, 1978), p. 30.

2. Val Adams, "Giant Give-Aways Planned by A.B.C.," *New York Times*, October 25, 1955, p. 67.

3. "Television Reviews," *Variety*, October 12, 1955, p. 34.

4. "Woman Wins $50,000," *New York Times*, November 13, 1955, p. 70.

5. Jon G. Smith, "She Kept on a-Goin': Ethel Park Richardson," *JEMF Quarterly*, Vol. 13, No. 47, Autumn 1977, pp. 105–111.

6. Richard F. Shephard, "Woman Wins First $100,000 TV Prize; Taxes Are Expected to Take $72,000," *New York Times*, December 11, 1955, p. 85.

7. "Boy Wins $100,000 on TV Show Here," *New York Times*, February 5, 1956, p. 1.

8. Anderson, *Television Fraud*, p. 32.

9. Mike Wallace and Gary Paul Gates, *Close Encounters: Mike Wallace's Own Story* (New York: William Morrow & Co., 1984), p. 17.

10. Maureen Dowd, "The Early Life of a Bedeviled Genius," *New York Times*, May 25, 1985, pp. 25–26.

11. "Television Reviews," *Variety*, April 11, 1956, p. 30.

12. Anderson, *Television Fraud*, p. 33.

13. Interview with Ralph Story, September 30, 1990.

14. Lilla Anderson, "Faith in His Fellow Man," *TV-Radio Mirror*, December 1956, p. 63.

15. Ibid.

16. Story.

17. Aline B. Saarinen, "TV Art Contest Wins a Public," *New York Times*, November 4, 1956, p. II-11.

18. Vincent Price, *I Like What I Know* (Garden City, NY: Doubleday & Co., 1959), p. 245.

19. Billy Pearson and Stephen Longstreet, *Never Look Back* (New York: Simon & Schuster, 1958), p. 342.

20. Gregory Merwin, "Quizzing The Master—Hal March," *TV-Radio Mirror*, May 1958, p. 81.

21. "Churchill's Son Bows Out of TV's $64,000 Question," *Los Angeles Times*, September 20, 1956, p. I-1.

22. David Wise, "$64,000 Programs Wanted to Use J. Edgar Hoover, Bishop Sheen," *New York Herald-Tribune-Post*, Special Dispatch, November 21, 1959.

23. Jack Gould, "End of An Era?" *New York Times*, December 22, 1957, p. II-13.

24. Erik Barnouw, *The Image Empire* (New York: Oxford University Press, 1966), pp. 61–65.

CHAPTER 21: HIGH STAKES HEROICS

1. Quoted in Hal Humphrey's "Around the Dials," *Philadelphia Inquirer*, January 23, 1957.

2. Bob Williams, "Quizzes Rule the Air Waves; Eight More Bow This Week," *Philadelphia Sunday Bulletin*, June 29, 1958, p. TF-2.

3. J. P. Shanley, "TV: Marathon Quiz," *New York Times*, October 10, 1956, p. 79.

4. "Feat of Balancing Wins $64,000 on TV," *New York Times*, September 16, 1956, p. 95.

5. Interview with Vicki Mills, June 24, 1984.

6. Ibid.

7. CBS television broadcast, *Name That Tune*, October 14, 1954 (New York: Museum of Television and Radio).

8. Ibid.

9. Letter from Sen. John Glenn, March 18, 1985.

10. Ibid.

11. Interview with Walt Framer, April 24, 1985.

12. Interview with Paul and Sally Bennett, February 12, 1990.

13. Sherrye Henry, "How They Began," *Parade Magazine*, February 1, 1987, p. 5.

14. J. P. Shanley, "Television: Knife Play," *New York Times*, September 8, 1956, p. 37. In 1960 two studio audience warmup men for the series were arrested on charges of splitting winnings with friends they put on the program.

15. Interview with Jan Murray, May 19, 1987.

16. "The Busy Middlemen in Giveaways," *Broadcasting*, Vol. 57, No. 6, August 10, 1959, p. 33.

17. "Television Reviews," *Variety*, September 19, 1956, p. 46.

18. Elizabeth Ball, "High Tension on 21," *TV-Radio Mirror*, June 1957, pp. 20–23, 72–73.

19. "Van Doren Dethroned on TV Quiz by a Woman Who Knows Kings," *New York Times*, March 12, 1957, p. 67.

20. "Television Reviews, *Variety*, July 10, 1957, p. 35. During the late 1950s CBS continued to bring new quizzes to network radio. A panel format (and 1957 summer replacement for Jack Benny), *Sez Who!* featured comedian Henry Morgan as moderator. In August 1959 it aired *Funny Side Up*, a Monday-through-Friday "It Pays to Be Ignorant"-styled series, with Bert Parks.

21. "Television Reviews," *Variety*, September 18, 1957, p. 34.

22. Interview with Win Elliot, May 28, 1985.

23. Ibid.

24. "Television Reviews," *Variety*, July 2, 1958, p. 30.

25. Alex McNeil, *Total Television*, 2d ed. (New York: Penquin Books, 1984), p. 104.

26. Helen Bolstad, "8 P.M., U.S.A.," *TV-Radio Mirror*, September 1958, p. 65.

27. CBS television broadcast, *The $64,000 Question*, April 9, 1957 (New York: Museum of Television and Radio).

28. Harry Castleman and Walter J. Podrazik, *Watching TV* (New York: McGraw-Hill Paperbacks, 1982), p. 125.

29. Quoted in the editorial "Relief at Last," *Philadelphia Inquirer*, September 24, 1957.

30. Ibid.

CHAPTER 22: THE CHIPS FALL

1. Kent Anderson, *Television Fraud* (Westport, CT: Greenwood Press, 1978), pp. 110–111.

2. Ibid., p. 111.

3. Ibid., pp. 112–113.

4. J. P. Shanley, "Television: '$64,000 Challenge,' " *New York Times*, April 9, 1956, p. 51. See "New Headache for TV," *Variety*, August 20, 1958, p. 23.

5. Gordon Cotler, "The Question about Quiz Shows," *New York Times Magazine*, December 1, 1957, p. 96.

6. Ibid.

7. Ibid., p. 98.

8. Earle McGill, *Radio Directing* (New York: McGraw-Hill Book Co., 1940), pp. 209–210.

9. Anderson, *Television Fraud*, p. 69

10. Ibid., p. 57.

11. Ibid., pp. 88–91.

12. Howard Rosenberg, "How Did the '50s Quiz-Show Scandal Ensnare a Tennessee Minister?" *Los Angeles Times Magazine*, November 5, 1989, pp. 20–24.

13. Harry Castleman and Walter Podrazik, *Watching TV* (New York: McGraw-Hill Paperbacks, 1982), p. 124.

14. Anderson, *Television Fraud*, pp. 134–135.

15. "Text of Van Doren Quiz Statement," *Los Angeles Times*, November 3, 1959, p. I-8.; Telenews newsreel, "Van Doren Confession," November 20, 1959 (Los Angeles: UCLA Film & Television Archive).

16. "FCC Proposes Law to Punish Air Deceptions," *Miami Herald*, February 12, 1960, p. 2-D.

17. Les Brown, *Encyclopedia of Television* (New York: Zoetrope, 1982), p. 345.

18. "Frederick Ford, 76; Led F.C.C. in Wake of 50's TV Scandals," *New York Times*, July 30, 1986, p. II-6; see also "Text of Attorney General's Report on 'Deceptive Practices' in Broadcasting Industry," *New York Times*, January 1, 1960, pp. C-10-12.

19. Interview with Dan Enright, May 13, 1987.

20. Castleman and Podrazik, *Watching TV*, p. 135.

21. Interview with Jack Narz, May 12, 1987.

22. Interview with Dennis James, May 10, 1987.

23. Castleman and Podrazik, *Watching TV*, p. 135.

24. Interview with Walt Framer, April 24, 1985.

25. Phil Meyer, "Miamians Debate Quiz Shows," *Miami Herald*, November 16, 1959.

26. Castleman and Podrazik, *Watching TV*, p. 134.

27. Drew Pearson, "Washington Merry-Go-Round," *Los Angeles Times*, October 30, 1959.

28. "Congress and the Quizlings," *Variety*, October 21, 1959, p. 28.

CHAPTER 23: VIANDS AND POPCORN

1. Erik Barnouw, *Tube of Plenty* (New York: Oxford University Press, 1975), p. 299.

2. Harry Castleman and Walter J. Podrazik, *Watching TV* (New York: McGraw-Hill, 1982), p. 145.

3. Barnouw, *Tube*, p. 300.

4. Cynthia Lowry, "Quiz Shows Nibbling Away TV Time Again," AP feature, *Miami Herald*, February 22, 1961.

5. Christopher P. Andersen, "Everything I've Done Has Been Terribly Chancy," *Parade Magazine*, March 29, 1987, p. 13.

6. Hugh Downs, *Yours Truly* (New York: Holt, Rinehart and Winston, 1960), p. 85.

7. Interview with Don Reid, April 1, 1985.

8. Maxene Fabe, *TV Game Shows* (Garden City, NY: Dolphin Book, 1979), p. 223.

9. Ibid.

10. Bart Andrews with Brad Dunning, *The Worst TV Shows Ever* (New York: E. P. Dutton, 1980), p. 61.

11. Ibid.

12. James Bacon, *How Sweet It Is: The Jackie Gleason Story* (New York: St. Martin's Press, 1985), pp. 169–170.

13. Dave Simms, "Television Treasure in Sand, *Miami Herald TV Preview*, December 17, 1967, p. 3.

14. Fabe, *TV Game Shows*, p. 290.

15. Chuck Barris, *Confessions of a Dangerous Mind* (New York: St. Martin's Press, 1984), p. 55.

16. Ibid., p. 56.

17. Ibid., p. 99.

18. Ibid.

19. Michael Drosnin, *Citizen Hughes* (New York: Holt Rinehart and Winston, 1985), pp. 145–155.

20. Andrews, *Worst TV*, p. 118.

21. Fabe, *TV Game Shows*, p. 230.

22. Jefferson Graham, *Come on Down!!! The TV Game Show Book* (New York: Abbeville Press, 1988), p. 41.

23. Television Program Listings, *New York Times*, October 3, 1969, p. 91.

24. Fabe, *TV Game Shows*, p. 124.

25. Interview with Mark Goodson, April 24, 1984.

26. Bill Todman, "Freedom of the Dial," *Variety*, January 5, 1949, p. 105.

27. John Crosby, *Out of the Blue* (New York: Simon & Schuster, 1952), p. 151.

28. Walter H. Waggoner, "William S. Todman, TV Producer, Dies," *New York Times*, July 31, 1979, p. II-4.

29. Goodson.

30. Ibid.

31. Waggoner, "William S. Todman," p. II-4.

32. Goodson.

33. Ibid.

34. Ibid.

35. Advertisement, "The British play twelve Goodson-Todman games," *Variety*, June 6, 1984, pp. 48–49.

CHAPTER 24: PLAY'S THE THING

1. Jefferson Graham, "Mark Goodson," *USA Today*, August 11, 1986, p. 4D.

2. Maxene Fabe, *TV Game Shows* (Garden City, NY: Dolphin Book, 1979), p. 181.

3. Tom Buckley, "Game Shows—TV's Glittering Gold Mine," *New York Times Magazine*, November 18, 1979, p. 172.

4. Interview with Frank Wayne, producer, April 25, 1984. Phil Wayne succeeded his father as producer in 1988, the year of his death.

5. Interview with Bob Barker, April 25, 1984.

6. Ibid.

7. Ibid.; interview with Johnny Olson, April 25, 1984.

8. "Bill Cullen," *Current Biography 1960* (New York: Wilson Co., 1960), p. 105; Cynthia Lowry, "Bill Cullen: Master of the M.C. Racket," *Miami Herald TV Preview*, April 9, 1967, p. 10.

9. Interview with Bill Cullen, April 26, 1984.

10. Annabelle Kerins, "Stay tuned, if you like to win prizes," *Newsday*, March 20, 1980, p. II-47.

11. Walter H. Waggoner, "Geraldine Souvaine, Producer of Features for Met's Broadcasts," *New York Times*, July 6, 1983, p. B9.

12. Interview with Bob Shannon, April 21, 1984.

13. Christopher Lydon, "F.C.C. Puts Limits on Networks' TV," *New York Times*, May 8, 1970, p. 1.

14. Ibid., p. 63; "TV Access Time: Mainly Quiz Shows," *New York Times*, September 5, 1975, p. 58.

15. "Television Reviews," *Variety*, July 25, 1984, p. 62.

16. Interview with Chuck Woolery, May 12, 1987.

17. "An Intimate Trip Behind the Pyramids," *Game Show Fever Magazine*, September 1987, p. 28.

18. "Radio Reviews," *Variety*, March 30, 1938, p. 35; Thomas A. DeLong, "Ad-libbers, Quizmasters Supplied Radio Word Factory," *Bridgeport Sunday Post* (CT), October 21, 1979, p. F2.

19. "Radio Reviews," *Variety*, October 27, 1943, p. 32.

20. Press bio of Arlene Francis, ca. 1972.

21. As quoted in Richard F. Shepard, "Wendy Barrie, Actress, Is Dead; Film and TV Personality Was 65," *New York Times*, February 4, 1978, p. 22.

22. Contract between Irene Beasley and Ted Bates, Inc., August 15, 1946, Broadcast Pioneers Library, Washington, D.C.

23. Interview with Dwight Weist, January 31, 1985.

24. Fabe, *TV Game Shows*, pp. 37–38.

25. "Radio Reviews," *Variety*, April 5, 1944, p. 28.

26. Cab Calloway and Bryant Rollins, *Minnie The Moocher and Me* (New York: Thomas Y. Crowell Co., 1976), p. 180.

27. "Radio Reviews," *Variety*, July 9, 1941, p. 26.

28. Lois Lowry, "How Does It Feel to Be on a TV Quiz Show? Don't Ask," *New York Times*, March 31, 1974, p. II-1.

29. Frank Giordano, "The Day I Laid an Egg on a Quiz Show," *New York Times*, February 2, 1975, p. II-27.

30. "Inflation Doubles '$64,000 Question,' " *New York Times*, August 19, 1976, p. 71.

31. Interview with Thom McKee, November 25, 1984.

32. Ibid.

33. Ibid.

34. Quoted in Susan Rosegrant, "He Knows His X's, Runs Up $230,000," *Miami Herald*, June 27, 1980, p. 19-A.

35. Interview with John Guedel, May 5, 1987.

36. Interview with Mark Goodson, April 24, 1984.

37. Harry F. Waters with John Yang, "Cheeky King Richard," *Newsweek*, June 25, 1979, p. 92.

38. Ibid.

39. Jefferson Graham, "The 'Wheel of Fortune' phenomenon," *USA Today*, March 25, 1985, p. 7D.

40. Peter J. Boyer, "As 'Wheel' Goes, So Go TV Profits and Careers," *New York Times*, May 8, 1986, p. C26.

CHAPTER 25: FLAVOR OF THE COMMON MAN

1. Milton Bracker, "No Question about Quiz Shows," *New York Times Magazine*, July 26, 1953, p. 17.

2. Andrew Pollack, "New Interactive TV Threatens the Bliss of Couch Potatoes," *New York Times*, June 18, 1990, p. 1.

3. Joseph N. Kane, Quiz Program Panel, Friends of Old-Time Radio Annual Convention, Newark, NJ, October 24, 1987.

4. Frank Rich, "Truth and Consequences: The Wit, Wisdom and Rude Shocks of Game Shows," *Time*, February 18, 1980, p. 85.

5. Mark Goodson, "TV Game Shows Are Hoodwinking Viewers Again," *New York Times*, May 9, 1976, p. II-27.

6. Tom Buckley, "Game Shows—TV's Glittering Gold Mine," *New York Times Magazine*, November 18, 1979, p. 170.

7. Max Lerner, *America as a Civilization* (New York: Simon & Schuster, 1957), p. 838.

8. John Hyldberg, Letter to the Editor, "Lonely Hearts," *New York Times Magazine*, August 9, 1953, p. 6.

9. Erma Bombeck, "At Wit's End: There's too Much Reality on TV," *Bridgeport Post* (CT), July 26, 1990, p. C7.

Select Bibliography

BOOKS

Allman, Kevin. *TV Turkeys: An Outrageous Look at the Most Preposterous Shows Ever on Television*. New York: Perigee Books, 1987.

Anderson, Kent. *Television Fraud: The History and Implications of the Quiz Show Scandals*. Westport, CT: Greenwood Press, 1978.

Andrews, Bart, with Brad Dunning. *The Worst TV Shows Ever*. New York: Dutton, 1980.

Ashley, Sally. *The Life and Times of Franklin Pierce Adams*. New York: Beaufort Books, 1986.

Barnouw, Erik. *A Tower in Babel: A History of Broadcasting in the United States to 1933*. New York: Oxford University Press, 1966.

————. *The Golden Web: A History of Broadcasting in the United States: 1933–1953*. New York: Oxford University Press, 1968.

————. *The Image Empire: A History of Broadcasting in the United States: 1953–1970*. New York: Oxford University Press, 1970.

————. *Tube of Plenty: The Evolution of American Television*. New York: Oxford University Press, 1975.

Barris, Chuck. *Confessions of a Dangerous Mind*. New York: St. Martin's Press, 1984.

Biow, Milton H. *Butting In . . . An Adman Speaks Out*. Garden City, NY: Doubleday, 1964.

Blumenthal, Norman. *The T.V. Game Shows: How To Get On and Win*. New York: Pyramid Books, 1975.

Boddy, William. *Fifties Television: The Industry and Its Critics*. Urbana, IL: University of Illinois Press, 1990.

Brooks, Tim. *The Complete Directory to Prime Time TV Stars, 1946–Present*. New York: Ballantine Books, 1987.

Brooks, Tim, and Earle Marsh. *The Complete Directory to Prime Time Network TV Shows*. New York: Ballantine Books, 1979.

Buxton, Frank, and Bill Owen. *The Big Broadcast: 1920–1950*. New York: Viking Press, 1972.

Castleman, Harry, and Walter J. Podrazik. *Watching TV: Four Decades of American Television*. New York: McGraw-Hill, 1982.

Cone, Fairfax M. *With All Its Faults: A Candid Account of Forty Years in Advertising*. Boston: Little, Brown, 1969.

Conrad, Peter. *Television: The Medium and Its Manners*. Boston: Routledge & Kegan Paul, 1982.

Crosby, John. *Out of the Blue: A Book About Radio and Television*. New York: Simon & Schuster, 1952.

DeLong, Thomas A. *The Mighty Music Box: The Golden Age of Musical Radio*. Los Angeles: Amber Crest Books, 1980.

Downs, Hugh. *Yours Truly*. New York: Rinehart & Winston, 1960.

Dunning, John. *Tune in Yesterday: The Ultimate Encyclopedia of Old-Time Radio, 1927–1976*. Englewood Cliffs, NJ: Prentice-Hall, 1976.

Fabe, Maxene. *TV Game Shows*. Garden City, NY: Dolphin Books, 1979.

Fates, Gil. *What's My Line? The Inside History of TV's Most Famous Panel Show*. Englewood Cliffs, NJ: Prentice-Hall, 1978.

Feldman, Ruth Duskin. *Whatever Happened to the Quiz Kids?* Chicago: Chicago Review Press, 1982.

Fox, Stephen. *The Mirror Makers: A History of American Advertising and Its Creators*. New York: William Morrow & Co., 1984.

Graham, Jefferson. *Come On Down!!! The TV Game Show Book*. New York: Abbeville Press, 1988.

Hall, Monty, and Bill Libby. *Emcee Monty Hall*. New York: Grosset & Dunlap, 1973.

Hickok, Eliza Merrill. *The Quiz Kids*. Boston: Houghton Mifflin, 1947.

Kane, Joseph Nathan. *How to Win on Quiz Shows*. New York: Bartholomew House, 1956.

Kieran, John. *Not Under Oath*. Boston: Houghton Mifflin, 1964.

Kirby, Edward M. *Star Spangled Radio*. New York: Ziff-Davis, 1948.

Lerner, Max. *America as a Civilization: Life and Thought in the United States Today*. New York: Simon & Schuster, 1957.

Levant, Oscar. *The Memoirs of an Amnesiac*. New York: Putnam's Sons, 1965.

———. *The Unimportance of Being Oscar*. New York: Putnam's Sons, 1968.

Linkletter, Art. *People Are Funny*. Garden City, NY: Doubleday, 1947.

Lowery, Fred. *Whistling in the Dark*. Gretna, LA: Pelican Publishing Co., 1983.

MacDonald, J. Fred. *Black and White TV: Afro-Americans in Television Since 1948*. Chicago: Nelson-Hall, 1983.

McGill, Earle. *Radio Directing*. New York: McGraw-Hill, 1940.

McNeil, Alex. *Total Television: A Comprehensive Guide to Programming from 1948 to the Present*. New York: Penguin Books, 1984.

Marx, Groucho, with Hector Arce. *The Secret Word is Groucho*. New York: Putnam, 1976.

Mehling, Harold. *The Great Time-Killer*. Cleveland: World Publishing Co., 1962.

Metz, Robert. *CBS: Reflections in a Bloodshot Eye*. Chicago: Playboy Press, 1975.

Muntean, Greg, and Gregg Silverman. *How to Become a Game Show Contestant: An Insider's Guide*. New York: Fawcett Columbine, 1987.

Noah, Robert. *All the Right Answers* (fiction). San Diego: Harcourt Brace Jovanovich, 1988.

Oakley, J. Ronald. *God's Country: America in the Fifties*. New York: Dembner Books, 1986.

Pearson, Billy, and Stephen Longstreet. *Never Look Back: The Autobiography of a Jockey*. New York: Simon & Schuster, 1958.

Price, Vincent. *I Like What I Know*. Garden City, NY: Doubleday, 1959.

Ray, William B. *FCC: The Ups and Downs of Radio-TV Regulation*. Ames: Iowa State University Press, 1990.

Rose, Brian G. (ed.). *TV Genres: A Handbook and Reference Guide*. Westport, CT: Greenwood Press, 1985.

Sackett, Susan, and Cheryl Blythe. *You Can Be a Game Show Contestant and Win*. New York: Dell Trade Paperbacks, 1982.

Scarne, John. *Encyclopedia of Games*. New York: Harper & Row, 1973.

Schwartz, David, Steve Ryan, and Fred Wostbrock. *The Encyclopedia of TV Game Shows*. New York: New York Zoetrope, 1987.

Schwartz, Marla Schram. *Be a TV Game Show Winner!* New York: Harmony Books, 1988.

Sherman, Allen. *A Gift of Laughter*. New York: Atheneum, 1965.

Shulman, Arthur, and Roger Youmer. *How Sweet It Was*. New York: Bonanza Books, 1966.

Summers, Harrison B. (ed.). *A Thirty-Year History of Programs Carried on National Radio Networks in the United States, 1926–1956*. New York: Arno Press and the New York Times, 1971.

Taylor, Robert. *Fred Allen: His Life and Wit*. Boston: Little, Brown, 1989.

Tobias, Andrew. *Fire and Ice*. New York: William Morrow, 1976.

Trebek, Alex, and Peter Barsocchini. *The Jeopardy! Book*. New York: Harper & Row, 1990.

PERIODICALS

Abarbanel, Don. "America's Most Popular Pastime: Crossword Puzzles." *MD Magazine*, November 1983.

Accinelli, Laura. "Game Show Mania: 70 Million Tune in to Win." *Game Show Magazine*, August 1986.

Adams, Val. "Lou Cowan: Quixotic Giveaway Producer." *New York Times*, June 26, 1949.

Alexander, Ron. "College Quiz Show, Favorite of the 60's, Tests Wits Again." *New York Times*, November 17, 1979.

Anderson, Jack. "Comeback: How TV's Dan Enright Bounced Back from the Biggest Mistake of His Life." *Parade Magazine*, December 1, 1985.

Andrews, Peter. "Television: The Hating Game." *Saturday Review*, March 29, 1980.

Belkin, Lisa. "Redefining Prime Time: It's All in Who You Ask." *New York Times*, August 11, 1987.

Bracker, Milton. "No Question about Quiz Shows." *New York Times Magazine*, July 26, 1953.

Bralove, Mary. "As the Scandals Fade, TV Game Shows Gain Another Big Following." *Wall Street Journal*, June 26, 1970.

Buckley, Tom. "Game Shows—TV's Glittering Gold Mine." *New York Times Magazine*, November 18, 1979.

Buder, Leonard. "Behind the $64,000." *New York Times*, August 7, 1955.

"Busy Miss Beasley." *New York Times*, November 9, 1947.

Cobb, Jane. "Living and Learning," *New York Times Magazine*, January 5, 1941.

Cotler, Gordon. "The Question about Quiz Shows." *New York Times Magazine*, December 1, 1957.

Dembart, Lee. "Groucho's 1950's Quiz Show Is a Hit All Over Again." *New York Times*, March 9, 1975.

Dempsey, John. "Gameshows Pace '85 Syndie Sales." *Variety*, November 14, 1984.

Duka, John. "From 'What's My Line' to 'Child's Play,' The Game's the Thing for Him." *New York Times*, December 5, 1982.

Dumont, Lou. "Horace Heidt." *Hobbies* Magazine, June 1982.

Dunlap, Orrin E. "Baffling the Board: Experts Face Second Year of Questioning as Listeners Ask for 'Info Please.' " *New York Times*, November 26, 1939.

"FCC Finds T'aint Easy Trying to Give Away a Giveaway Ruling." *Variety*, August 24, 1948.

Ferretti, Fred. "Fleeting Fame: When Quiz Kids Grow Up." *New York Times*, December 26, 1982.

"Giveaways vs. Horatio Alger." *Variety*, February 7, 1940.

Gloetzner, John. " 'Talkies' Hit Show Work, Mitchell Turns 'Answer Man.' " *Bridgeport Sunday Post*, September 25, 1938.

Goodson, Mark. "Confessions of a Quizo-Phrenic." *Variety*, January 5, 1949.

———. "TV Game Shows Are Hookwinking Viewers Again." *New York Times*, May 9, 1976.

Gottschalk, Jr., Earl C. "How to Win (or at least have fun) on TV Game Shows." *Family Circle*, April 5, 1977.

Gould, Jack. "Jack Benny or Jackpot?" *New York Times Magazine*, August 15, 1948.

———. " 'Give-Away' Issue." *New York Times*, August 28, 1949.

Graham, Jefferson. "Game Shows Win Heart of Heartland." *USA Today*, July 5, 1985.

———. "Mark Goodson: For the Creator of 'The Price Is Right,' the Name of the Game Is Longevity." *USA Today*, August 11, 1986.

Green, Tom. "Home Tapes Reveal a Splice of Life." *USA Today*, March 5, 1990.

"Growth of Vox Pop Programs." *Variety*, February 10, 1937.

Hutchens, John K. "Who Thought Up the Quiz Show?" *New York Times Magazine*, August 23, 1942.

———. "Chiefly of High Finance." *New York Times*, February 28, 1943.

Jennings, C. Robert. "Quiz Shows: The Woman Question." *New York Times Magazine*, February 9, 1958.

Joel, George. "Quid-pro Quiz," *The Nation*, November 16, 1940.

Kalb, Bernard. "Bennett Cerf: He Also Works in Video." *New York Times*, August 2, 1953, p. II-9.

Lev, Michael. "Game Shows Return as Prime-Time Contestants." *New York Times,* July 30, 1990.

Lindsay, Robert. "School Is Back in Session for 'The Quiz Kids.' " *New York Times,* April 13, 1980.

Lowry, Cynthia. "TV Quizmasters, Yesterday's Heroes." *Miami Herald,* December 13, 1959.

McEvoy, J. P. "The Quiz Kids," *Reader's Digest,* October 1940.

Marks, Leonard. "Legality of Radio Giveaway Program." *Georgetown Law Journal,* Vol. 37, 1948–1949.

Millner, Cork. "The TV Games People Play." *Saturday Evening Post,* January/February 1981.

O'Brien, Richard. "Quiz Is No 'I.Q.' " *New York Times,* August 7, 1938.

Reploge, E. E. "Television—A Medium of the Future." *Broadcast Advertising,* November 1929.

Robinson, Henry Morton. "Information Please." *Reader's Digest,* January 1939.

Rosenberg, Howard. "How Did the '50s Quiz-Show Scandal Ensnare a Tennessee Minister?" *Los Angeles Times Magazine,* November 5, 1989.

Roush, Matt. "No Question That 'Jeopardy!' Is a Hit." *USA Today,* April 24, 1986.

Russell, Norton. "They're Human, After All: Four Musketeers of 'Information Please.' " *Radio Mirror,* July 1939.

Sabulis, Thomas. "The Luck of the Draw." *Parents' Choice,* Vol. 3, No. 2, 1980.

Salmans, Sandra. "Why TV Audiences Love to Play Games." *New York Times,* April 28, 1985.

Shah, Diane K. "The Good Fortune of Pat Sajak." *New York Times Magazine,* December 11, 1988.

Stahl, Bob. "Postwar Pains, Strikes Keep Tele from Public." *Variety,* January 8, 1947.

Todman, Bill. "Freedom of the Dial." *Variety,* January 5, 1949.

Waters, Harry F., with Michael A. Lerner. "What a Deal!" *Newsweek,* February 9, 1987.

"Who Is Ward Byron?" *SPERDVAC Radiogram,* July 1985.

Index

ABOUT THE AUTHOR

THOMAS A. DeLONG is the author of the ASCAP-Deems Taylor Award-winning *The Mighty Music Box: The Golden Age of Musical Radio* and coauthor of *The Museum of Broadcasting's Classical Music Collection* and *The Telephone Hour: A Retrospective*, both issued by the Museum of Television and Radio in New York. His biography of conductor-showman Paul Whiteman *(POPS)* was published in 1983. He also has written more than 30 articles on broadcasting for newspapers and magazines and has served as guest curator of exhibitions on radio, television, popular music and films. Chairman of the Board of the Westport School of Music in Connecticut, he holds advanced degrees from Columbia University and New York University Graduate Business School. His association with broadcasting began as an undergraduate at Williams College.